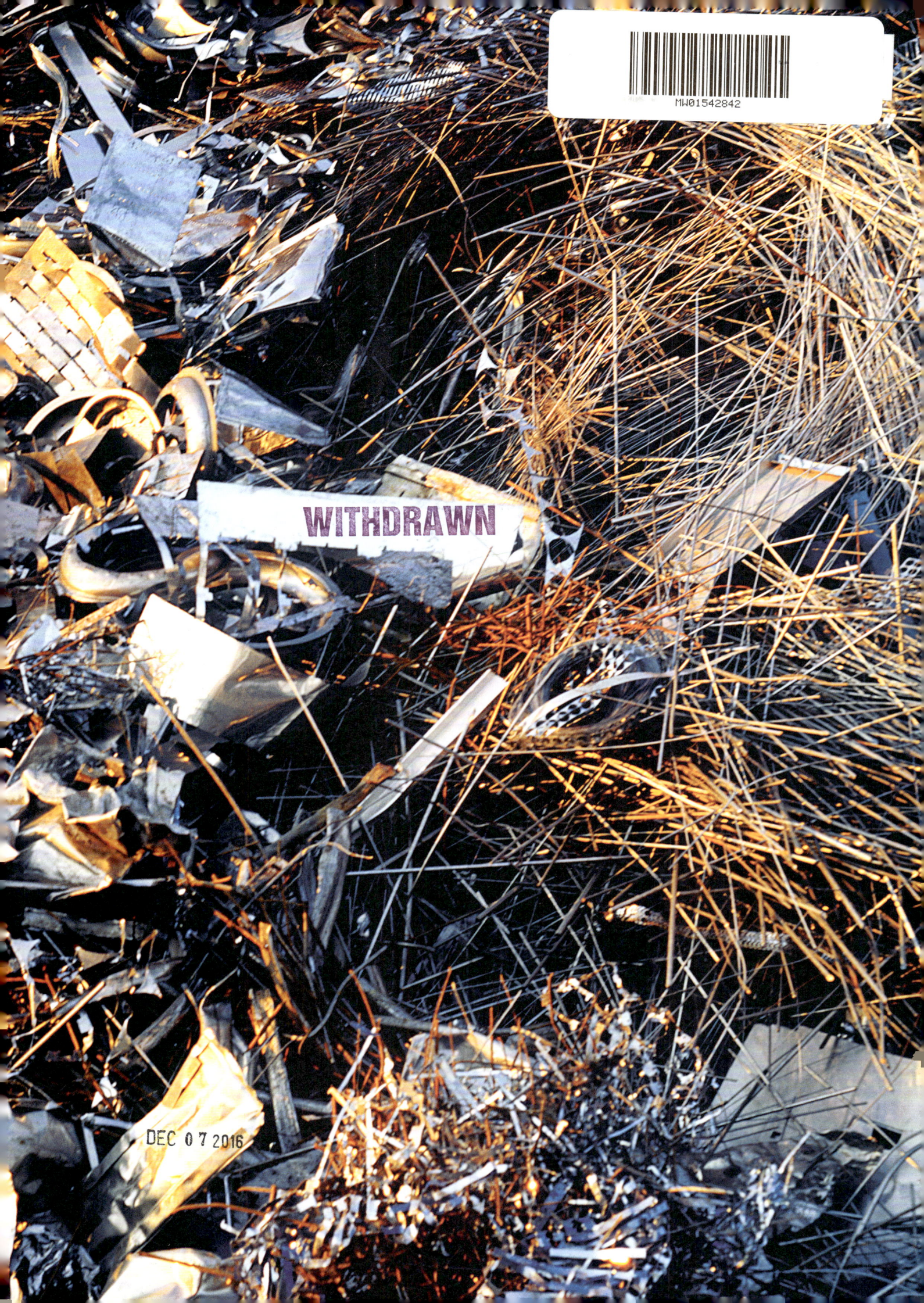

Doug Aitken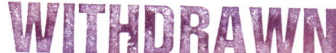

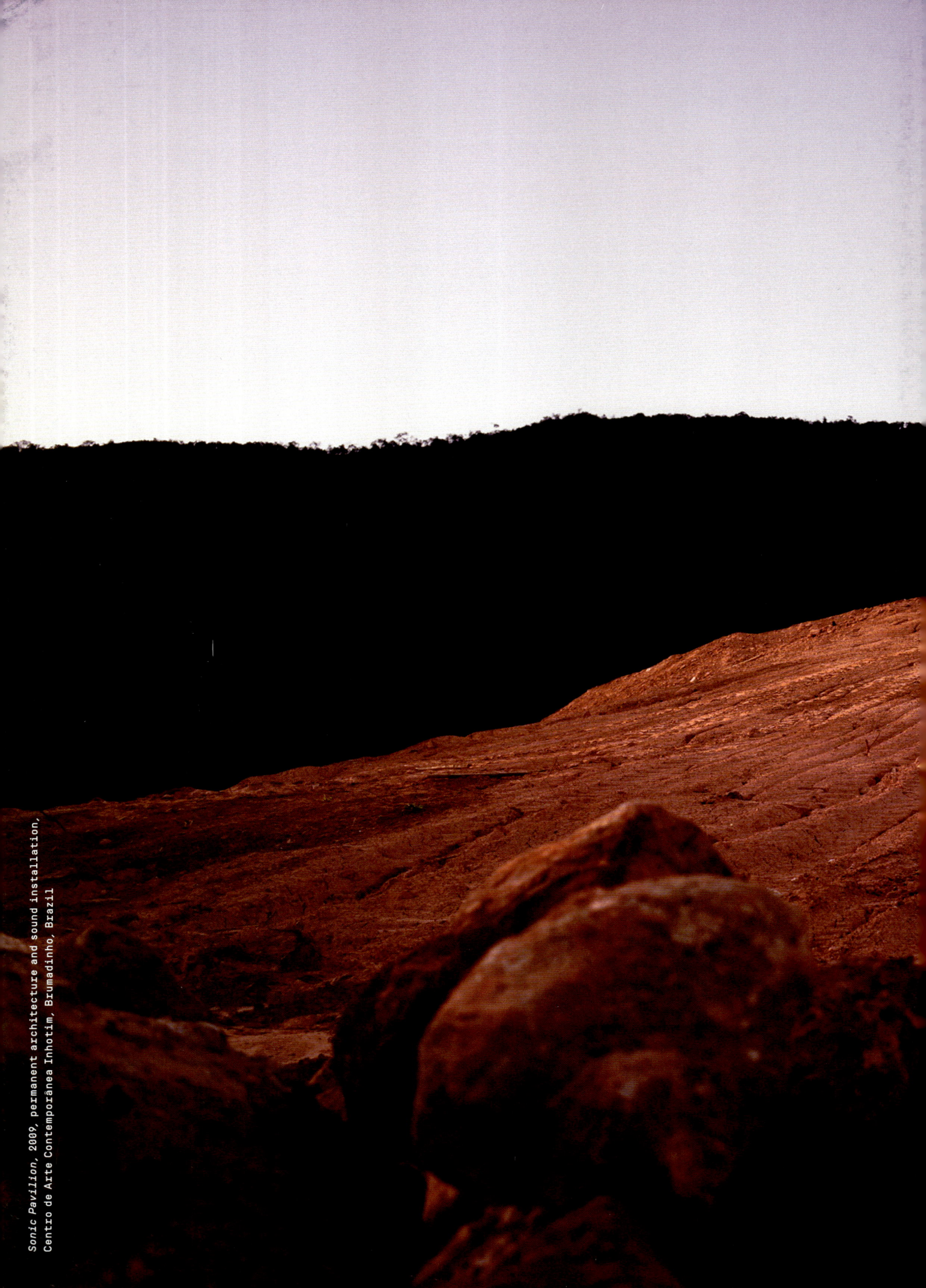

Sonic Pavilion, 2009, permanent architecture and sound installation, Centro de Arte Contemporânea Inhotim, Brumadinho, Brazil

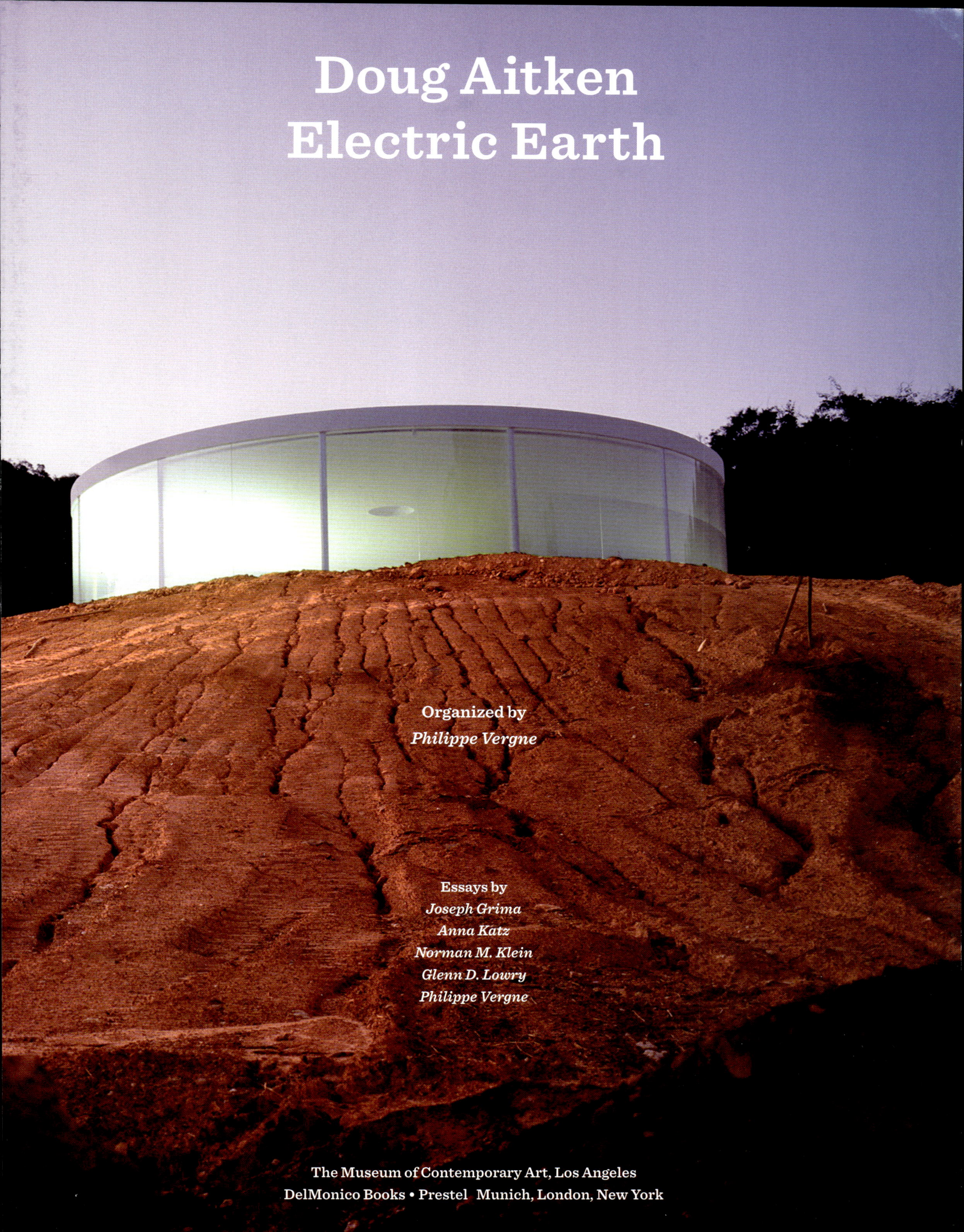

Doug Aitken
Electric Earth

Organized by
Philippe Vergne

Essays by
Joseph Grima
Anna Katz
Norman M. Klein
Glenn D. Lowry
Philippe Vergne

The Museum of Contemporary Art, Los Angeles
DelMonico Books • Prestel   Munich, London, New York

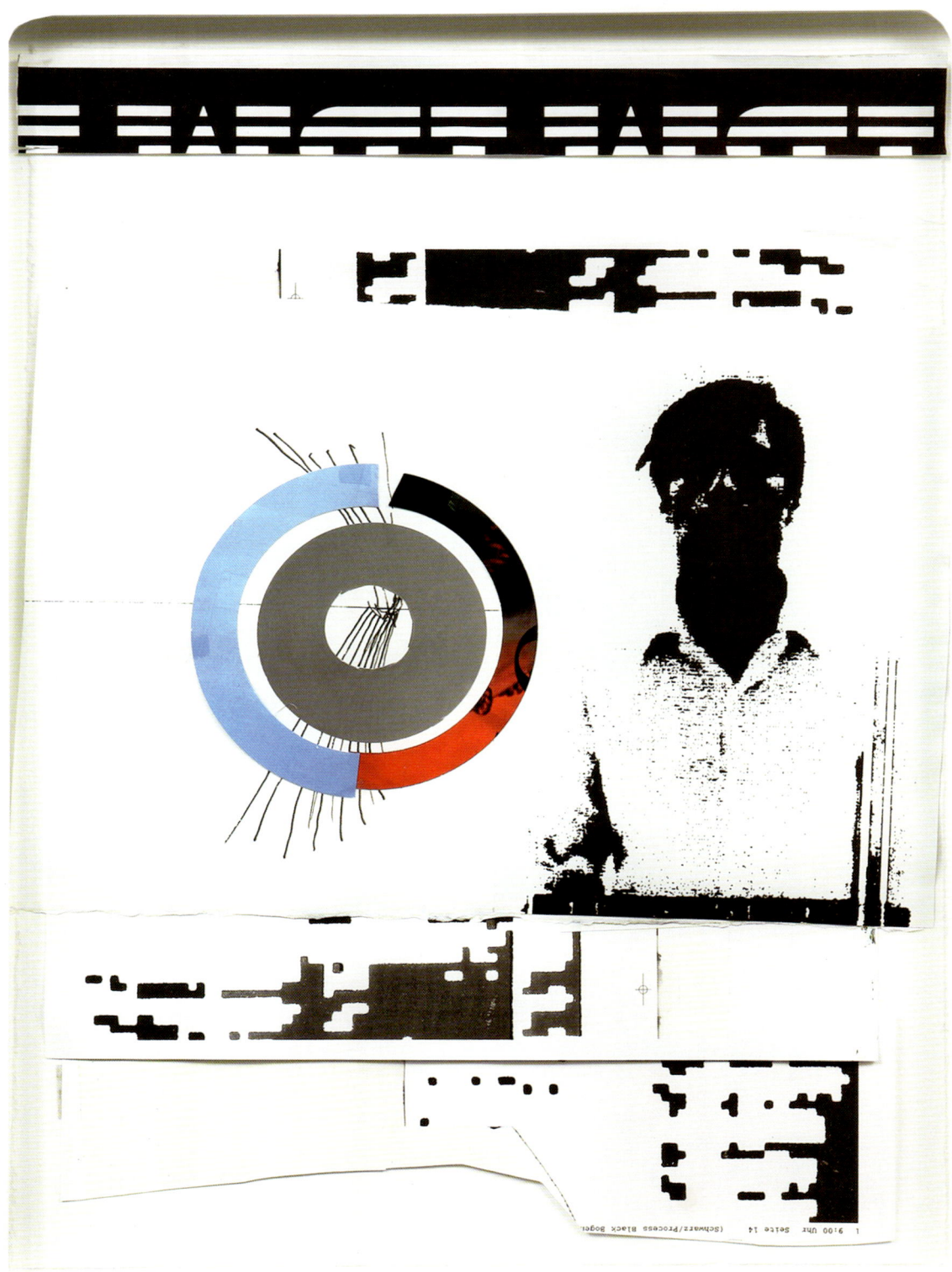

Director's Foreword and Acknowledgments
Philippe Vergne
7

You Are Here and So Am I

Philippe Vergne

12

Doug Aitken, Mapmaker

Anna Katz

185

From *sleepwalkers* to *Station to Station*:

Inverting the Museum

Glenn D. Lowry

197

An Architecture for the Now

Joseph Grima

207

A Granular History of Space:

Doug Aitken

Norman M. Klein

214

Exhibition Checklist
224

Image Captions
227

Selected Exhibition History and Bibliography
232

Contributors
258

Photography Credits
260

Lenders to the Exhibition
260

Artist's Acknowledgments
263

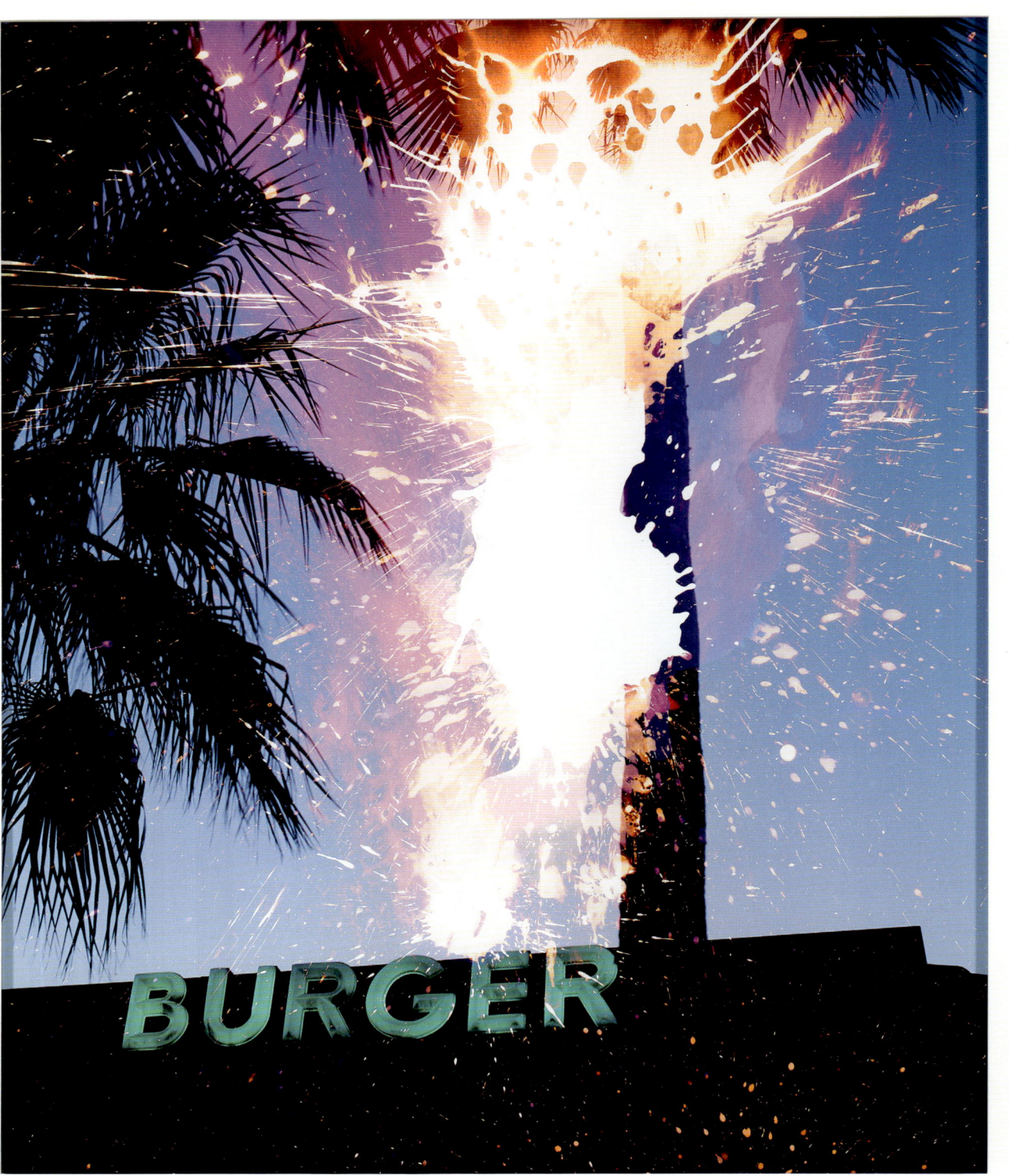

desire (chemical spills), 2009

Director's Foreword and Acknowledgments

For more than twenty years, Doug Aitken has shifted our perceptions of images and narratives. His multichannel video installations, sound works, sculptures, photographs, publications, happenings, and architectural interventions have manifested the nature and structure of our ever-mobile, ever-changing, image-based contemporary condition. Aitken has invented an immersive aesthetic rooted in interdisciplinary collaborations, the availability of images, and the vulnerability of individuals, calling into question the relentless human, industrial, urban, and environmental entropy that defines twenty-first-century existence.

 Doug Aitken's long affiliation with MOCA began in 2000, when the museum acquired *electric earth* (1999), as a partial and promised gift from David Teiger in honor of Jeremy Strick. Staggered across four rooms, this landmark eight-channel video installation (which premiered at the 1999 Venice Biennale, produced under the patronage of Fondazione Sandretto Re Rebaudengo) secured Aitken's position as a formidable creator of nonlinear, nonnarrative film and quickly became a cornerstone of our collection. The acquisition of *electric earth* attests to not only the museum's ongoing mission to collect, present, and interpret the art of our time, but also our profound commitment to artists in *their* time, as they produce their work. Our dedication is demonstrated both at home and abroad in our support of international artists, as well as those based in Los Angeles.

 Doug Aitken: Electric Earth—the artist's first full-scale midcareer North American survey—has been organized in close collaboration with the artist and his studio. This relationship exemplifies the very best of what it means for MOCA to be the artist's museum—to embrace the artist's vision, nurture a reception for the work, produce original scholarship through publications, and make the work widely accessible to our audiences. Likewise, this exhibition is a testament to MOCA's belief in the urgency of contemporary expression: Aitken's work across mediums and disciplines engages with some of the most central concerns of our moment, from catastrophic environmental depredation to unprecedented technological mediation; self-contained, decentralized communication; and the incursion of commerce into every aspect of our social relationships. The uniqueness of Aitken's work is its endless search for creative forms, structures, and spaces in his determination to expose audiences to these ideas and, in so doing, bring audiences together.

Doug Aitken: Electric Earth would not have been possible without the support of MOCA's Board of Trustees, indefatigable champions of contemporary art. Their commitment to artists, to an ambitious program of exhibitions, educational initiatives, and publications, and to identifying and presenting the most significant and challenging art of our time makes them integral to our mission. In particular, I wish to recognize board co-chairs Lilly Tartikoff Karatz and Maurice Marciano for their leadership and friendship, and Carolyn Powers and Mandy and Cliff Einstein for their early support.

I am extremely grateful to the individual collectors, public museums, and foundations that have graciously loaned works from their collections. An exhibition of this magnitude could not have taken place without the generosity of our funders. Lead support is provided by the Annenberg Foundation, The Eli and Edythe Broad Foundation, Aileen Getty Foundation, Eugenio Lopez, LUMA Foundation, Maurice Marciano, Carolyn Powers, and Fondazione Sandretto Re Rebaudengo. Major support is provided by Mandy and Cliff Einstein, Mimi and Peter Haas Fund, and Panasonic. Generous support is provided by Jill and Peter Kraus, the National Endowment for the Arts, Maria Seferian, and Julia Stoschek Foundation e. V., Düsseldorf. Additional support is provided by Juliet McIver, Eileen and Peter Michael, and David and Angella Nazarian. Supporters of the exhibition catalogue include 303 Gallery, Galerie Eva Presenhuber, Regen Projects, Los Angeles, and Victoria Miro Gallery. Exhibitions at MOCA are supported by the MOCA Fund for Exhibitions with lead annual support provided by Delta Air Lines, Shari Glazer, Hästens, and Sydney Holland, founder of the Sydney D. Holland Foundation. Generous funding is also provided by Jerri and Dr. Steven Nagelberg, and Thao Nguyen and Andreas Krainer.

I wish to express my warmest thanks to MOCA Chief Curator Helen Molesworth, who recognized the importance of this project from its inception and offered invaluable guidance throughout. *Doug Aitken: Electric Earth* could not have been realized without the extraordinary dedication of Anna Katz, the Wendy Stark Curatorial Fellow at MOCA, who guided the process of this exhibition and demonstrated an astonishing ability to handle a complex project, from exhibition making to managing the production of the publication and bringing together the public programs. Sincere thanks to Jill Davis, Director of Exhibition Management, and Sarika Sanyal, Exhibition Management Coordinator, for overseeing all practical and budgetary matters, keeping us on course at every turn. Patrick Weber, Director of Exhibition Production, as well as David Bradshaw, Technical Manager, tackled this exhibition's not inconsiderable technological, fabrication, and installation challenges with intelligence and aplomb. Patrick was aided immeasurably by Josh Weisberg of WorldStage Event Services, Neil Shaw of Menlo Scientific Acoustics, and Steve Jones. Thank you to Sandy Davis, Head Registrar, and Emily Willmann, Assistant Registrar, for seeing to every aspect of artwork transport and care. Michael Harrison, Chief Financial Officer/Chief Operating Officer, has been an essential partner, as have been Colleen Russell Criste, Chief Development Officer, along with Sarah Cohen and Andrew Gould, and Sarah Lloyd Stifler, Chief Communications Officer, and her team, including Marco Braunschweiler, Eva Seta, and Jin Son. Indeed, though *Doug Aitken: Electric Earth* was first conceived over private conversations with Doug Aitken when I first arrived in Los Angeles to assume my post as Director of MOCA, the successful actualization of the project has depended, in one way or another, on the efforts of every member of the museum's staff; each can claim a share in this exhibition; each makes working at MOCA a true joy. For her daily grace under fire, I owe special thanks to Niyah Rahmaan, Executive Assistant to the Director.

It gives me great pleasure to thank our tour partner, the Modern Art Museum of Fort Worth, for joining in our admiration for Doug Aitken's work and for bringing the exhibition to its audiences. Thanks are due in particular to Director Dr. Marla Price, Chief Curator Michael Auping, and Assistant Curator Alison Hearst.

The Doug Aitken Workshop is a workshop in the truest sense, and it has been a privilege to work with Carolyne (Bunny) Jurriaans, Studio Manager/Producer; Conner MacPhee, Designer; Dylan Marcus, Graphic Designer; Austin Meredith, Editor; Max Schwartz, Image Editor and Archivist; and Stephanie Willsey, Designer, all of whom assisted with every stage of exhibition, catalogue, and exhibition tour planning. Aitken's galleries have also provided crucial support in the same vein. Thank you to Cristian Alexa, Brian Doyle, Jessica Heerten, and Lisa Spellman of 303 Gallery; Björn Alfers, Andreas Grimm, Eva Presenhuber, and Markus Rischgasser of Galerie Eva Presenhuber; Erin Maans, Victoria Miro, and Glenn Scott Wright of Victoria Miro Gallery; and Lindsay Charlwood, Jane McCarthy, Katy McKinnon, and Shaun Caley Regen of Regen Projects.

This catalogue was beautifully designed by Lorraine Wild and Marina Mills Kitchen of Green Dragon Office, both of whom have provided remarkable insight into the body of work. Thank you to Donna Wingate of Artist and Publisher Services for her incisive editorial direction and to Mary DelMonico, Karen Farquhar, and Ryan Newbanks of DelMonico Books • Prestel for their superbly skillful production services. This book's contributing authors have shed new light on Aitken's imagery and materials, strategies and methods, and contexts and ambitions: Joseph Grima, Anna Katz, Norman M. Klein, and Glenn D. Lowry.

Personally, I would like to thank Sylvia Chivaratanond and Indra Vergne for their emotional support and for allowing their lives to be adjusted, and stretched, to the needs of such a project.

Lastly, I must extend my most heartfelt thanks to Doug Aitken, whose work and long friendship have been an inspiration. His deep interest in fully immersive experiences that transcend the temporal and spatial confines of a conventional exhibition and his collaborative spirit have helped all of us reimagine the nature of what a work of art can be, of what an art experience can do. I value his vision and his determination to effect change.

Philippe Vergne
Director
The Museum of Contemporary Art, Los Angeles

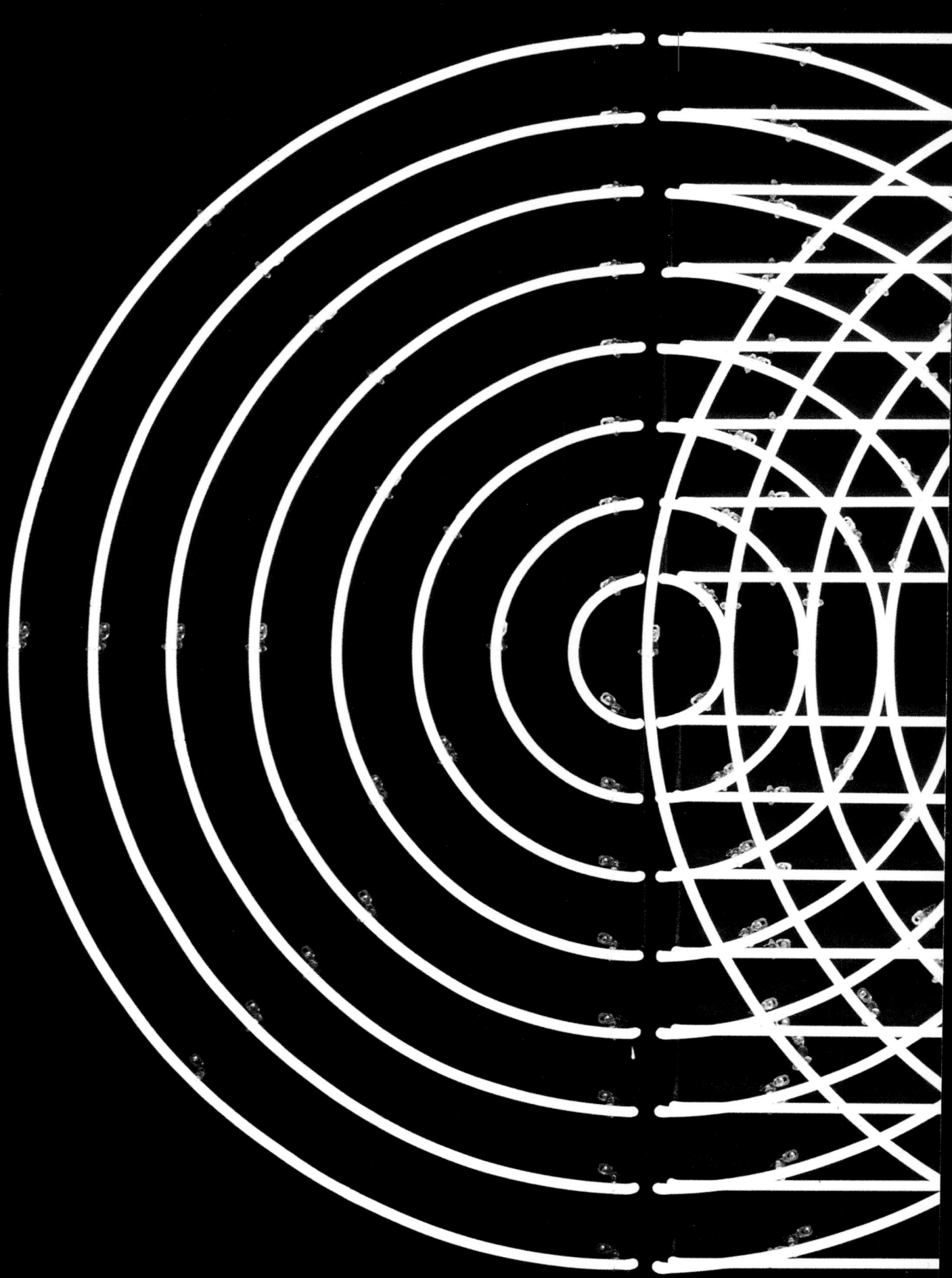

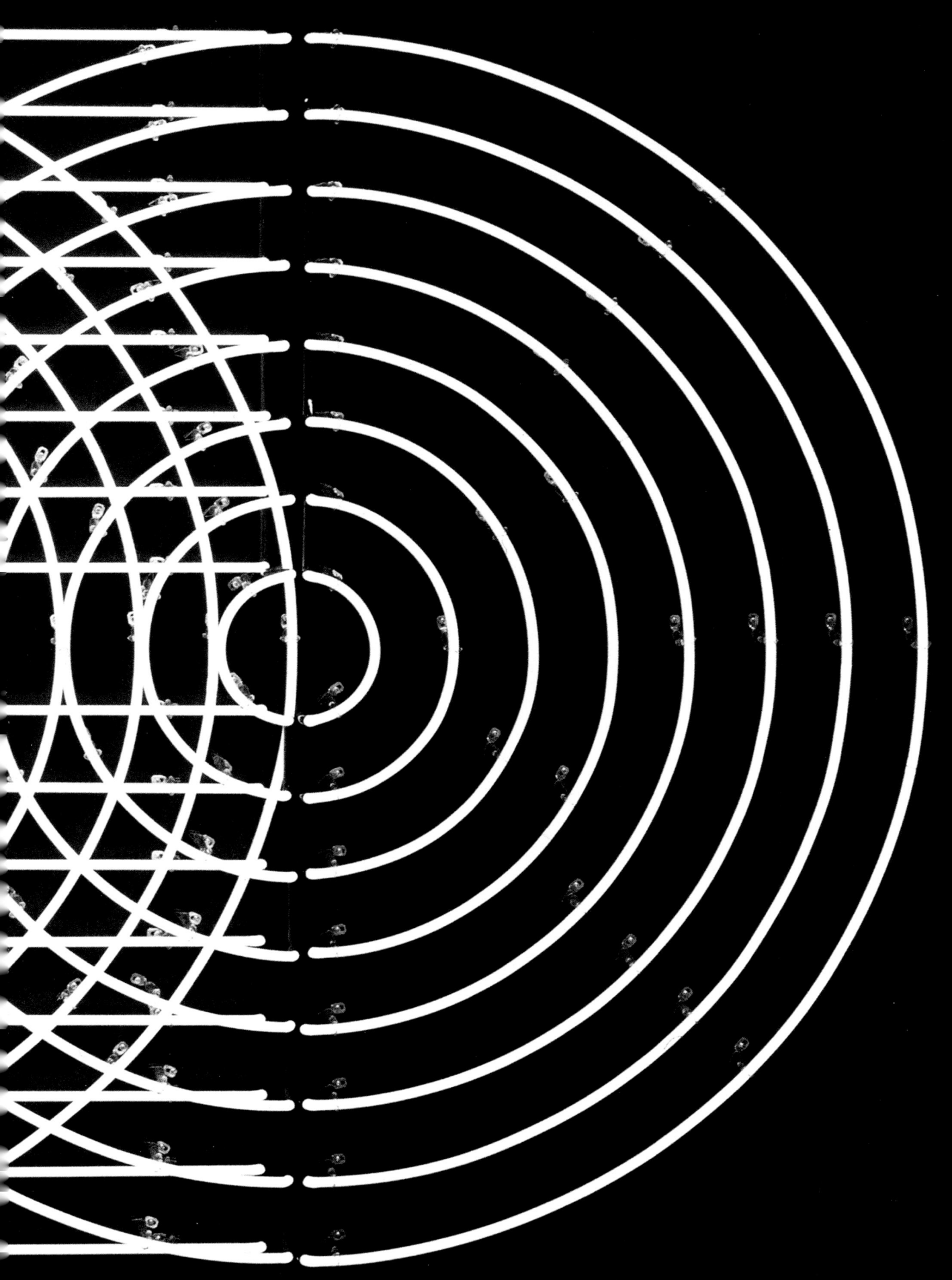

You Are Here and So Am I

Philippe Vergne

"The museum should be a structure for broadcasting, an antenna that reaches far and wide, well beyond its own walls": these are the words of artist Doug Aitken, spoken as we began the process of assembling this exhibition. His statement reveals his interest in the museum space and its ability not only to present his artwork but to meet—and, indeed, even exceed—the creative needs of our time.

For more than twenty years, Aitken has distinguished his oeuvre through experimentation with video, sound, photography, sculpture, and architecture. From early single-channel works based on the appropriation and reediting of preexisting Hollywood images, such as *i'd die for you* (1993; page 238), to fully immersive installations in which images and sounds overwhelm the senses, such as *electric earth* (1999; pages 120–131) and *Black Mirror* (2011; pages 132–143), to performances and programmed events, such as *Station to Station* (2013; pages 42–49), and architecturally scaled projections on buildings, such as *sleepwalkers* (2007; pages 200–201, 234) and *lighthouse* (2012; page 232), his work has been fully dedicated to capturing our contemporaneity, to presenting a landscape of the now, be it literally a landscape, or actually the many material and immaterial landscapes that constitute our times, or the psychological landscape of today's human condition, alienated or elated.

Almost eighteen years ago, Aitken and I began speaking about his work with regard to the strategies and aesthetics of the entertainment industry. At that time, he stressed that if his work should be contemplated within the context of mass culture, he was interested in the language of communication rather than that of the world of entertainment, and he has reiterated this statement to me over the years when discussing his core concerns as an artist.

Communication was also a key concern for the artist Walter De Maria. Shortly before he passed away in 2013, he and I discussed possible parallels between his own work, *The Vertical Earth Kilometer* (1977; fig. 1), installed permanently in Kassel, Germany, and Aitken's *Sonic Pavilion* (2009; pages 2–3, 233), an architectural work at the Centro de Arte Contemporânea Inhotim in Brazil. De Maria's work is a one-kilometer-long brass rod, two inches in diameter, buried vertically in the earth with the top flush to the surface of the ground. *Sonic Pavilion* is a small, round glass building, high on a hilltop, at the center of which is a cavity that descends vertically 202 meters into the ground, rigged with geologic microphones to amplify the sounds of the earth within the pavilion in real time. Both works may be seen as processes of capturing seismic waves, but as De Maria pointed out, Aitken's work emerges from his agility with our culture, in which communication and its delivery systems are now as intuitive as breathing.

It is important to understand that Aitken's work emerged from Los Angeles in the early 1990s, an environment defined by storytelling and images; from the aridity of a landscape irrigated by narrative and artificially generated water; from a tech paradise that sprouted from a pink stucco impression of impermanence. Whereas experimental predecessors such as Nam June Paik, Dan Graham, and Bruce Nauman held the phenomenological experience of the work as central, Aitken emerged as part of the third generation of artists, in the mid-1990s, to work with video and moving images. He never questioned or challenged the medium of video, per se, nor had he any particular interest in "quoting" or being contextualized as part of anything other than his own specific moment. There is no trace of nostalgia in his approach. Rather, Aitken possesses an acute knowledge of the aesthetics of the late 1960s, including the liberation and experimentation of that moment; a spirit of defiance toward traditional modes of representation, such as painting and sculpture; and the understanding that new times present new needs that require new modes for ideation.

Aitken belongs to a generation of artists such as Philippe Parreno, Pierre Huyghe, and Dominique Gonzalez-Foerster, for whom film functions as a medium for experience, and exists as form as much as subject matter. This generation learned from Daniel Buren, Jean-Luc Godard, and Michelangelo Antonioni that film is a language perpetually engaged in telling the story of film as much as the story of any plot. Aitken's moving-image work derails the conventional wisdom of cinema—more specifically, of Hollywood—within which a movie is a story (and a good story makes for a good movie). Aitken aspires to emancipate his work from any parasitic dependency on the traditional models of narrative or story arc, based on a beginning, middle, and end. He reduces the filmic image to its most essential functions: duration, recording, indexical presence. But he does so without indulging in a grainy, reductionist aesthetic of conceptual and postconceptual moving-image works. This strategy merges his work—almost symbiotically—with aspects of mass media and commercial industries, and critically does not shy away from an aesthetic informed by mass communication, advertising, and mainstream commercial films.

The results of his experiments are aimed toward a target no less ambitious than the dissolution of boundaries between contemporary artistic production and the commercial aesthetic strategies that form the pillars of such culturally dominant fields as communications, mass media, digital platforms, and, especially, the entertainment industry. As opposed to being a mimetic strategy, it is one motivated by the desire to recapture our visual culture from the strictures of the entertainment and media worlds, and to consummate a union between true, independent artistic production and the culture's most advanced visual techniques and technologies. Indeed, Aitken's recuperation of film and video is motivated less by their visual imagery than by their formal codes of communication, and his method is to create, and simultaneously disrupt, narratives that are defined as much by the logic of editing as they are by the content of pictures.

Aitken's narratives can be both truncated and open-ended. They loop around central themes, fragments of their own structures, generating repetitions and a sense of *déjà vu, déjà entendu* that extends time and creates space. Images' durations generate the shapes of his installations. It is undeniable that Aitken has studied and integrated the history of avant-garde filmmaking and editing from early innovators such as Tony Conrad, but Aitken has transcended the constraints of minimal or postminimal systems and serial logic. As the artist has said, the structure of editing for the images, as well as, I suppose, for the soundtracks, takes a contrarian position vis-à-vis the systematic, rational logic of minimalism.

Aitken's relationship to systems is to undermine them. When editing, if a structure emerges, his first instinct is to fight against it, to free himself from the constraint, and to liberate his own ability to produce. Structure might be necessary, but only to be overcome. The word "liberate" is intentionally chosen here, as I would think that this need to liberate the editing logic of his work is not a formal manner, but a deeply personal way to be in the world that might explain Aitken's defiance toward and mistrust of existing formats—architectural, social, or institutional. To a certain extent, this mistrust indicates a deep attachment to his independence and the economy of work that he has created for himself.

The most direct antecedent (that I believe is a touchstone for Aitken) is the composer and performer Terry Riley and his major work *In C* (1964; fig. 2). The score was conceived as a series of musical rules and predefined relationships that other interpreters, musicians, and performers could use, reshape, and tweak in order to produce a personal work. The rhythmic anchor is based on a pattern of repetition; the neutral grid is a backdrop for rhythmic disruptions and rotations. It generates a progression of melodic sounds for Riley, and for Aitken, images: gradual changes in the cycle of information in which variations and constants emphasize the disruption as well as the return of identical modules—musical for Riley, visual and sound-based for Aitken.

The balance between the constrained and the free, the ordered and the open, the personal and the collective, is what makes the work original. Unlike Riley, Aitken acts as his own interpreter, managing a balance between the free and the ordered as a strategy to intervene in any threads of narrative flow that we might begin to see, so as to actually present us with *time*, as experienced through moving images. His editing logic creates a visual and temporal space conceived to suggest the expectation of narrative order, a tension toward "what comes next," a dynamic that is endlessly pointing forward, giving rise to an open form—improvised and interfaced with thematic relations between sounds and images that strategically dissolve and reconstitute a visual, time-based, and harmonic landscape. This sense of pacing, of interrupted moments, of shifting and floating, is simultaneously a summary of a narrative and the negation of that narrative.

Aitken's repetitions of images might seem disorienting, and their effects—musically and visually—amount to the use of the fragment as a dynamic, such as a voice reciting "Check in, check out," which is a part of the audio in *Black Mirror*. What we see and hear is never the same, though never totally different: a gradual relocation of meaning, never completely a repetition. The fragmentation of images, sounds, and narrative is continually servicing any risk of historical or narrative linearity. Communication in our world is relentlessly constant—and uninterruptible—in ways that Marshall McLuhan's communication theory of a global village could never have anticipated.[1] Perhaps as a metaphor for this, if the loop appears integral to Aitken's aesthetic, we discover that the loop is never simply a loop. What he suggests through his editing logic is a spiraling dynamic, embedded with certain assumptions about time and space in which the lines of communication are never down. As shown in some of the *ultraworld* collages (2005–2008; pages 4, 16–27), the waves pass through as well as emanate from the body.

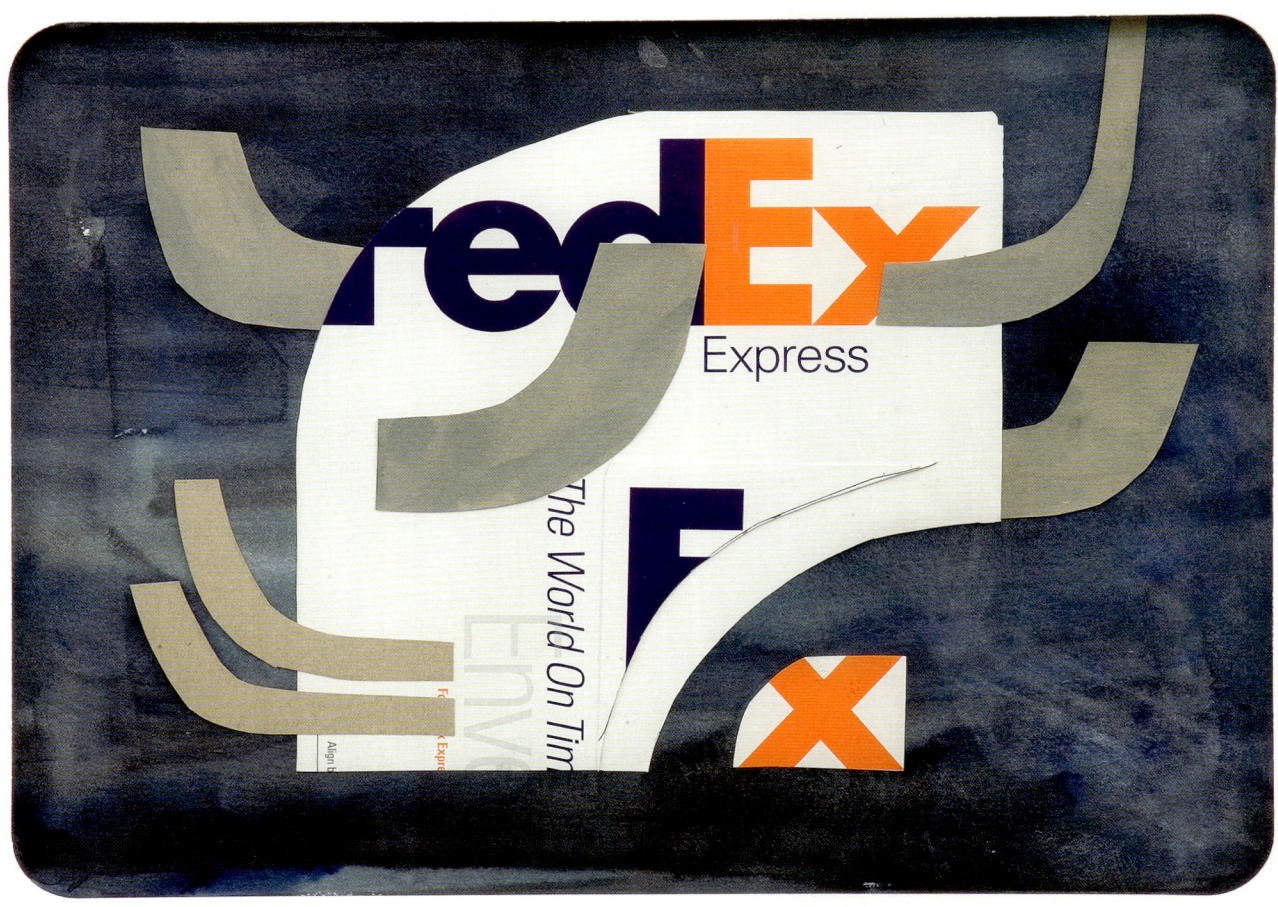

To begin taking in Aitken's aesthetic, *ultraworld*, a series of modestly sized, handmade, and neatly presented collages, is of specific importance. It is concentrated both as an iconography that feeds his work and as a kind of aesthetic system—if one can use that word—of montage, juxtaposition, and fragmentation. Contained within it, we find images of architecture that collapse with body fragments: an eye dominating a rhizomatic volume; the profile of a man framing two towers; a fragmented image of Manhattan onto which the IBM logo is superimposed, which is at the center of an expanding network of lines emanating from it; a body lost, suspended above an anonymous urban landscape; the split face of a young woman topping a cardboard cutout of Manhattan; a black-and-white image of a young man juxtaposed with a circular concentric shape of a broken pie chart with black-and-white, fragmented urban landscape imagery; text, cut off from its source, "Sun Sinking into the Santa Monica Bay," floating in the middle of a dark, lavish, watery surface. These collages map out a field of possible activities and territories. Many of the elements that constitute Aitken's aesthetic are to be found in this work—landscapes, fragmentations, disarticulation of linearities, graphics, bodies, networks, editing processes—in a direct, analog, handmade format that offers guidance to the artist's entire oeuvre. *Ultraworld* stands as a matrix for an aesthetic that might attempt to capture and formalize a state of being in a world saturated by ultracommunication.

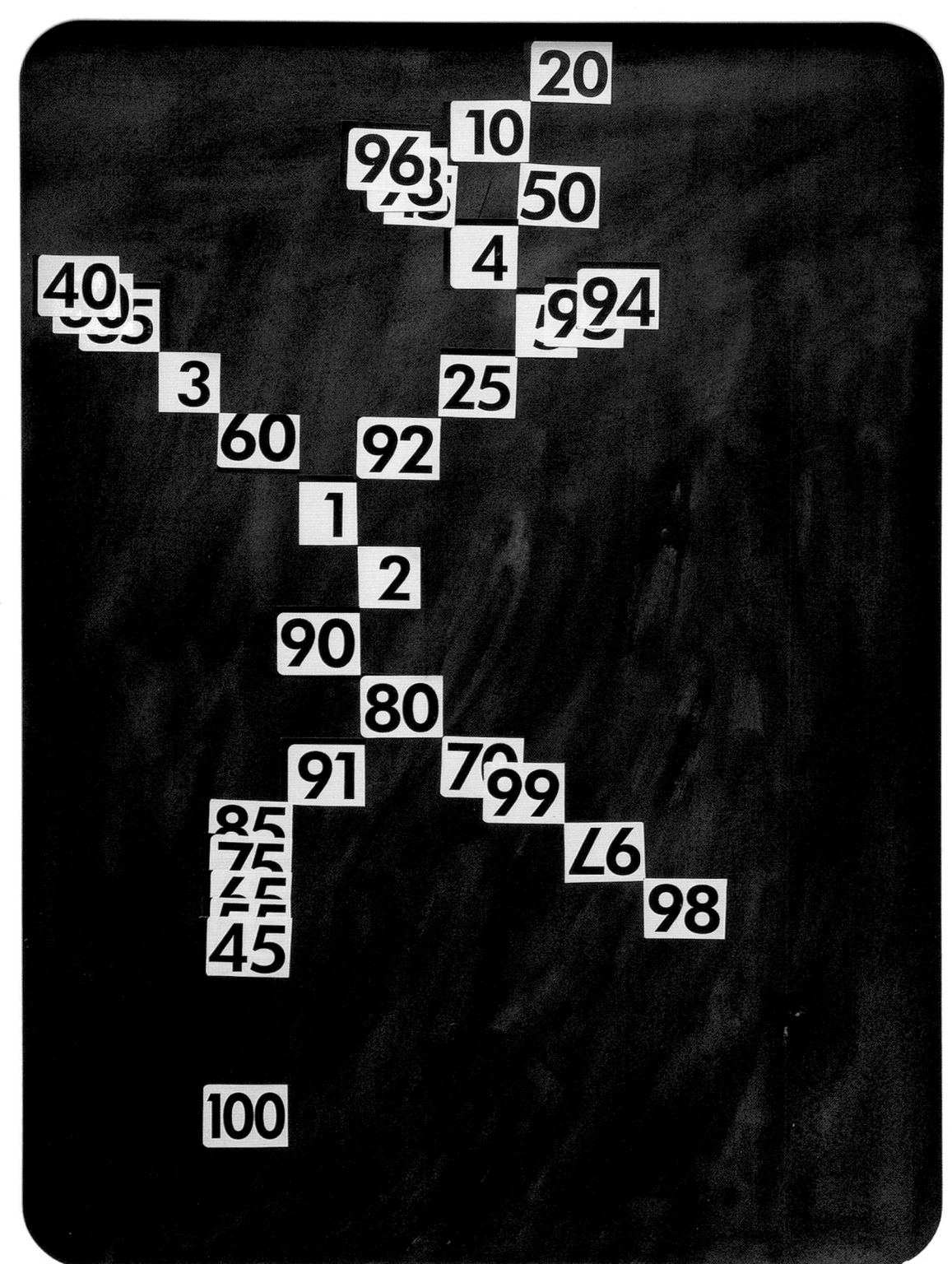

opposite: ultraworld K, 2007
ultraworld M, 2007

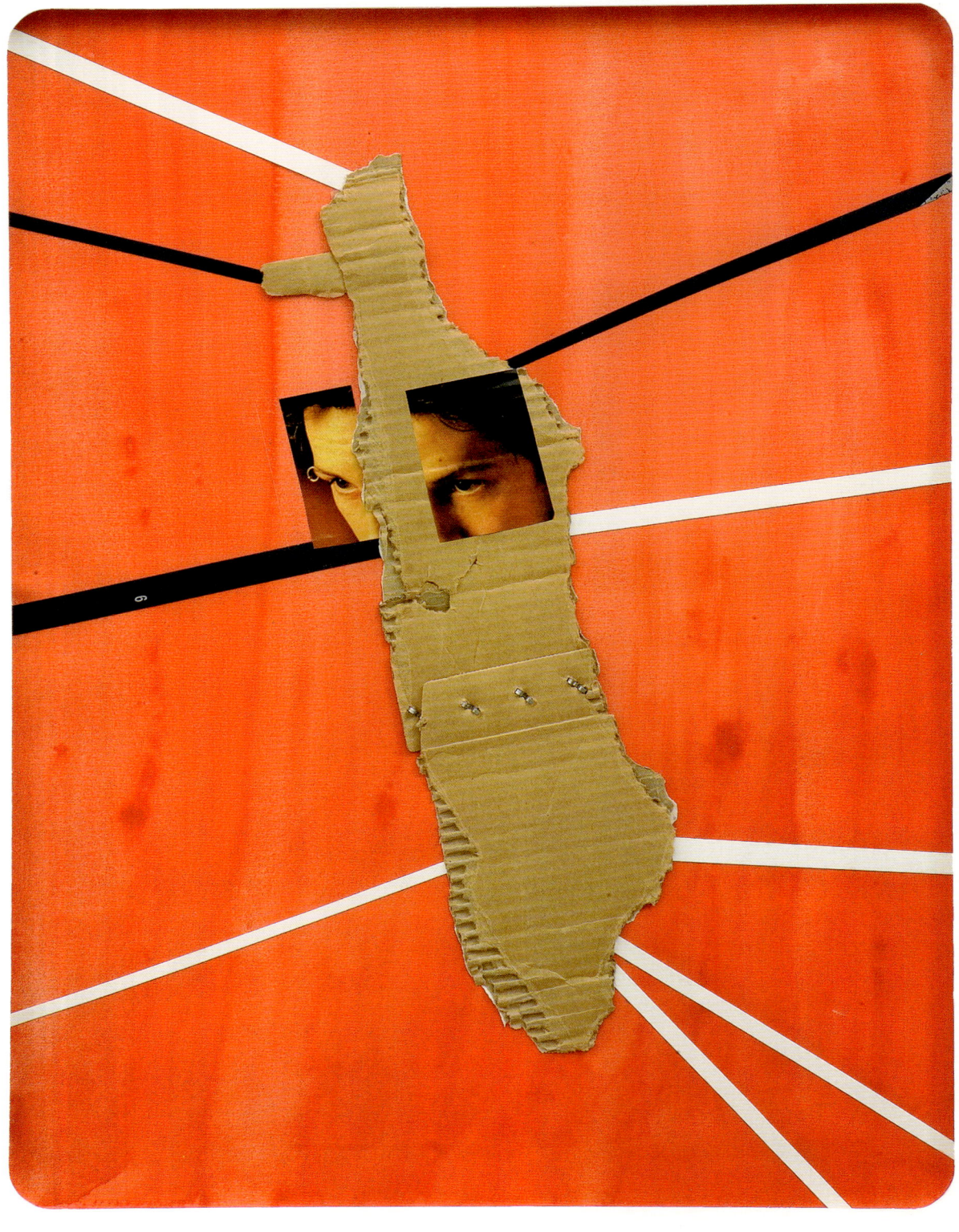

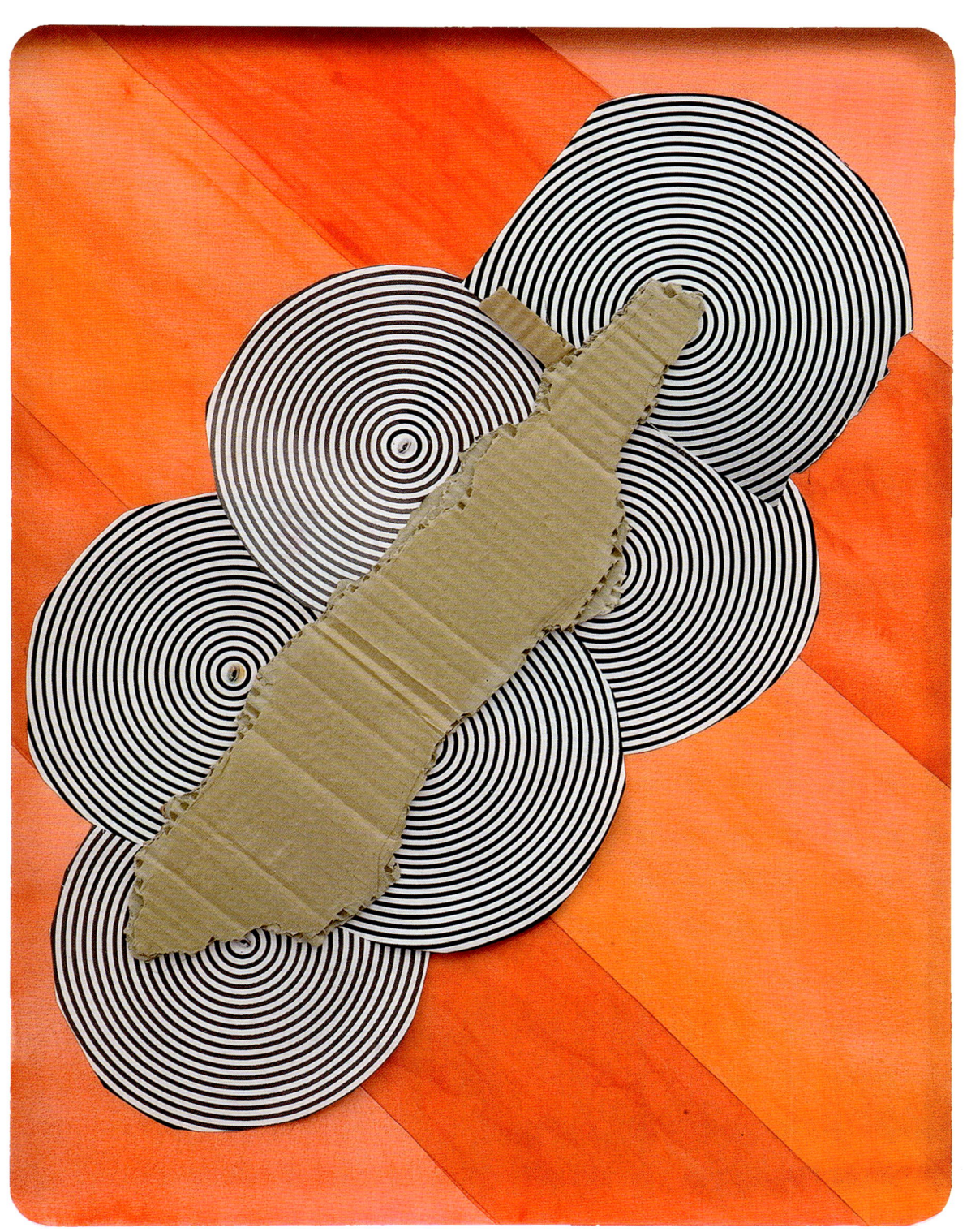

ultraworld V, from set ultraworld T-W, 2006-2008

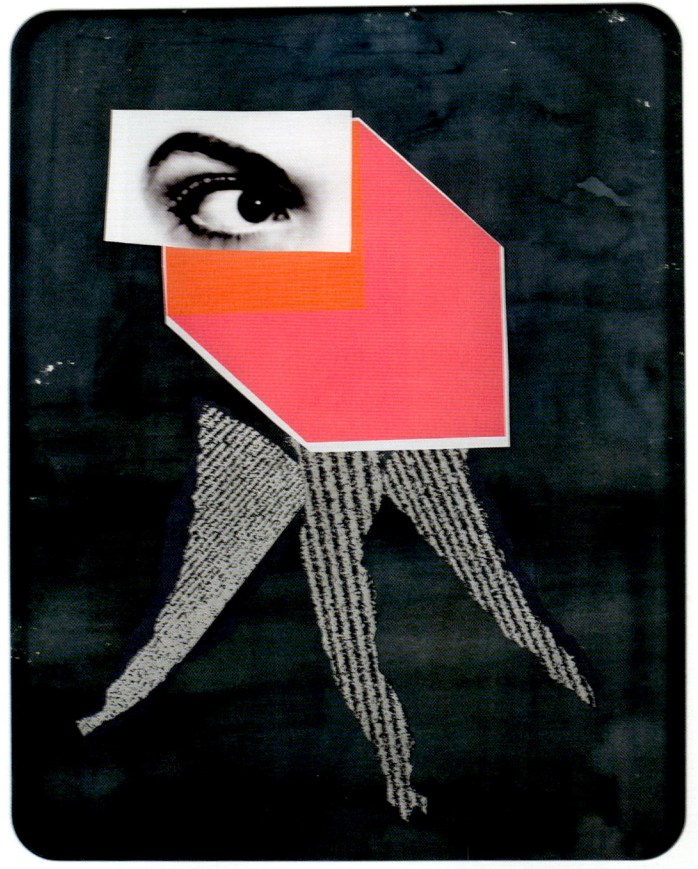

ultraworld N, 2007

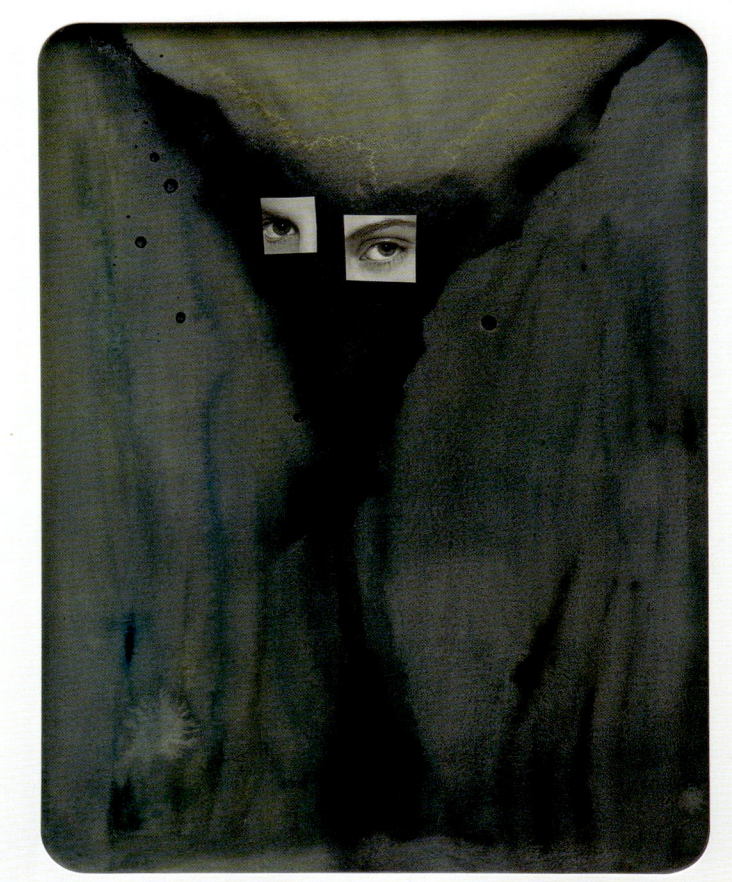

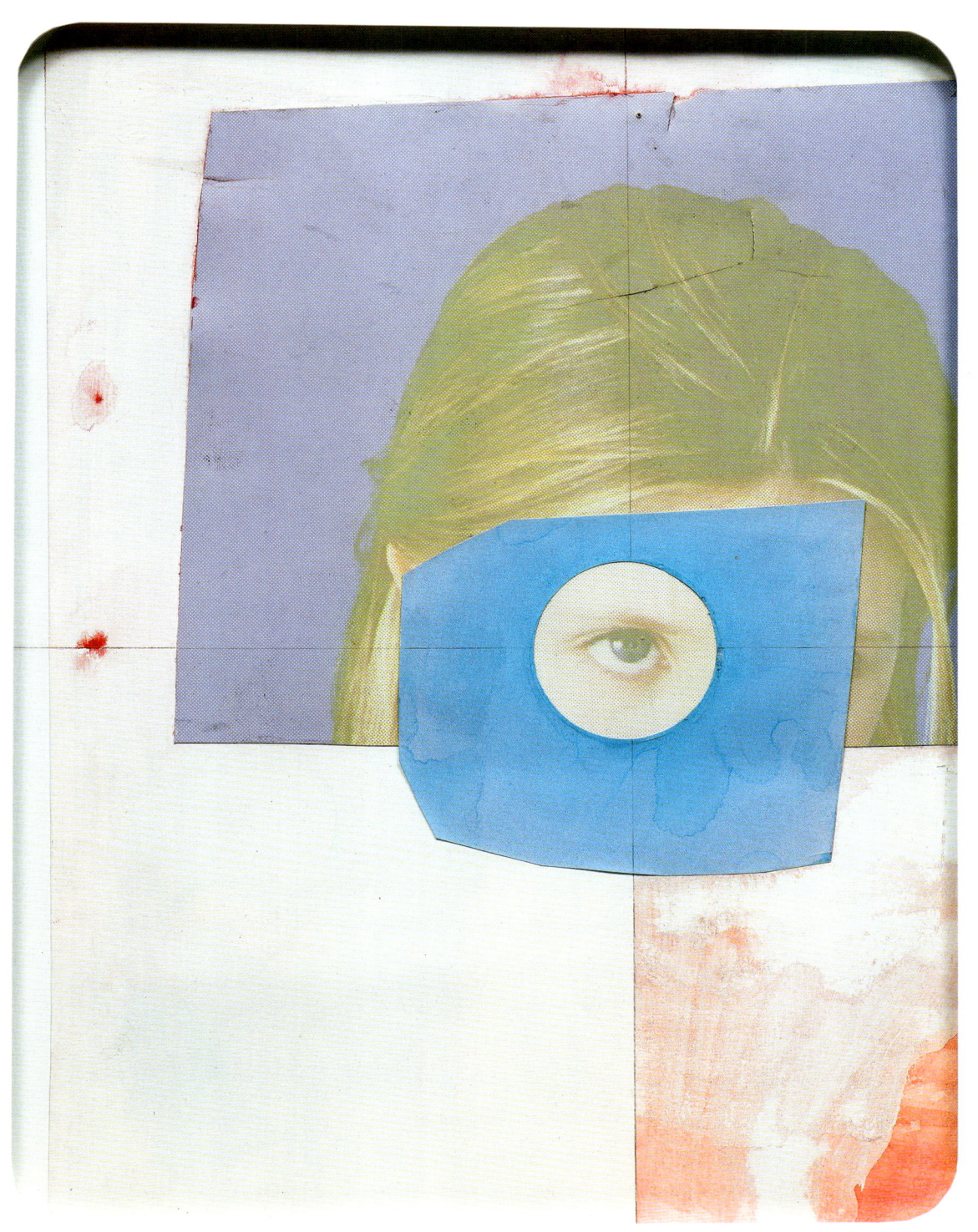

Untitled, 2005-2010

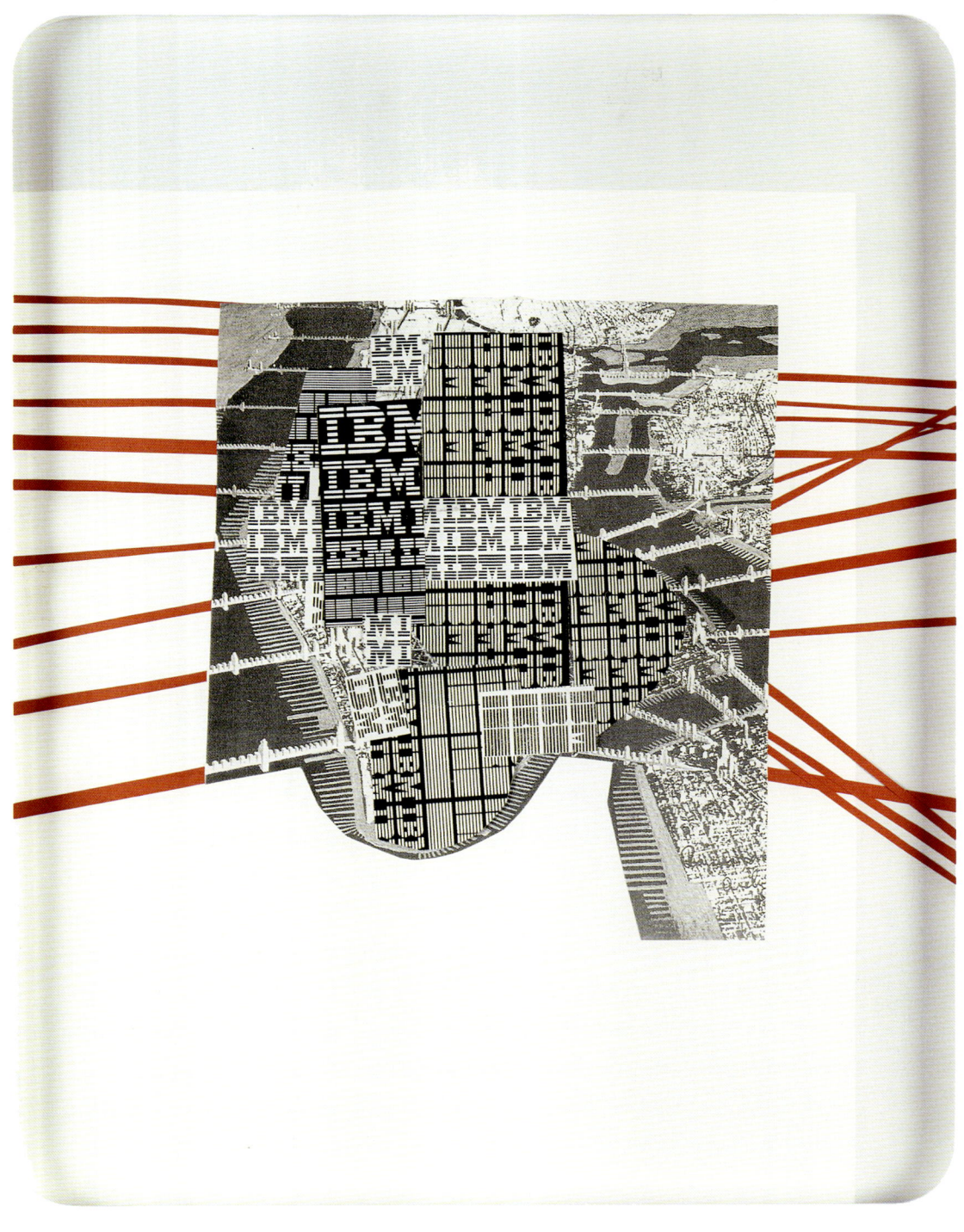

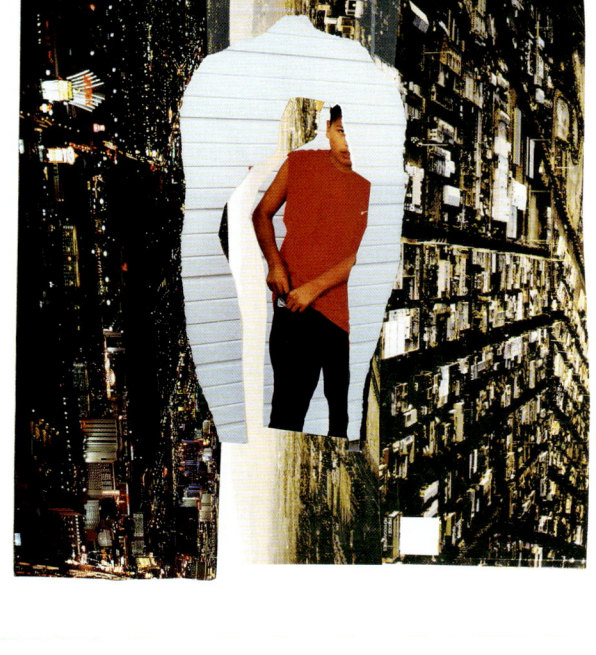

ultraworld B, 2005

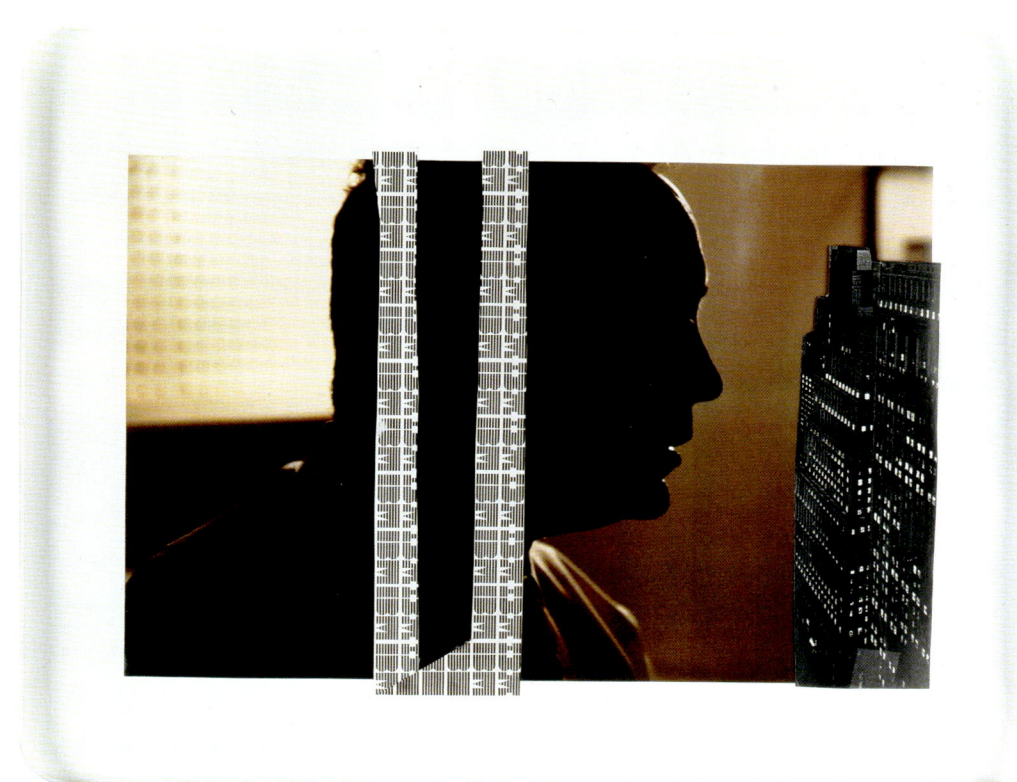

ultraworld C, 2005

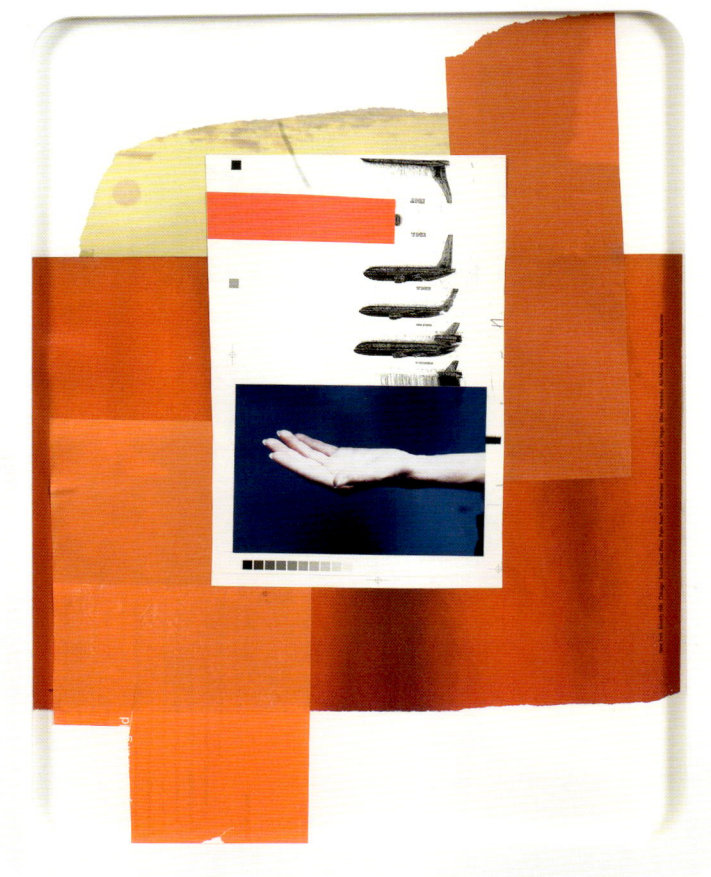

ultraworld W, from set ultraworld T–W, 2006–2008

Sun Sinking into the Santa Monica Bay, 2010

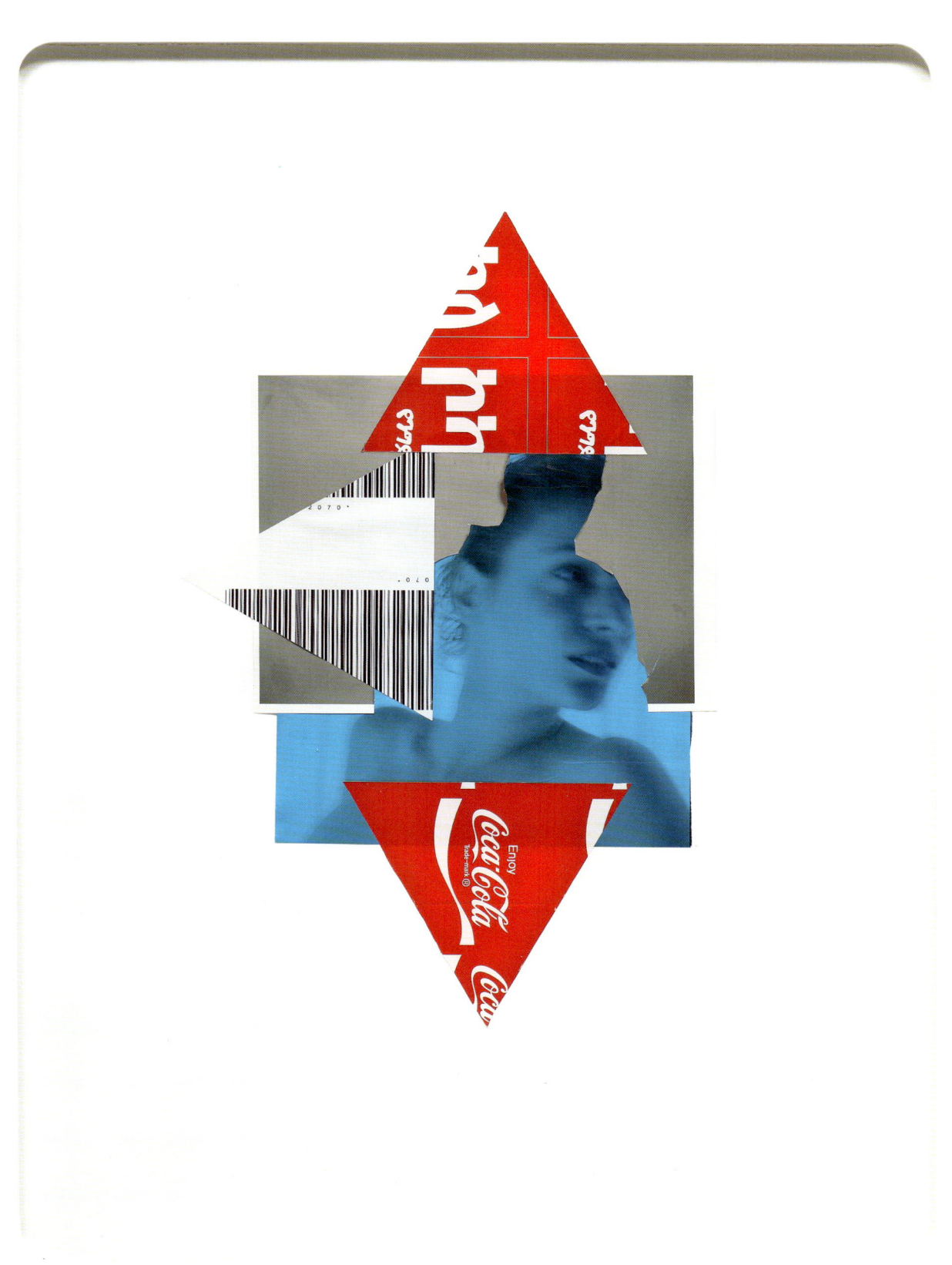

Untitled, 2005-2010

ultraworld T, from set ultraworld T-W, 2006-2008

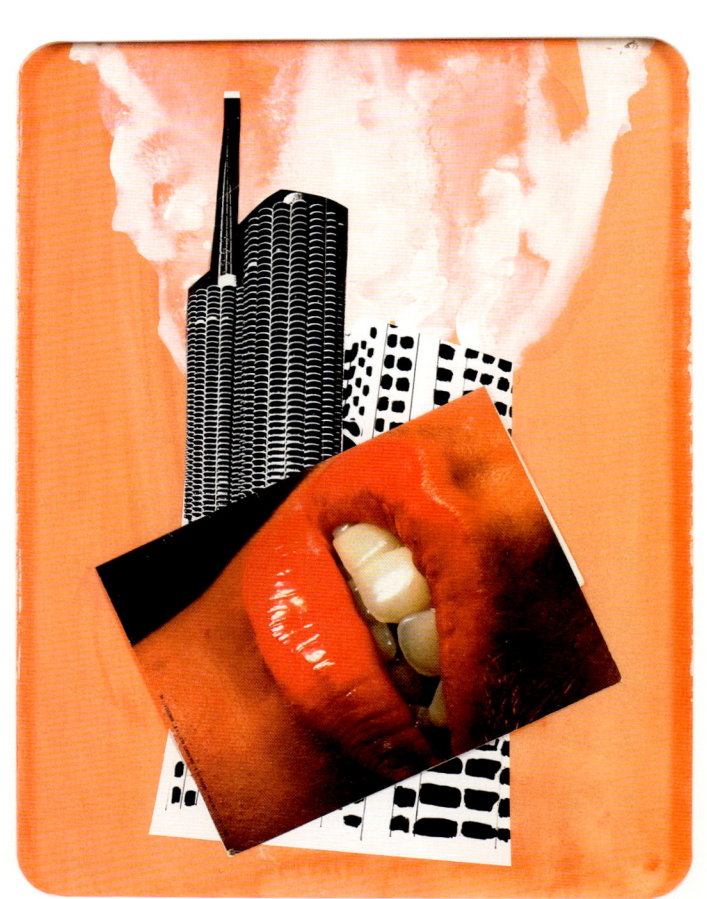

ultraworld U, from set ultraworld T-W, 2006-2008

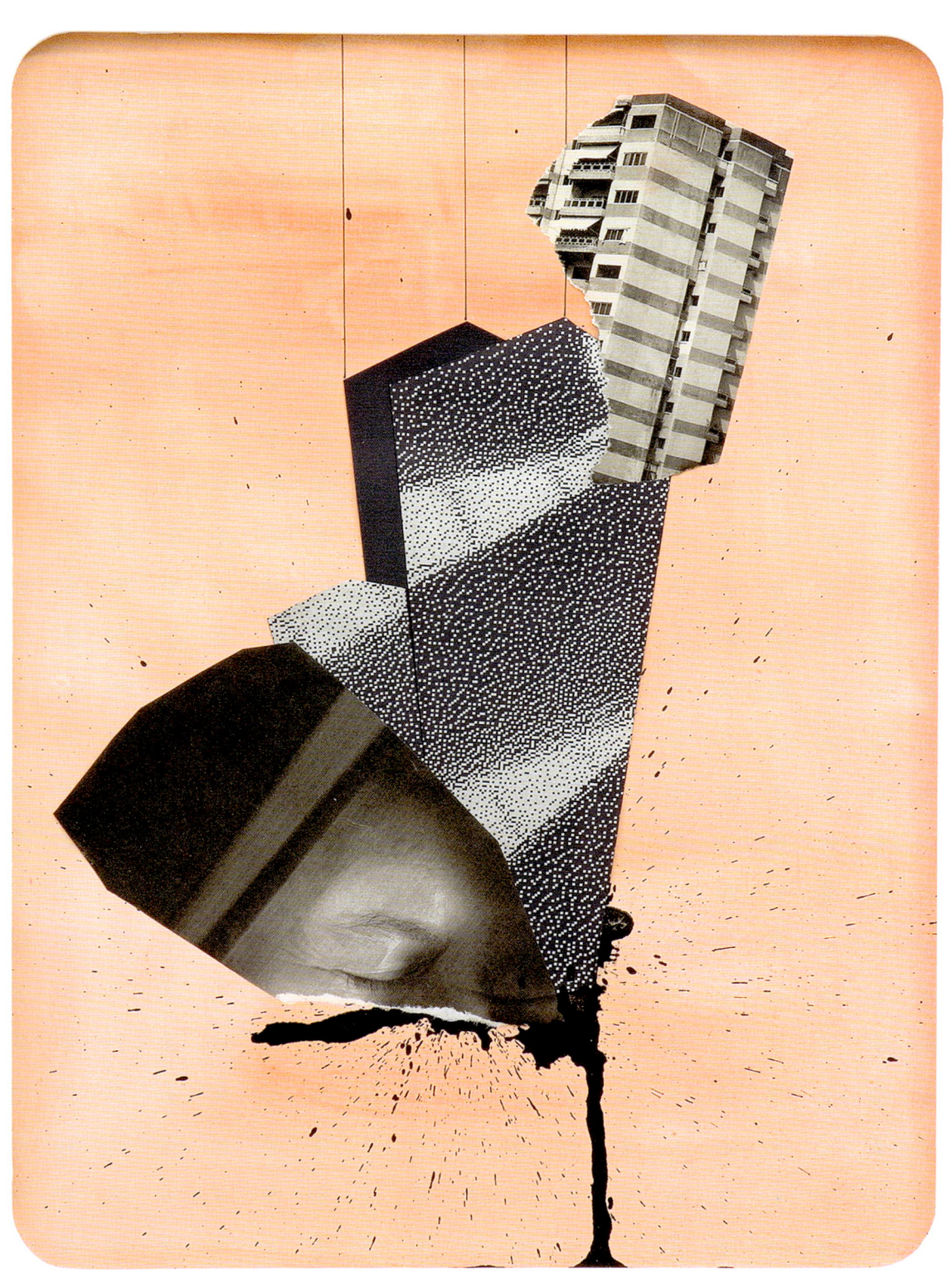

ultraworld I, 2007

Most of Aitken's installations, such as *diamond sea* (1997; pages 74–85), *electric earth*, *Black Mirror*, and *SONG 1* (2012 / 2015; pages 168–177), all of which are present in this exhibition, are composed of multiscreen videos locating viewers at the center of theater-in-the-round architectures built of images and sounds, overstimulating the senses and pulling viewers into the work by turning them into protagonists. We are almost always viewers-in-common. We experience Aitken's project by joining in his world, accepting his invitation to a communal experience.

Aitken's fluid architectures of images, sounds, and voices are the panopticon liberated from surveillance and punishment, gathering places as in his photographic work titled *conspiracy* (1998; pages 114–115) and are a true implementation of Herbert Bayer's *Diagram of the Field of Vision* from circa 1930 (fig. 3). In the corner of this diagram is an individual with a unique eye in place of his head—an ultraperceptive cyclops standing in a field of a kaleidoscopic architecture of screens, capable of seeing in all directions at once, creating a forest of simultaneous images. A typographer, graphic designer, architect, art director, sculptor, environmental designer, painter, and member of the Bauhaus, Bayer was active at a time when the notion of a mass-media world and culture was being invented. He saw in exhibition spaces a place from which information would emanate, arenas for mass communication bringing together film, radio, avant-garde theater, and advertising in ways that would revolutionize modern life. The exhibition space could become a new frontier for innovation in art and mass communication—and a form of radical and political optimism where art and mass communication could coexist in one form, where design would be integrated with industrial production.

Often considered foundational to the installation art that would emerge in the late 1960s and 1970s, Bayer's diagram in many ways resonates with Aitken's work. Aitken's immersive strategies for installations not only push our understanding of perception but also—owing to Aitken's range of interests and practices (architecture, film, and graphic design, for example)—subtly bend our experience toward the anticipatory, toward what comes next. Similar to Bayer's diagram, Aitken's installations create a space for simultaneous and instantaneous awareness of the many events unfolding around an observer's immediate present, the collapse of any linear read of aural and visual triggers— a collapse of time into space for increased and instinctive levels of awareness. The impact of mass communication on perception might just come from the knowledge that the etymological root of the word "communication" is *to make common* to many.

Aitken's work could be about what we share, and an attempt to define a form, in the gestalt meaning of form, to reclaim—or to conspire to reclaim— what we have in common. A form made of images, sounds, and at times concepts, such as a theater in the round—a shared, circular place, so present in Aitken's aesthetic—defies the linear strategies of conventional broadcast media and narrative storytelling. His circles, *Sonic Pavilion, don't think twice II* (2006; pages 10–11), *Sonic Fountain* (2013; pages 30–32, 34–35), *conspiracy, SONG 1*, and *these restless minds* (1998; pages 92–99, 101), among others, are public arenas, as the place of the *polis*. Examples include the Hirshhorn Museum and Sculpture Garden's iteration of *SONG 1* projected on the facade of its circular architecture; *sleepwalkers* was similarly projected on the facade of The Museum of Modern Art; *migration (empire)* (2008; pages 144–155) became the surface of the Carnegie Museum of Art in 2008. The images, their open loops of circulation, the voices they bring, might then have been how these institutions reclaimed for a time their place in the *citée*, reclaimed their publicness by somehow blowing open, metaphorically or not, their walls, and what their walls mean in terms of the institutional and authoritative status of the museum.

What we experience as communal is inherently immersive. Sounds in particular, or the absence of sound, in the form of either man-made sounds or nature-made music, play a critical role in Aitken's work. Again, the importance of Riley's *In C* could offer clues as to Aitken's approach to film, conceived with a core musical logic in mind. Sounds, especially voices, provide an auditory dimension in Aitken's work that simultaneously competes with and complements his visuals. Sounds participate as events, fusing the sensorial experience of his work as a whole. Sound as applied by Aitken is often out of sync with any prescribed ideas of narrative. This strategy requires viewers to pay attention to what they are hearing and seeing in a manner rather different from conventions they are familiar with.

Aitken's deep interest in a specific history of musical and sound experimentation inspired the structures of such works as *Sonic Fountain* and *Sonic Pavilion* as well as the unrealized *silent pavilion* (2008; fig. 4). *Sonic Fountain* consists of a square grid of rods suspended from the ceiling, and from which water drips, falling into an open pool of milky-white water carved into the gallery floor. Microphones within the pool are selectively amplified so that the wet drumming of drips is controlled as a varying rhythmic, almost symphonic pattern; amplified throughout the space, Aitken's sound pulsates time itself in a particularly contemplative manner, dismantling any delineation between sound and music, between irregular motions and vibrations and vibrations regularly and harmonically ordered.

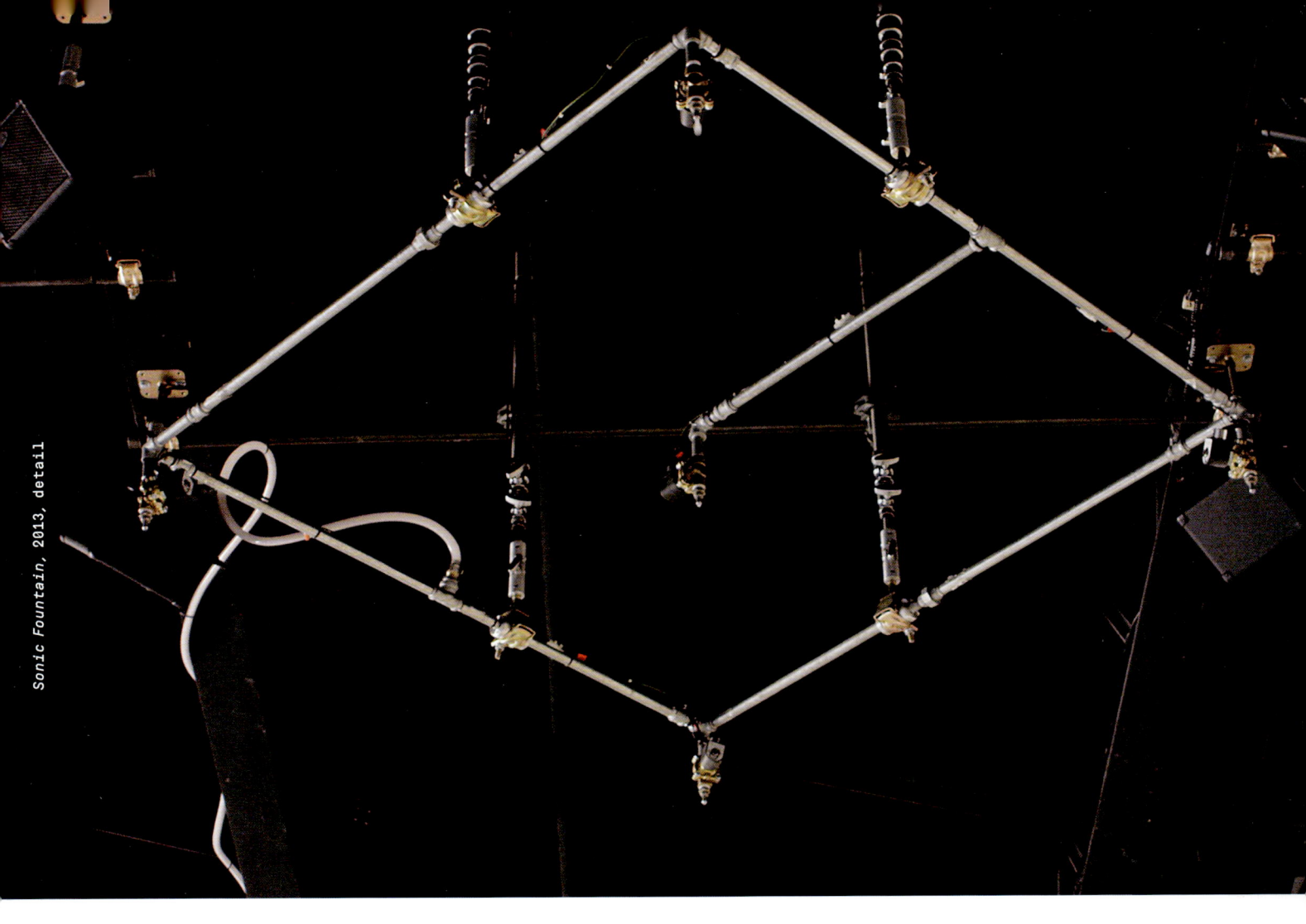

Sonic Fountain, 2013, detail

SONIC FOUNTAIN

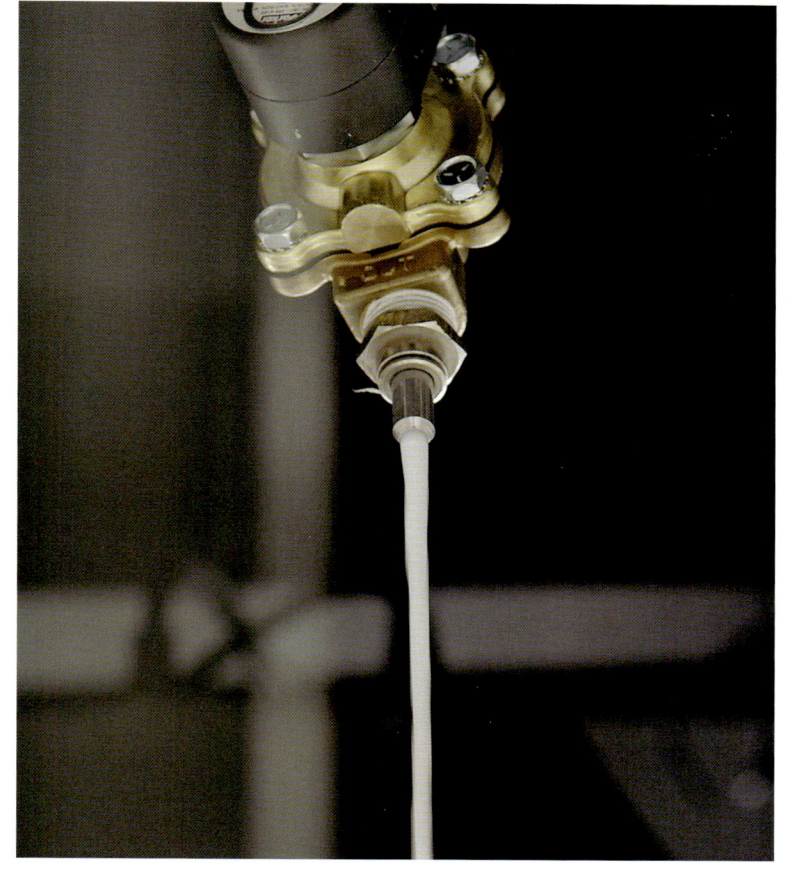

Sonic Fountain, 2013, detail

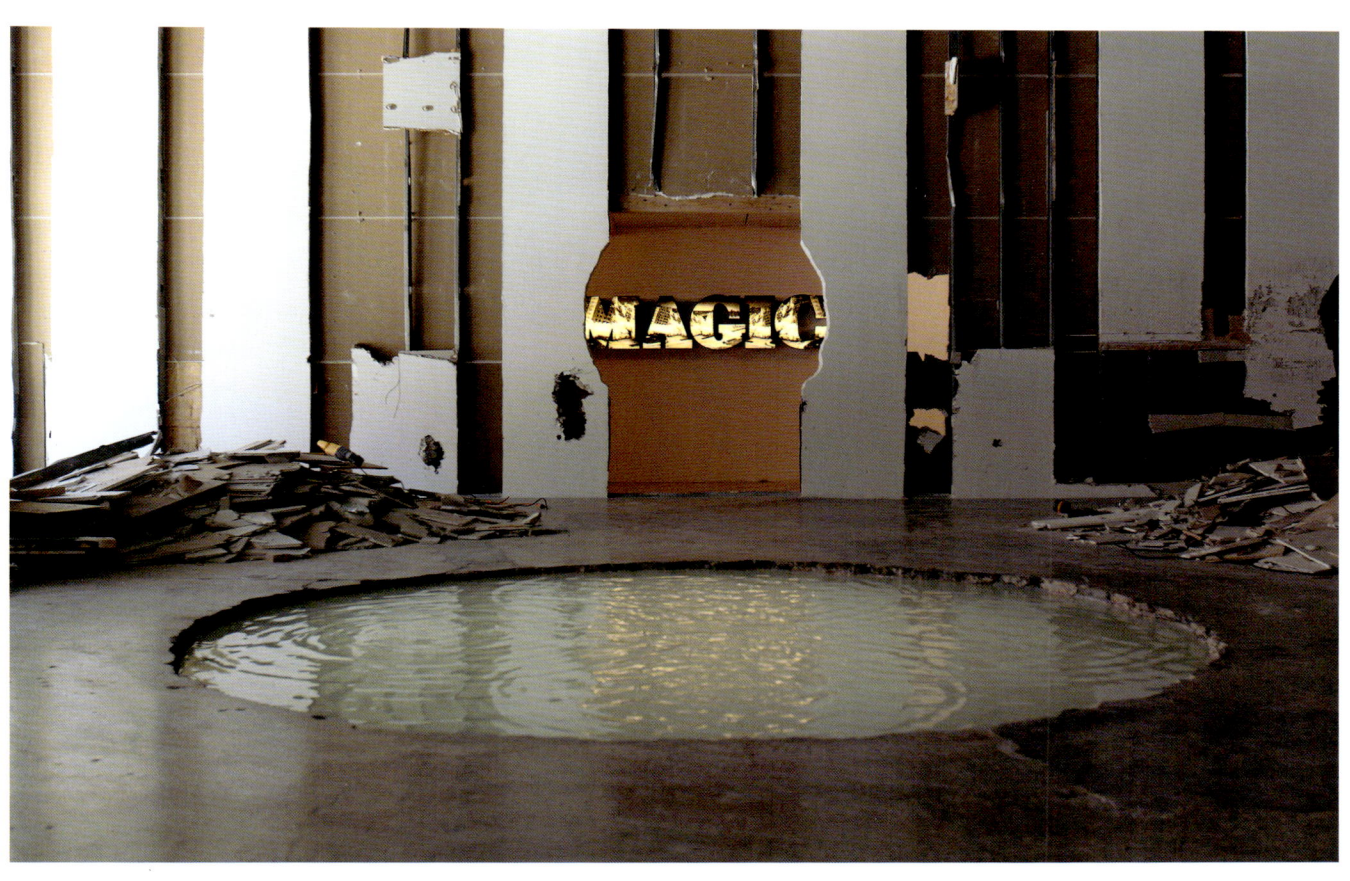

Sonic Fountain, 2013, installation view from 100 YRS (part 2) performance, 303 Gallery, New York

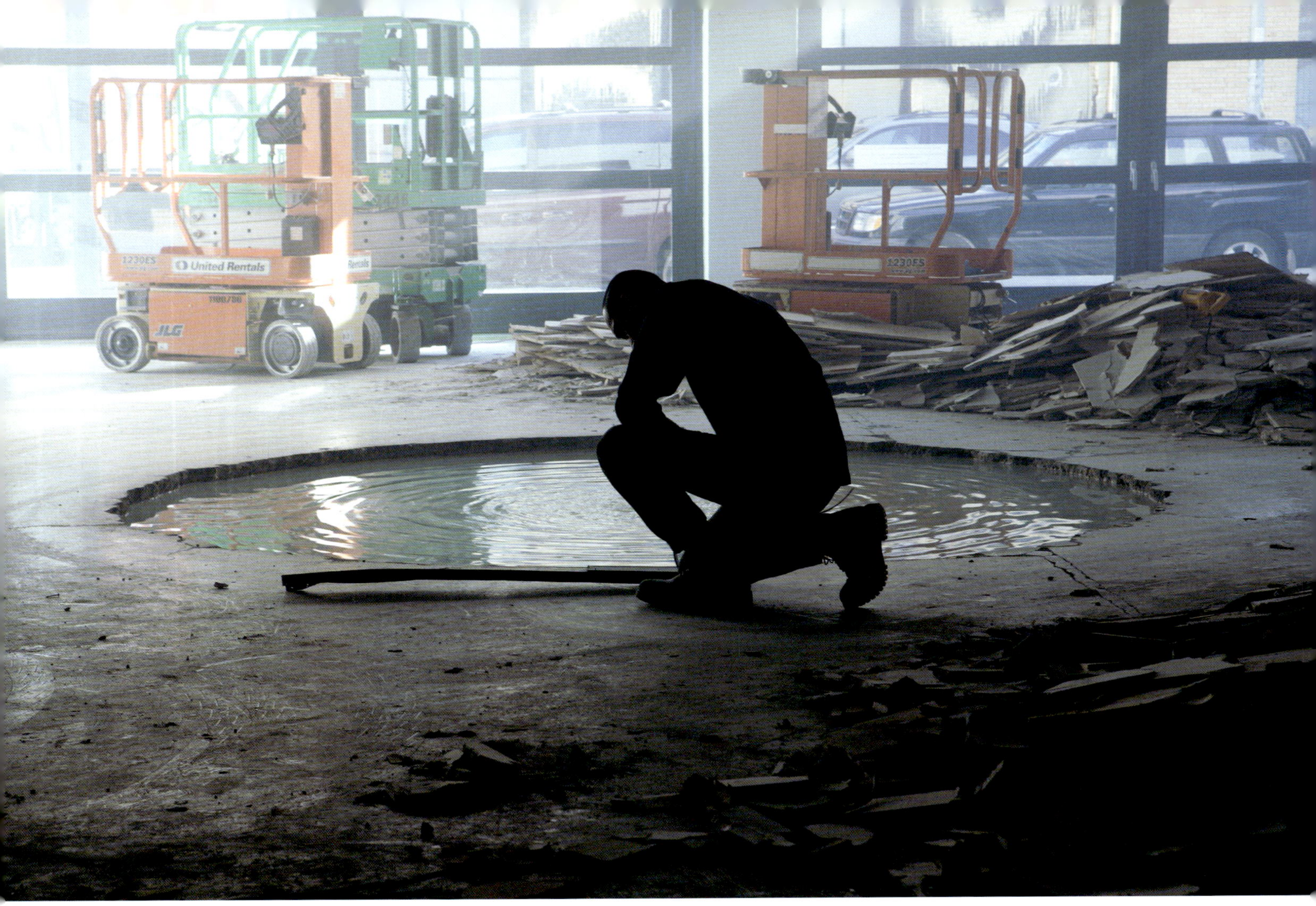

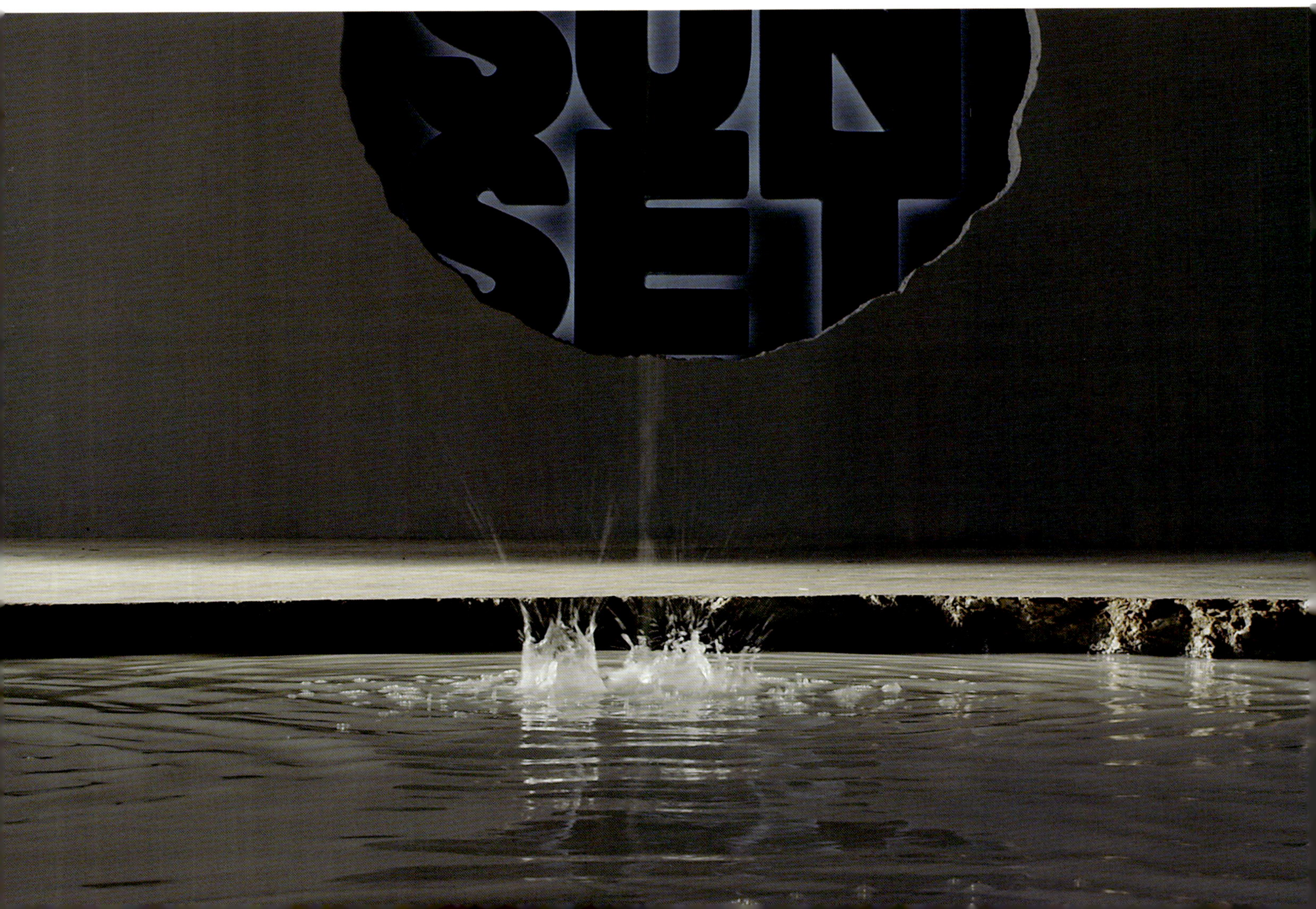

Sonic Fountain and the use of water as an instrument must be inserted into a lineage of musical experimentation in which John Cage and the Fluxus movement, and George Brecht in particular, play a significant role. It is within this legacy that Aitken's work must be evaluated. As humorously mentioned by Douglas Kahn in *Noise Water Meat*, when Jackson Pollock stopped dripping in 1952, Cage started pouring and began to experiment with water as music.[2] Cage's experiments ranged from blowing a duck whistle into a bowl of water to the use of a "water gong," a Chinese gong plunged into a tub of water during the production of a tone.[3]

If Aitken's editing strategies produce an extension and contraction of time, his sound work allows us to hear time as an aural/musical structure. *Sonic Fountain*'s patterned drops of water make us see in space the pattern of hearing, which is also an undulation. Hearing occurs when the air between a sound and its auditor is struck and undulates spherically, falling on the ears, as the water in a pool undulates when a drop of water reaches it. In a theater in the round, sounds and voices spread and rise into the audience similarly, horizontally but also vertically, in an ascending motion. As these circles of sounds and water expand and contract, vertically and horizontally, they define spherical space as an agora—a place to congregate—the same kind of circular space that appears so often throughout Aitken's project: a shared space, common to many. Such is the case with the diagram of two expanding and concentric circles of fluorescent light that composes the pattern of Aitken's wall work *don't think twice II*, which almost stands as a programmatic scheme for his approach to architecture and space.

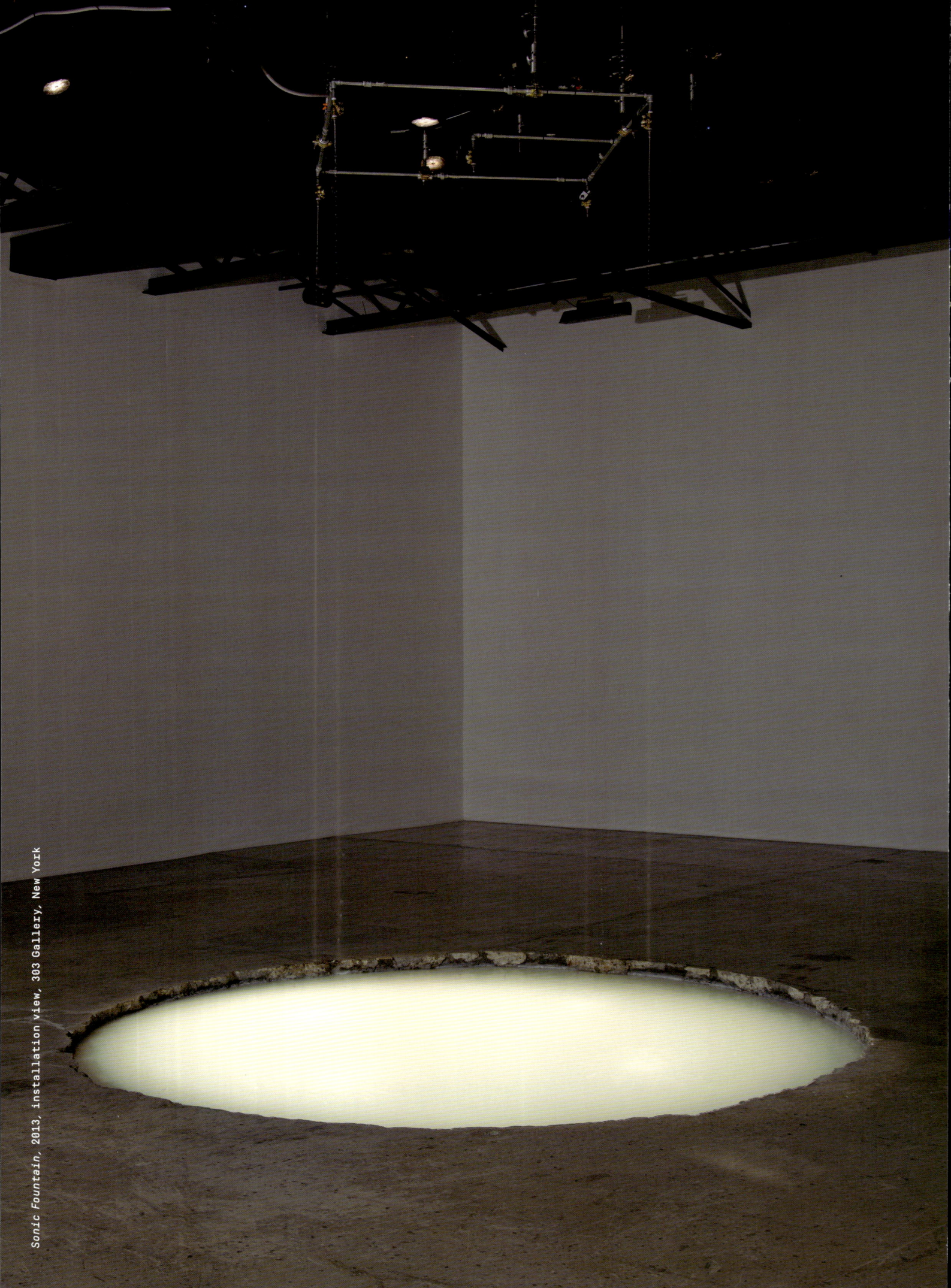

Sonic Fountain, 2013, installation view, 303 Gallery, New York

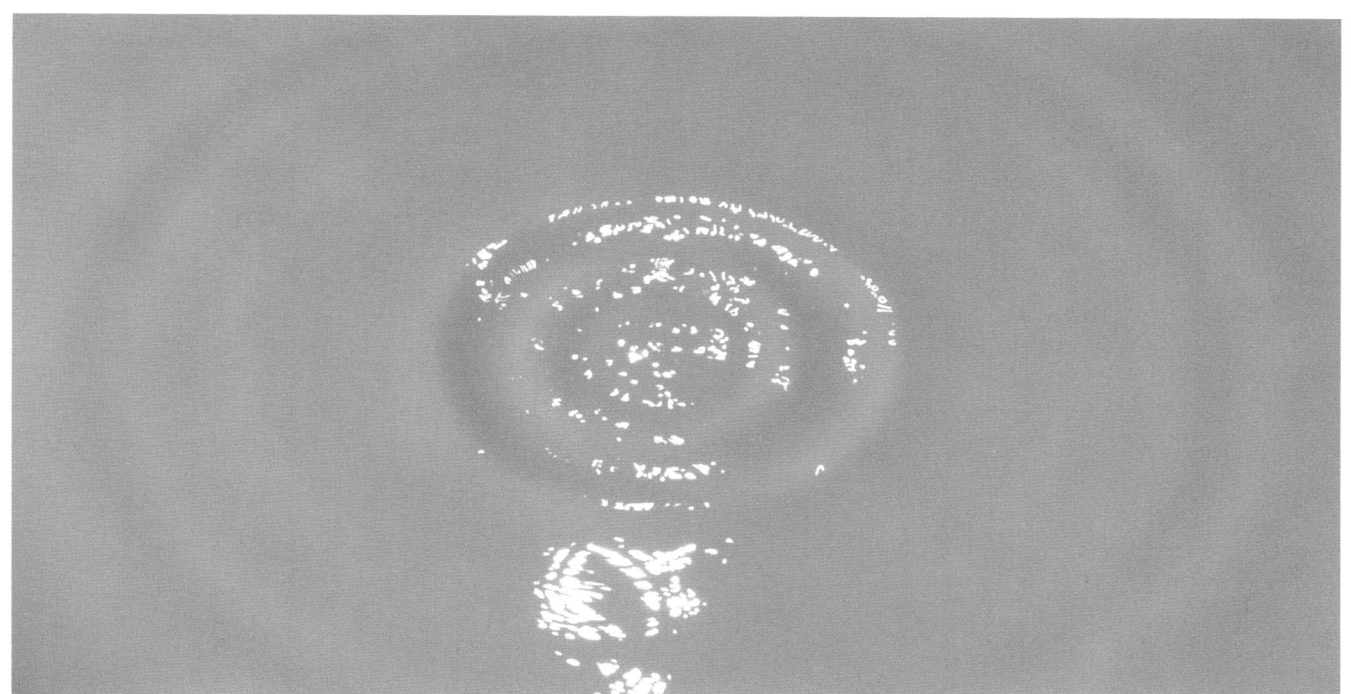
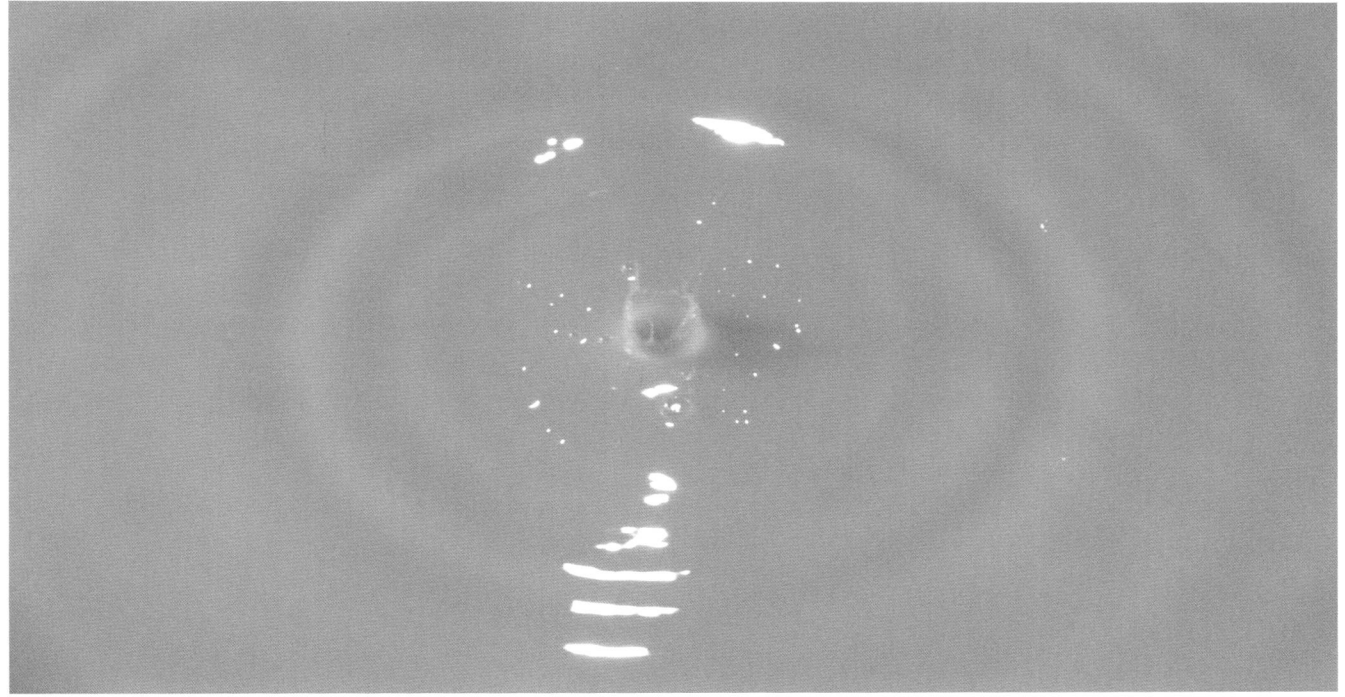

Sonic Fountain, 2013, details

As described earlier, *Sonic Pavilion* is a circular glass building capturing and broadcasting the seismic waves of the earth, extant at all times, in an infinite gradation—even when impossible to perceive. As such, this work makes audible a reality that exists well below our perceptual abilities. The sounds of nature, earth, and water are in one way or another taken out of their own acoustic chambers in order to be amplified through a process in which nature is transformed into art. *Sonic Pavilion* is the architectural extension of Robert Morris's *Box with the Sound of Its Own Making* (1961), a wooden box containing and literally playing the sounds of its own making.

With *silent pavilion*, it is John Cage again who must be cited for the importance of *4'33"* (1952) as well as his essay "The Future of Music: Credo" (1937), in which "noise" functions as the locus for experimental music, equipped with means for electronic amplifying systems turning a variety of minuscule sounds into music—turning the world into one sound event where everything is musical. Furthermore, Cage's experiments with the anechoic chamber are an important precedent, as are the anechoic chamber and other sensory environments conceived by Robert Irwin, James Turrell, and scientist Ed Wortz for the Los Angeles County Museum of Art's Art and Technology Program in 1969. Beyond sonic, auditory experimentation, what all of these initiatives share is simply the fact that a work of art is not an object anymore, but an immersive, sensorial, and spatial experience; a phenomenological experience that defies conventional acts of perception previously limited to standing in front of an object or an image. This is an idea that is deeply rooted in Aitken's aesthetic. Aitken's unrealized *silent pavilion* is a modernist pavilion in which three walls are covered with sound-isolation padding while a fourth, glass wall faces the surrounding landscape. Inside this silence generator, one would be left with a vista and the sounds produced by the body: heartbeats, footsteps, swallowing—the sounds that constitute us. And in *silent pavilion* the body itself becomes an emitting entity, engaged in transmission. Even with all these silencing devices, the pavilion stresses the impossibility of absolute silence and isolation.

More so than any notions of representation, at the core of Aitken's work we find the artist addressing the very nature of communication: how we communicate, what we communicate, what communicates, and what is communicated. Spaces, relationships, emissions, and receptions: What do these create? And within such spaces, what is the nature of the experiences we share? What content do we have in common? Aitken creates and captures—both metaphorically and literally—magnetic fields: fields of emissions that surround us, constitute us, alienate us, and, ultimately, pass through us. It almost echoes Lamartine's question "Inanimate objects, do you have a soul?" In the presence of objects such as the dozens of empty, seemingly mute billboards that Aitken has photographed (*the mirror #9*, 1998; pages 38–39), we ask: Does the absence of imagery or any promotional argument on their surface mean they are dormant? Or do they continue to be active, transmitting, messaging? And if so, what is their message?

Could it be that in our media-defined and communication-saturated cultural and technological environment, media has become a species? Aitken has managed to develop an aesthetic that steps back from traditional mediums, though not only painting and sculpture. His work is articulated in and around both telecommunication technology (transmission, projection, telephony, and cinema) and recording media (photography, phonography, and, again, cinema, which finds a place in both categories). Aitken's aesthetic is characterized by the notion of transmission, while the storage mode of recording is defined by inscription on a surface or in a material. The transmission of media is an idea that is based on broadcasting, emitting, and, I would add, glowing. It is about electricity, magnetic fields, electromagnetic aura, or, in fact, a pure aura of a moment in history, of a material, and of course of a person. Nature is heard in his work, waves of electronic communication are sent out, felt. To put it simply, Aitken's work is extroversion.

The print *the mirror #11 (rise)* (1998; pages 40–41) is a stereotypical postcard view of Los Angeles at night, showing lines of illuminated boulevards shooting toward the horizon. Cars and streetlamps provide illumination that, by now, has been seen thousands of times in movies, advertising, and art. The image itself is either clichéd or iconographic, a generic appropriation with no specific source. It is a commonplace view, a shared thing. We all know it and its location, and for these reasons, it may just be impossible to produce or reproduce. It is an image caught in its own feedback loop—one that never leaves, one that will only ever continue to reemerge. Every day.

Another way to look at *the mirror #11 (rise)* would be to see it as a buzzing, humming, overloaded circuit board, bearing highly charged electronics carrying electricity, an electromagnetic cartography charting any interferences that would signal or betray the presence of a city. It is actually scientifically possible to locate a city by its electronic leaks from sources as diverse as cars, lightbulbs, computers, and electrical grids. Cities permanently leak and transmit energy and information, and there is no silence in a world where the electromagnetic charge is so deeply burned into the environment.

the mirror #9, 1998

MIRROR SERIES

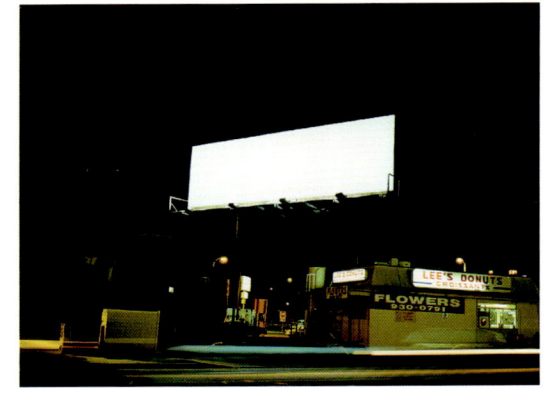
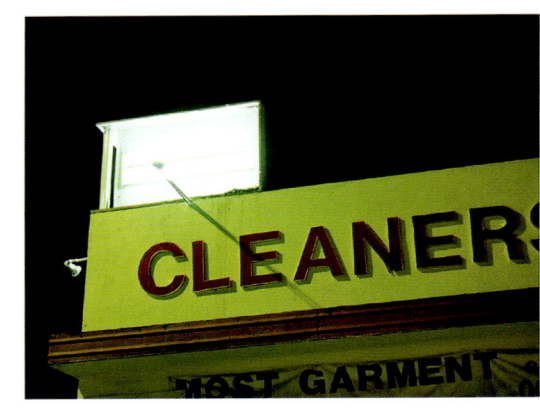
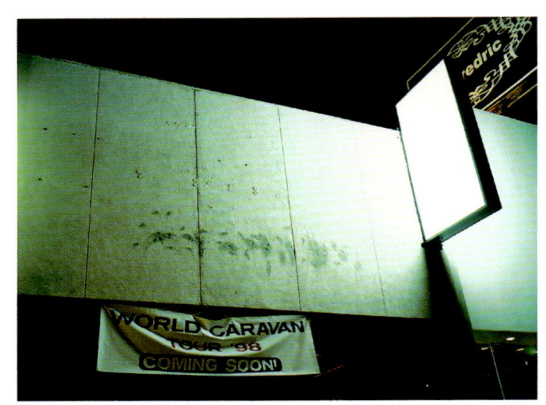
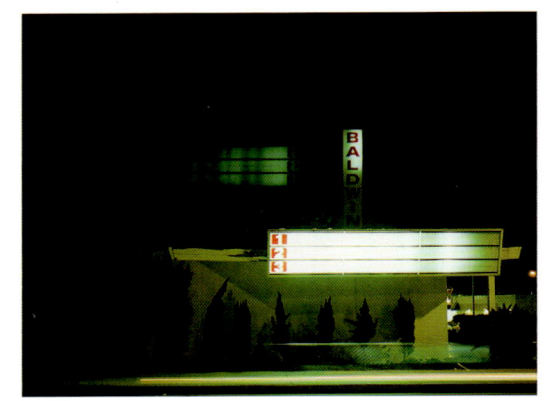
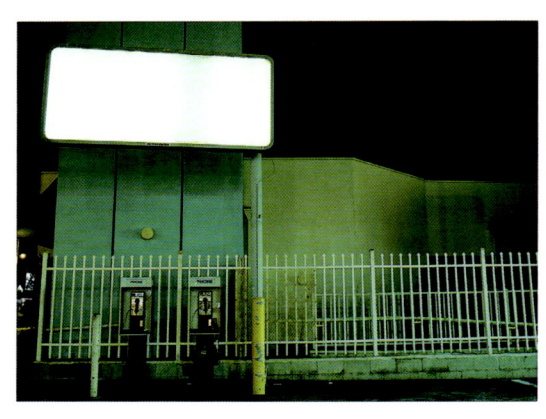

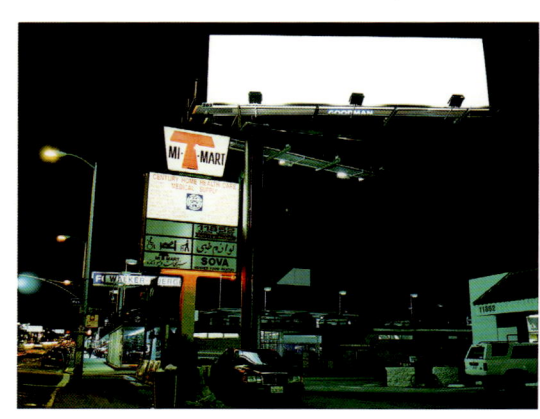

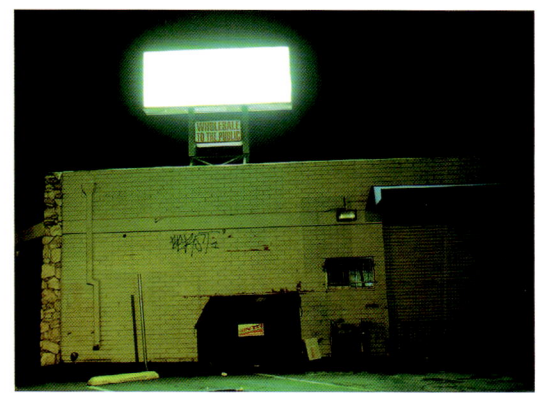
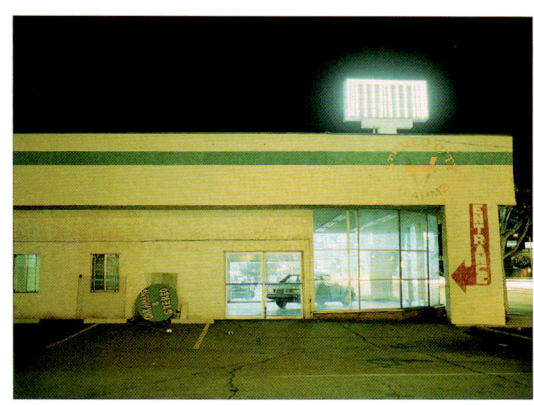
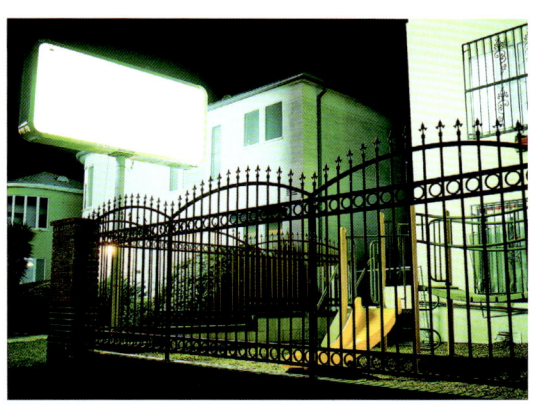
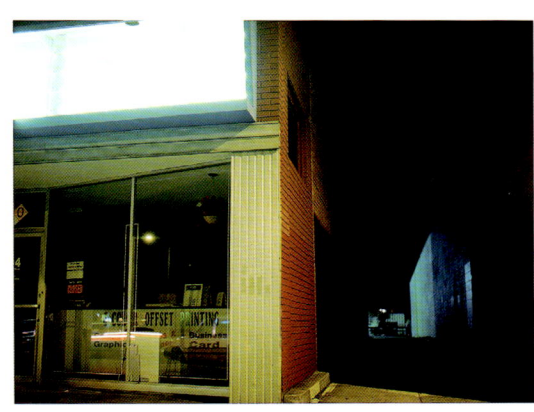
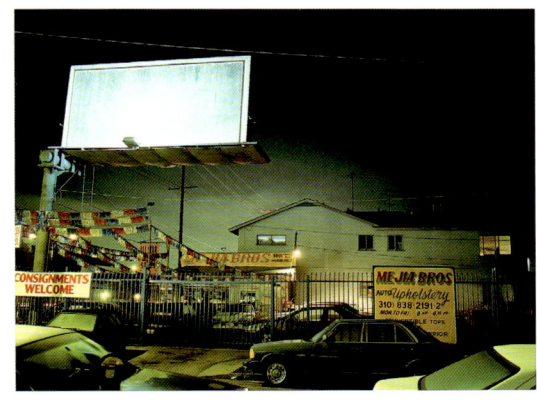
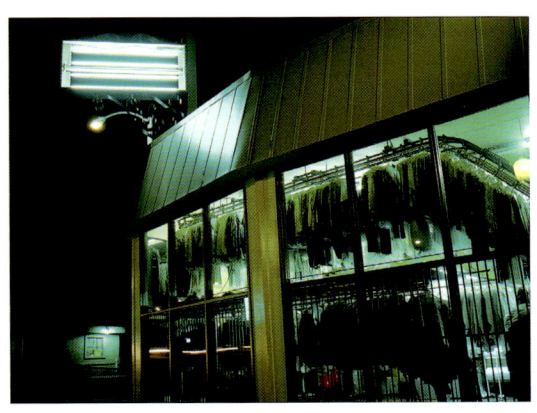
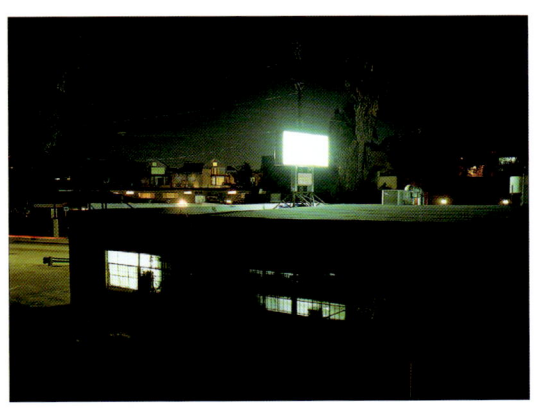

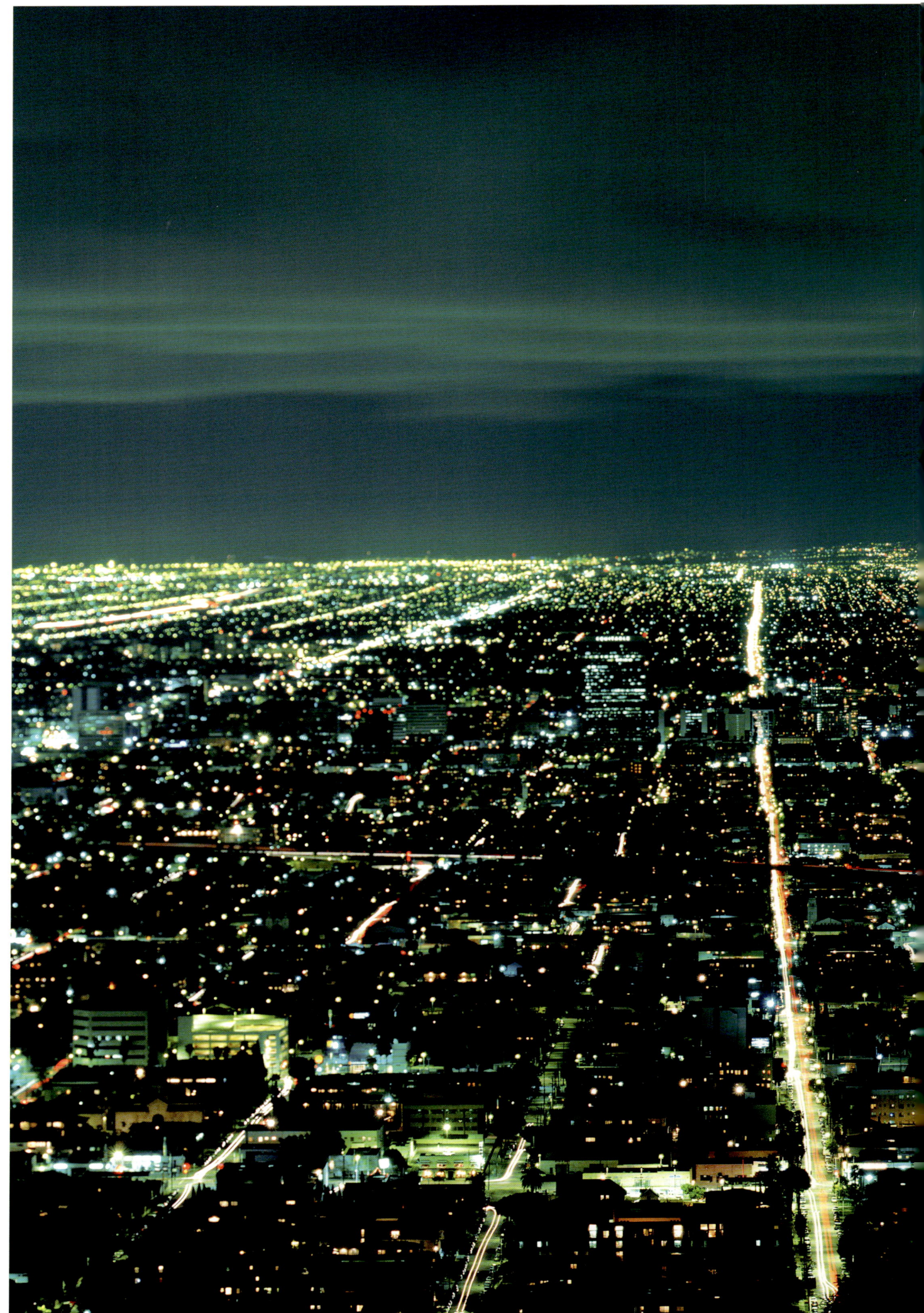

the mirror #11 [rise], 1998

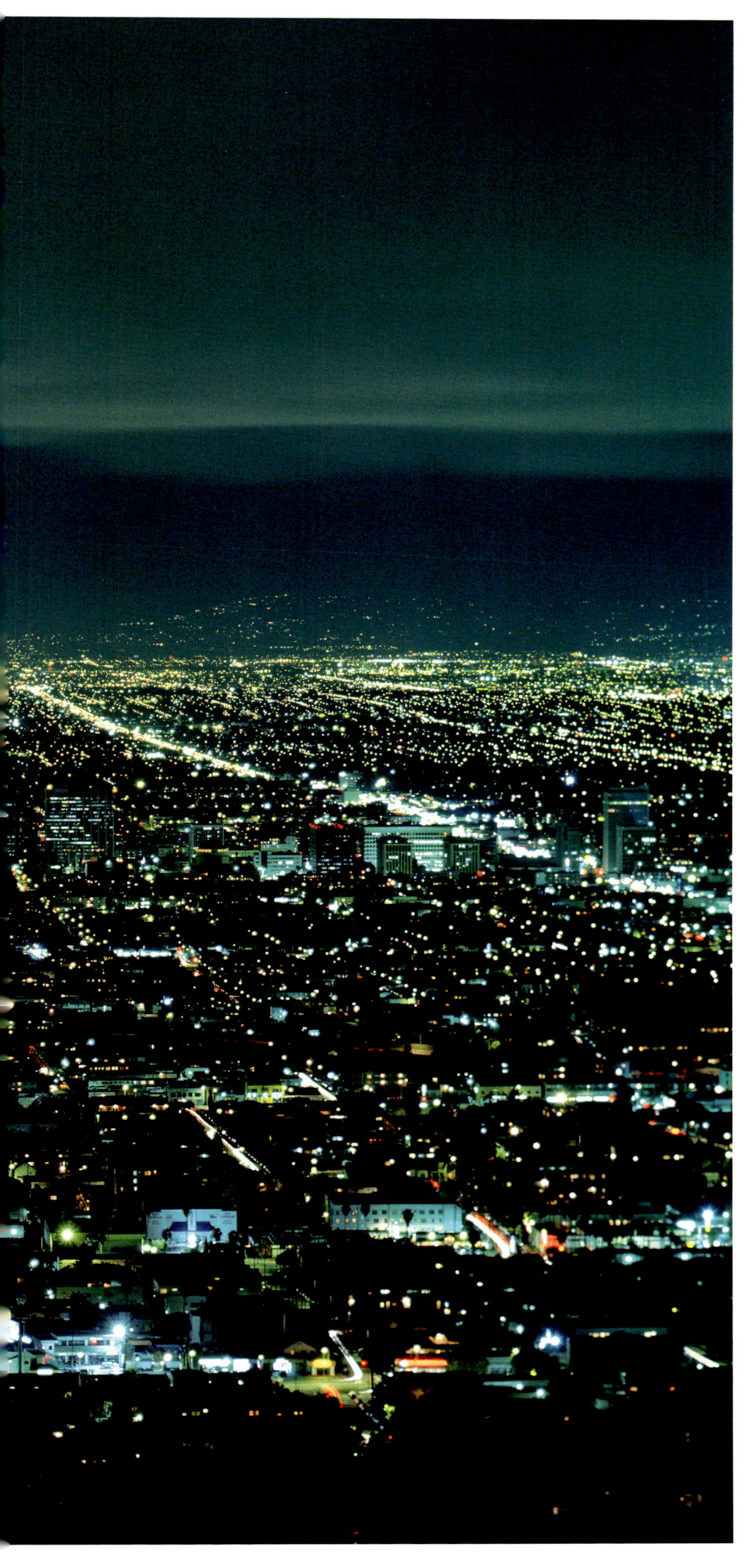

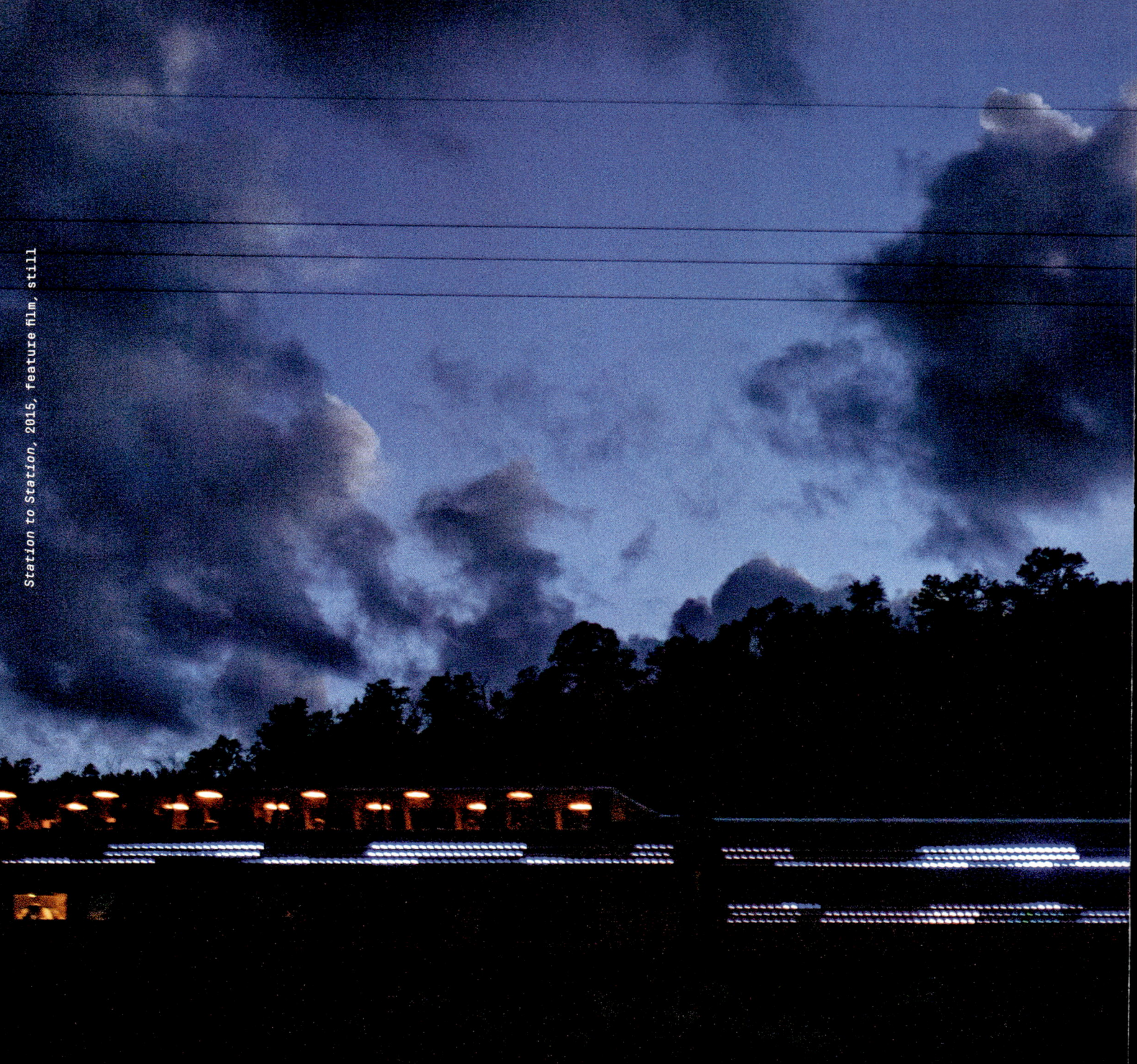

Station to Station, 2015, feature film, still

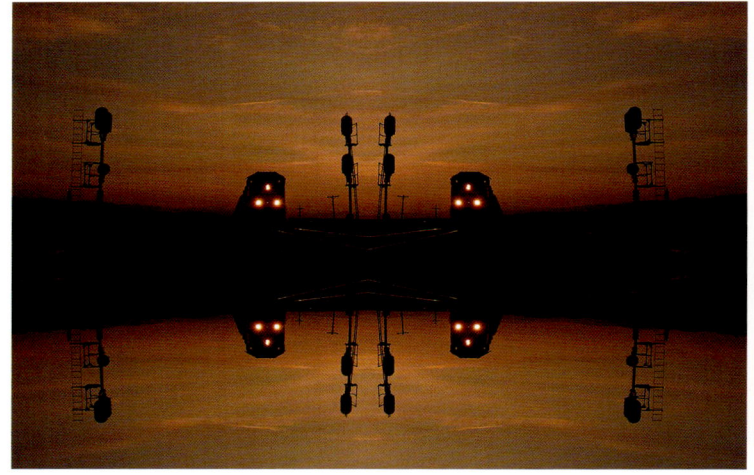
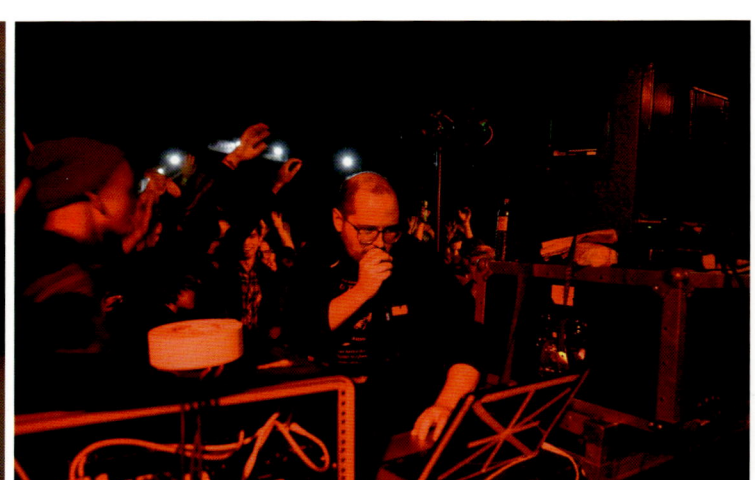

Station to Station, 2013 [left to right: Station to Station, 2015, feature film, still; Dan Deacon performs; the Oakland happening; Jonah Bokaer's AIRLOCKS]

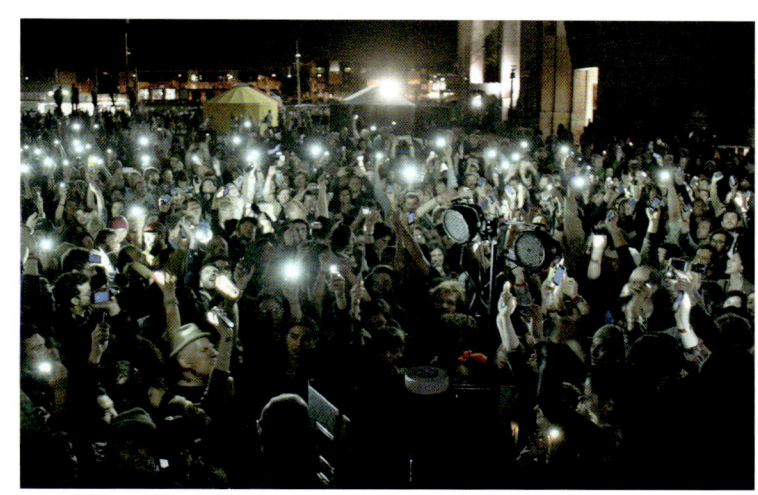
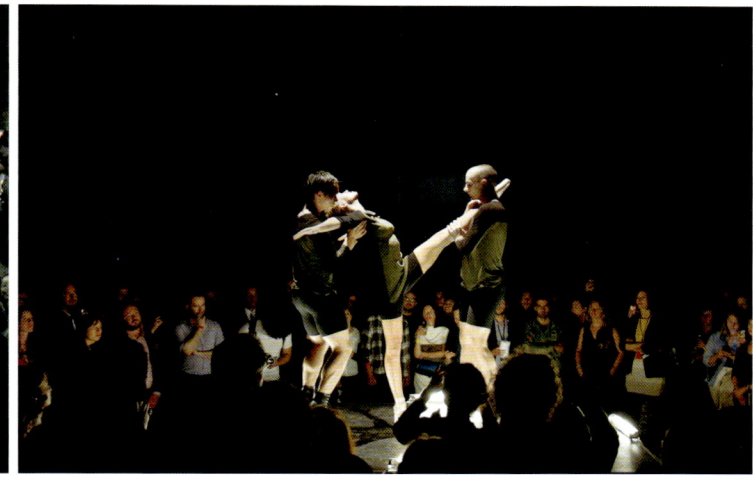

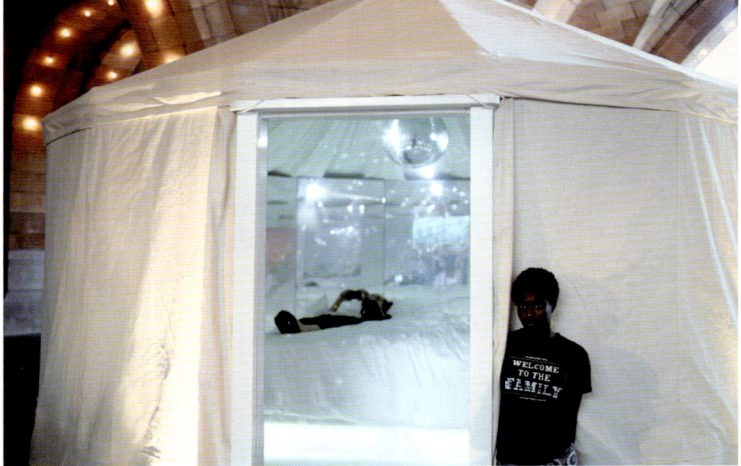
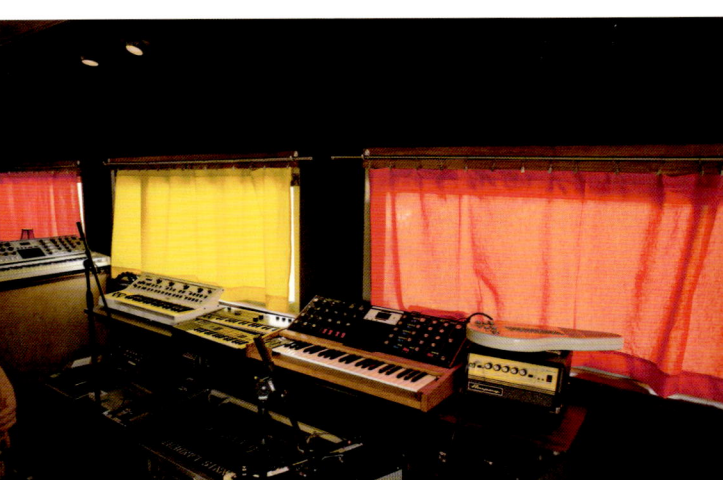

Station to Station, 2013 (left to right: Urs Fischer's yurt; the Station to Station train recording car; Aaron Koblin and Ben Tricklebank's *Light Echoes*; Jackson Browne)

      With *Station to Station*, Aitken continued to build on notions of transmission and media. *Station to Station* was an event conceived as a cross-country train journey—twenty-three days in duration—from New York to San Francisco. During the trip, numerous artists such as Urs Fischer, Ariel Pink, Rirkrit Tiravanija, Thomas Demand, Cat Power, Liz Glynn, Giorgio Moroder, and Olafur Eliasson came together to populate the vehicle and to participate in events and performances at stops along the route. The entire "work" was documented and edited into a feature film, constructed from sixty-two one-minute fragments, charting a creative cartography of the journey and the terrain of the country. It could be said that *Station to Station*'s medium was the land, and its making constituted Aitken's programming of the journey's content along the antennae of railways. With the development of the railroads, advanced network distribution was established to transport goods and information across the United States. Additionally, the postal system traveled along these same railways, as did the telegraph system, an early manifestation of electronic and information transmissions. Some, at that time, believed that the metallic parallel tracks of the railroad themselves held the potential for transmitting signals.

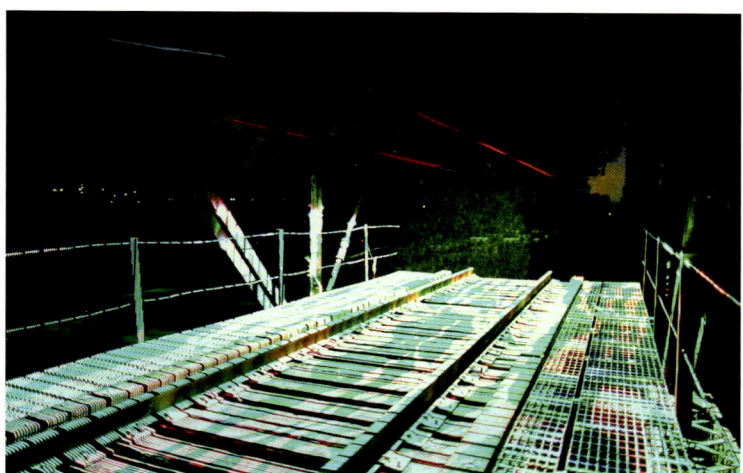 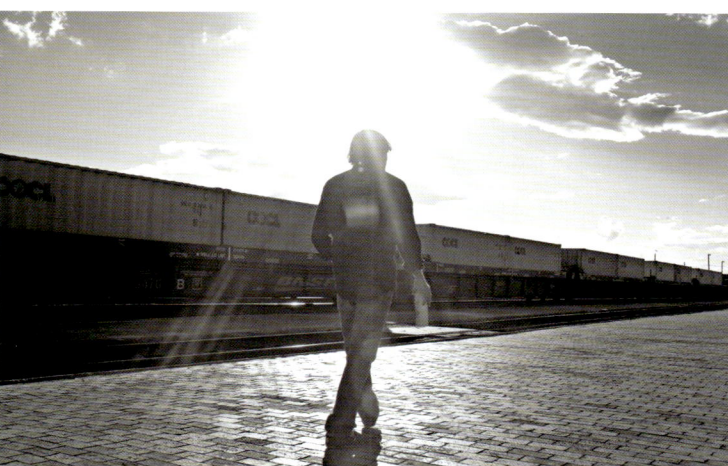

Additionally, beyond being an artwork of the land and its potential, *Station to Station* is a contemplation of the process of creativity. By bringing together these creative minds, Aitken presents us with an archaeology of today's creative world—mobile and across disciplines. This is also at the center of *THE SOURCE (evolving)* (2012–ongoing; pages 50–57), an architectural pavilion designed in collaboration with David Adjaye, principal architect of Adjaye Associates, that hosts six simultaneous and alternating video projections that record interviews with some of the most experimental and imaginative figures of our time.

Aitken's ability to capture and formalize this notion of permanent transmission is also seen in his sculptures and photographic lightboxes. *Sunset (black)* (2012; pages 58–59), a wall sculpture spelling the word "sunset," is composed of dark foam and epoxy and backlit with LEDs. Like *the mirror #11 (rise)*, *Sunset (black)* stratifies a dark cliché of the Los Angeles of James Ellroy or Steve Erickson. It is an active object: its LED glow pushes it off the wall from behind and projects it toward the viewer, somehow modifying its surroundings and the way it is perceived. The sculpture becomes conductive, leaking information and energy.

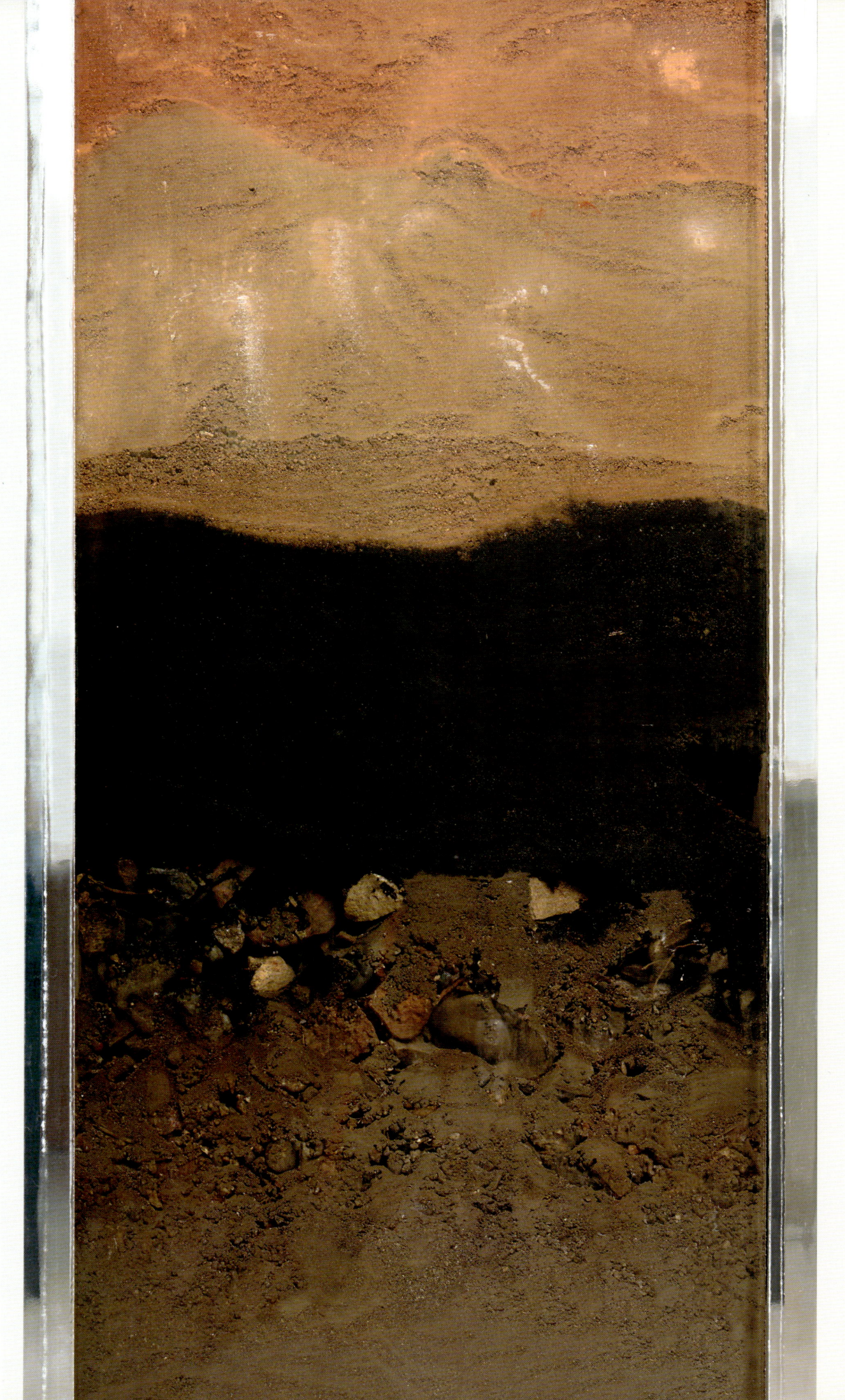

Station to Station [Volume], 2013, detail
opposite: *Station to Station [Volume]*, 2013

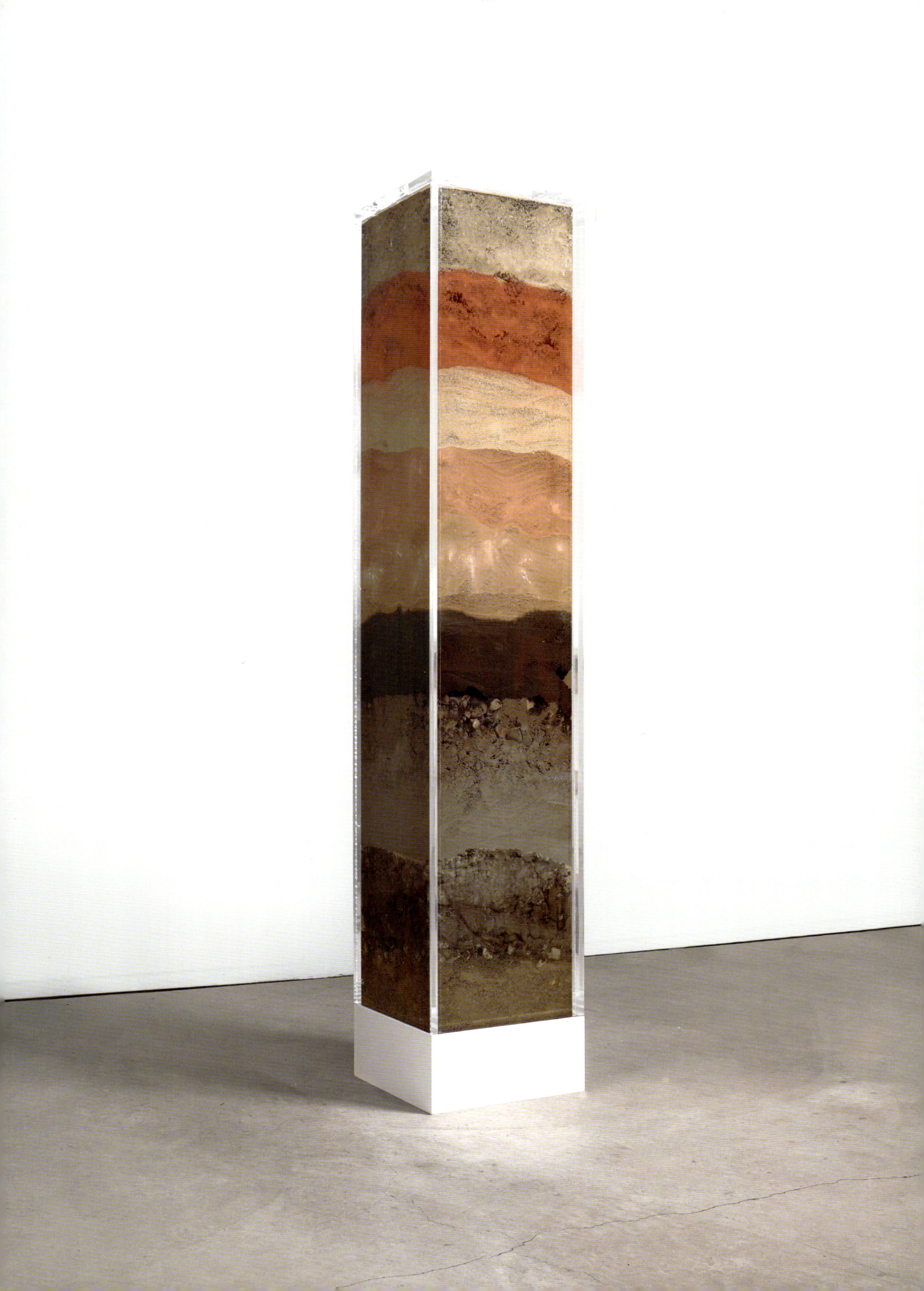

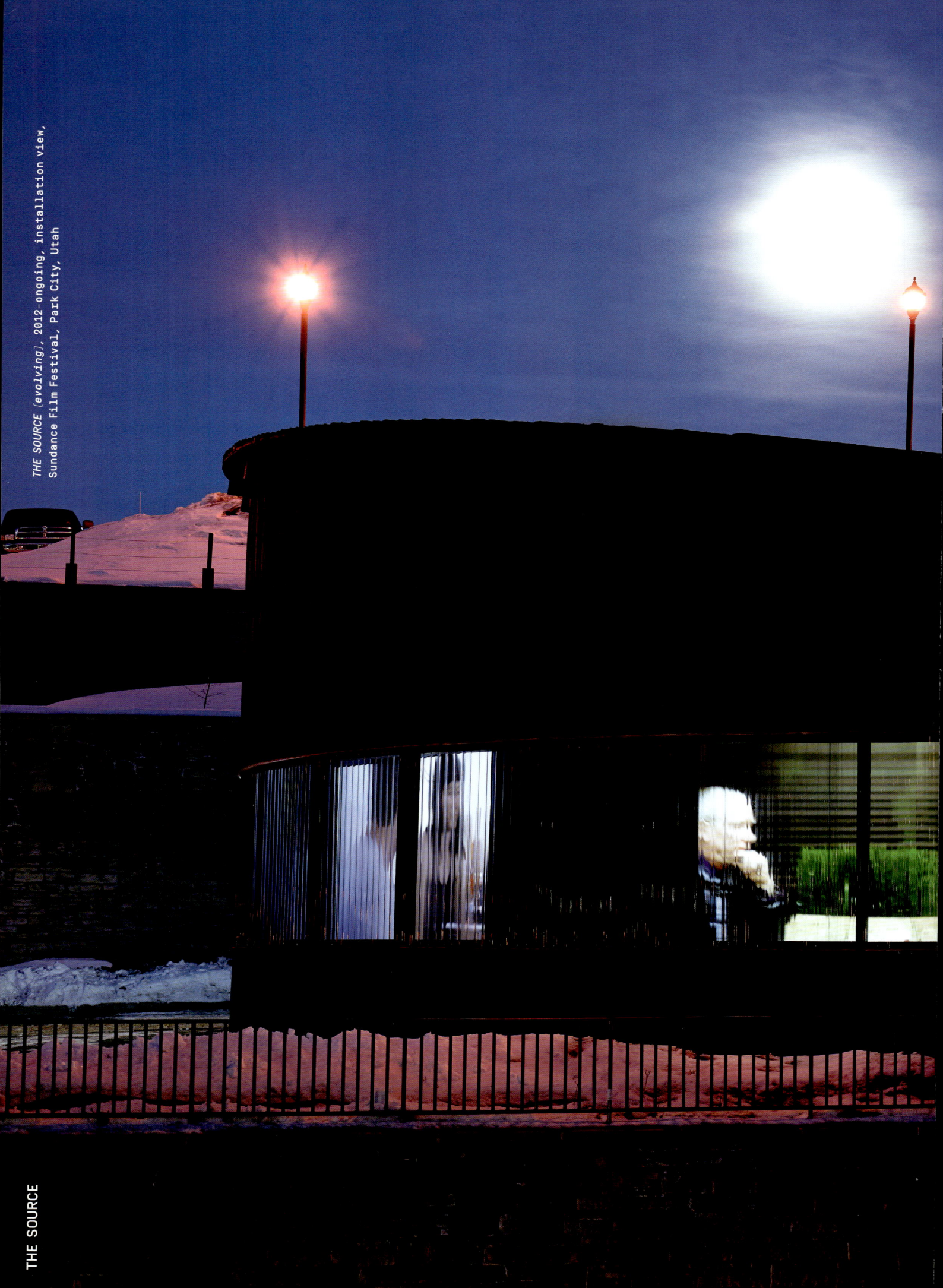

THE SOURCE (evolving), 2012–ongoing, installation view, Sundance Film Festival, Park City, Utah

THE SOURCE

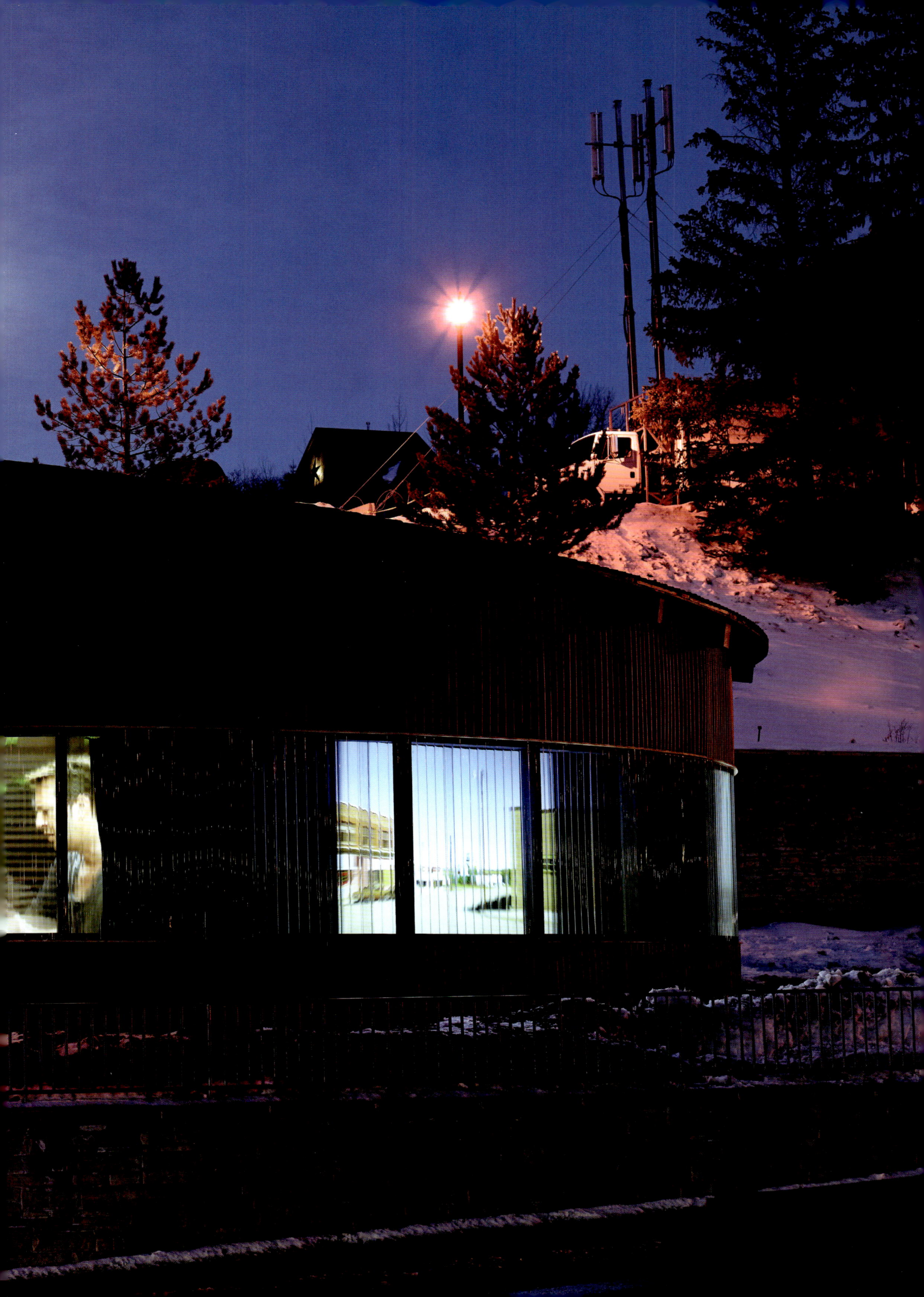

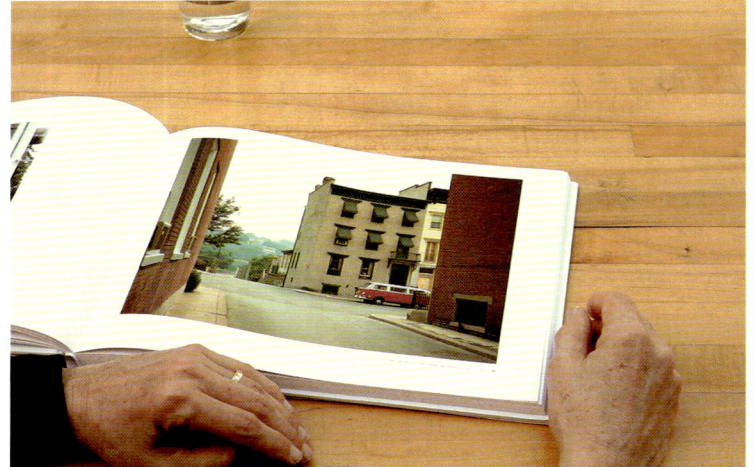 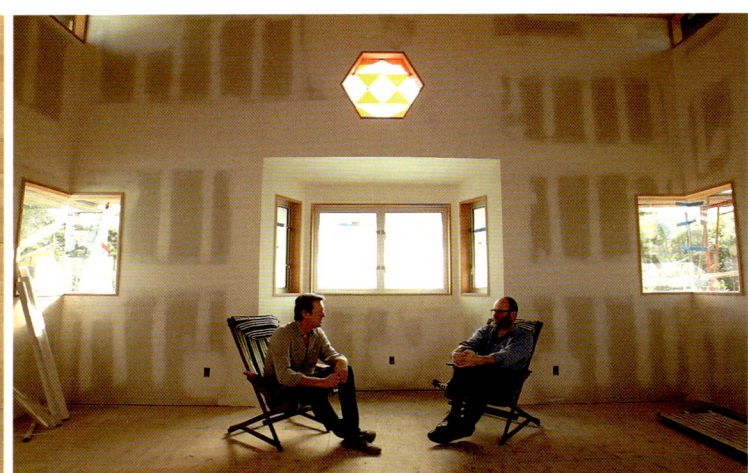

THE SOURCE [*evolving*], 2012–ongoing, stills
[left to right: Stephen Shore; Thomas Demand; Paolo Soleri; Jack Pierson]

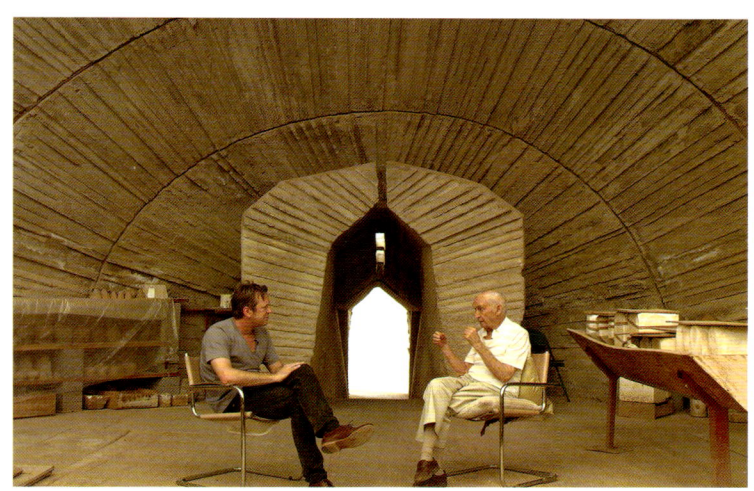 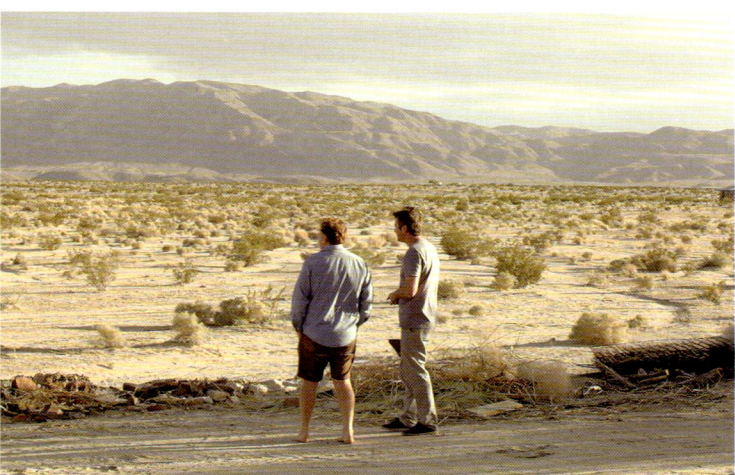

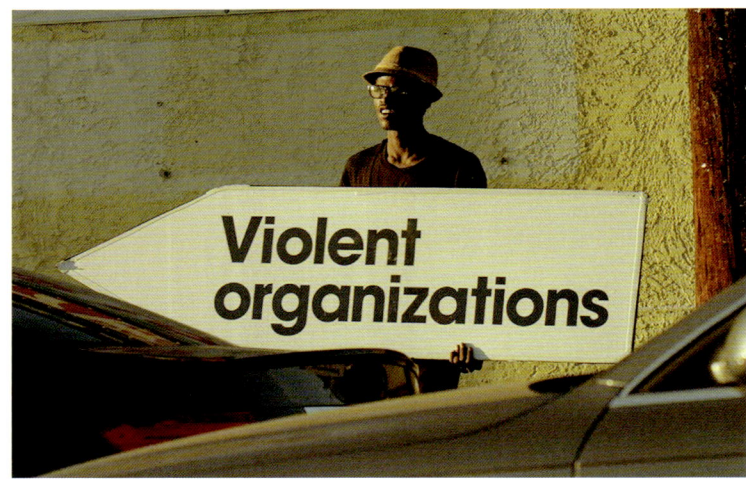
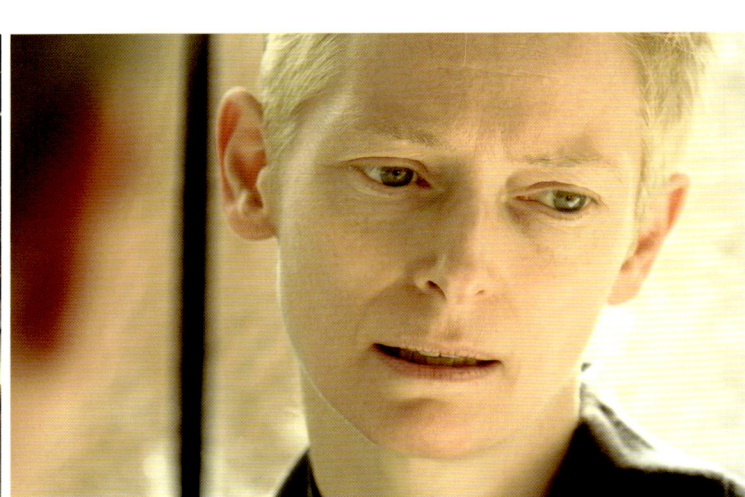

THE SOURCE (evolving), 2012-ongoing, stills
[left to right: landscape signs (sign happening), 2014;
Tilda Swinton; David Adjaye; Liz Glynn]

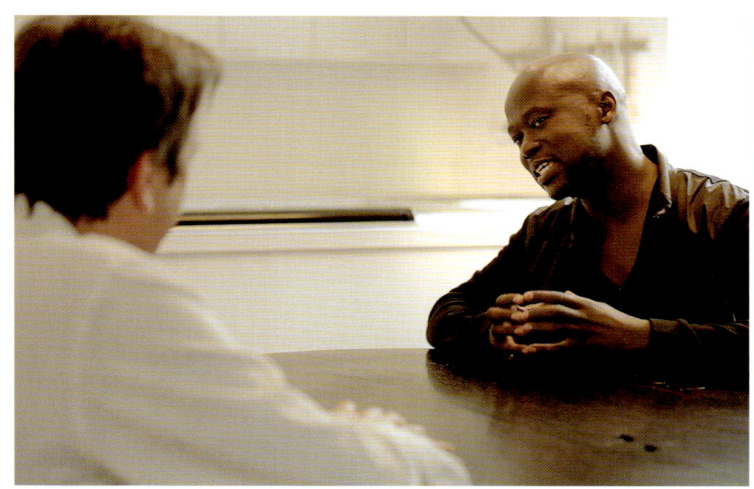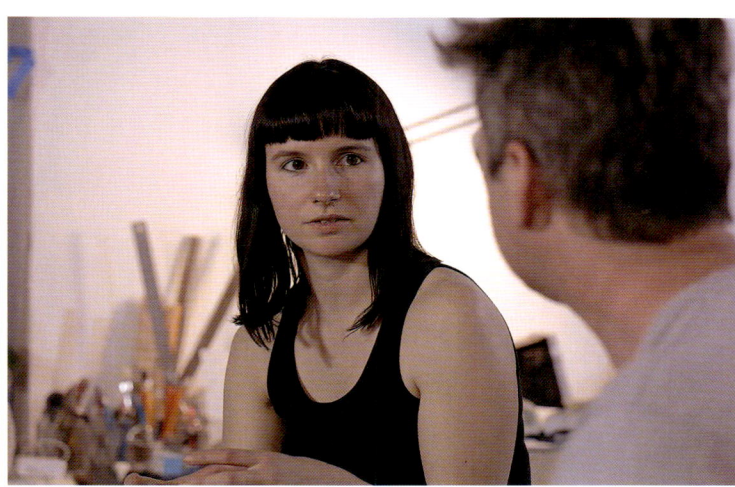

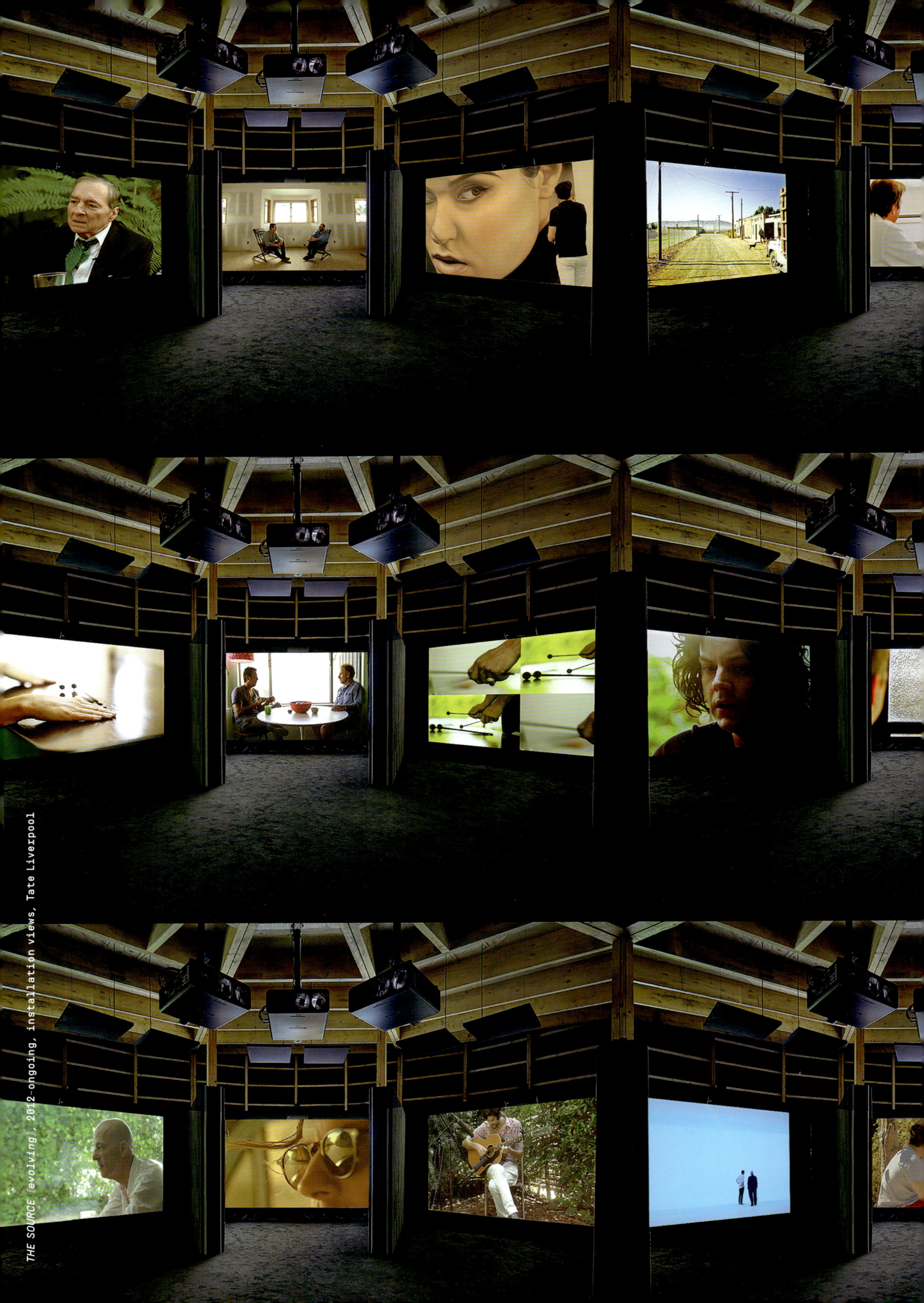

THE SOURCE (evolving), 2012-ongoing, installation views, Tate Liverpool

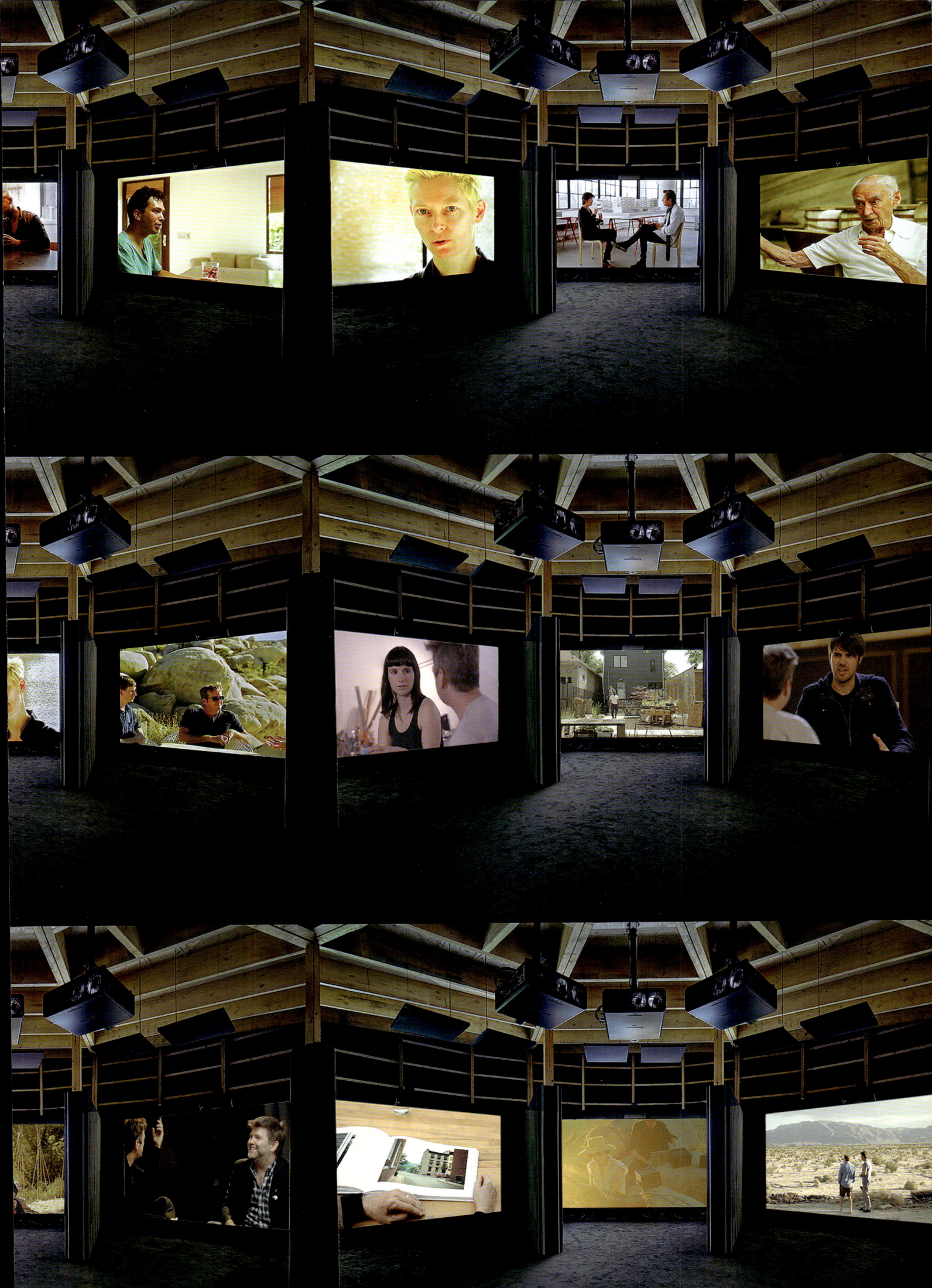

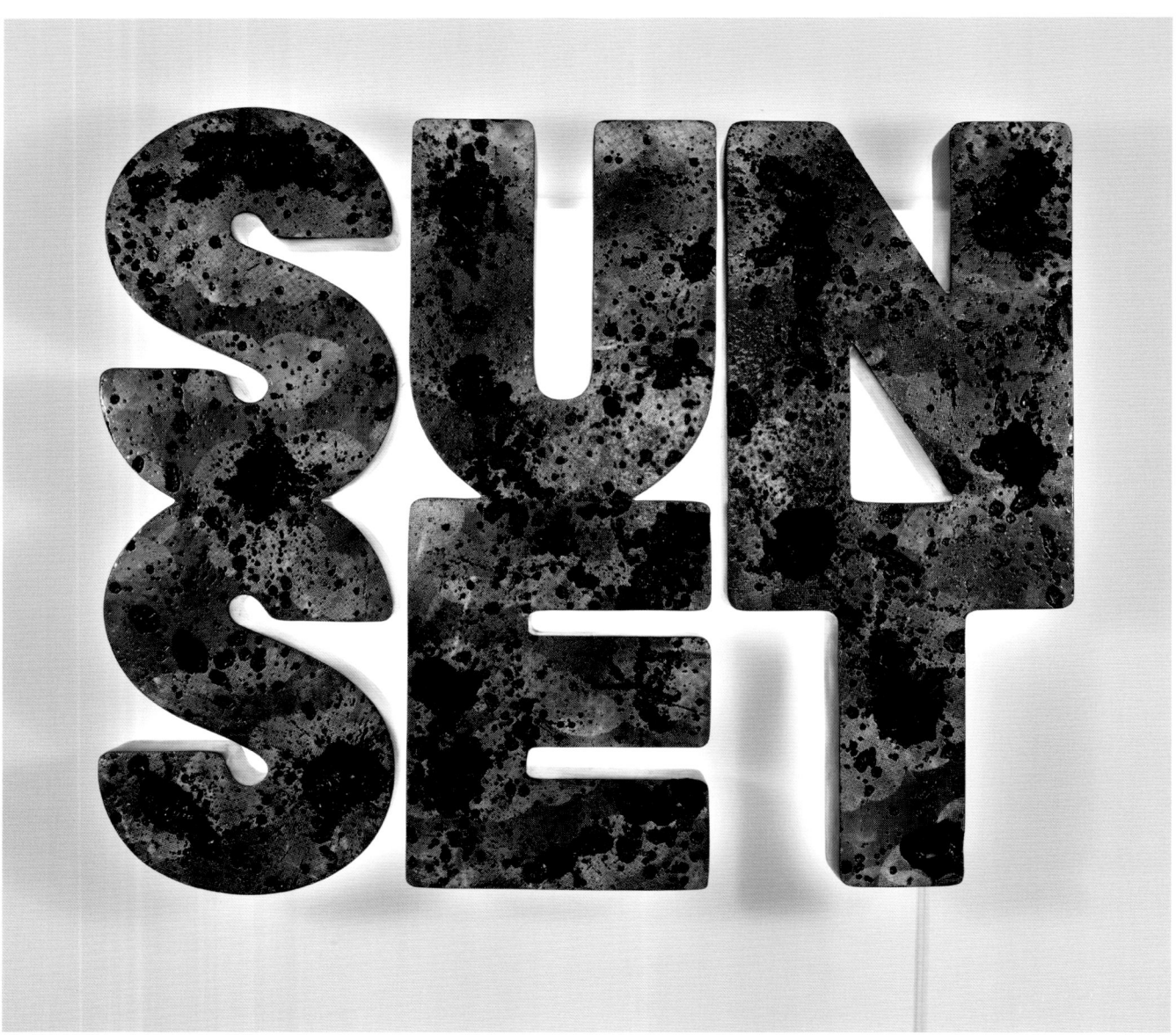

Sunset (black), 2012
opposite: *Sunset (black)*, 2012, detail

SUNSET (BLACK)

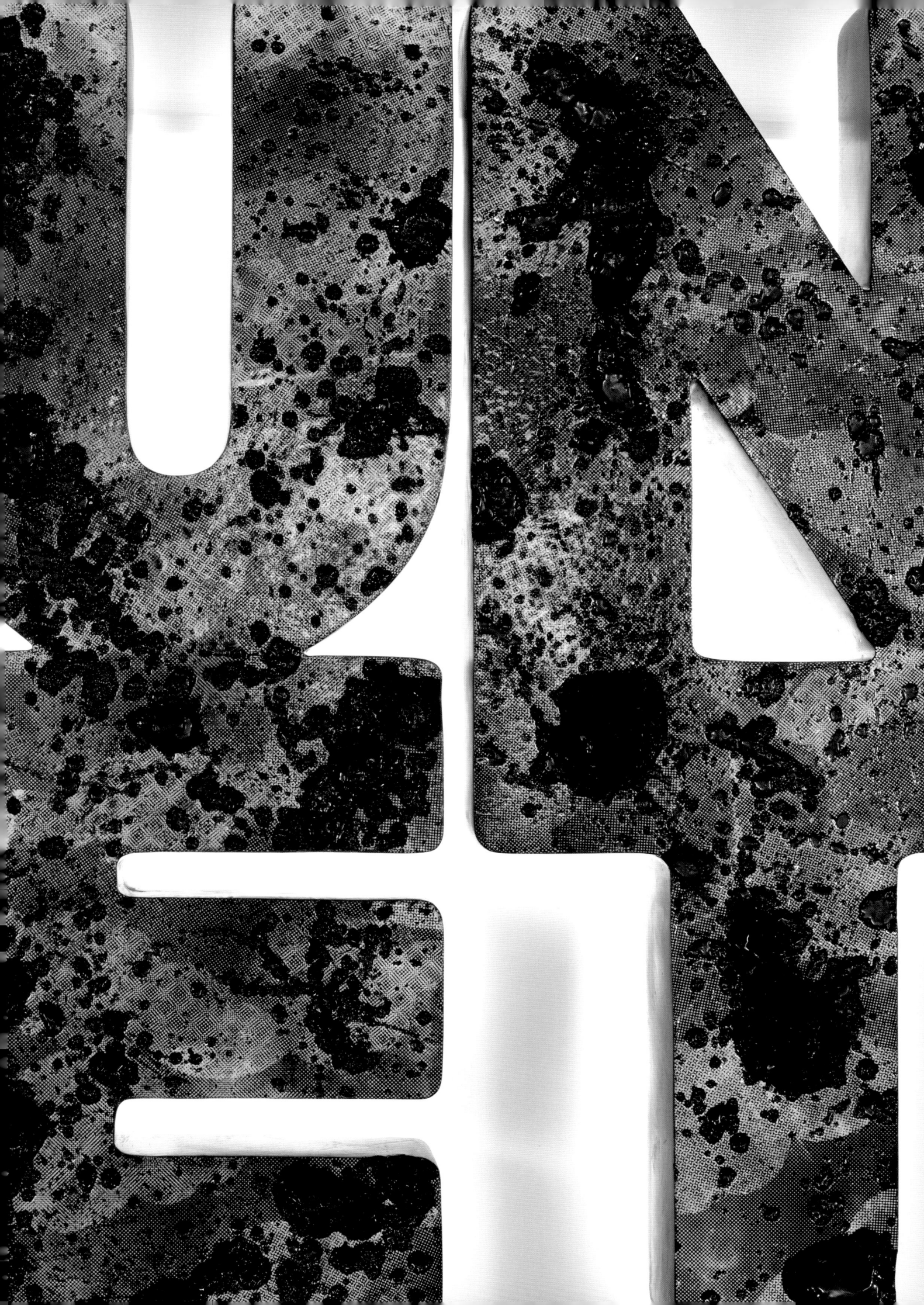

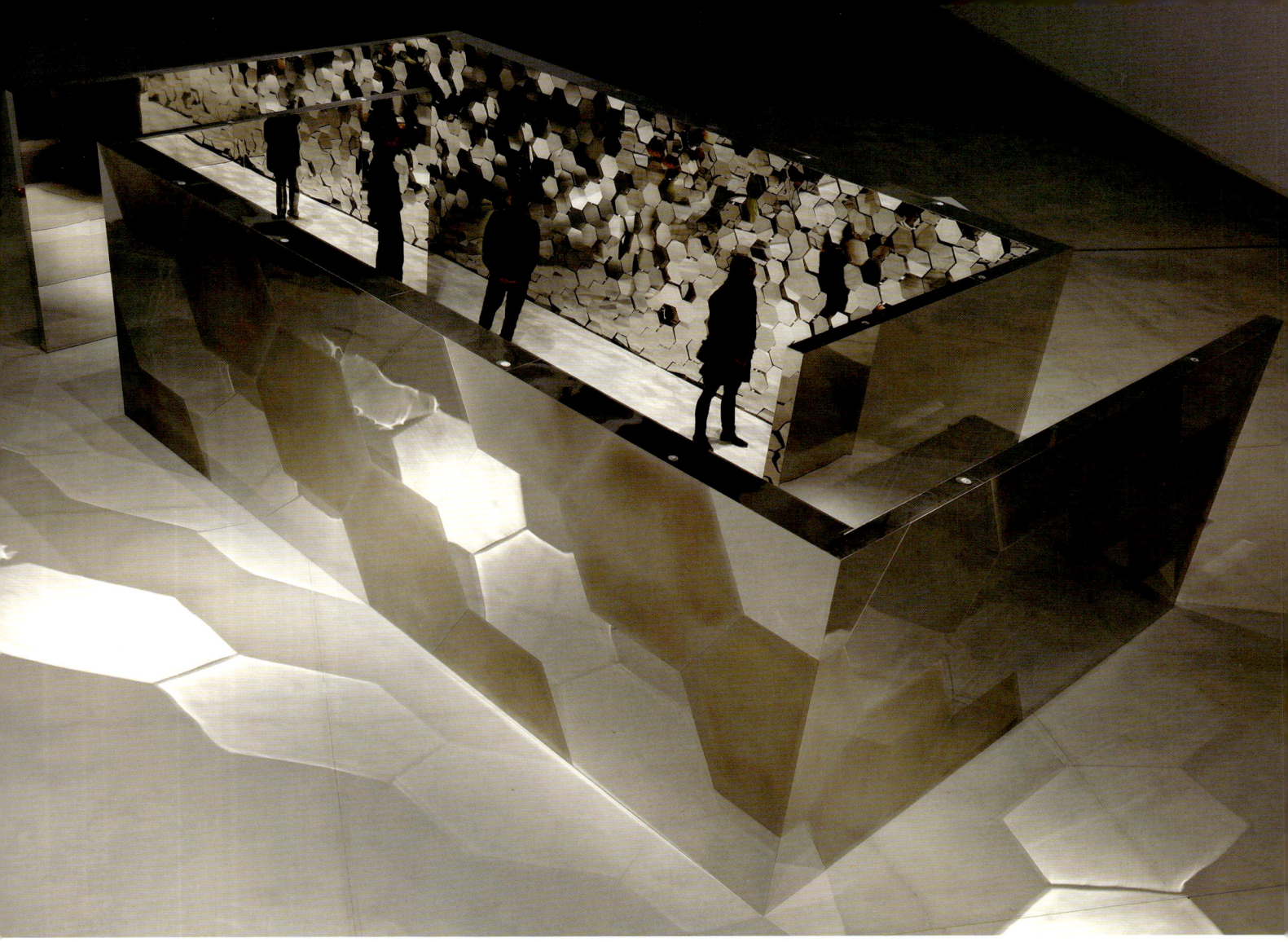

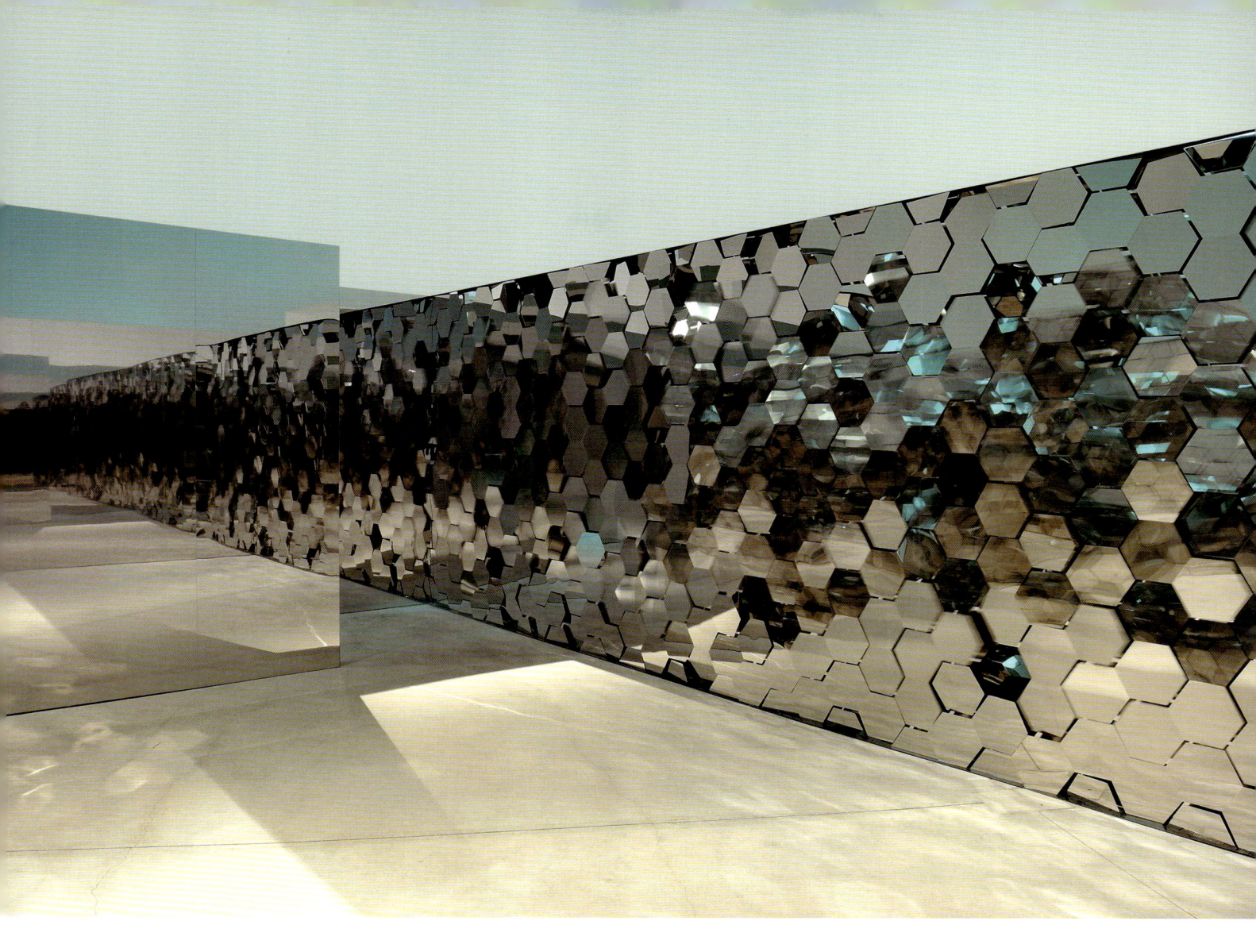

no history, 2005, installation views, LABoral Centro de Arte y Creación Industrial, Gijón, Spain

END [*mirror*], 2014

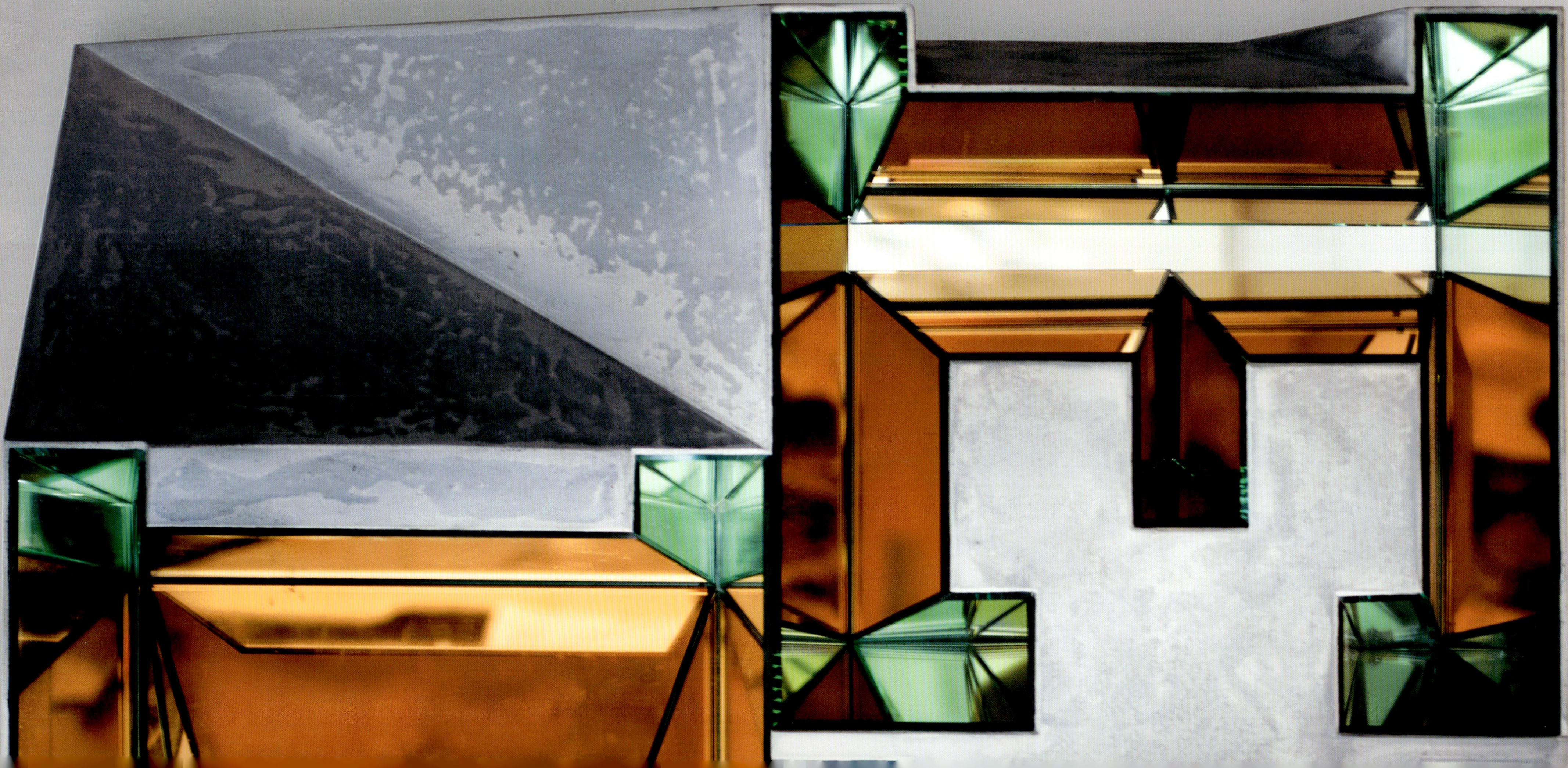

END [MIRROR]

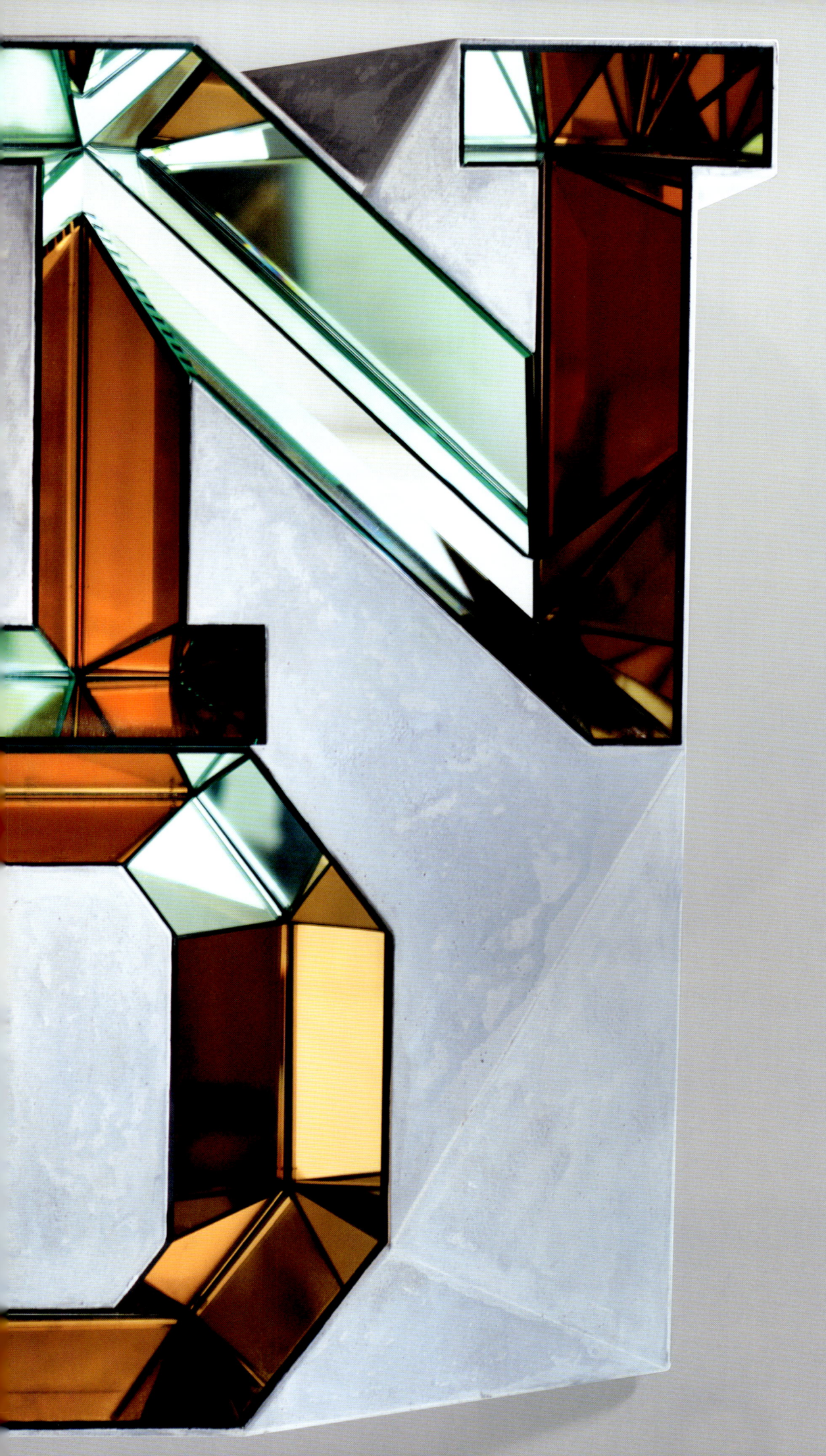

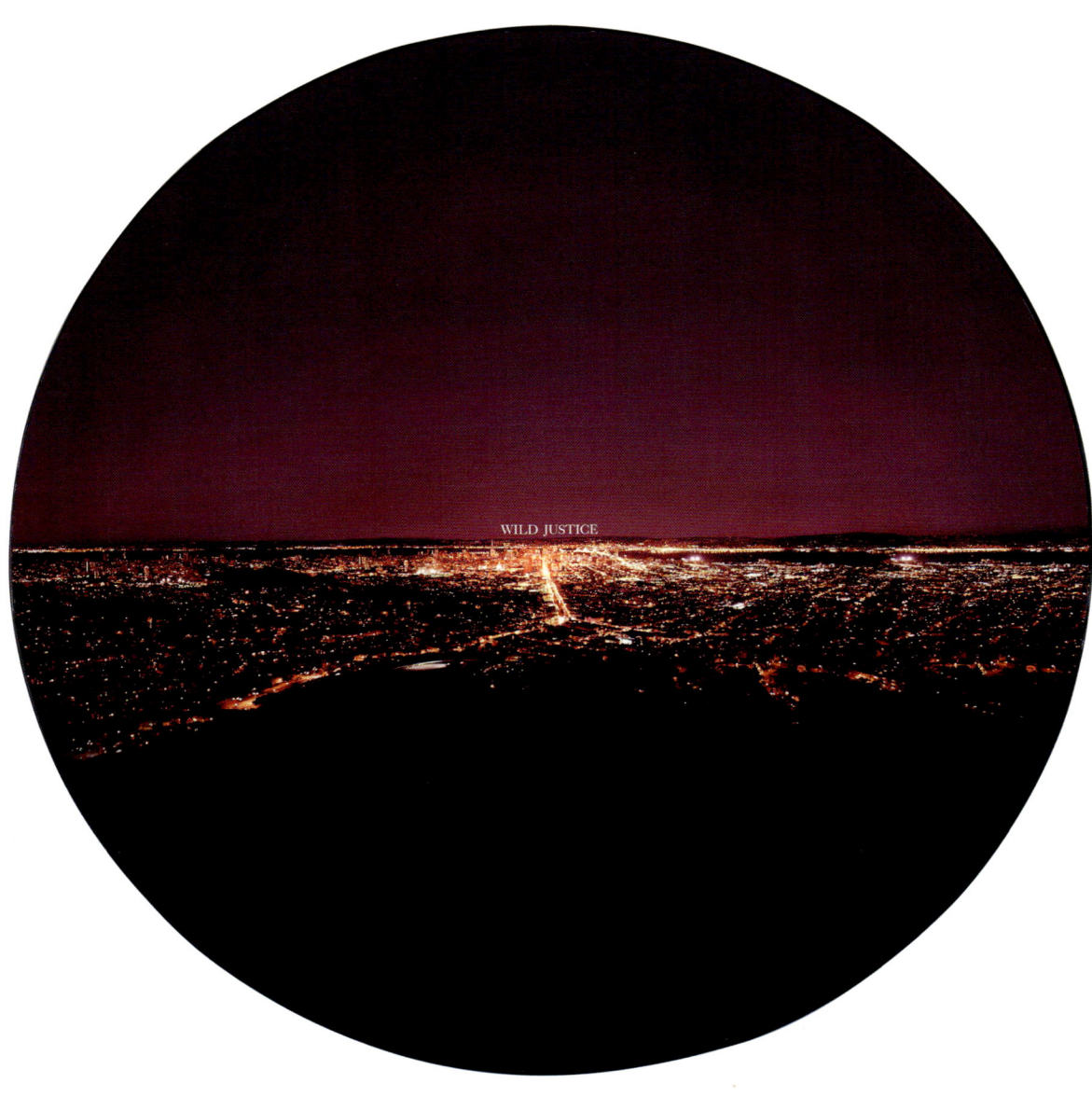

WILD JUSTICE, 2014
opposite: WILD JUSTICE, 2014, detail

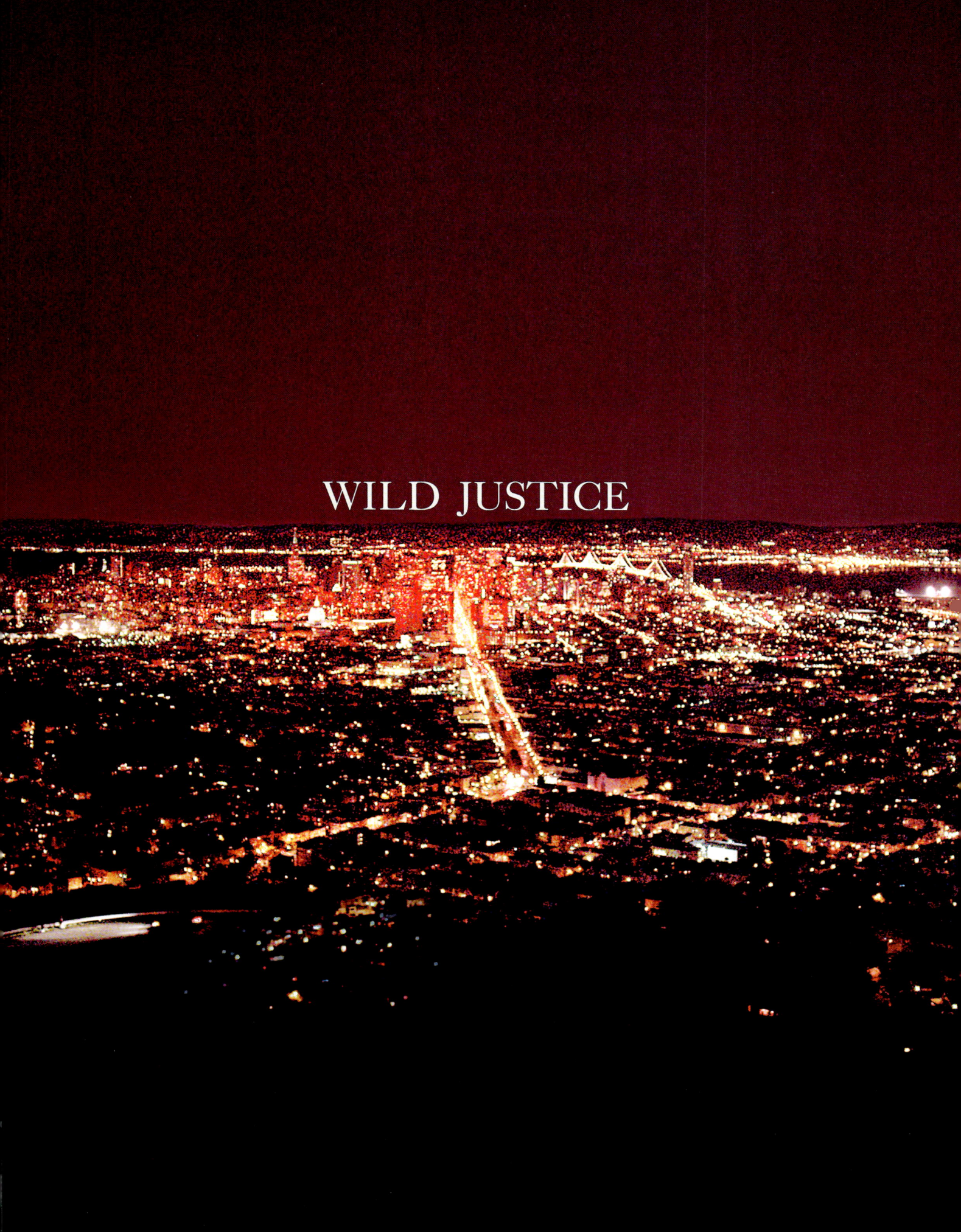

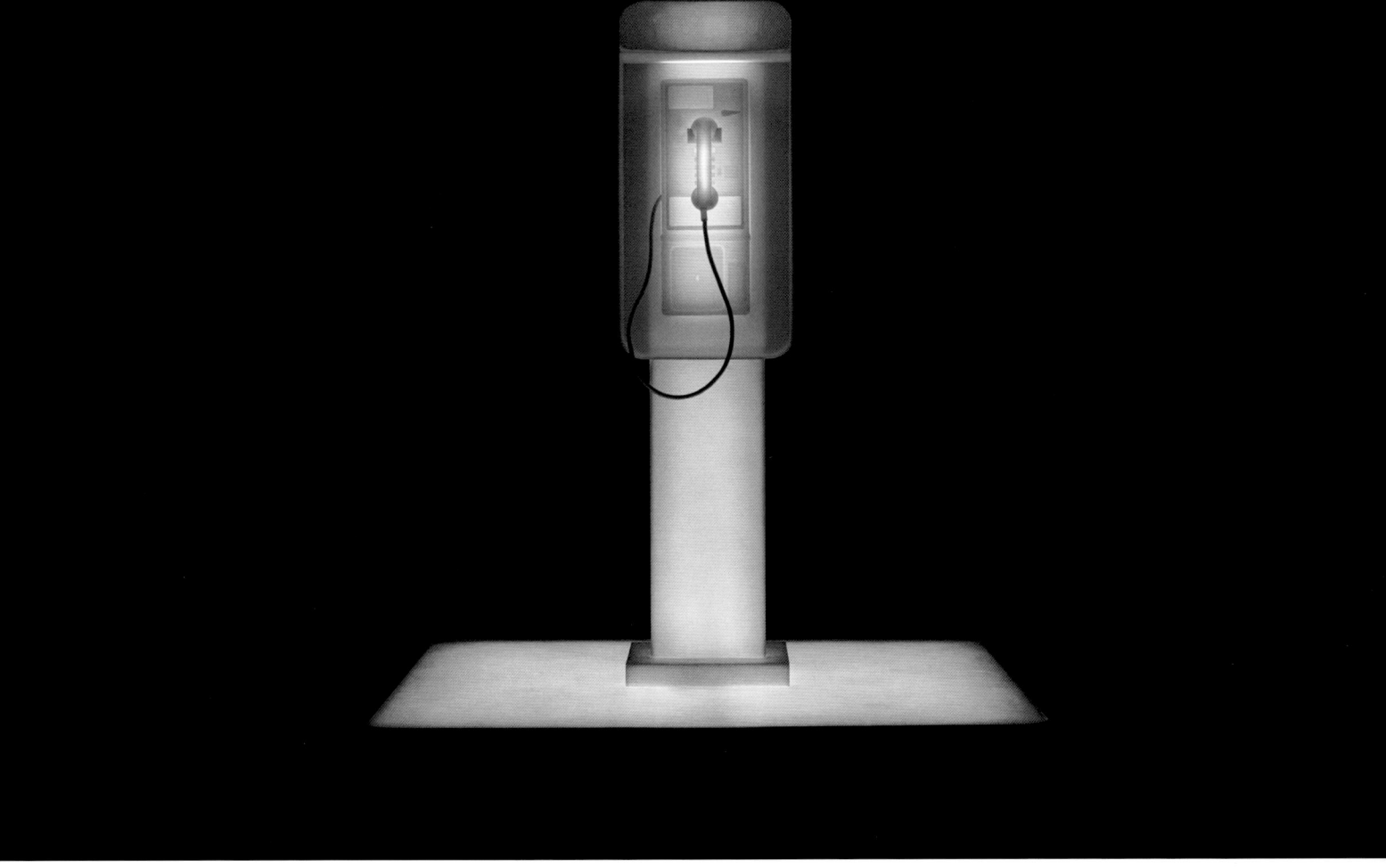

TWILIGHT

Similarly conductive, perhaps even to a higher degree, is Aitken's free-standing sculpture *twilight* (2014; pages 66–71). This work takes the form of an outdated pay phone, an anachronistic object cast in translucent resin and acrylic, and rigged with a kinetic LED system that brightens or dims according to the density of people around it. Its light pattern emits the language of an object, a visual music that, like one's laptop, is never off, leaking information as it dozes and stirs. Its effect is mesmerizing and immaterial, possessing beauty beyond the point of seduction. It is actually rather dark in a "We never sleep, we always watch" sense. And this is an essential part of Aitken's strategy: behind such visual lust we find a darker reality, that of sunshine and noir.

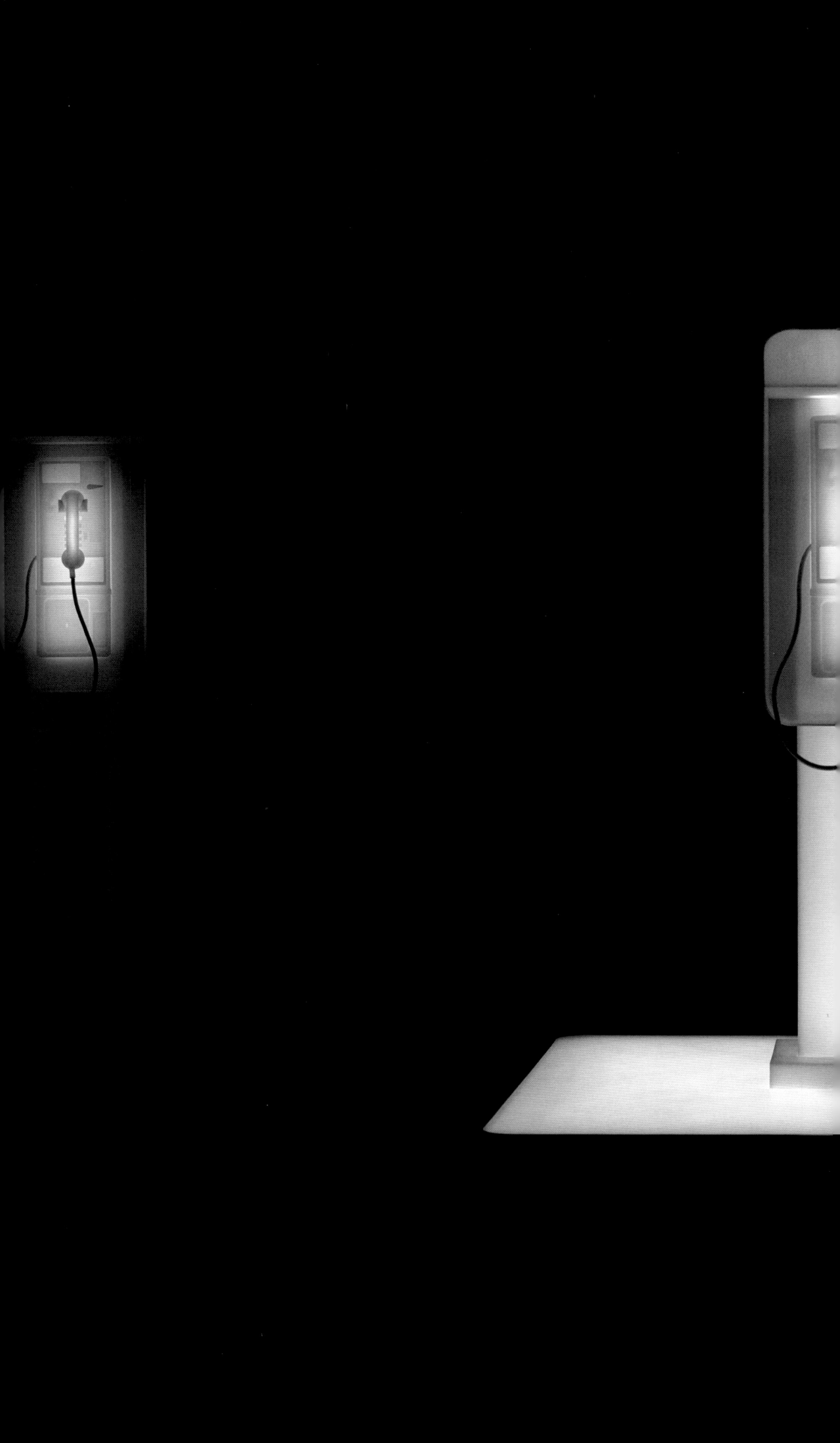

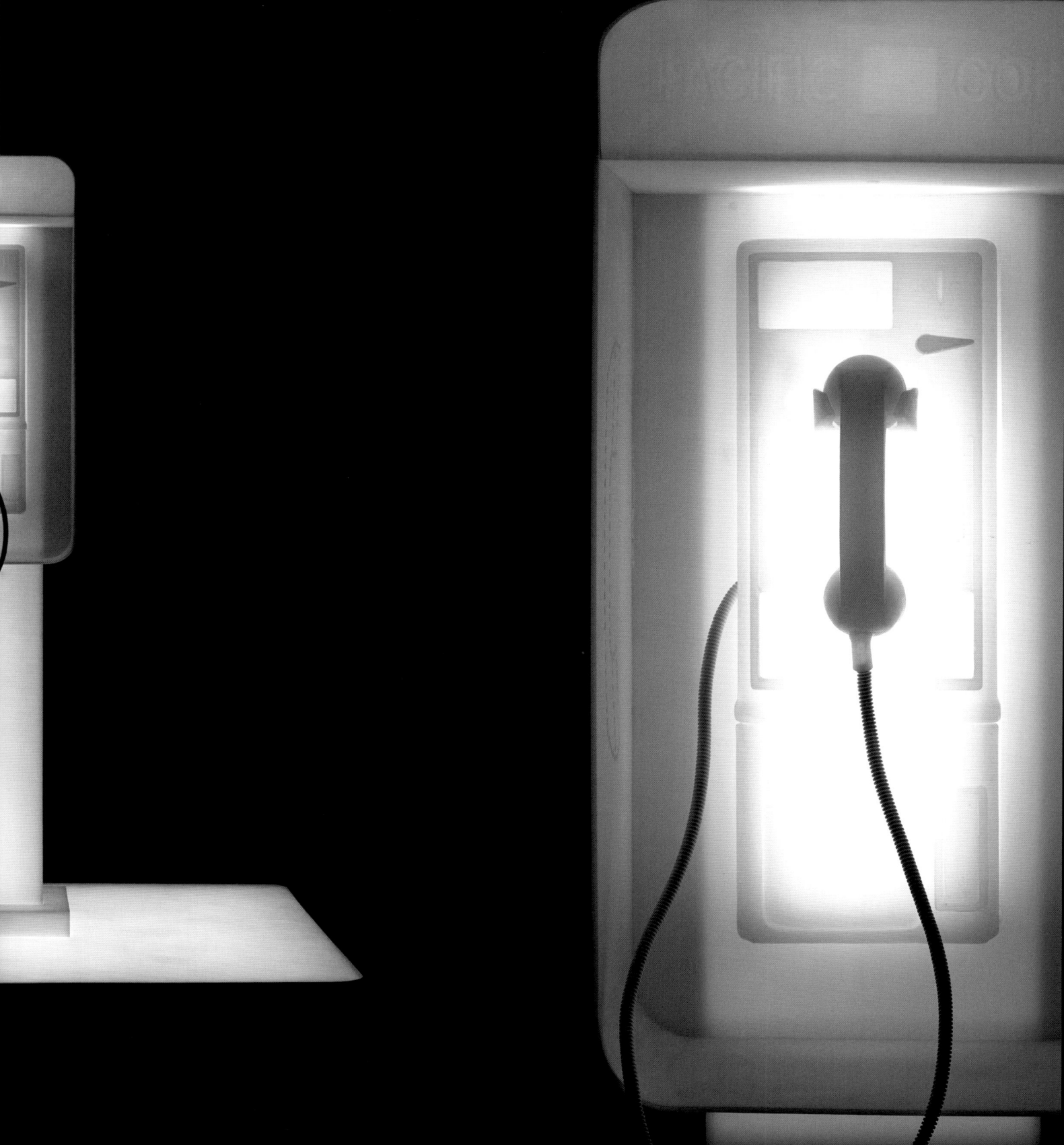

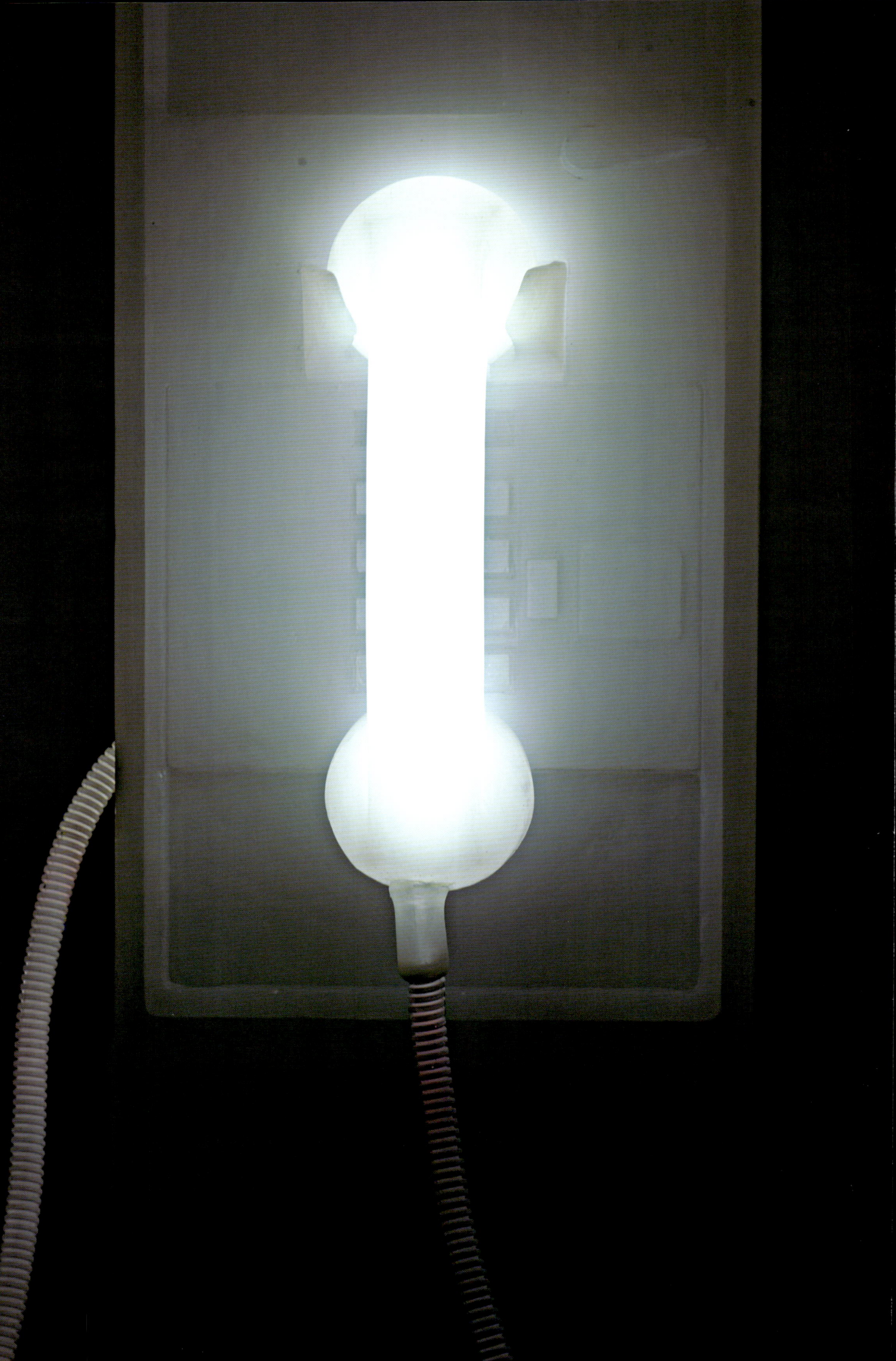

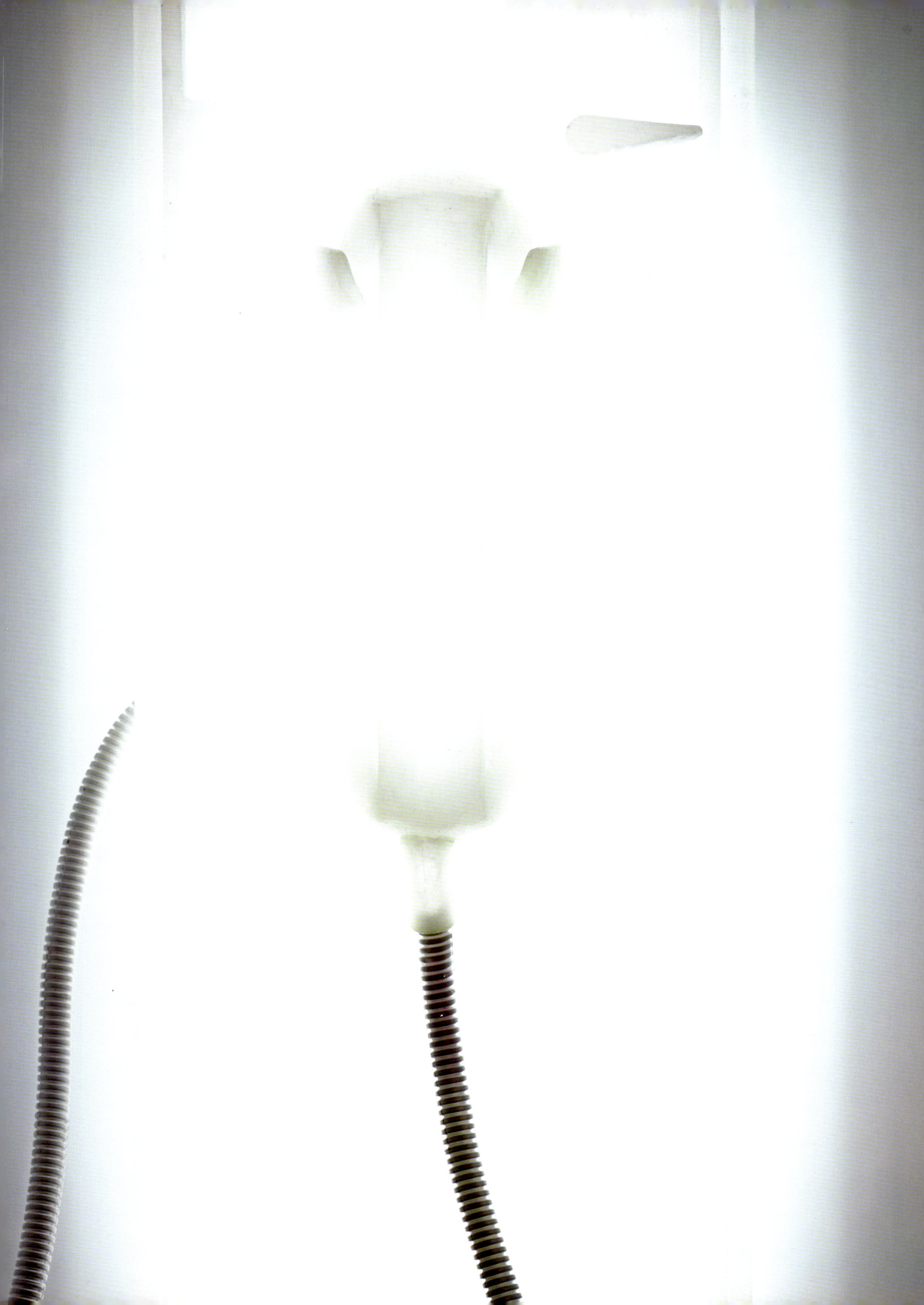

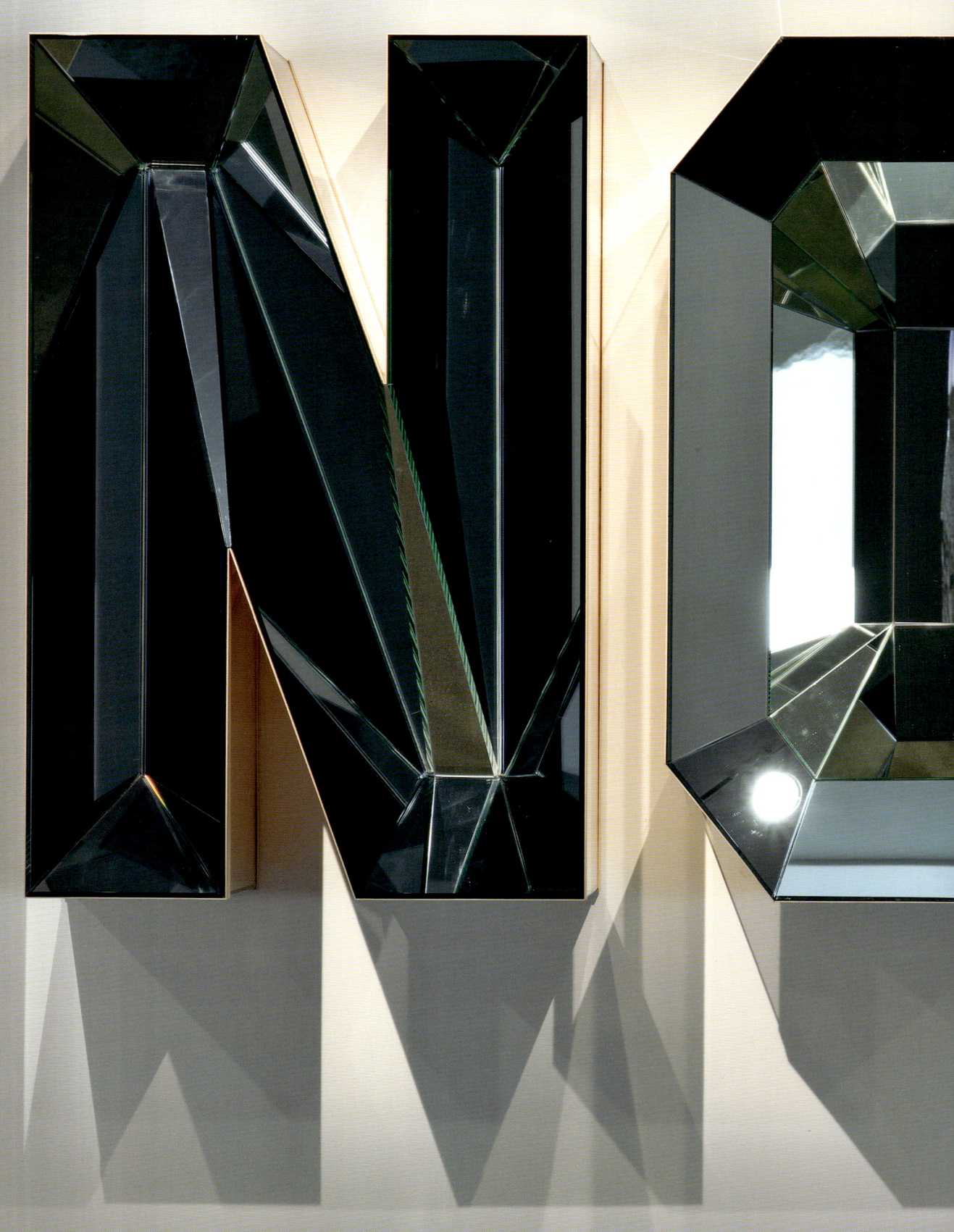

NOW [Blue Mirror], 2014

NOW [BLUE MIRROR]

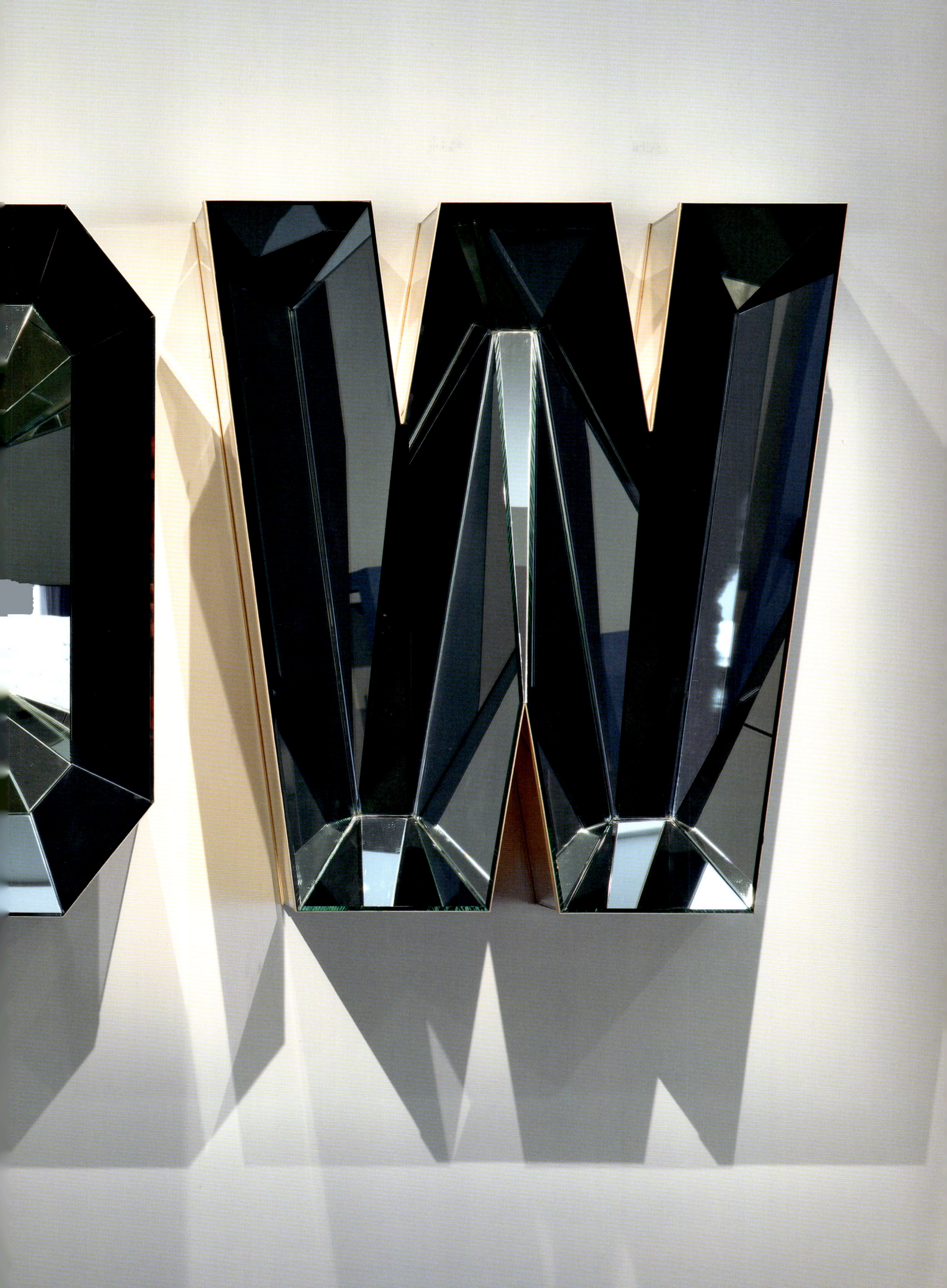

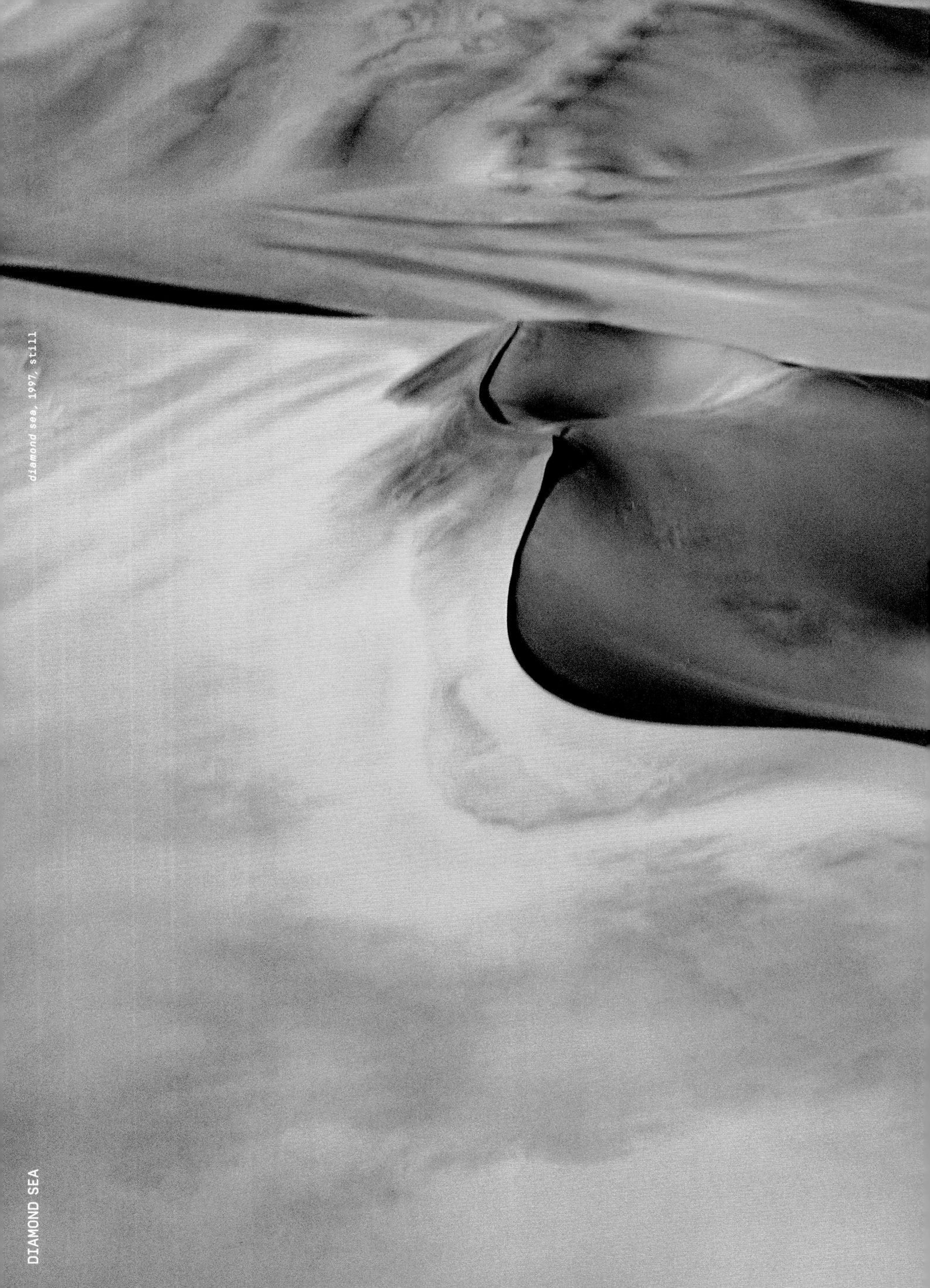

DIAMOND SEA

diamond sea, 1997, still

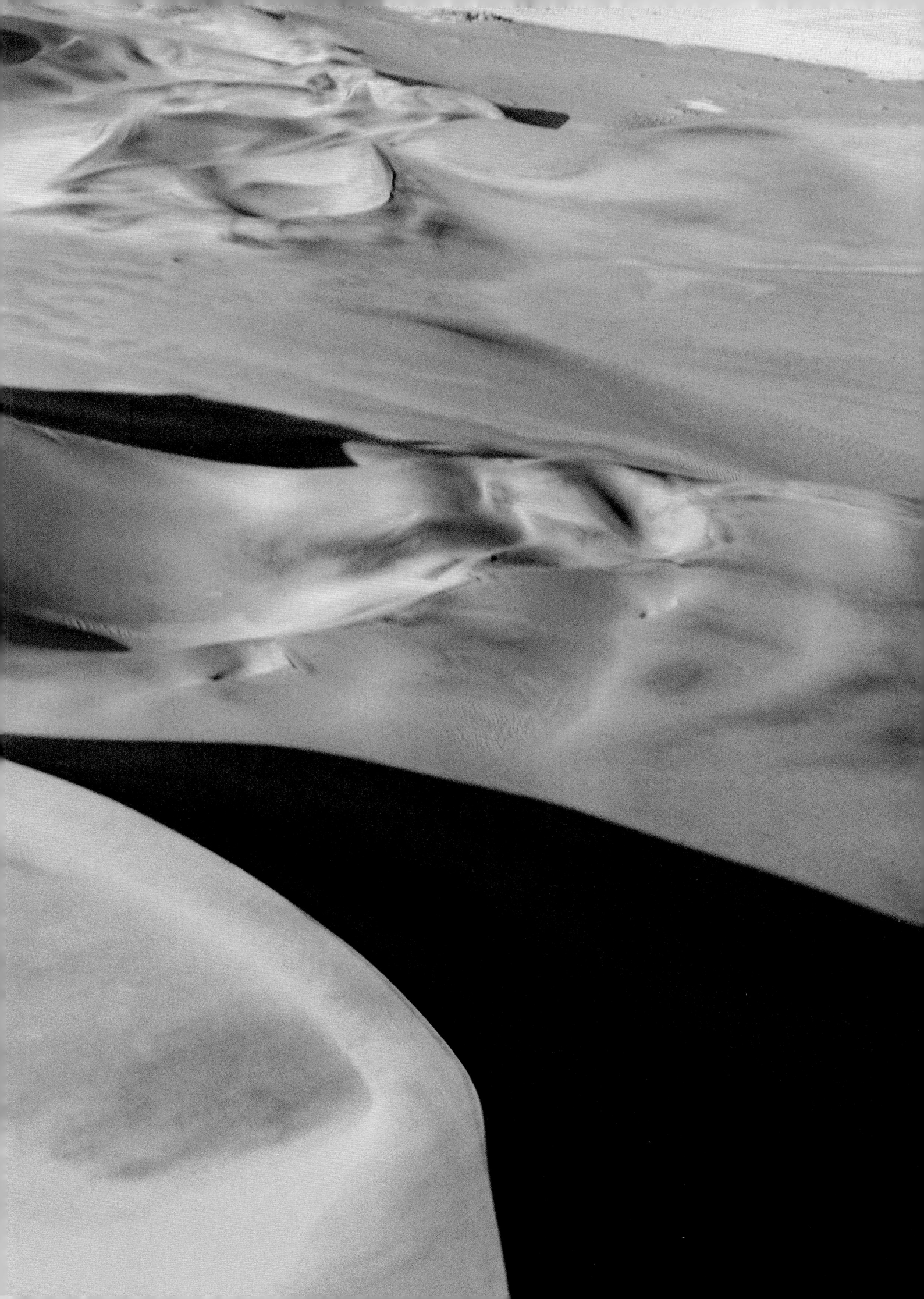

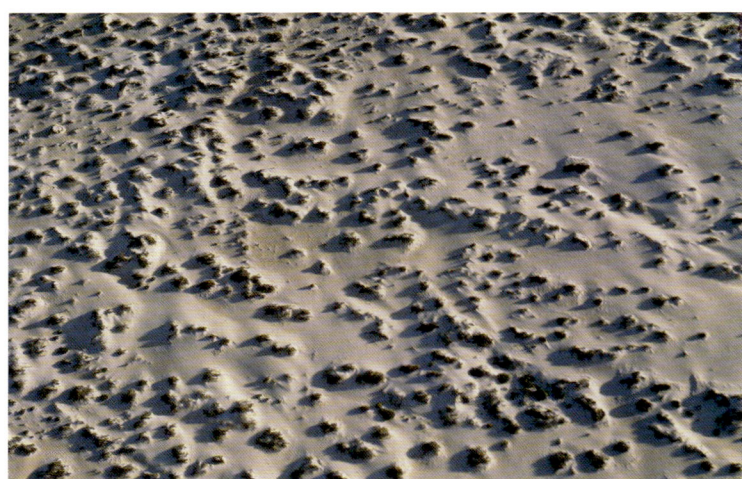
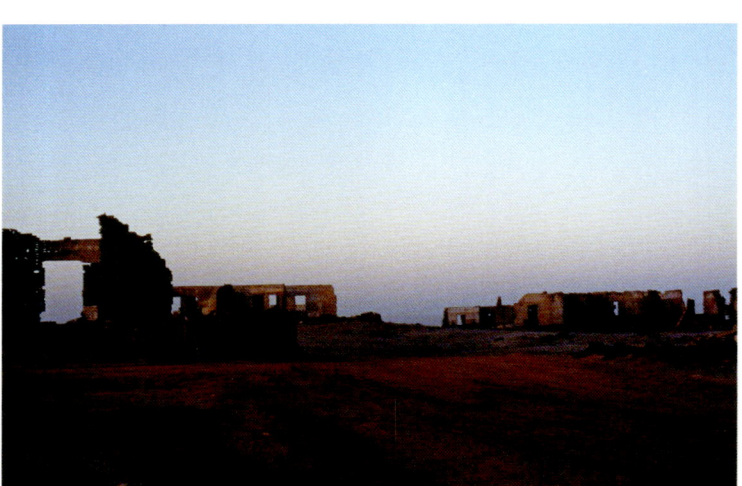

diamond sea, 1997, stills

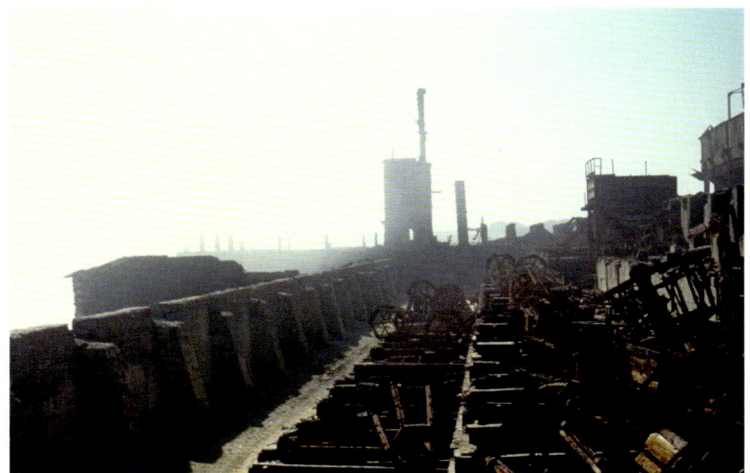 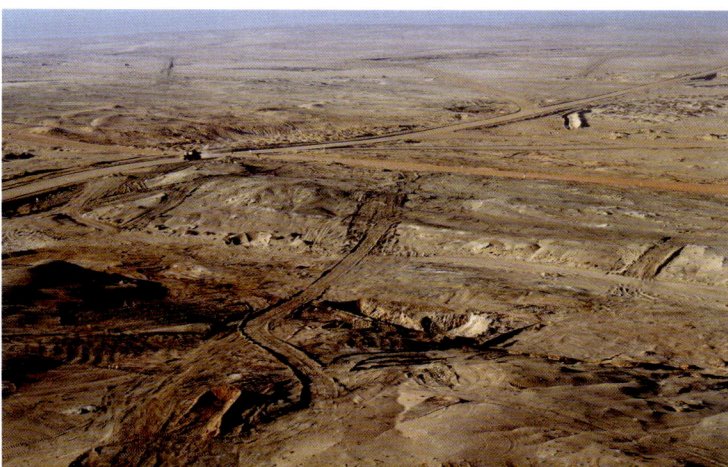

As we have established, Aitken's work and its aesthetic have been informed and shaped by an understanding of an avant-garde history of the interrelationship between art, communication, music, technology, and electronic innovations in transmission strategies. But how do his forms articulate his content, his ideas? We must return to the idea of what is common to many, what brings us together as a group, the questions that constitute us as a group: questions of the environment and its alterity, of the human condition in a culture of permanent, nonstop communication, and of global trade and its impact on our lives.

Aitken's installations delimit landscape. They are presented in the form of immersive landscapes as much as they depict any landscape: manmade landscapes, landscapes devoid of human presence, cityscapes, all displaying a sense of foreboding entropy, such as *diamond sea* and *these restless minds*. The former is a mesmerizing stroll through an off-limits and hyperguarded region of the Namib Desert known as Diamond Area 1 and 2, a forty-thousand-square-mile piece of land sealed since 1908 and hosting the world's largest and most profitable computer-controlled diamond mine.

diamond sea, 1997, still

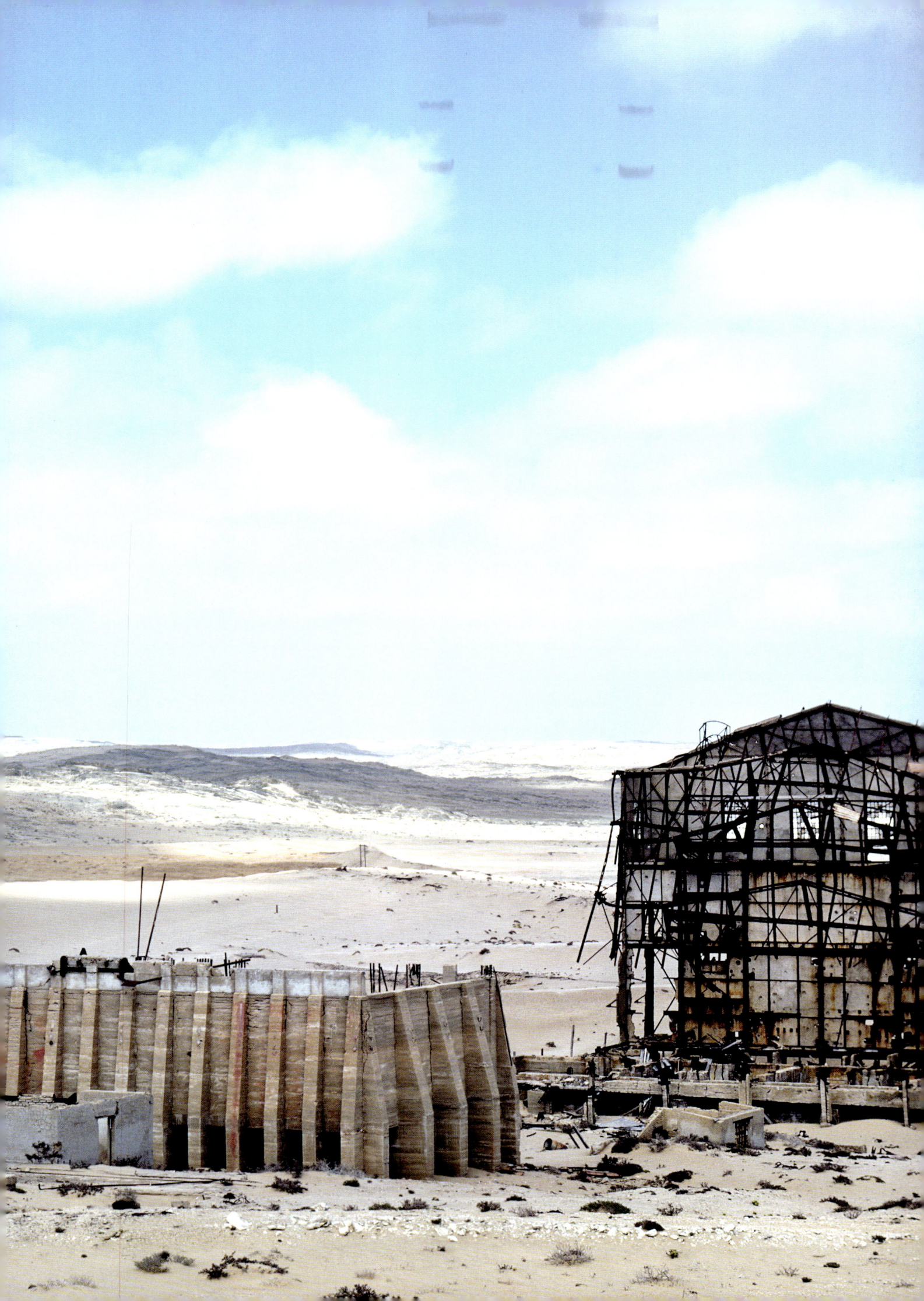

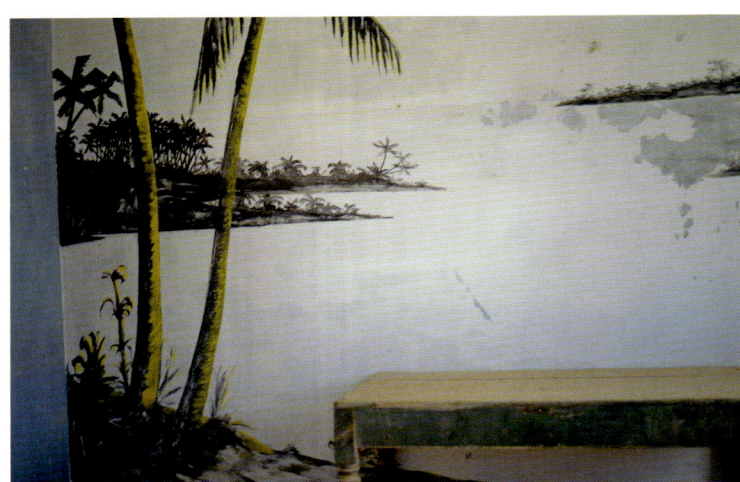 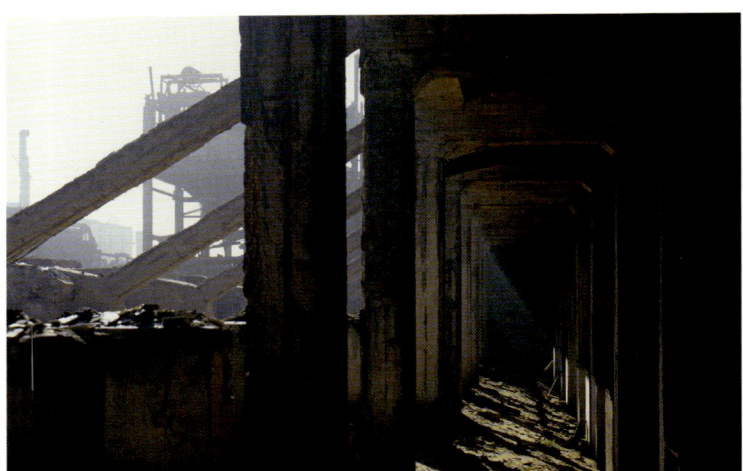

diamond sea, 1997, stills

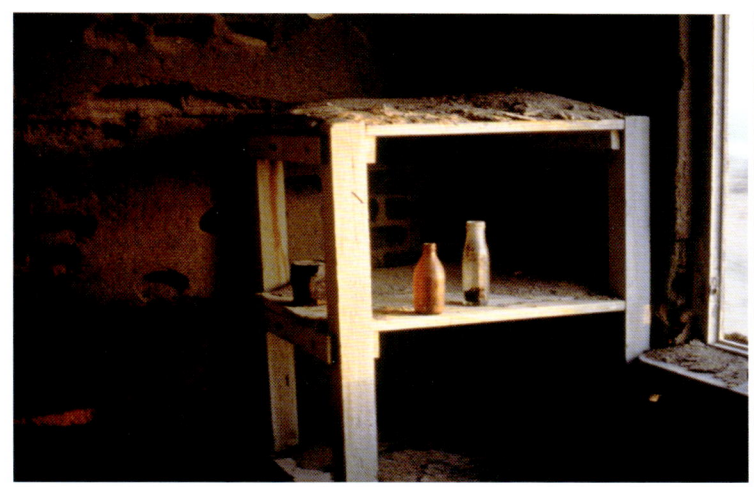
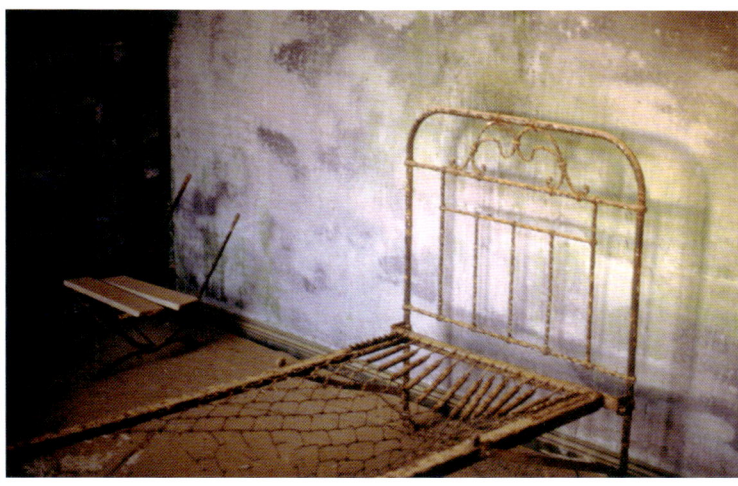

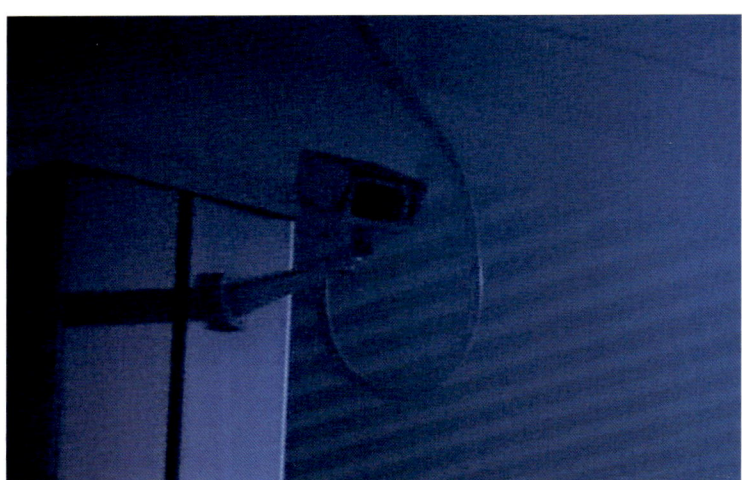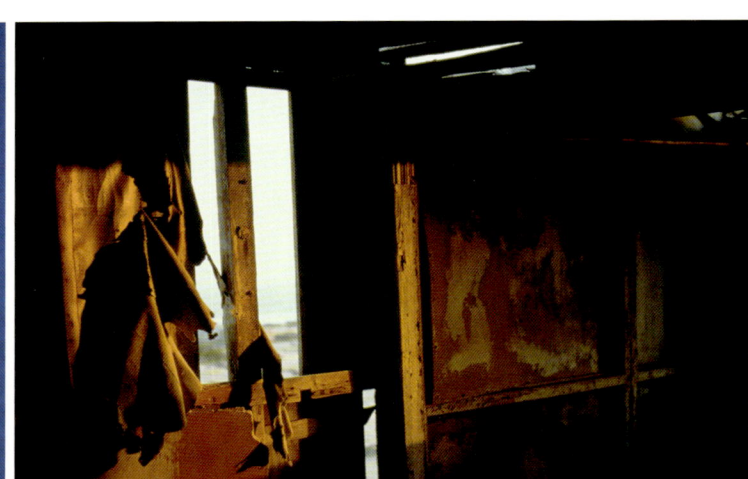

diamond sea, 1997, stills

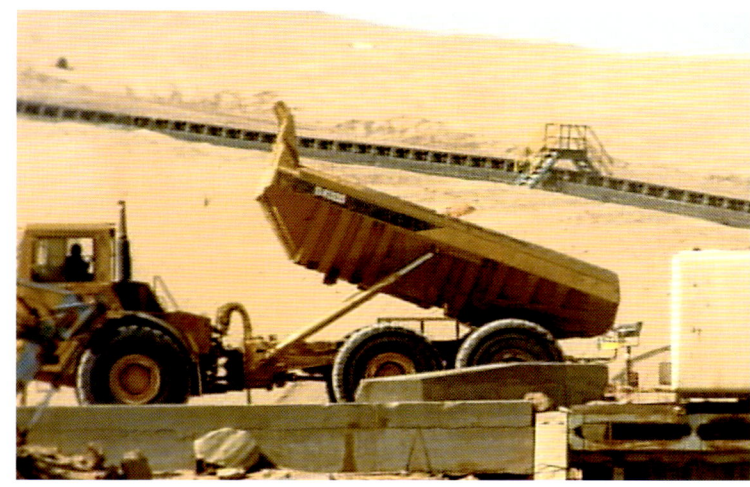 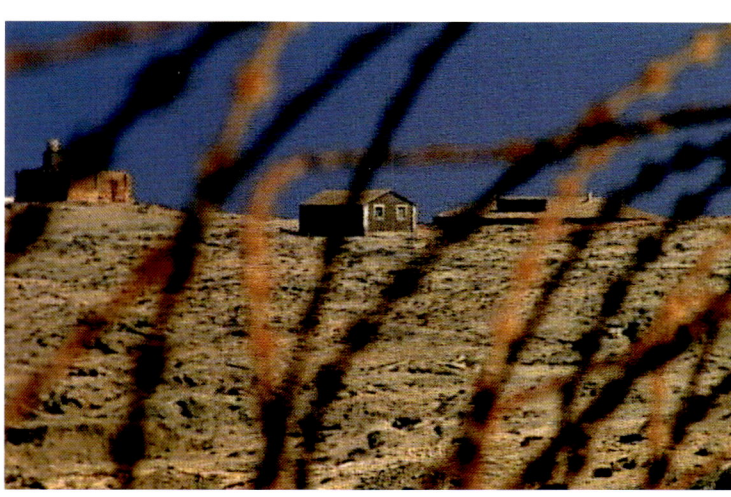

diamond sea, 1997, installation views, Schirn Kunsthalle, Frankfurt

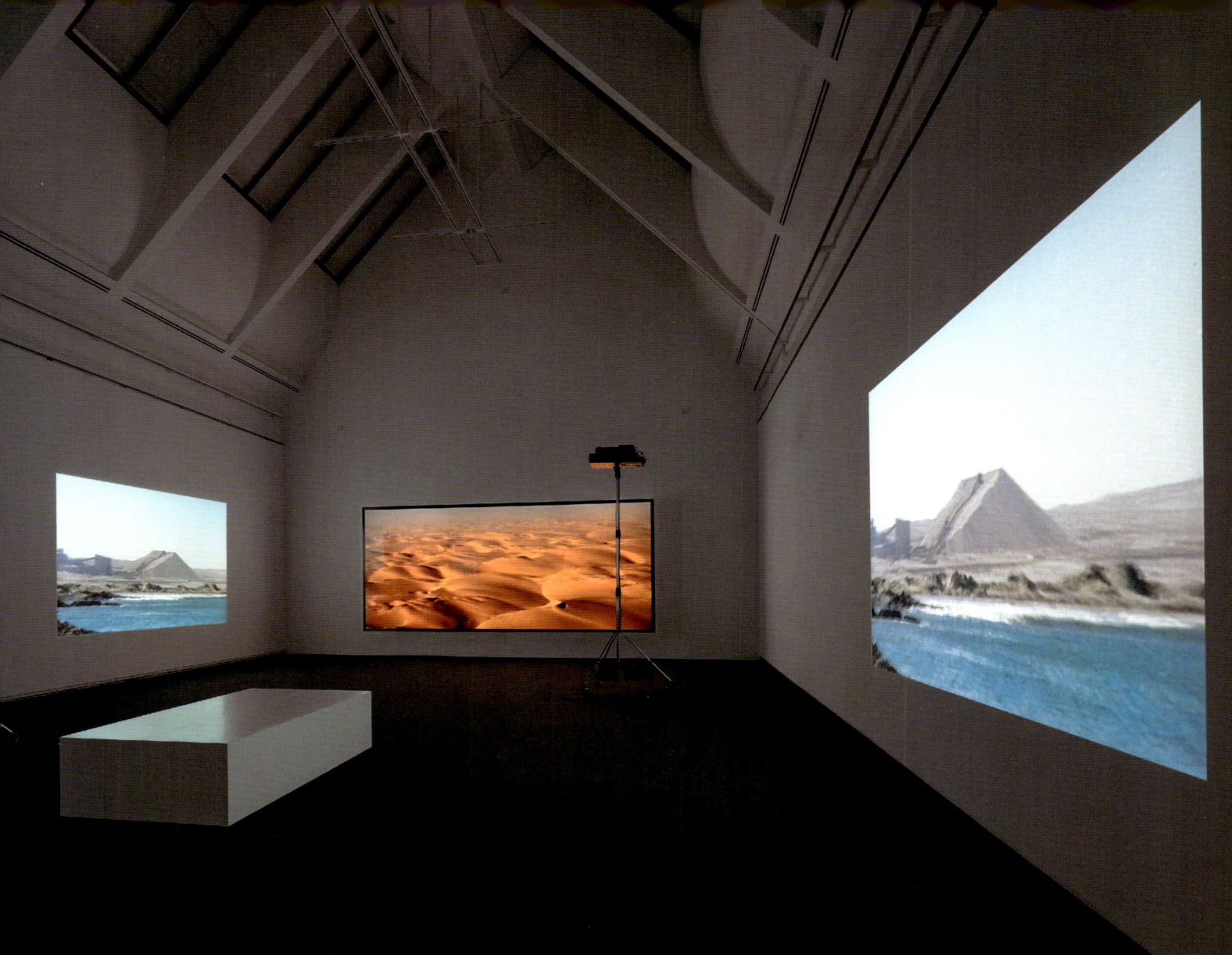

    The installation—two projections, one suspended monitor, and one large lightbox—places the viewer directly in the center of this forbidden landscape, a decaying vista, where machines extract the earth's matter in a continuous loop, while architectural ruins show the vanishing traces of a long-gone human presence. The camera roams among geologic, desert residue and machinery, under the perfect sky of an industrial arcadia. We see no life-form other than wild horses running aimlessly in the dunes. We are left facing what we have produced and are still producing in an economy of useless luxury and vanity: environmental destruction, pollution, obsolescence, and waste—the industrial wasteland. Paradoxically, we are visually seduced: we cannot take our eyes off it, as the landscape is ultimately luscious, sensual, and photogenic in its decay, under the cold sun of economic prosperity.

NEW SHELTER II   *new shelter II, 2001 / 2016*

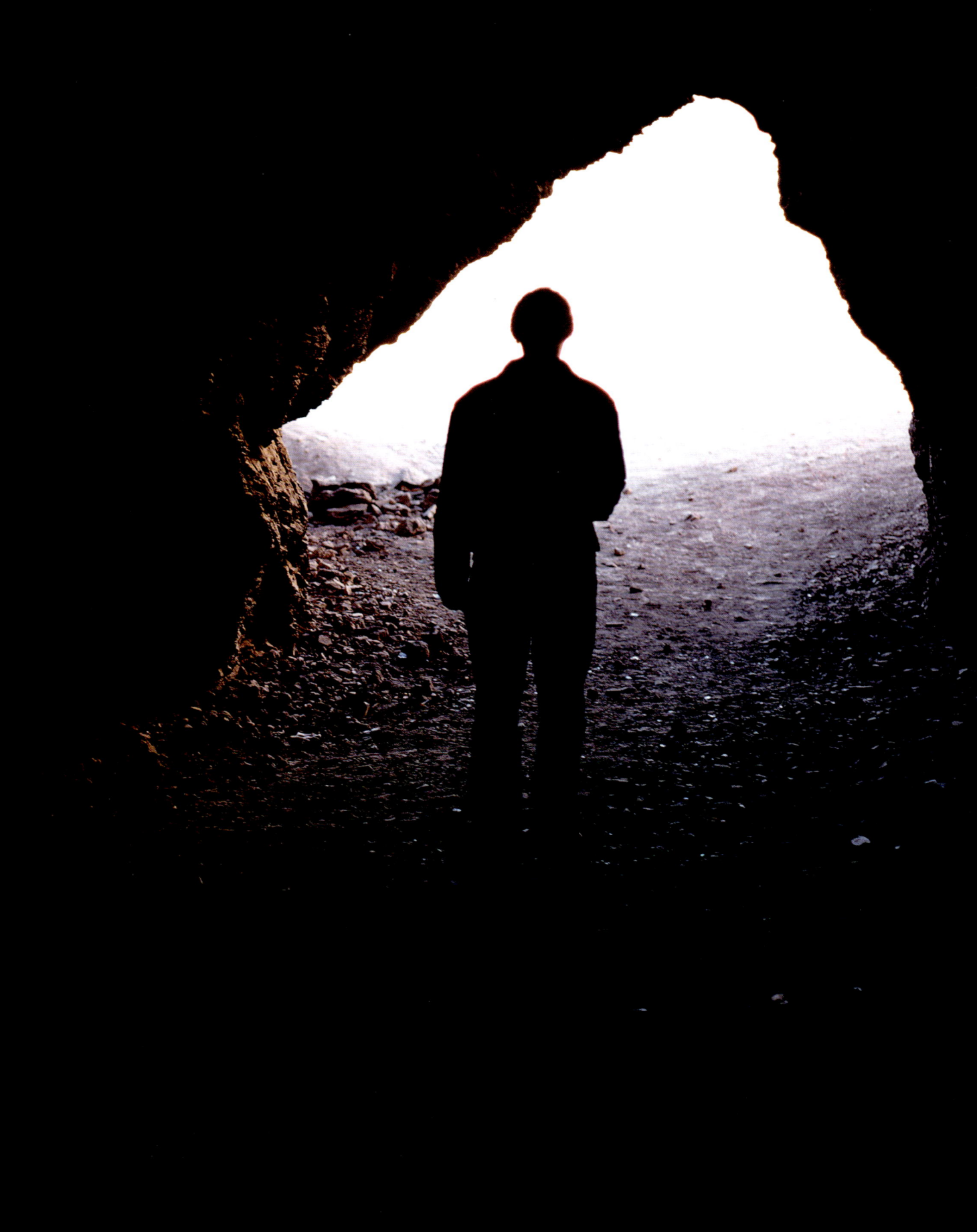

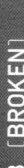

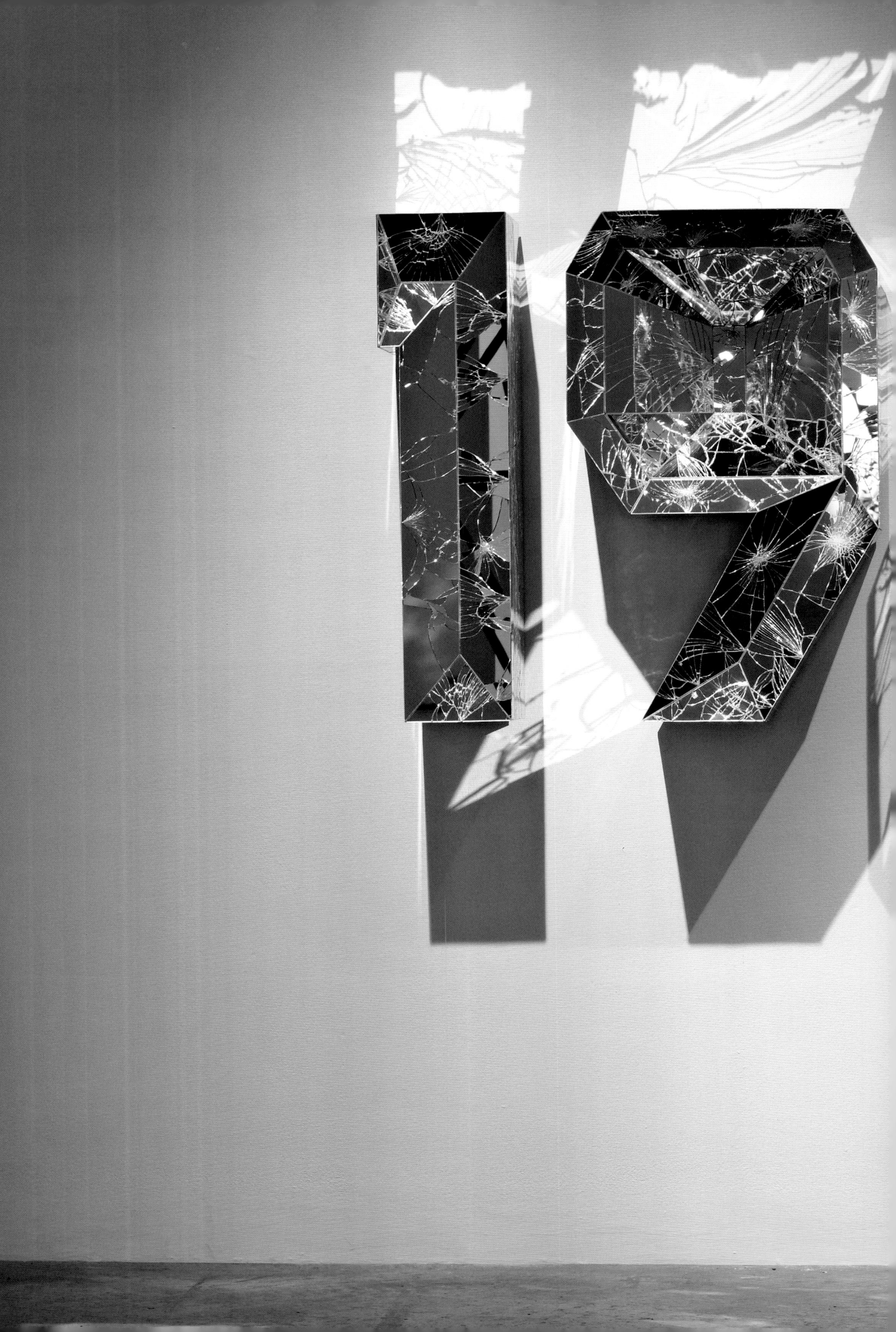

1968 [broken], 2011

1968 [BROKEN]

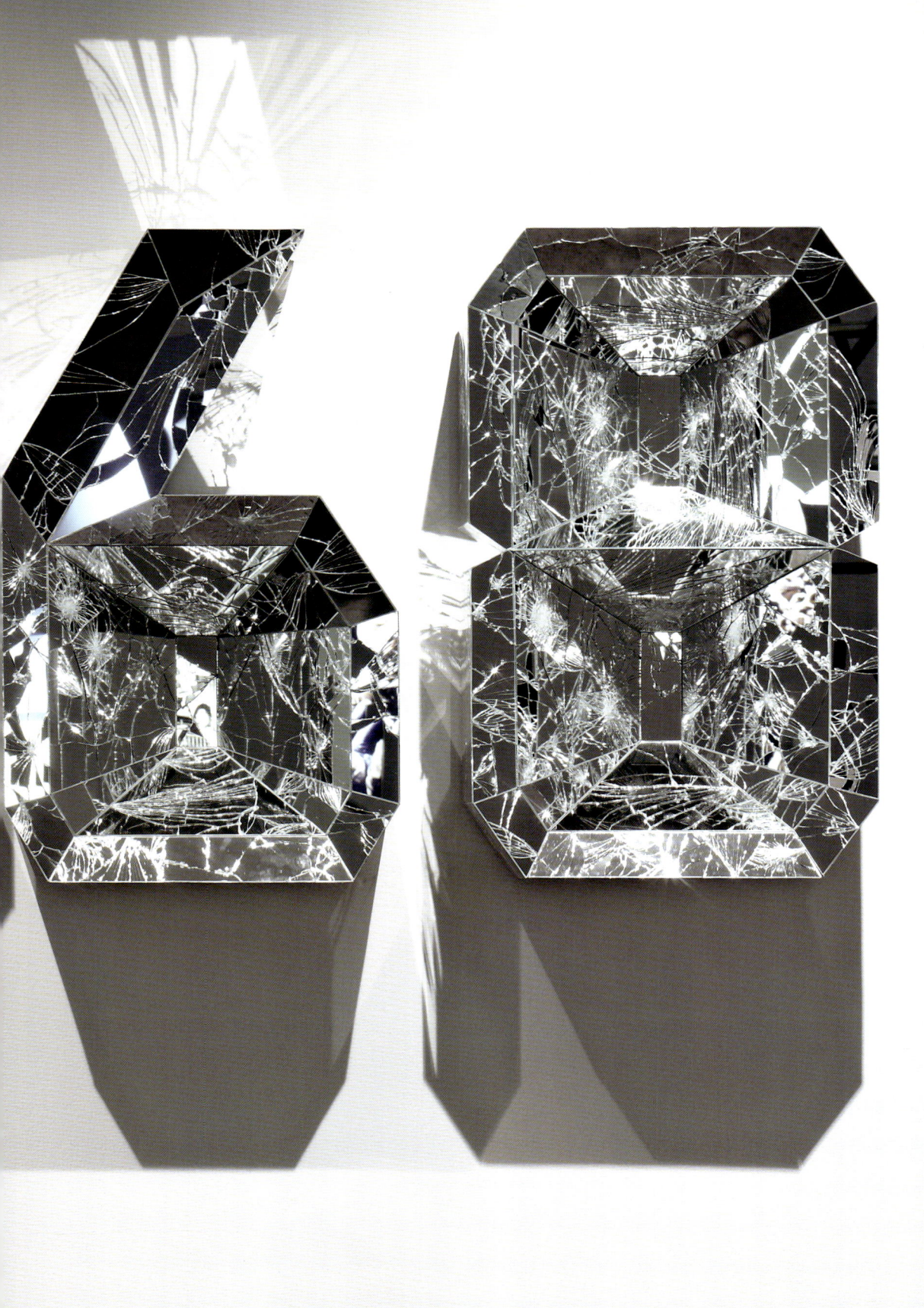

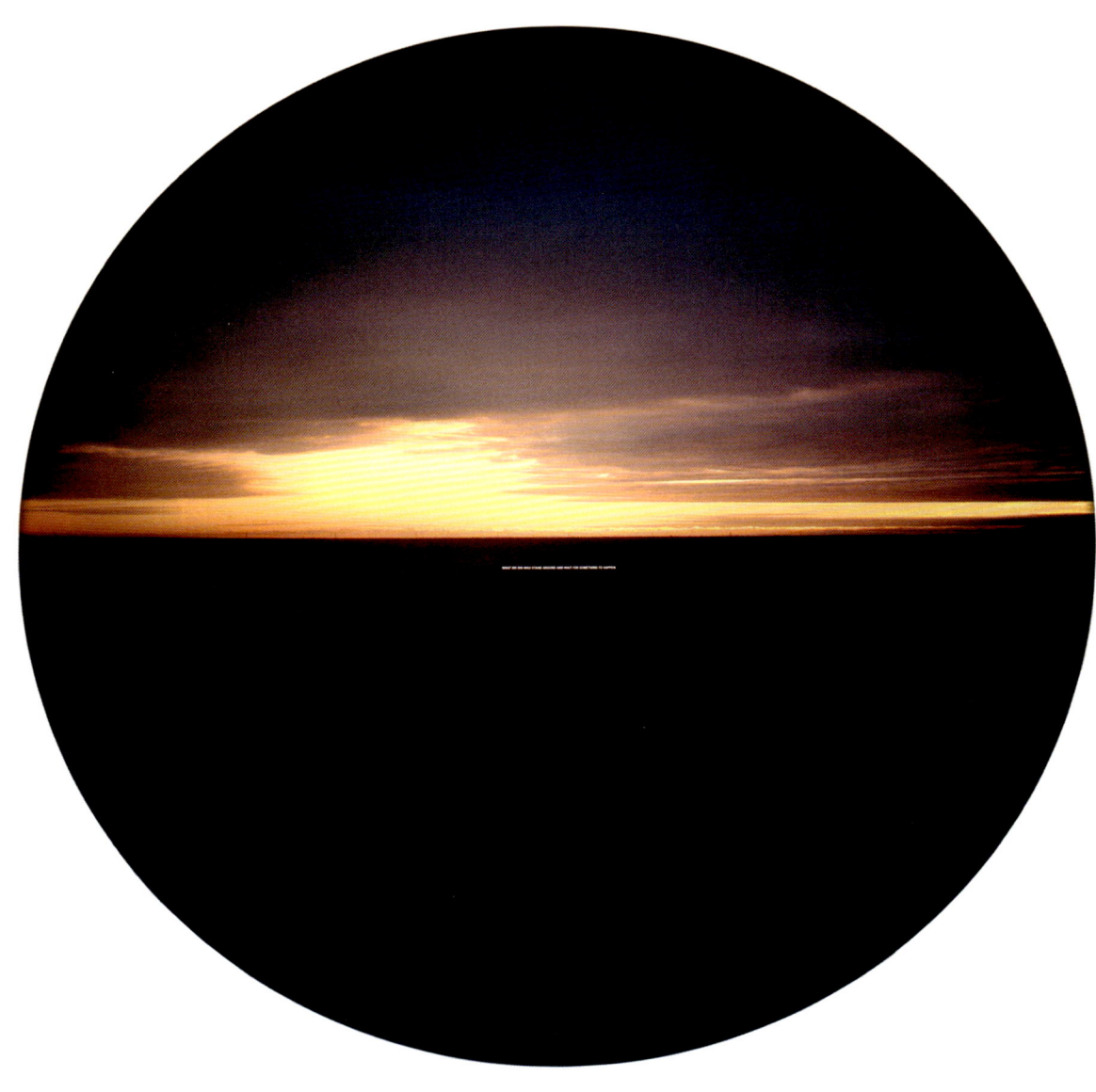

WHAT WE DID WAS STAND AROUND AND WAIT FOR SOMETHING TO HAPPEN, 2011
opposite: WHAT WE DID WAS STAND AROUND AND WAIT FOR SOMETHING TO HAPPEN, 2011, detail

WHAT WE DID WAS STAND AROUND AND WAIT FOR SOMETHING TO HAPPEN

WHAT WE DID WAS STAND AROUND AND WAIT FOR SOMETHING TO HAPPEN

these restless minds, 1998, still

THESE RESTLESS MINDS

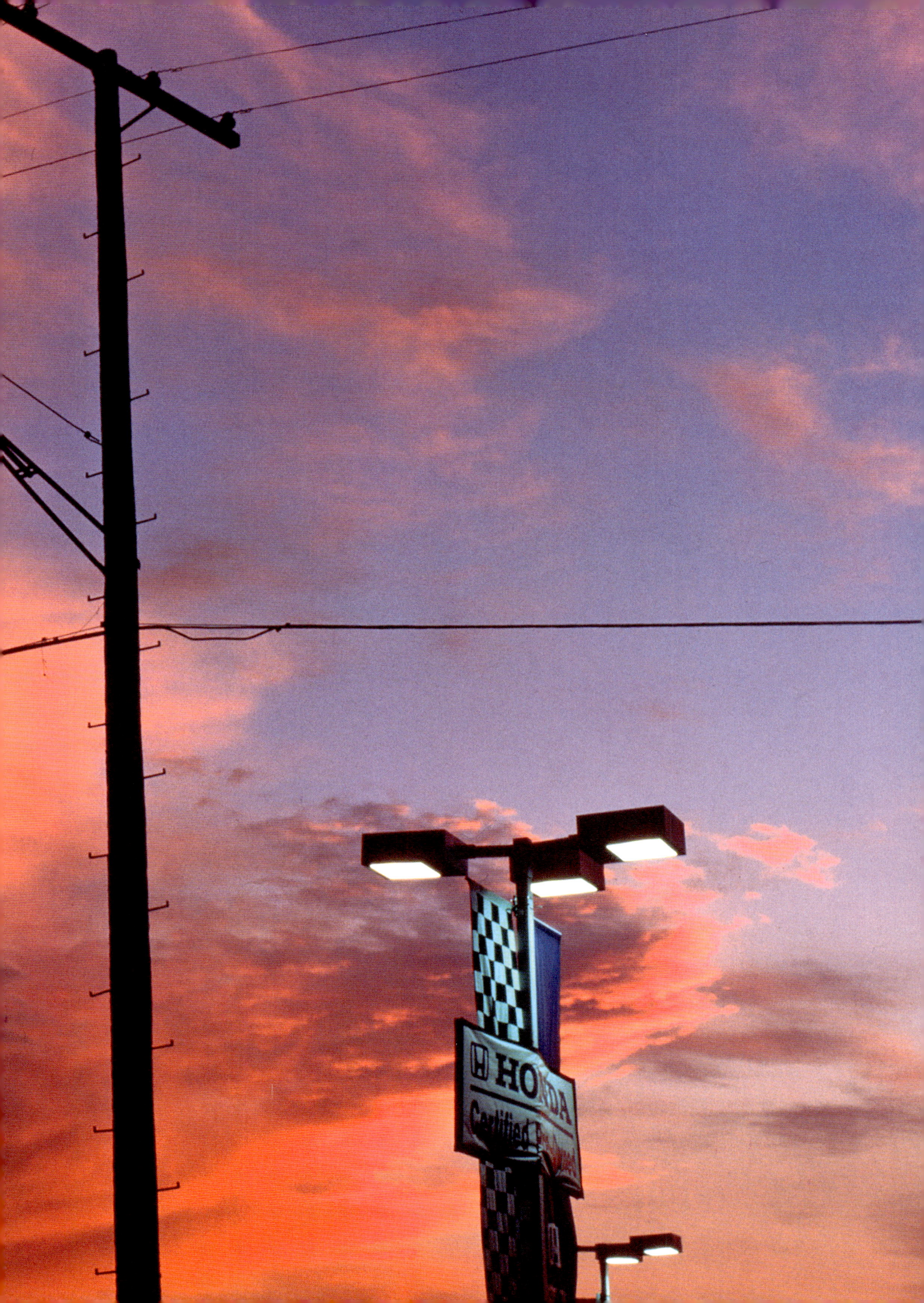

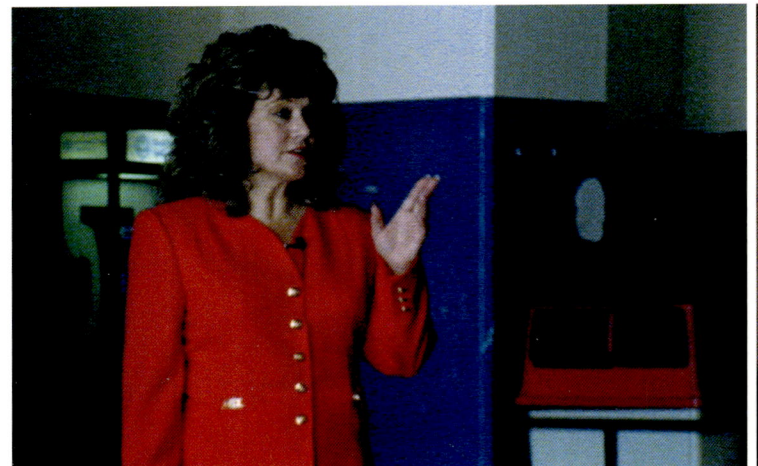
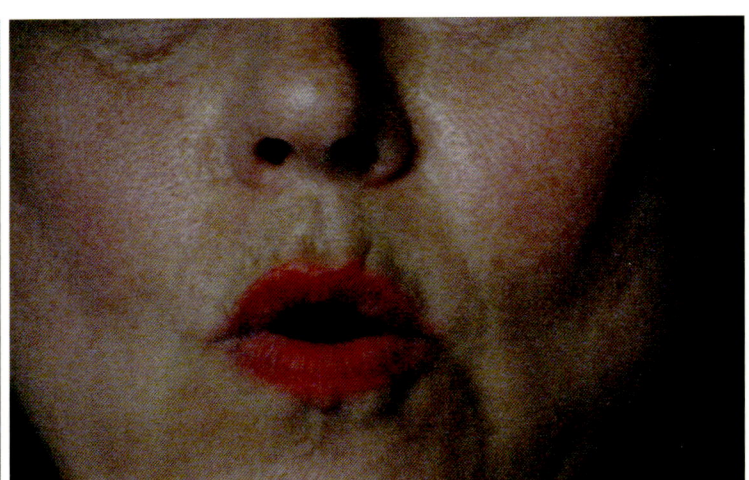

these restless minds, 1998, stills

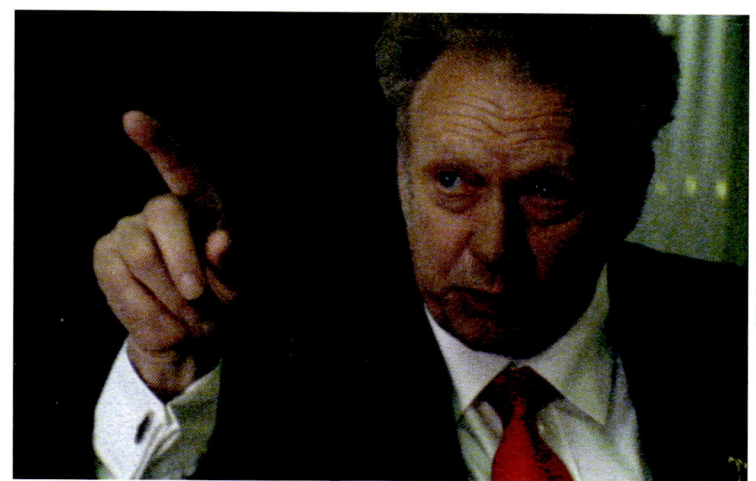 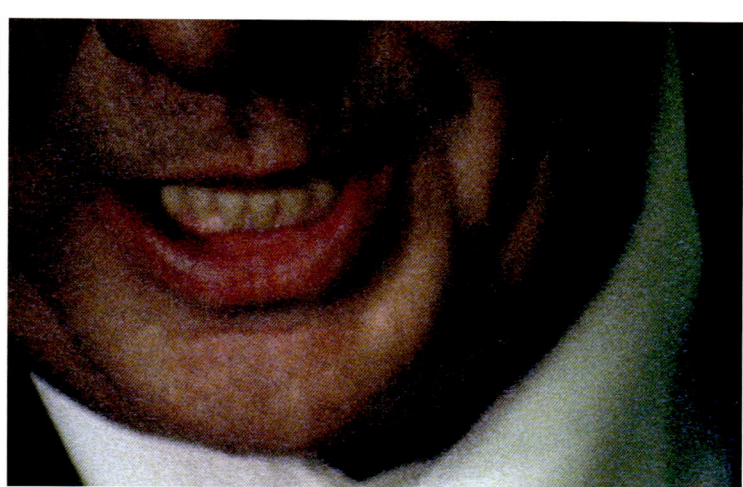

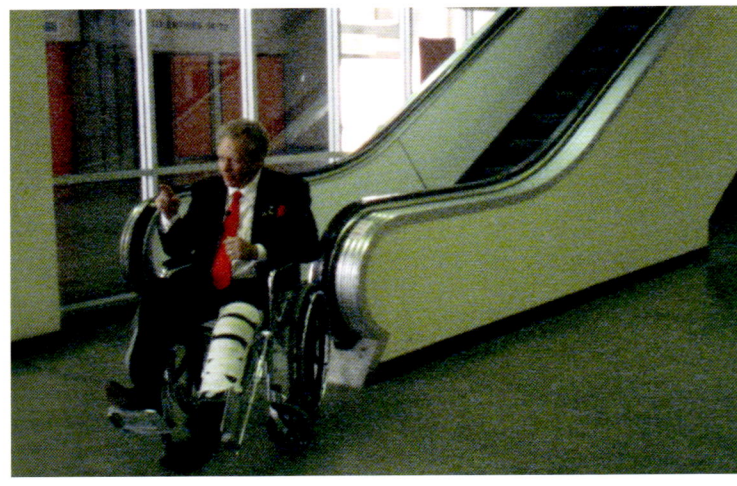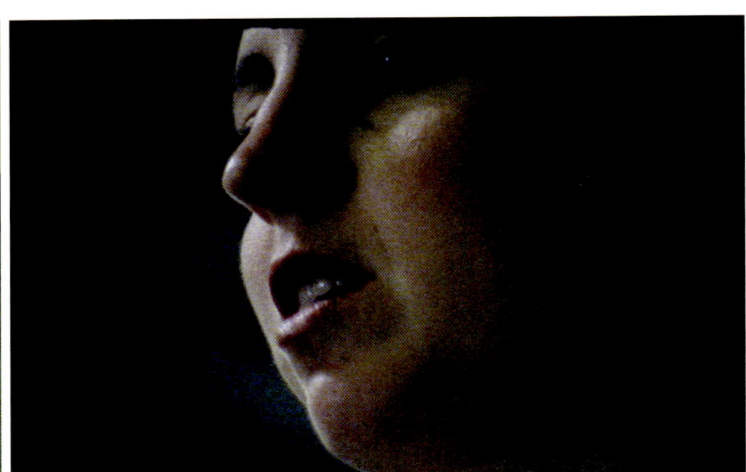

these restless minds, 1998, stills

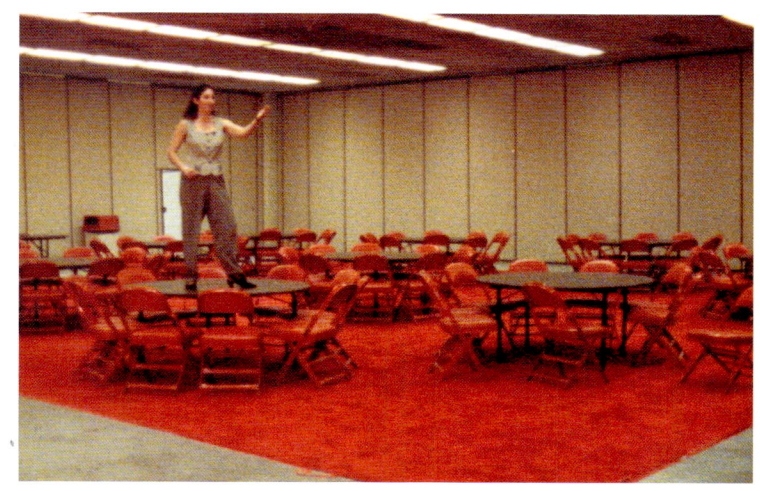 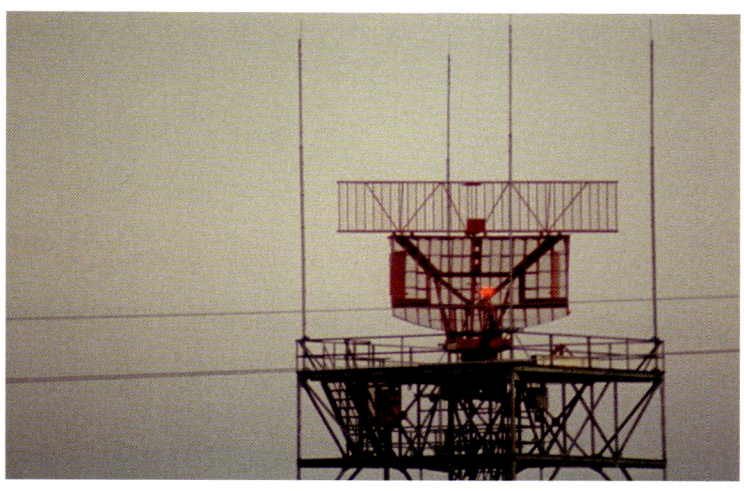

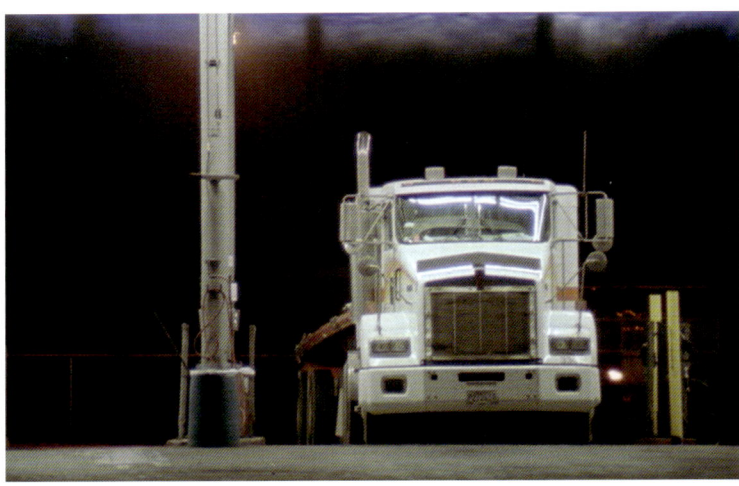
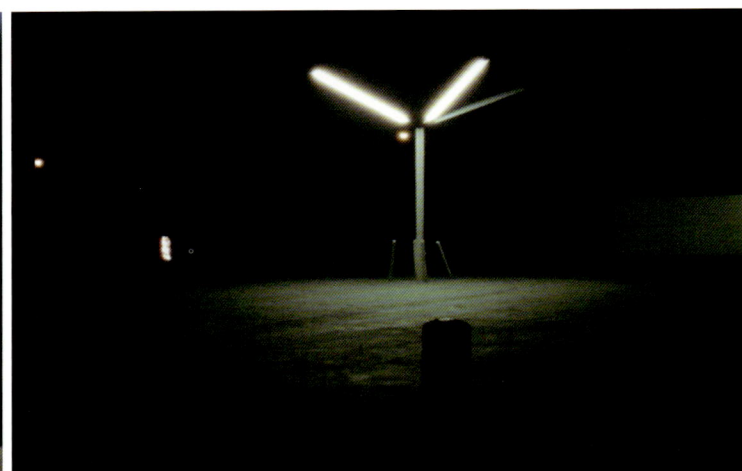

these restless minds, 1998, stills

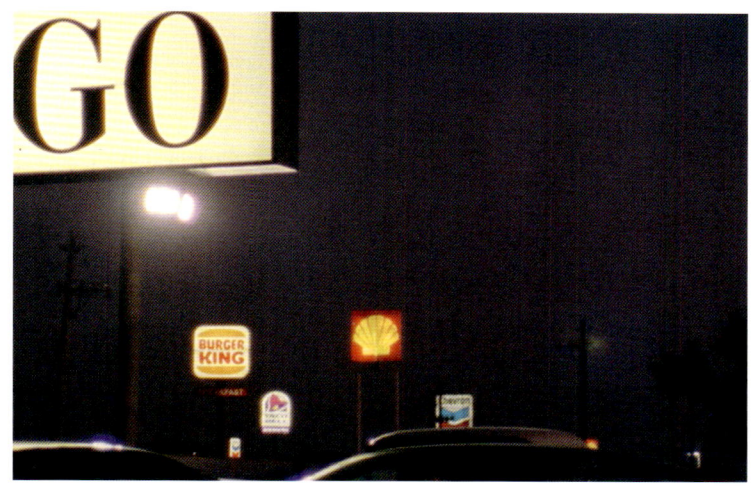
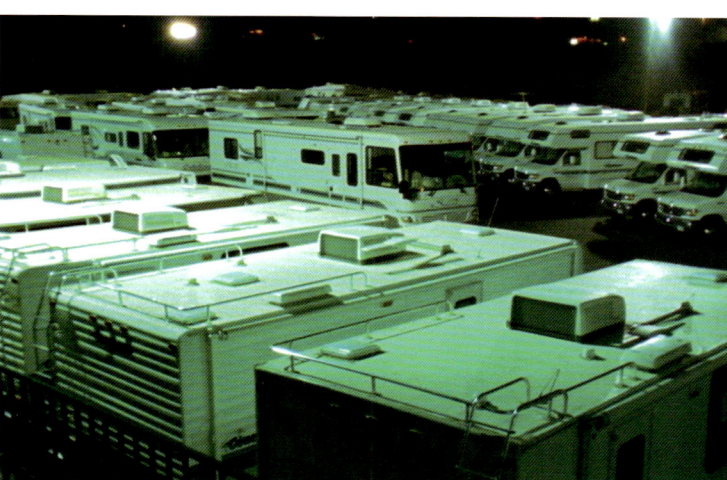

Economic prosperity—or the transactional aspect of it—is also at the center of the installation *these restless minds*. The installation is a theater, a wooden structure with circular benches under a hanging set of three video monitors that resemble the vernacular devices one would find in an airport or a sports bar. On the screens, we see auctioneers located in unlikely, uncanny places such as empty parking lots, motel swimming pools, elevators, bingo rooms, and highway underpasses, all in the hypnotic thrall of their monotonous chants. Their voices are marvelous, abstract, and serial. But set against vast landscapes in the American West, where aridity meets desolation, the predominant feeling is that our dreams are being auctioned off in a place that does not belong to anyone—a veritable no-man's-land. And these are not even the big dreams. They are the mundane, small-scale aspirations: getting by, making ends meet in one's own house—even a trailer—a home, with some small measure of comfort. Or what Aitken has referred to as "ninety-nine-cent dreams."

    This vocal liberation from syntax and meaning accentuates a further subordination to the dominating social value of being sold—and buying into— a conception of life, experiences, and relationships that are degraded to exchangeable commodities, if you can afford them. And in this irrigated paradise, nobody will place a reserve on your dreams and life expectations. In this place, the despoliation of the landscape matches that of the social body falling off the grid of social organization, of socialization.

these restless minds, 1998, installation view, 303 Gallery, New York

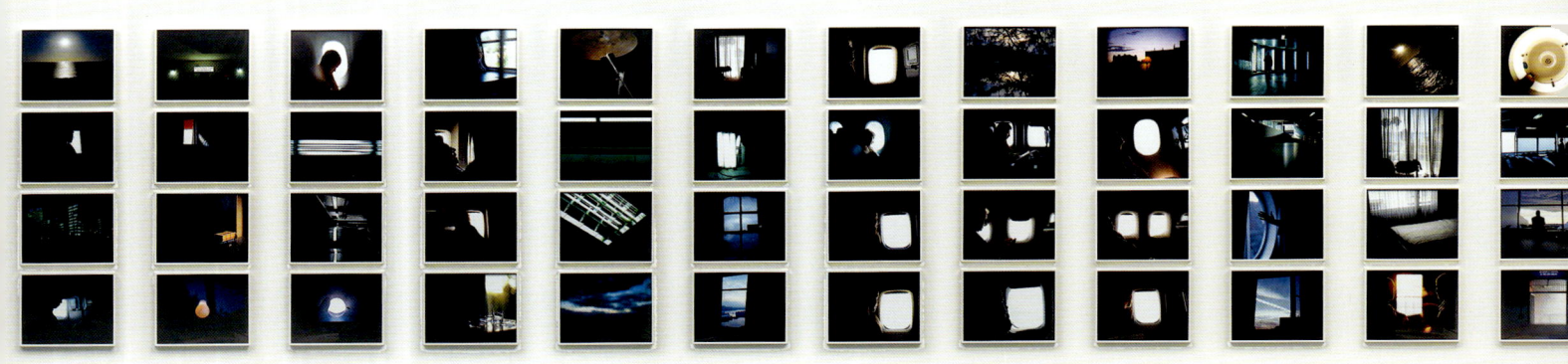
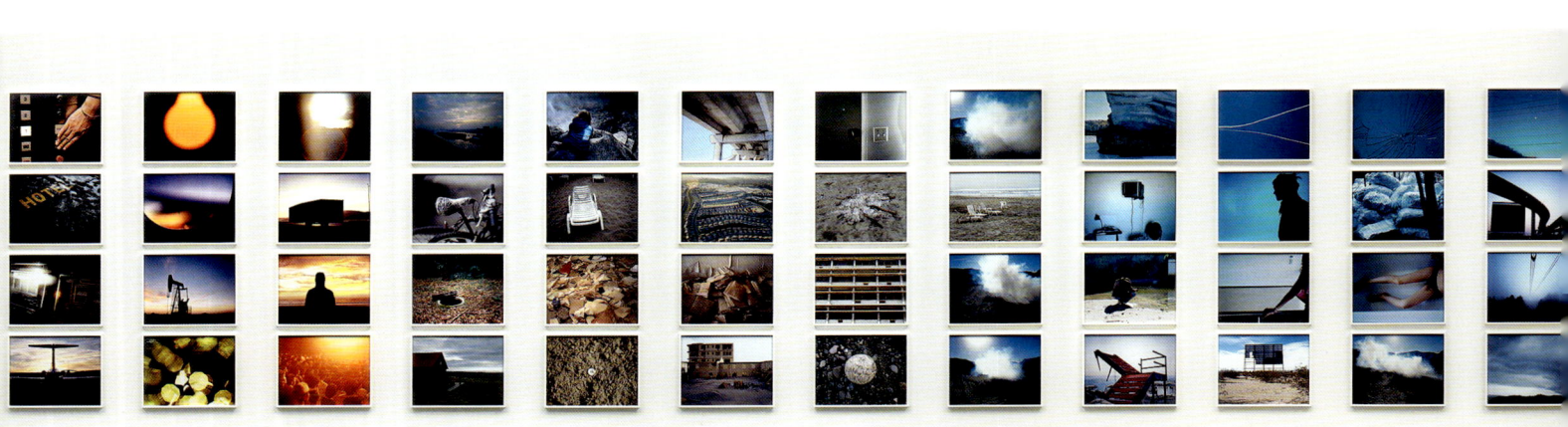

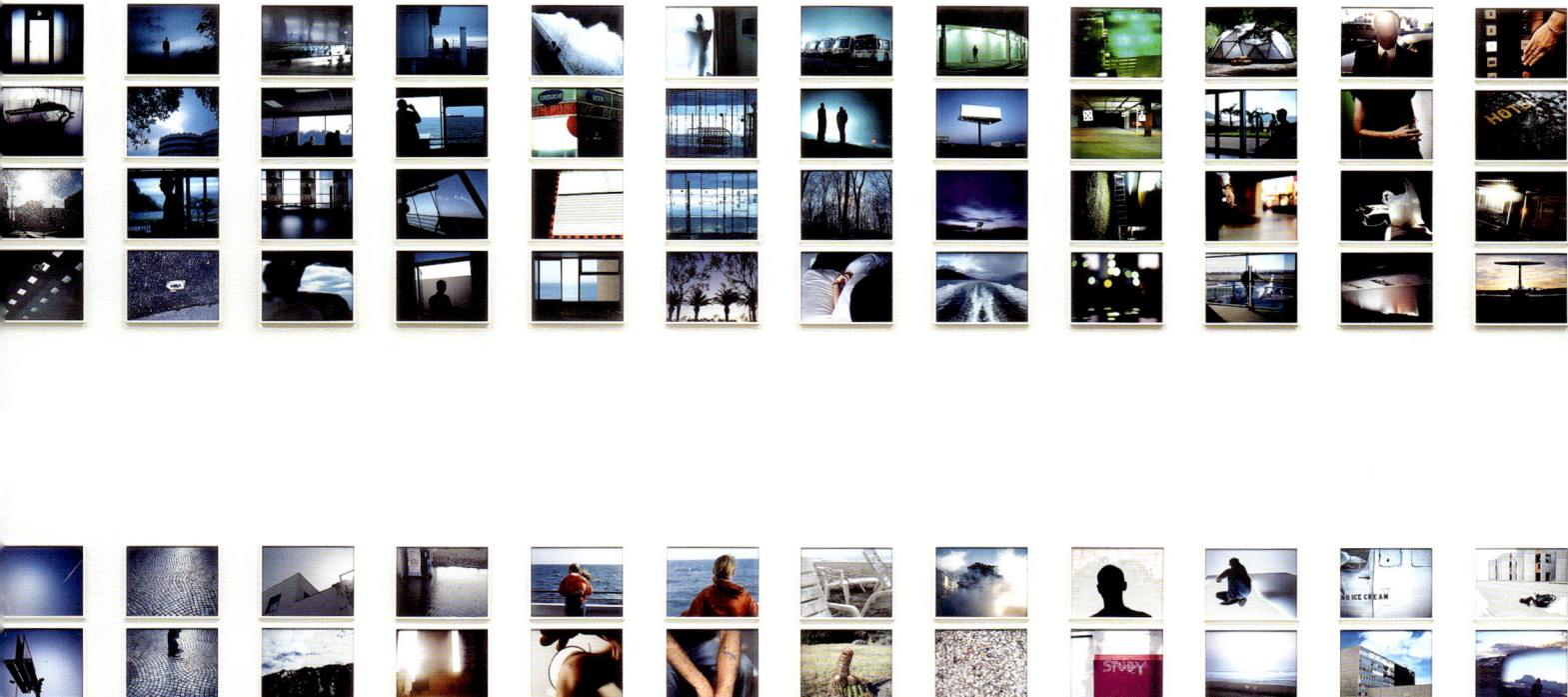

99c dreams, 2008, detail

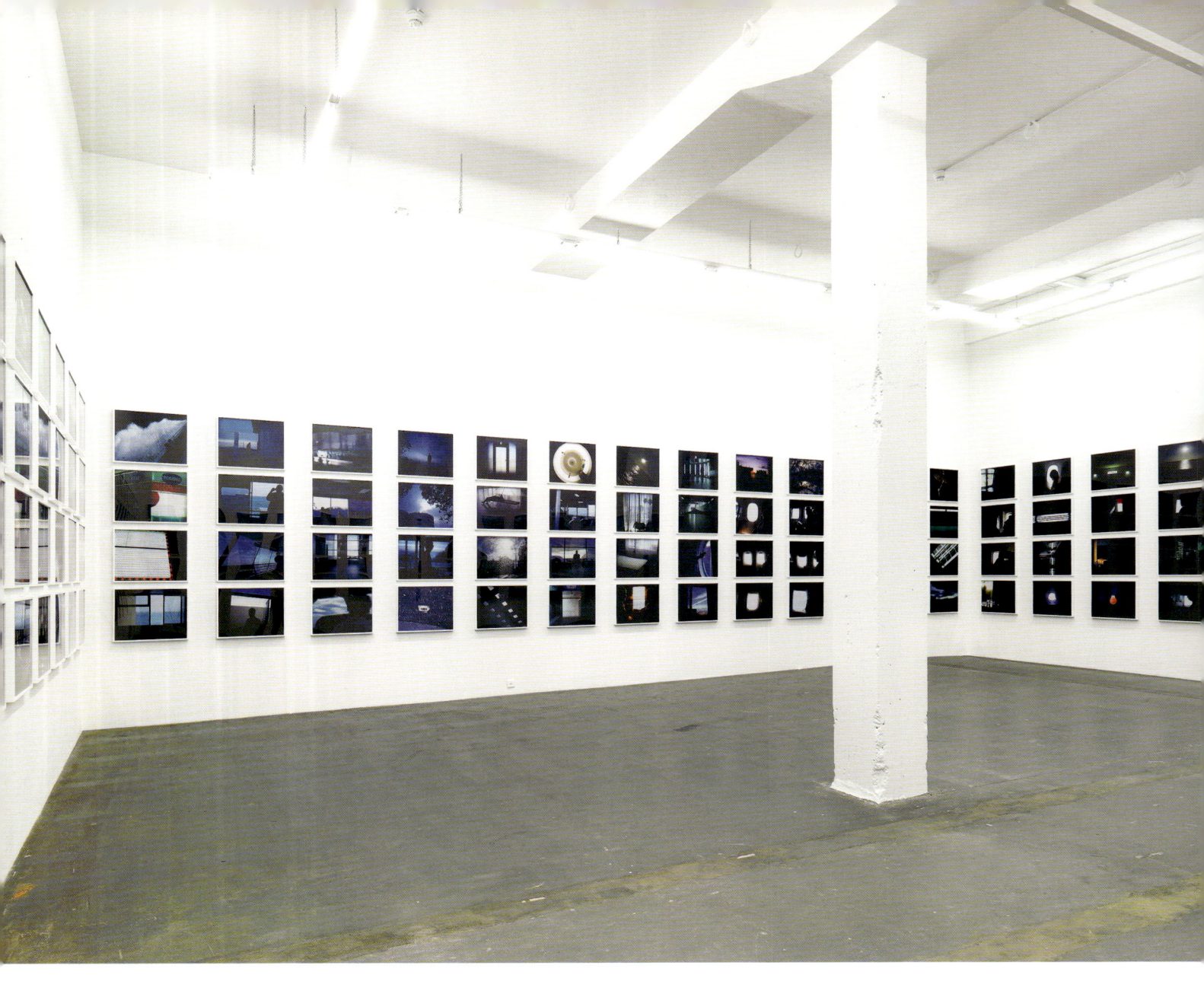

99c dreams, 2008, installation views,
Galerie Eva Presenhuber, Zurich
following spread: 99c dreams, 2008, detail

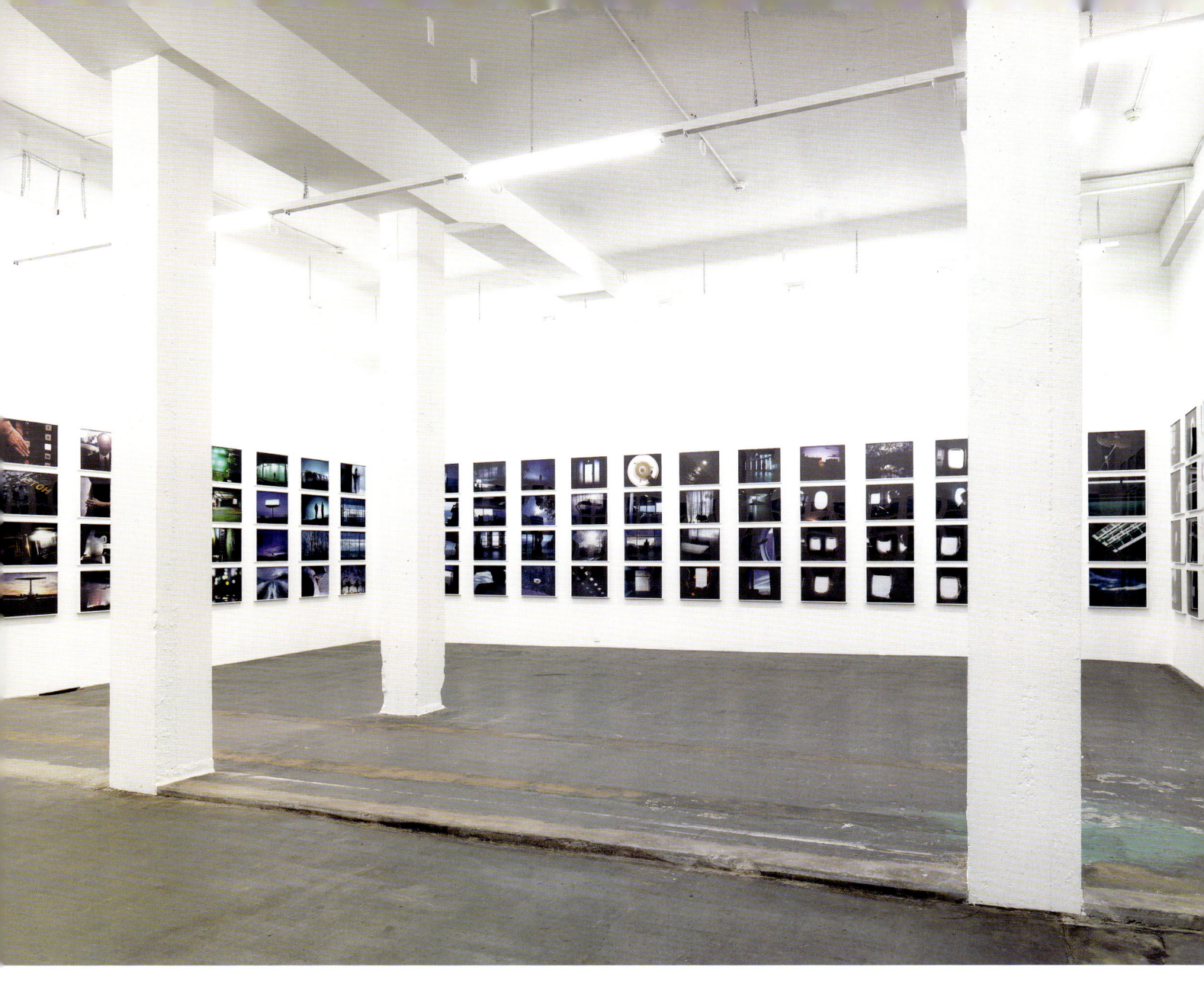

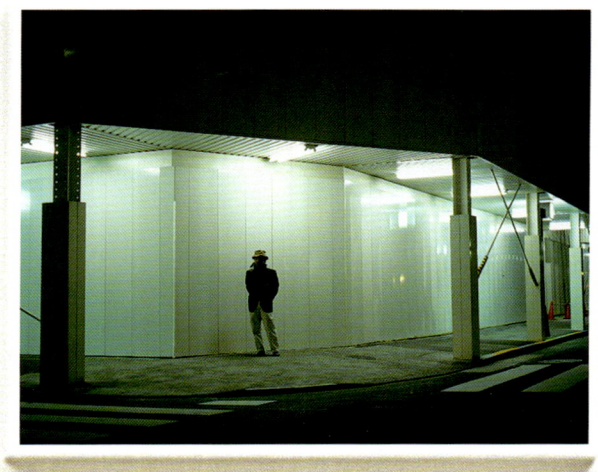
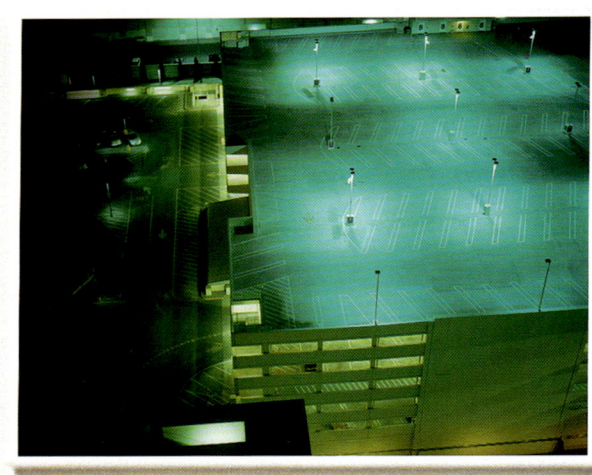
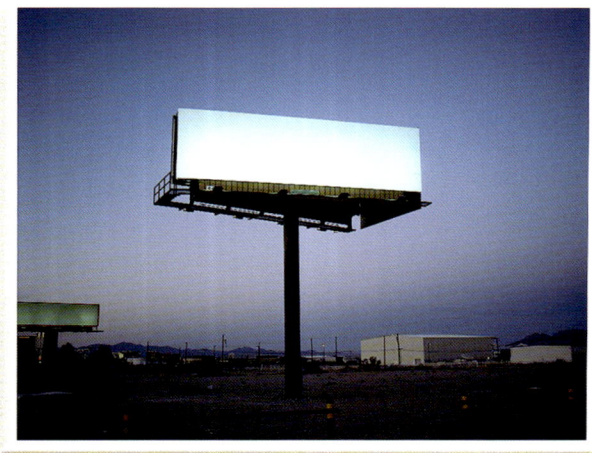
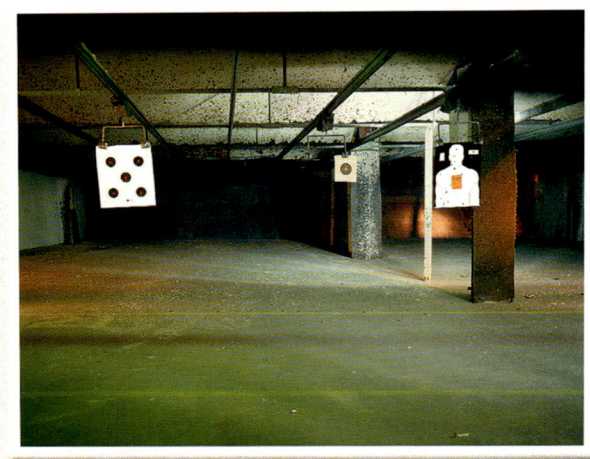
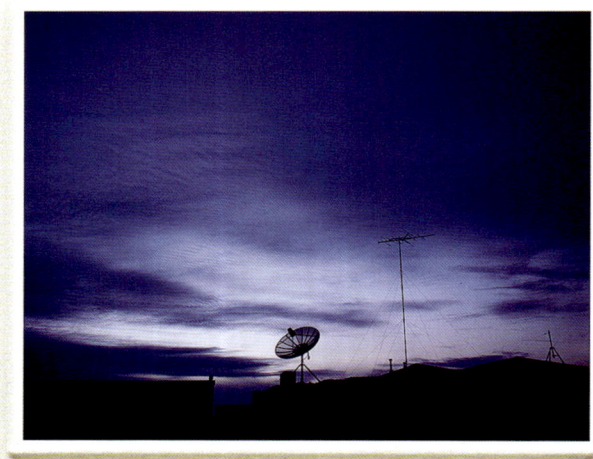
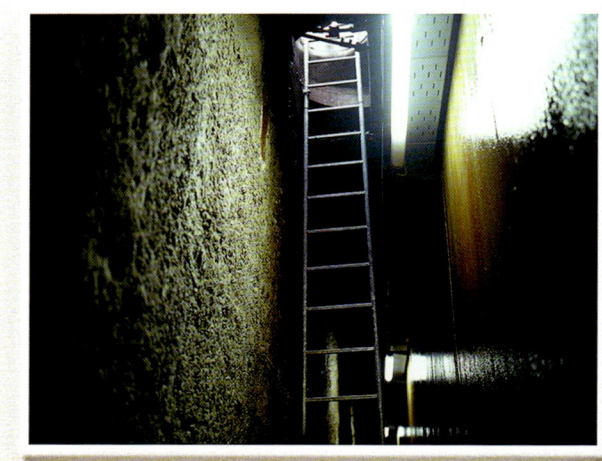
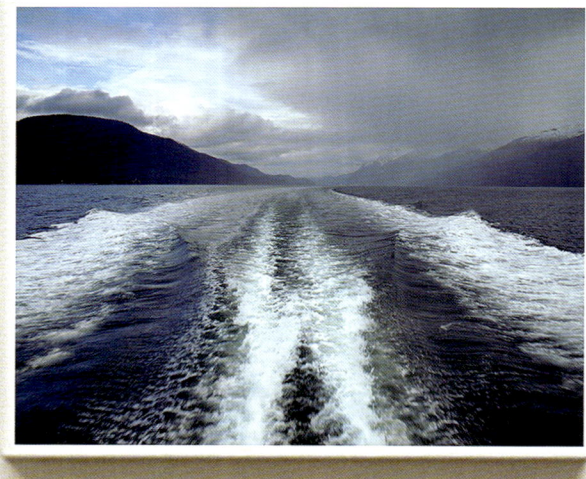
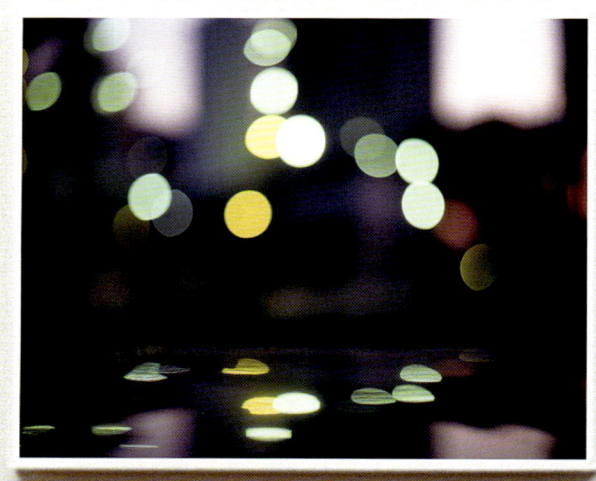

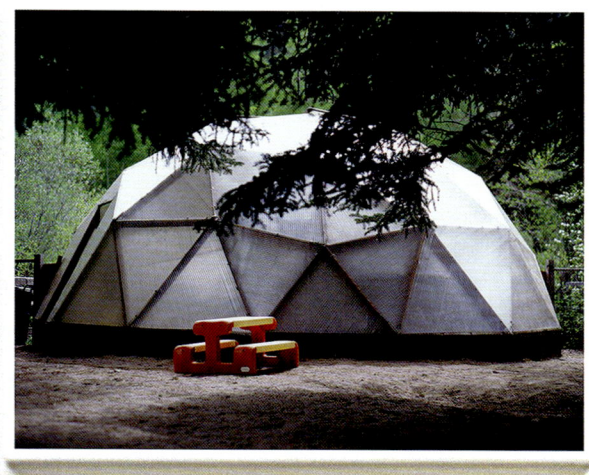
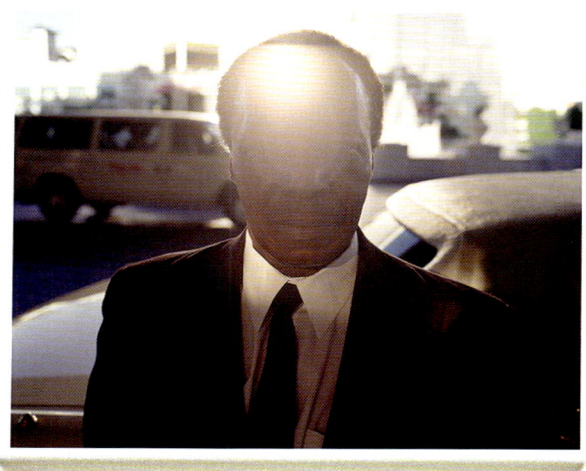
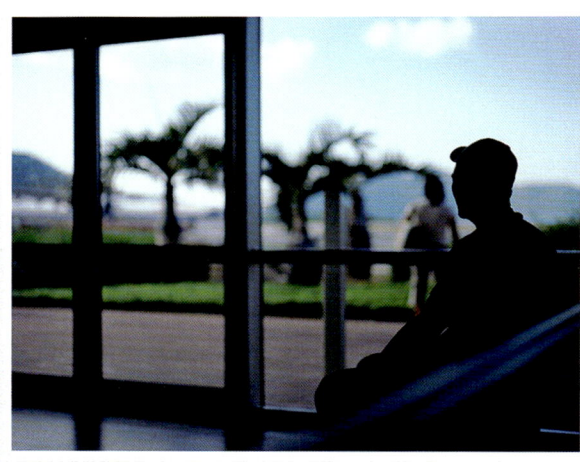
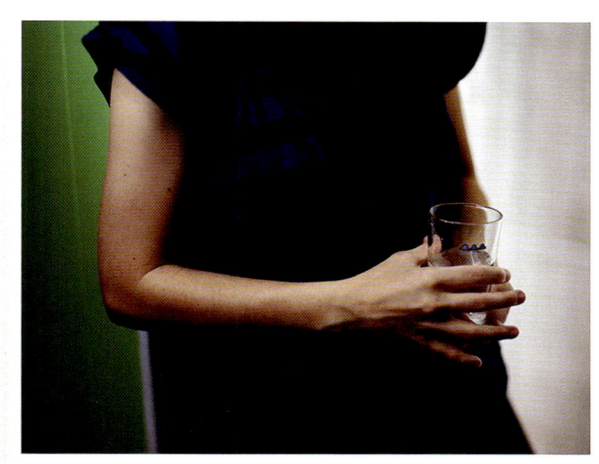
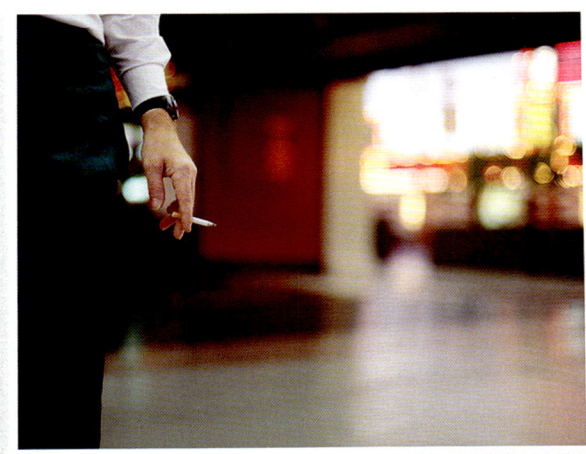
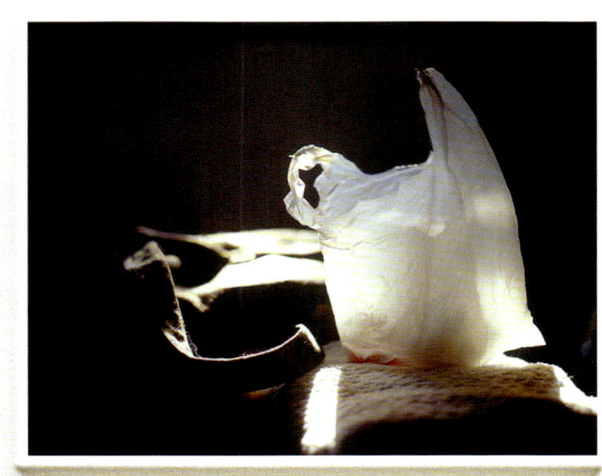
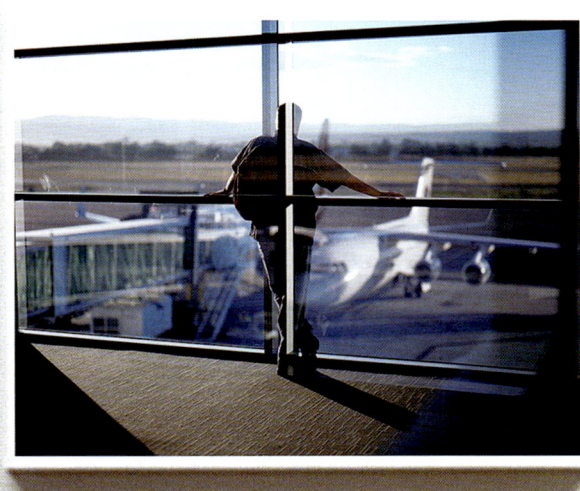
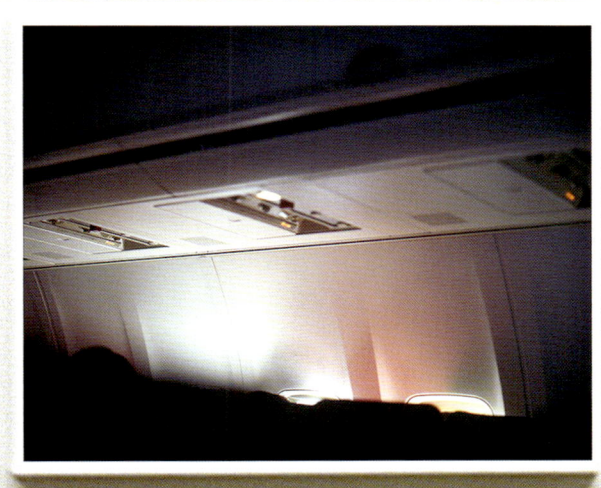

passenger, 1997

PASSENGER

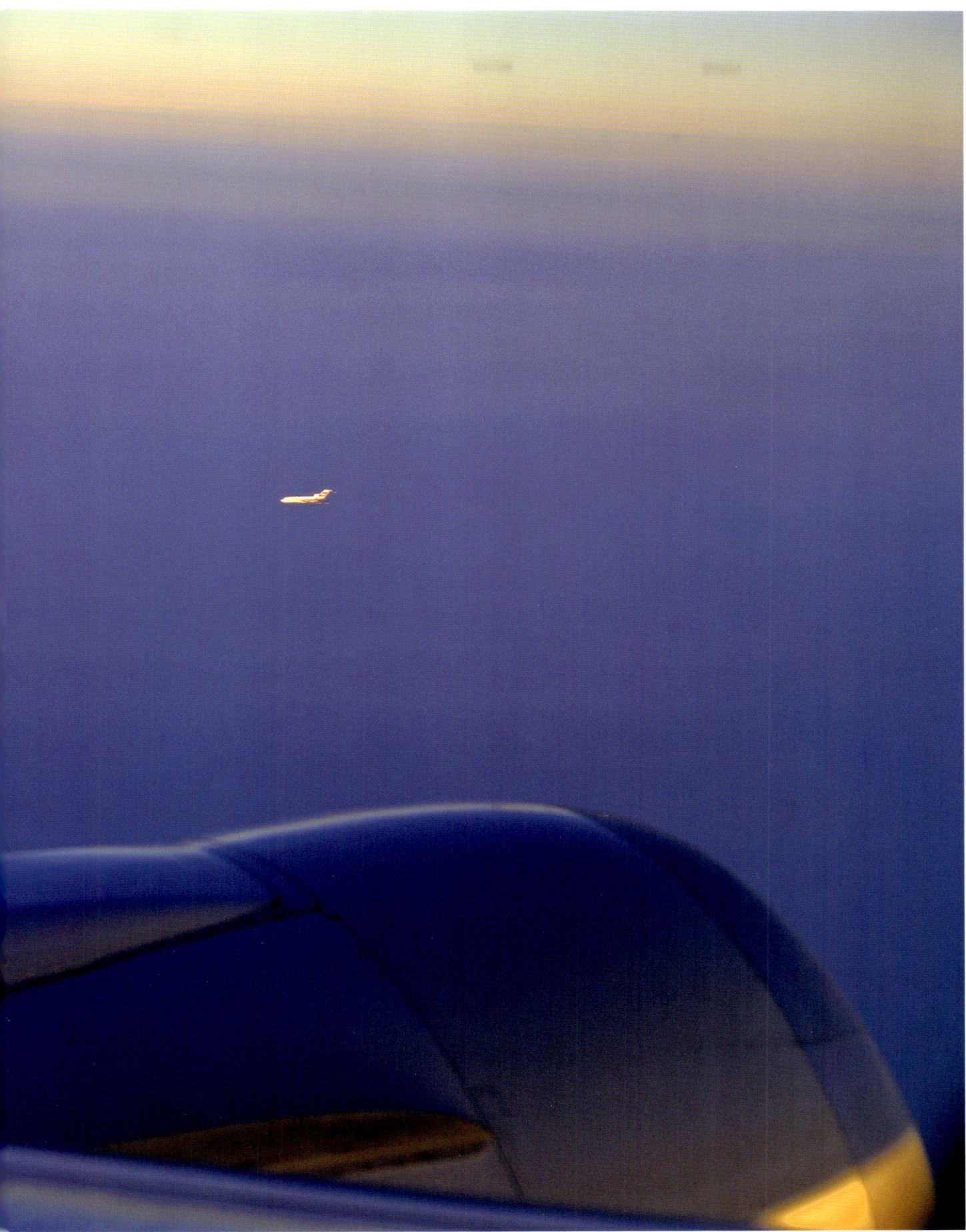

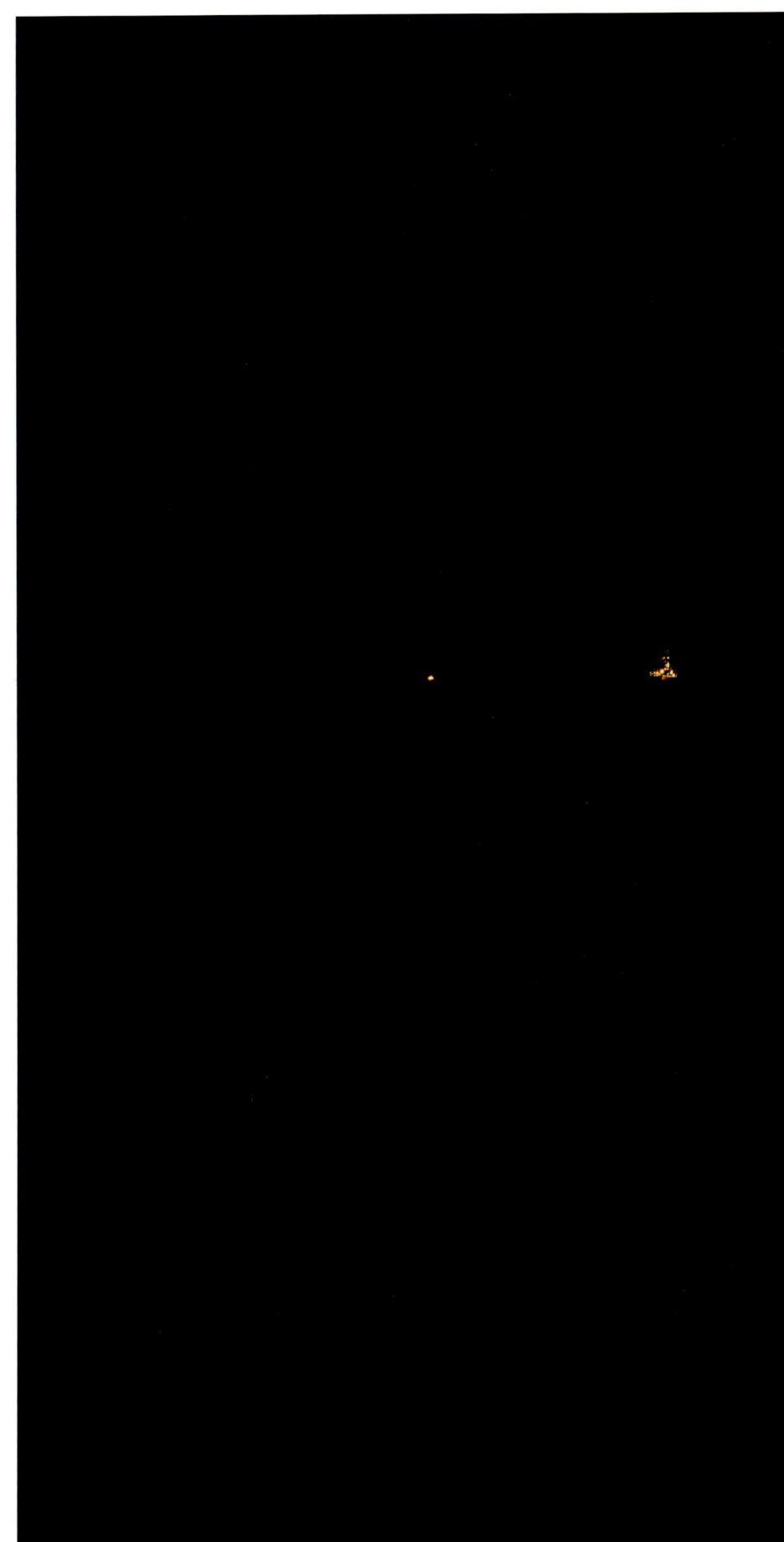

untitled [Santa Barbara Offshore Platforms] I, 1998

UNTITLED [SANTA BARBARA OFFSHORE PLATFORMS] I

conspiracy, 1998

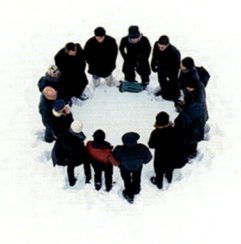

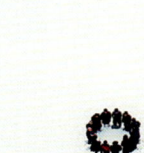

CONSPIRACY

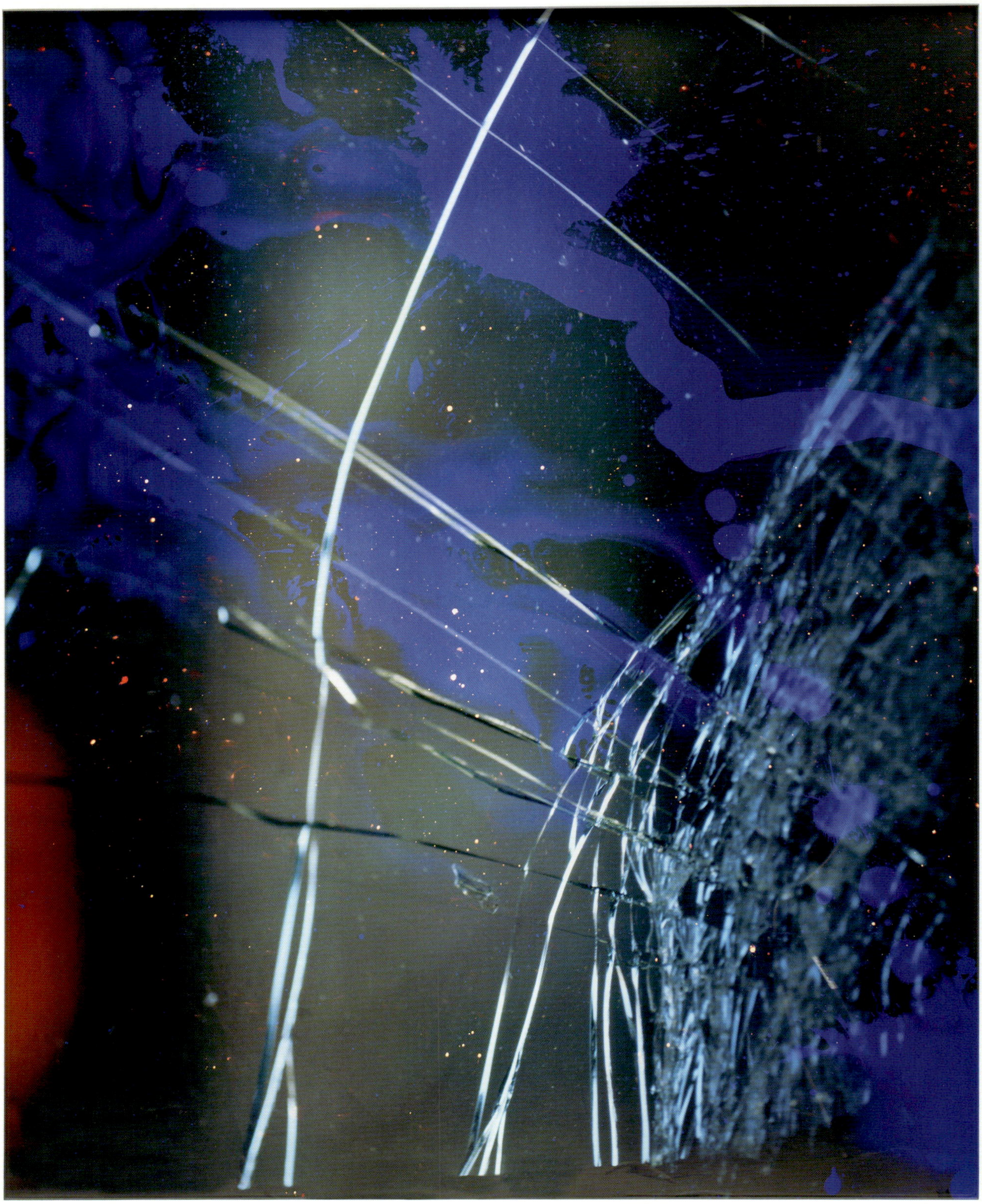

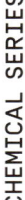

open door [chemical series], 2007

CHEMICAL SERIES

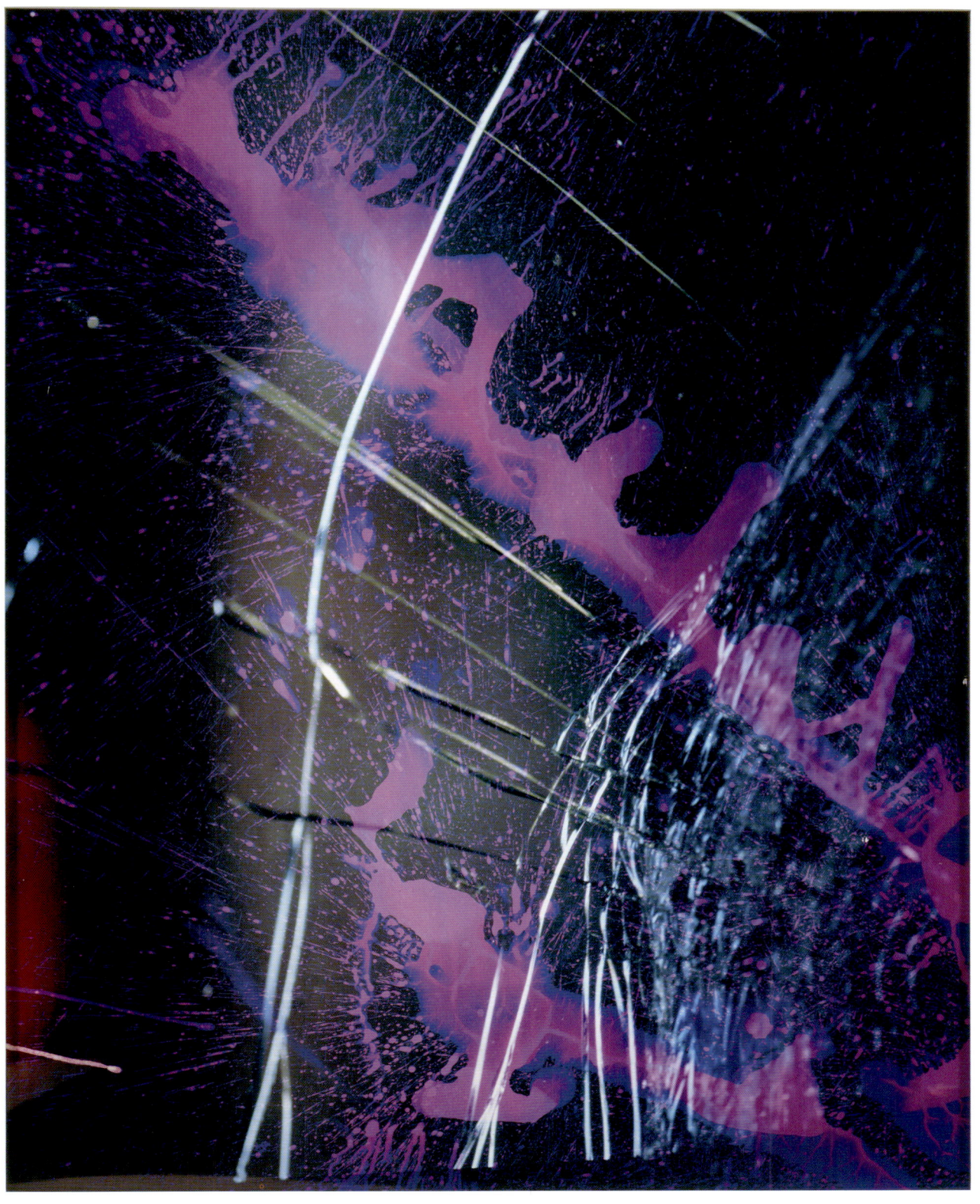

points of transition (chemical series), 2007

sleeper [chemical series], 2007

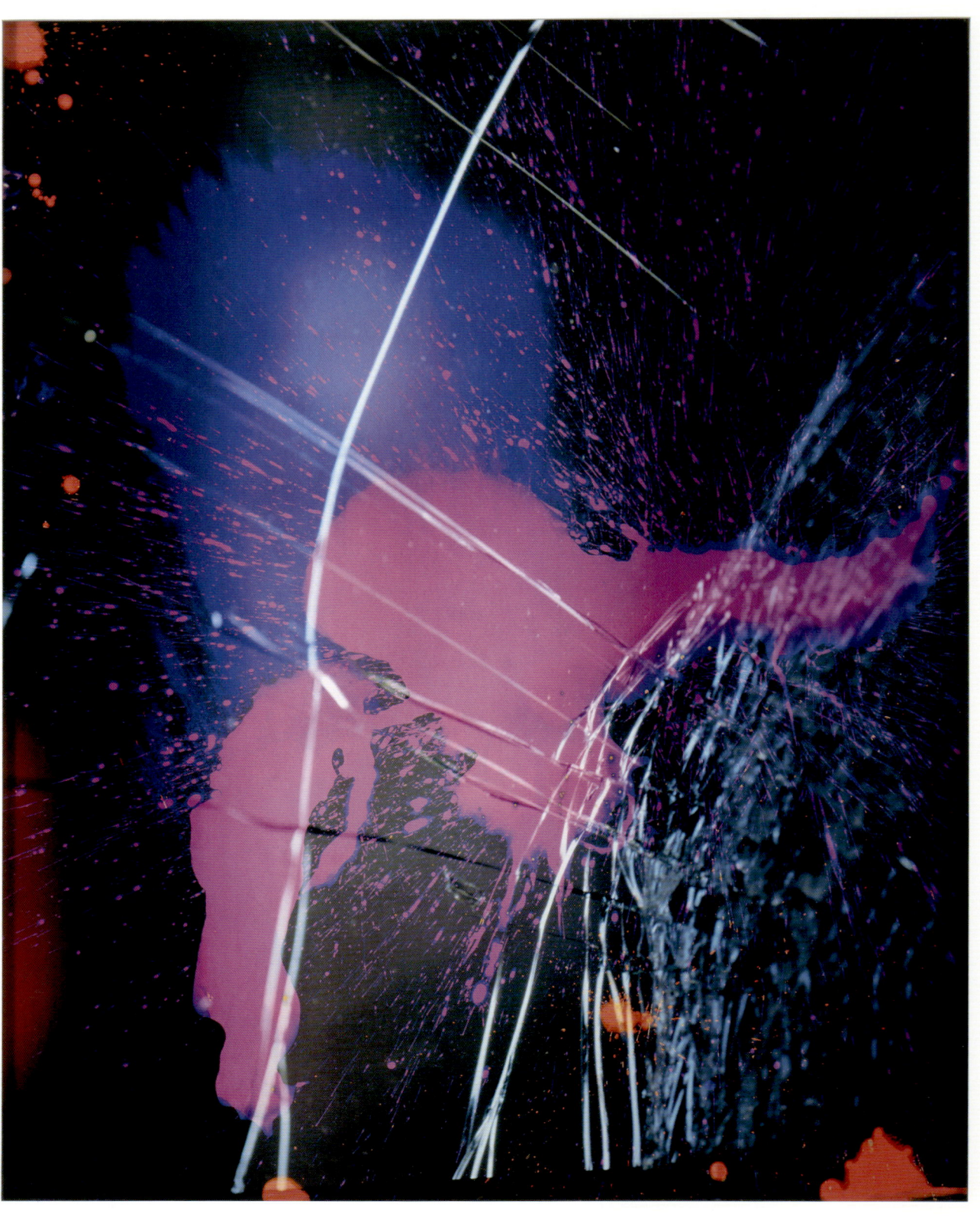

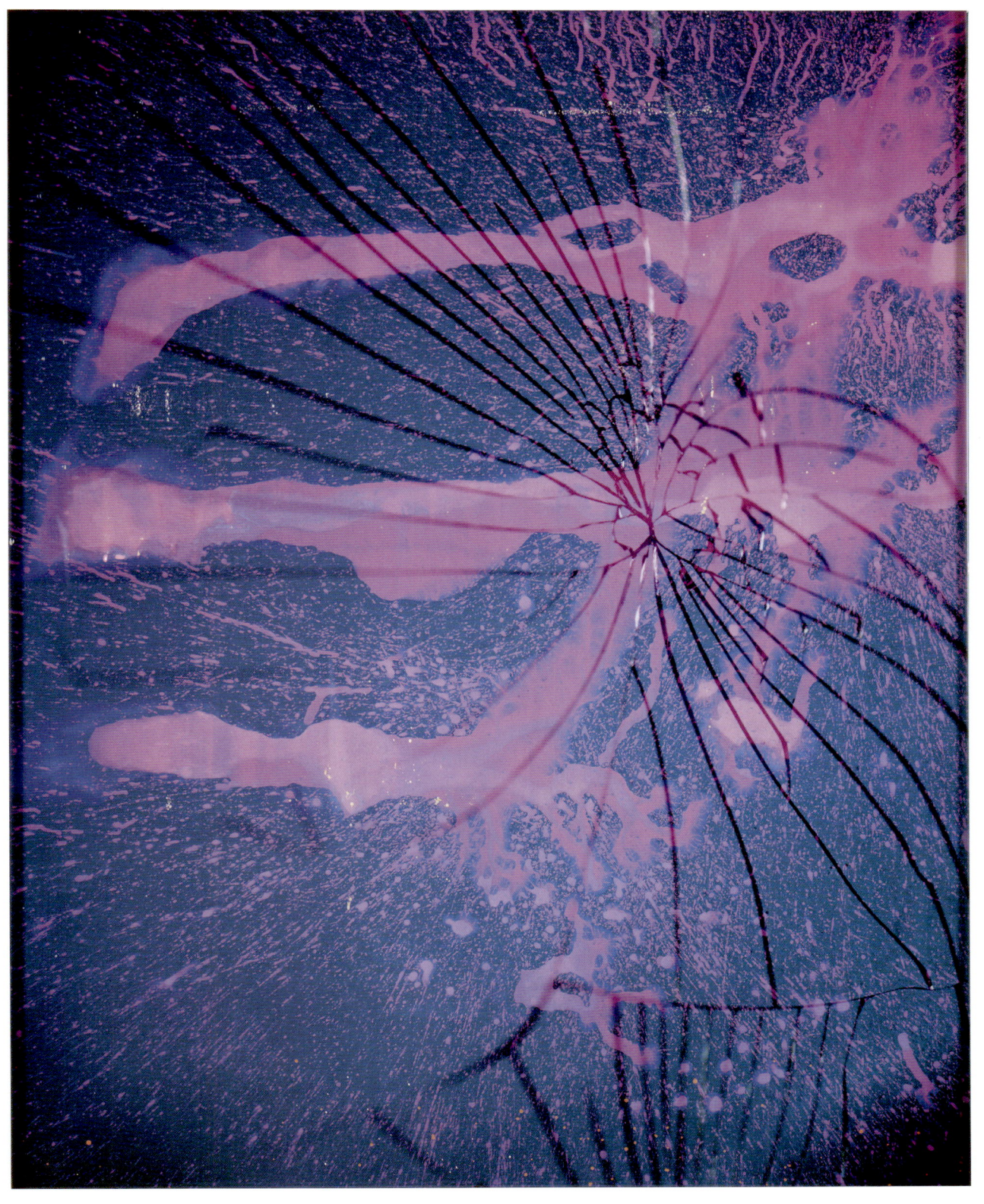

station to station [chemical series], 2007

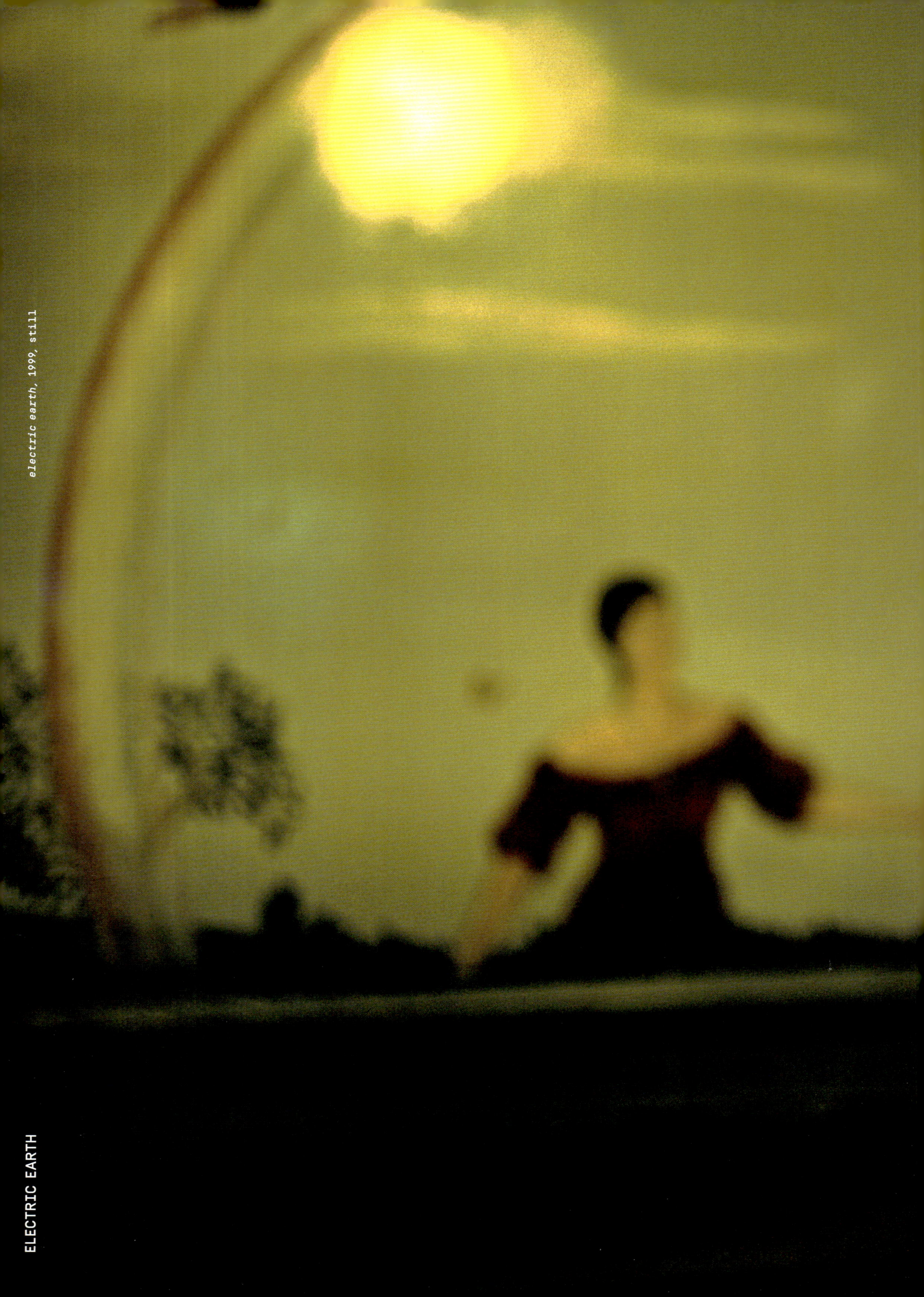

ELECTRIC EARTH

electric earth, 1999, still

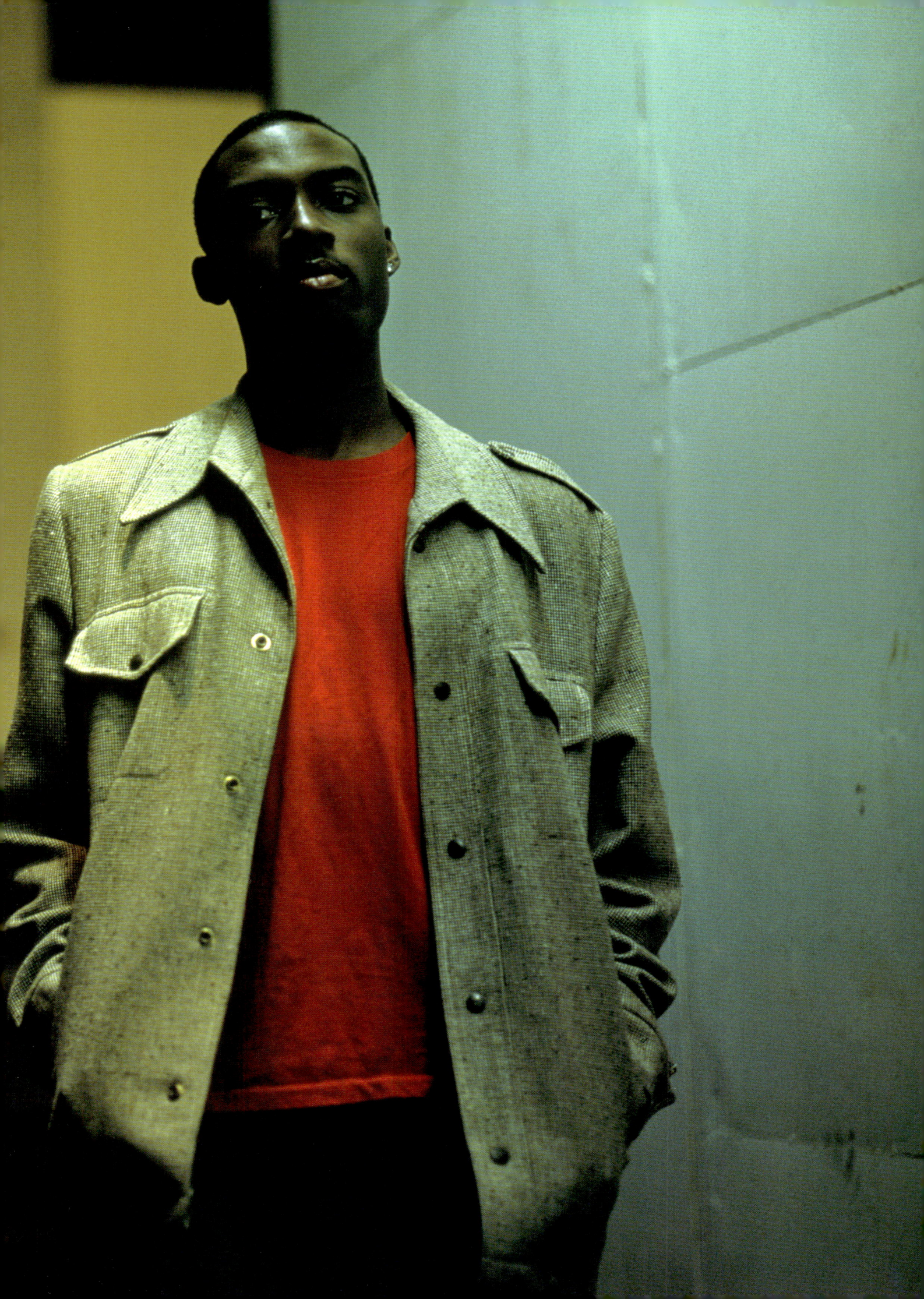

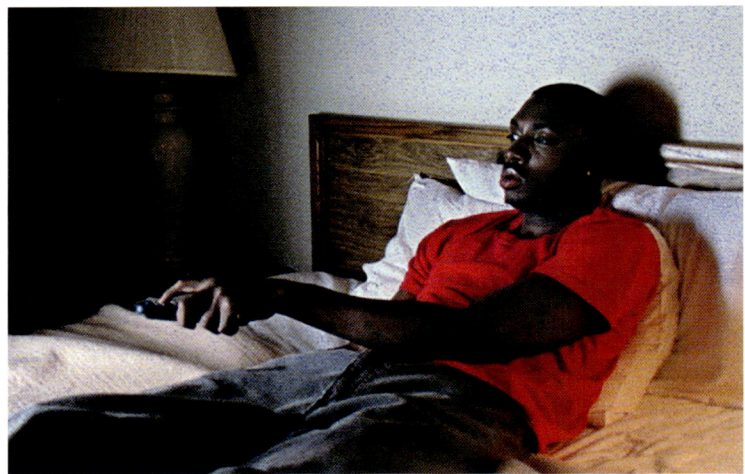
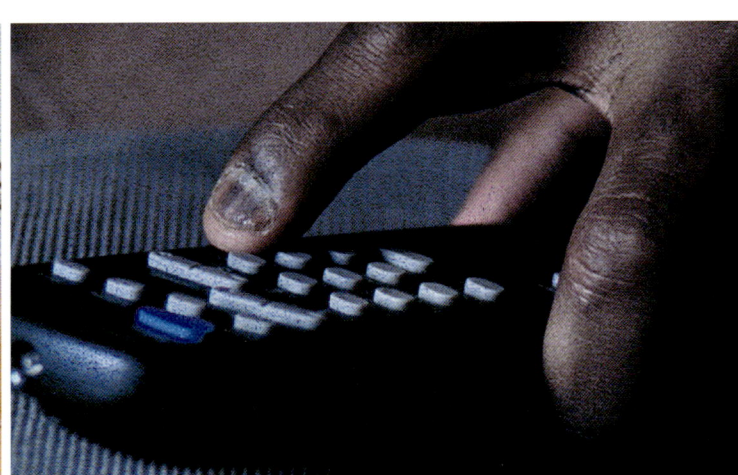

electric earth, 1999, stills

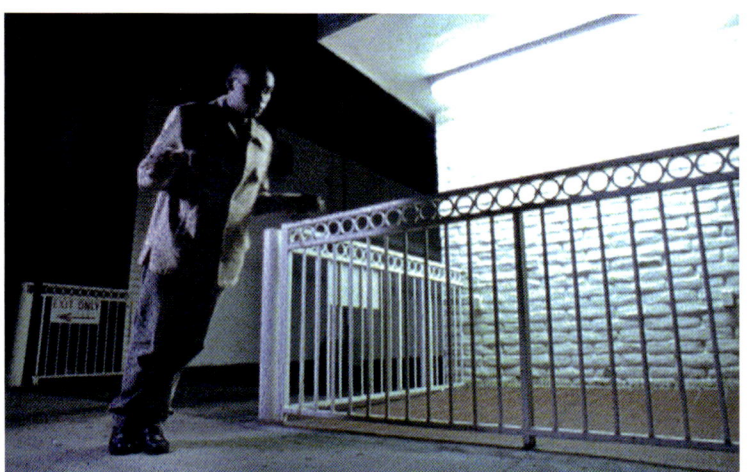 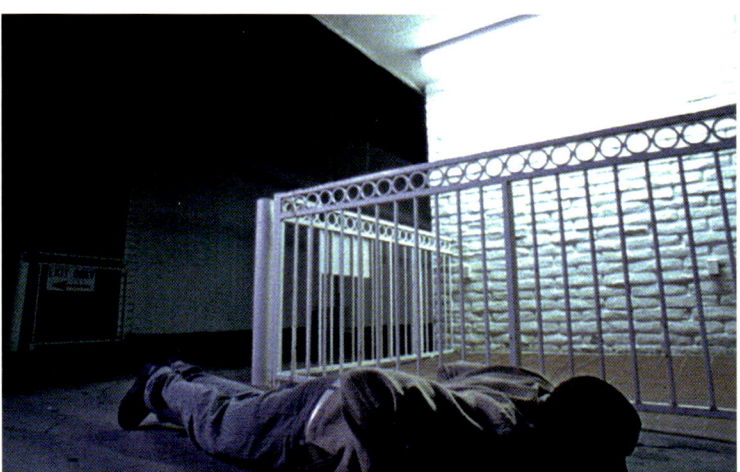

"Off the grid" could perhaps be the subtext for contemplating the forms and conditions of dislocations: an urban example, *electric earth*, and another, in the jet-set/jet-lag case of *Black Mirror*. An eight-screen, multichannel installation, *electric earth* defines a maze-like architecture of moving images and transparent screens. As viewers enter the space, they witness and accompany a young man on a journey, shuffling along in a choreographed, staccato manner, some conflation of hip-hop moves, physical impairment, and avant-garde dance. Each gesture is an event unto itself: he crosses through an urban landscape characteristic of Los Angeles but that could be anywhere one might confront a feeling of loss: laundromats, car washes, parking lots, airports, deserted streets. At times he falls to the ground, avoiding the inquisitive gaze of surveillance cameras; at times his hands face the sky, mimicking the finger motions of a trumpet player, while an airplane takes off, leaving him on the ground, leaving him behind. Leaving. Within the space, viewers, whose shadows are cast onto the screens, encounter sonic events, acoustic occurrences, constellations of sounds from mechanical noises, digital tuning, street soundscapes, a composed heterophony punctuated by the protagonist's voice. The entire installation seems to be acoustically porous and transparent to the world surrounding the protagonist.

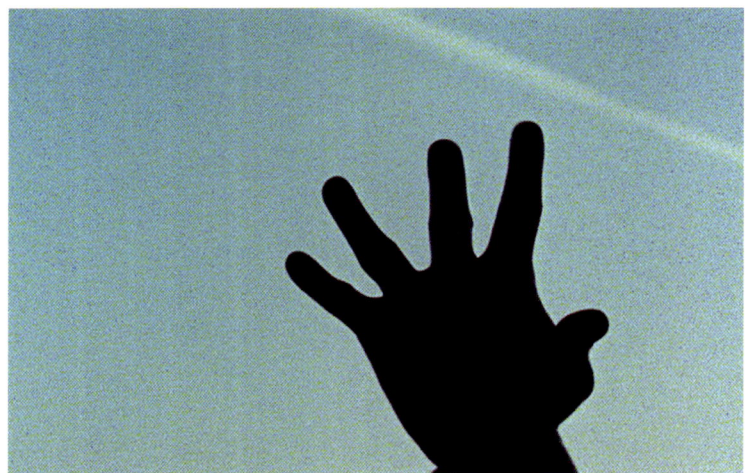 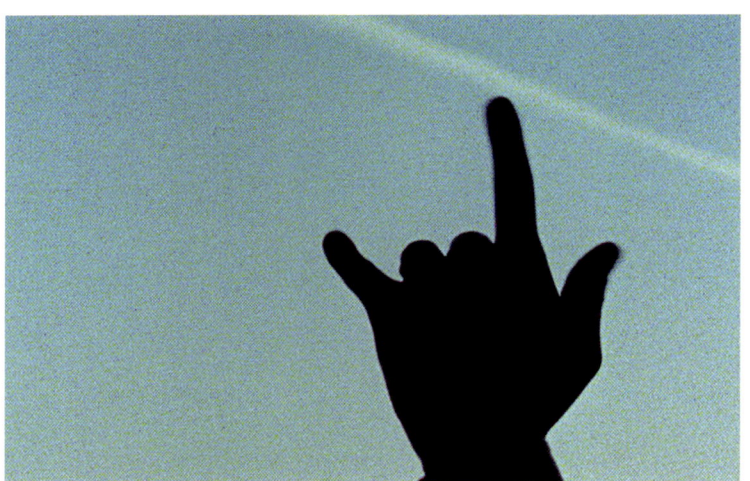

electric earth, 1999, stills

The subject's movements appear to be reacting to the movements of some kind of energy field around him, as if all the molecular agitation linking his anatomy to the materiality and the energy of the environment were prescribing his bodily movements, and these movements were a manifestation of the transmitted energy and magnetic forces overwhelming him and feeding him at the same time. His body has become a transducer, the medium through which electrical, electromagnetic, and acoustic energy flows. His body functions as an antenna misdirecting self-determination. As he moves about within and during the environmental chaos he has become a part of, he adapts himself; he grows adept at soubresauts and brusque, abrupt twists and shifts, with his legs, his mind, all his senses. His restless motions seem self-generated though also imposed, as we can no longer distinguish the source of the initial impulse. "A lot of times I dance so fast that I become what's around me. It's like food for me. I, like, absorb that energy. Absorb that information. It's like I eat it. That's the

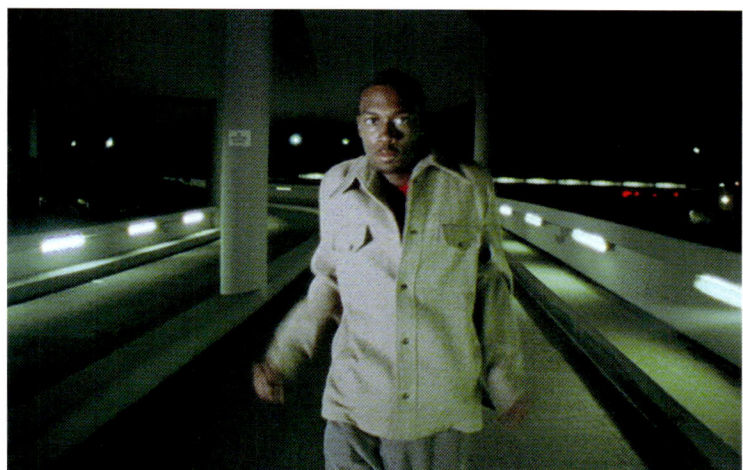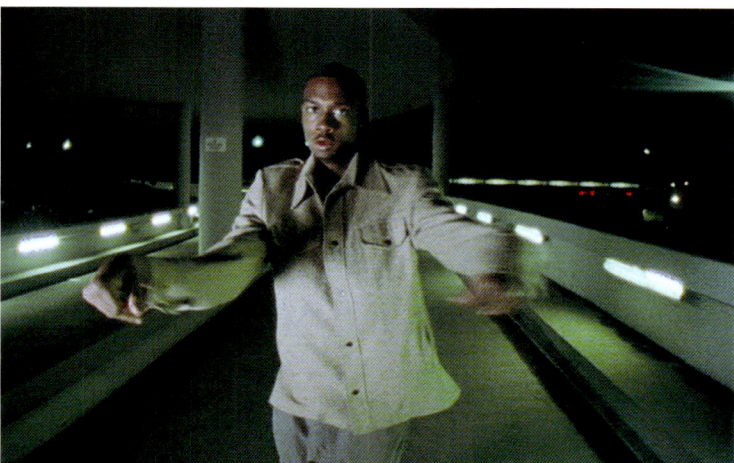

only now I get" says the voice with a schizophrenic tension. As if the constant and fractured stimulations provoke the jerky moves from one posture to another, from one thought to another, from one fragment to another fragment of life, the body becoming the nexus that multiple wave lines approach and press against. In a kind of crescendo, he seems to experience an epileptic or convulsive seizure. A seizure occurs when patterns of awareness and action, the combination of knowing, feeling, and doing, all reach a crisis, disrupting the continuity of transactions, exchanges between an organism and its environment. *Electric earth* captures the contradictions and ambiguities of such a state of being when one is fed, energized by the electricity, information, solicitations, and endless possibilities offered by the environment. This convulsive seizure becomes a new condition. With permanent waves of seismic, auditory, digital, and communicative interferences, nothing separates us anymore from the improbability of the world—or, actually, from the hyperprobability of our world.

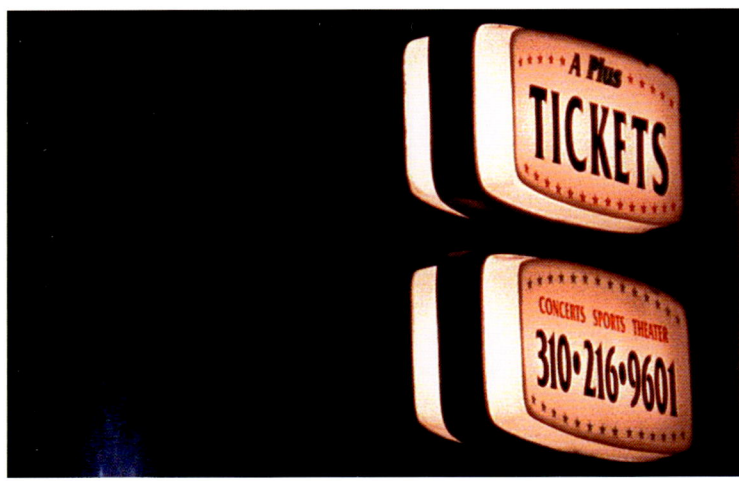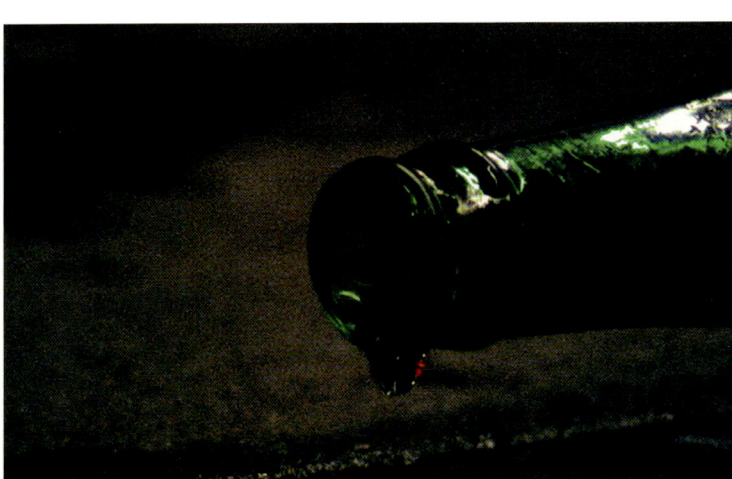

electric earth, 1999, stills

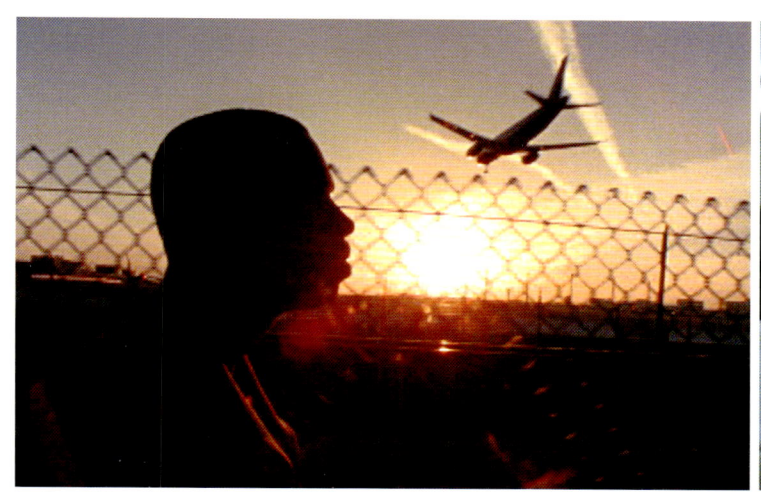 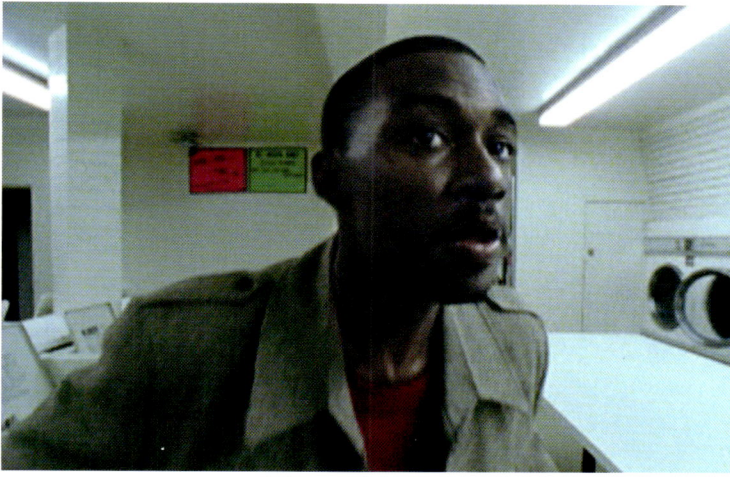

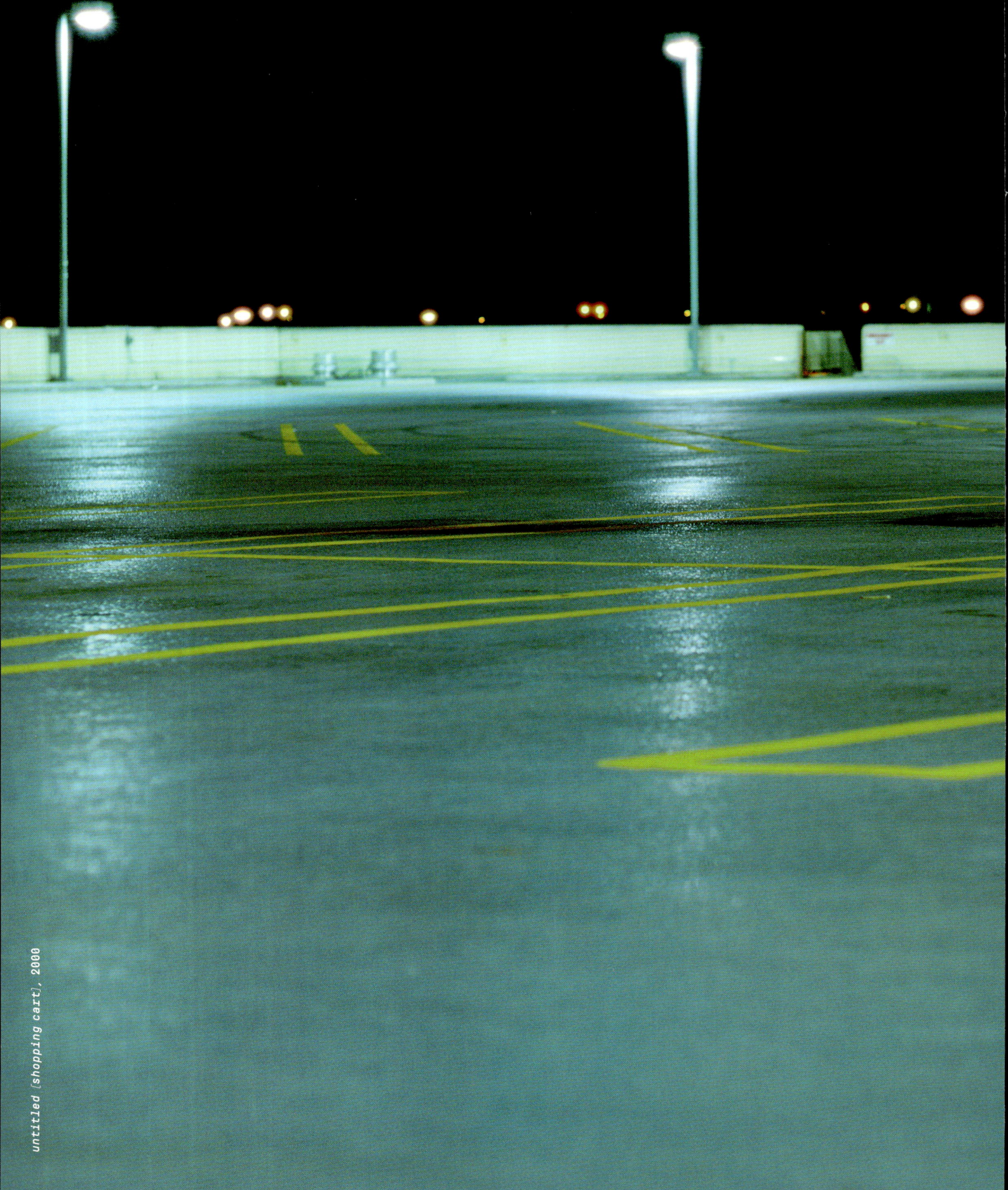

untitled (shopping cart), 2000

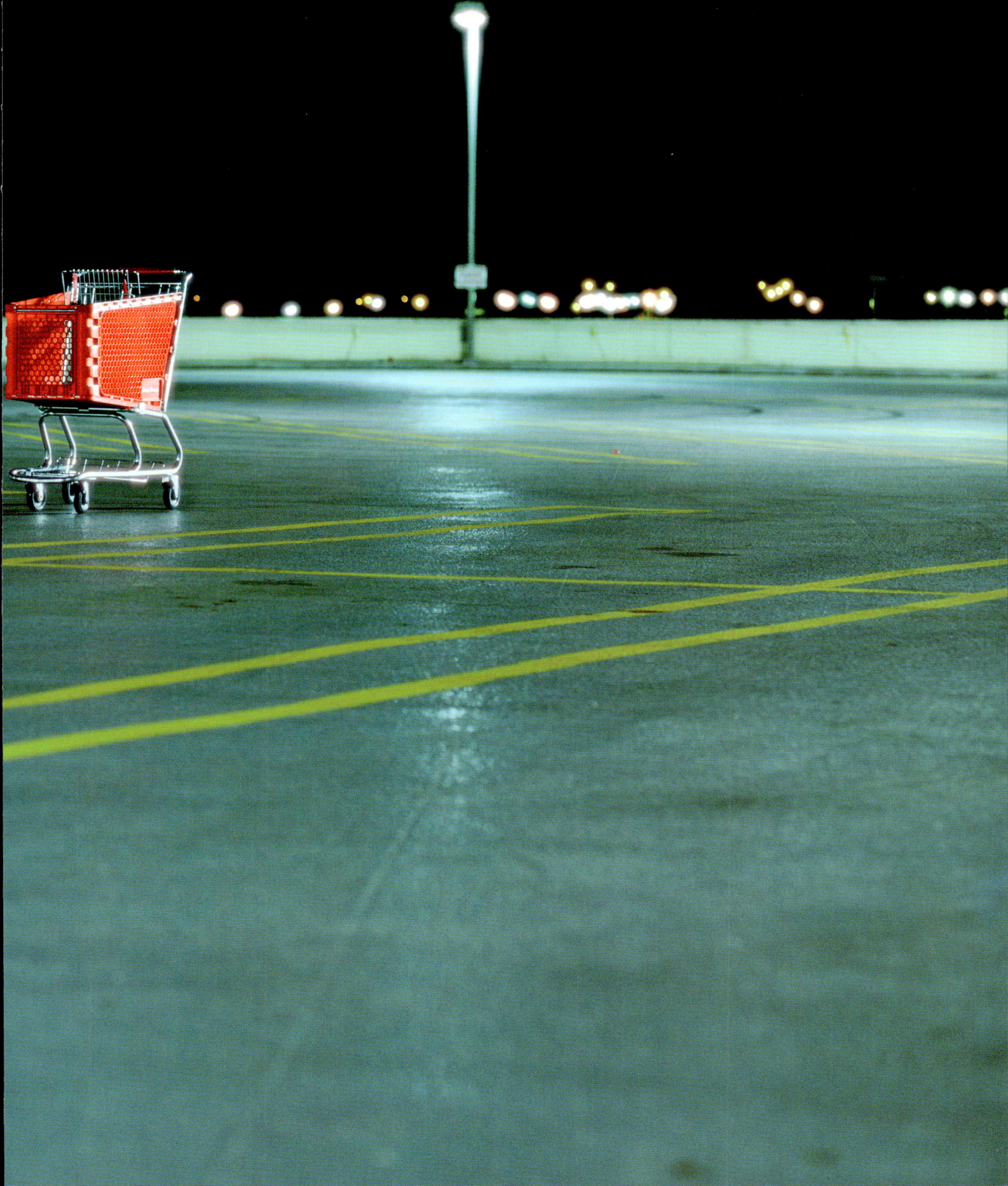

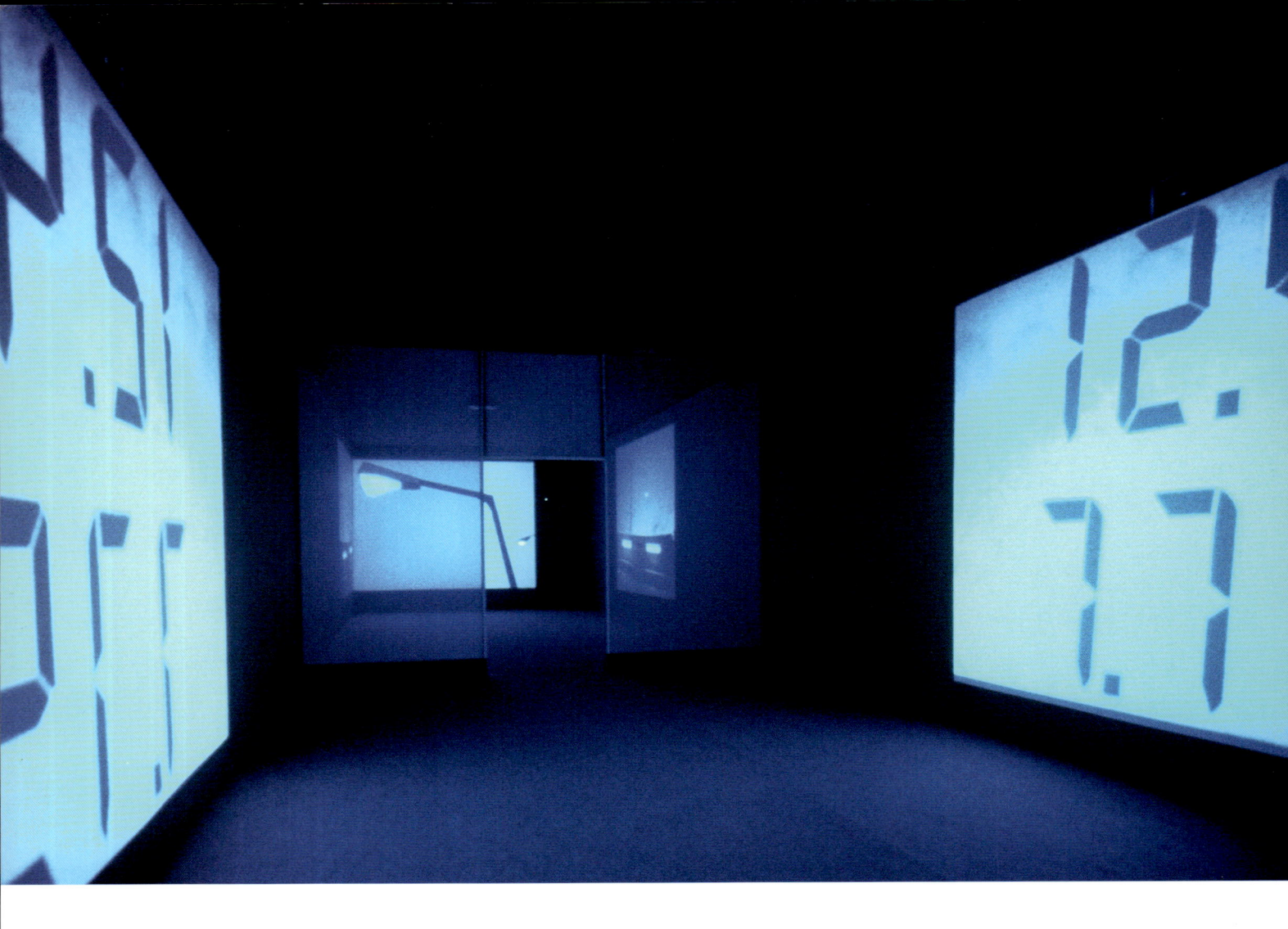

electric earth, 1999, installation view, 48th Venice Biennale, Venice, Italy
opposite: electric earth, 1999, installation view,
The Museum of Contemporary Art, Los Angeles

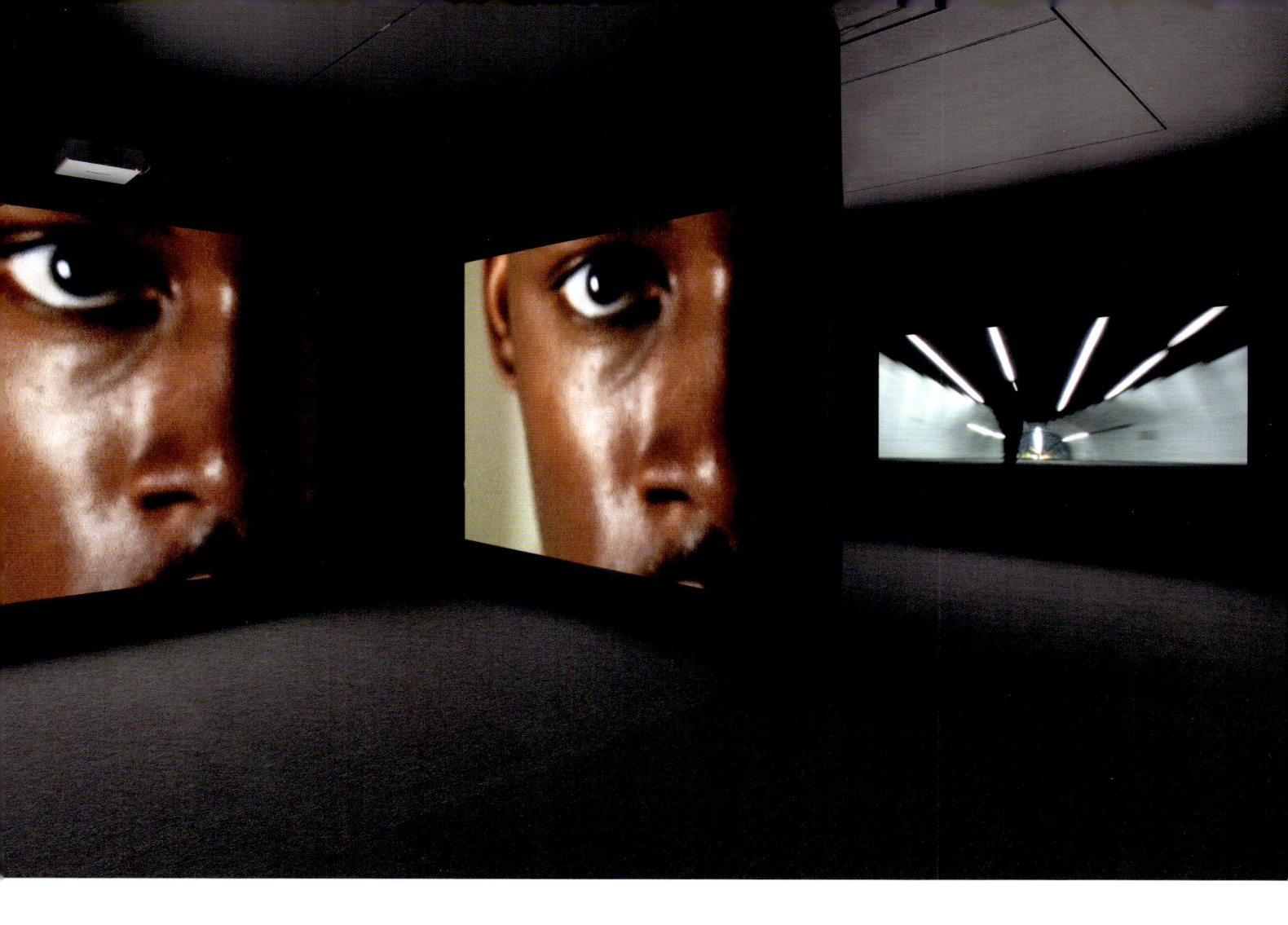

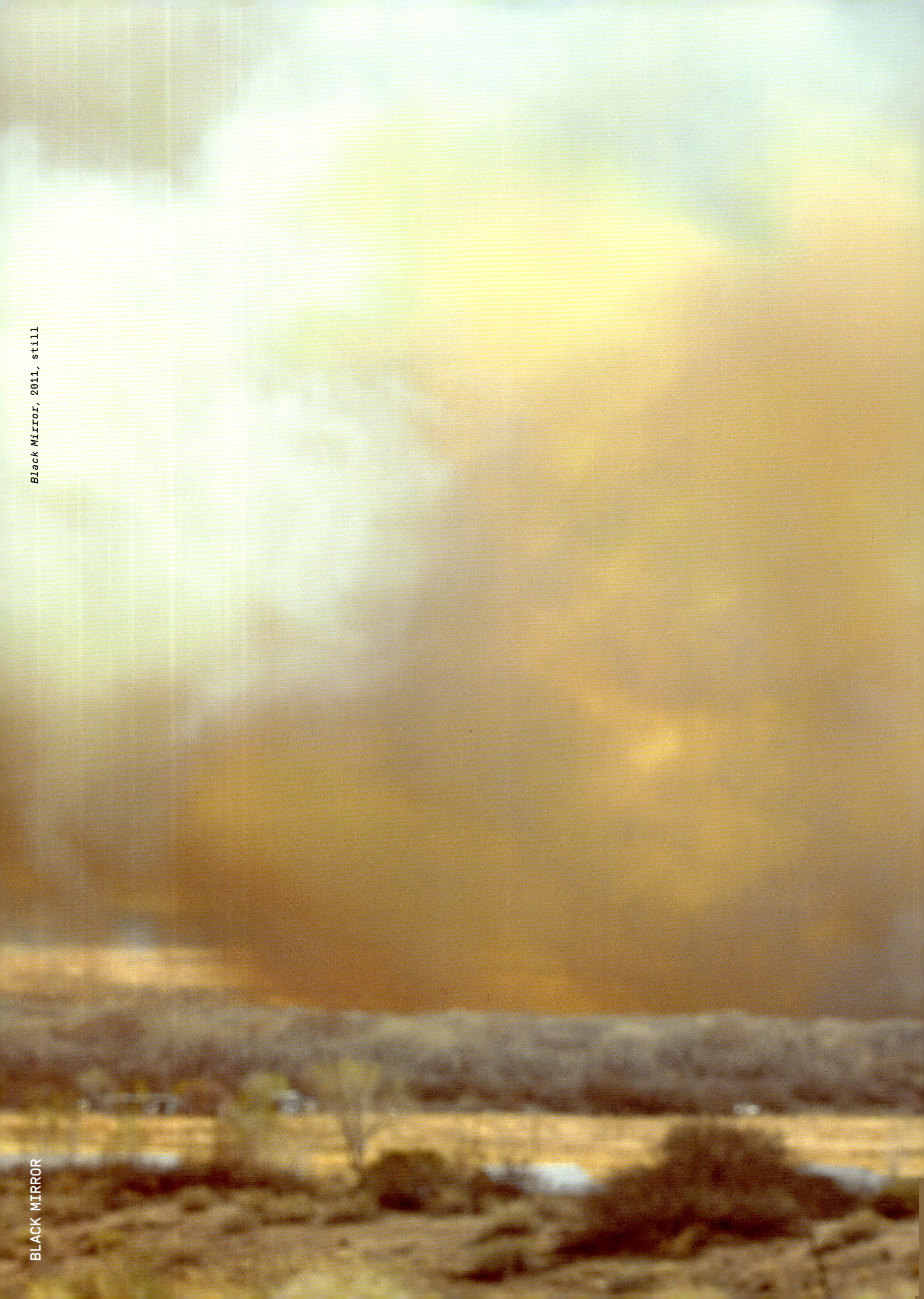

Black Mirror, 2011, still

BLACK MIRROR

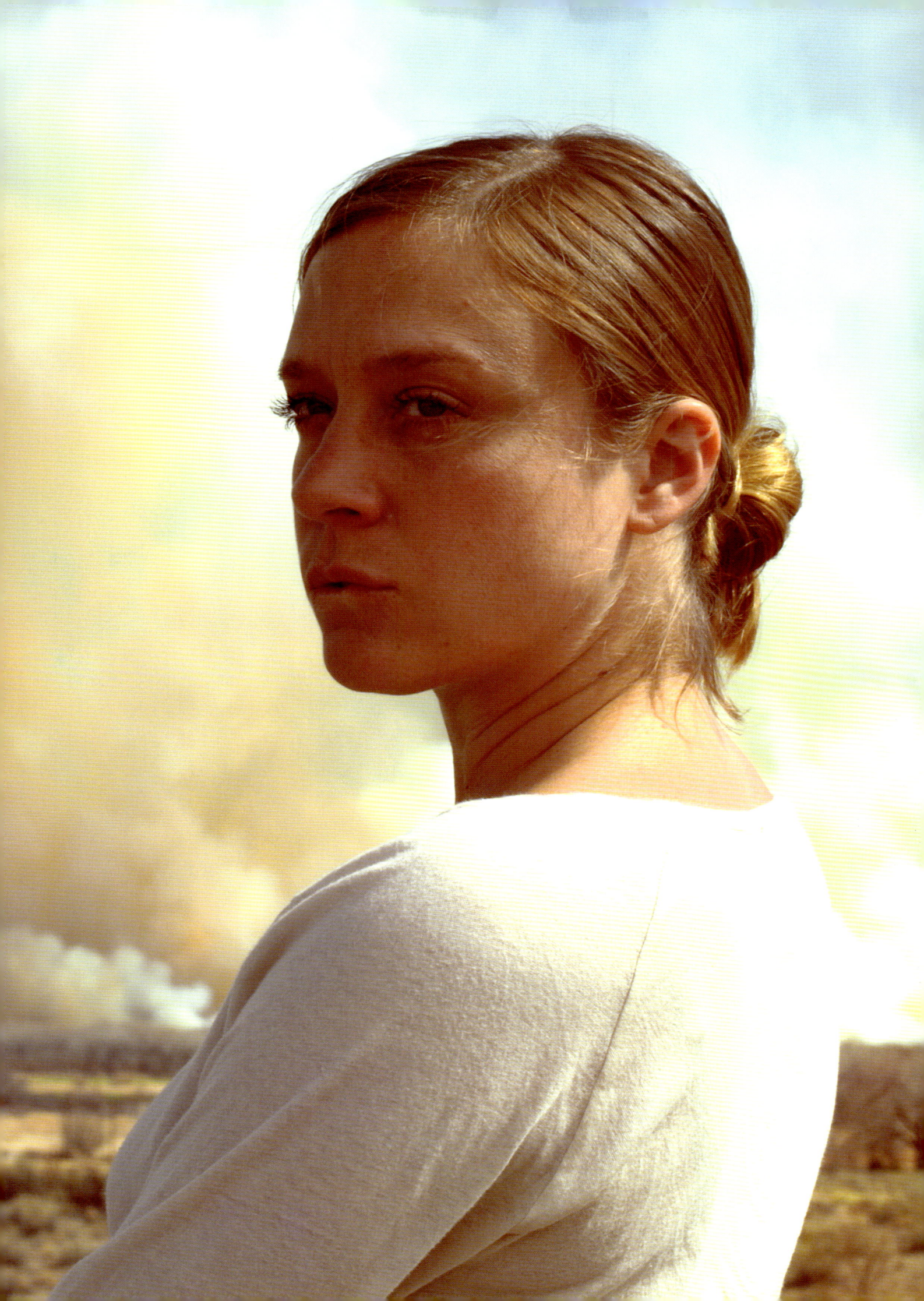

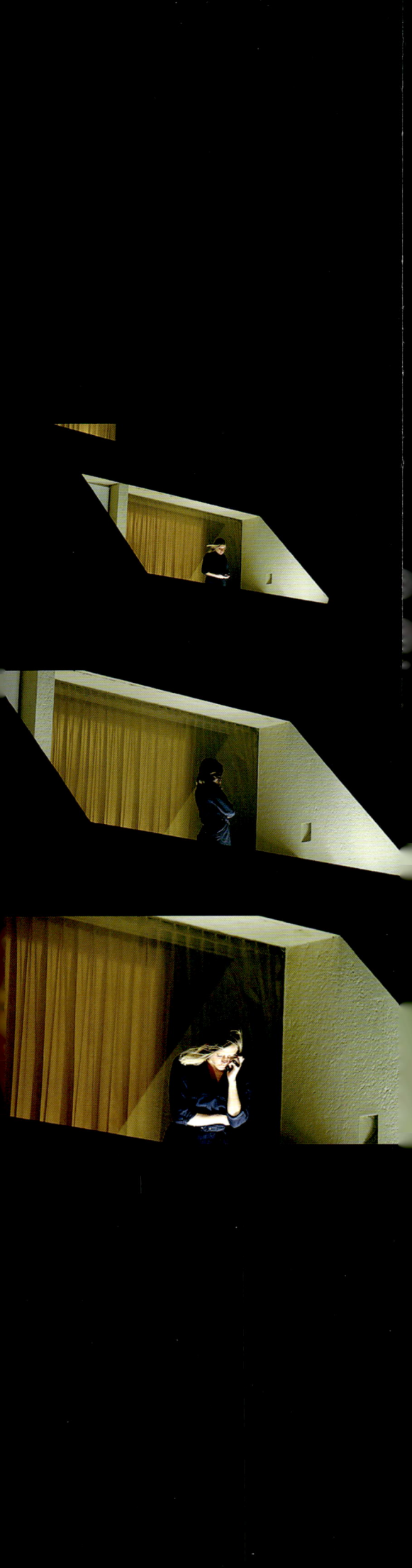

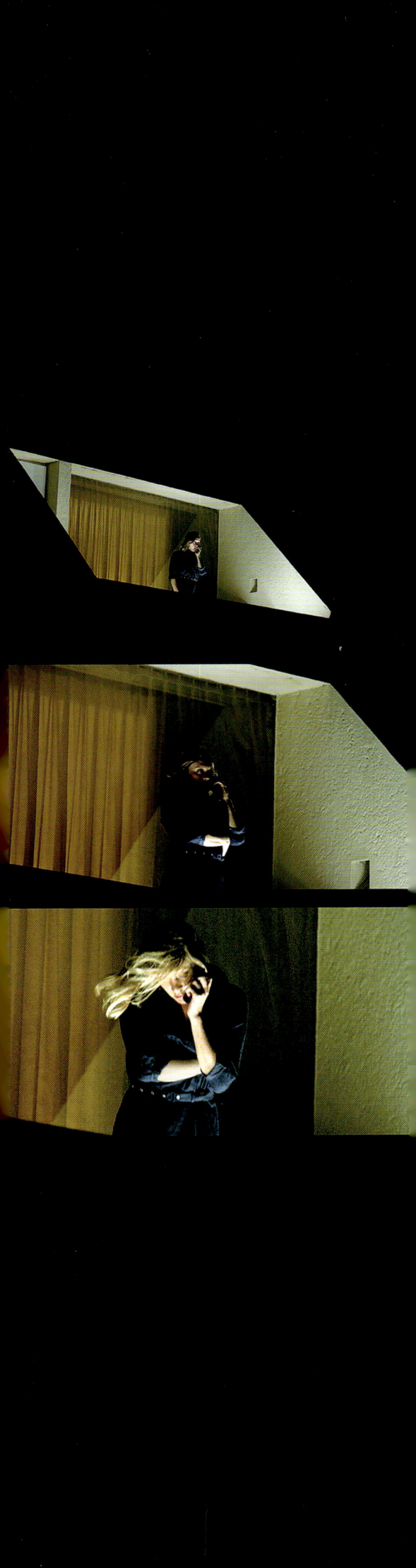

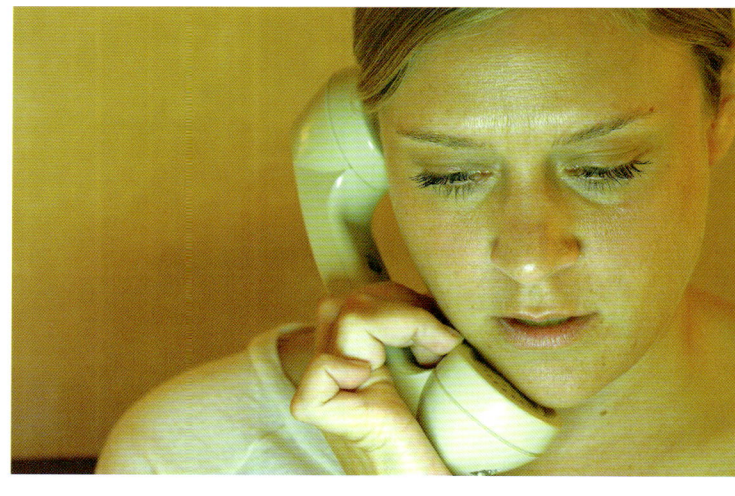 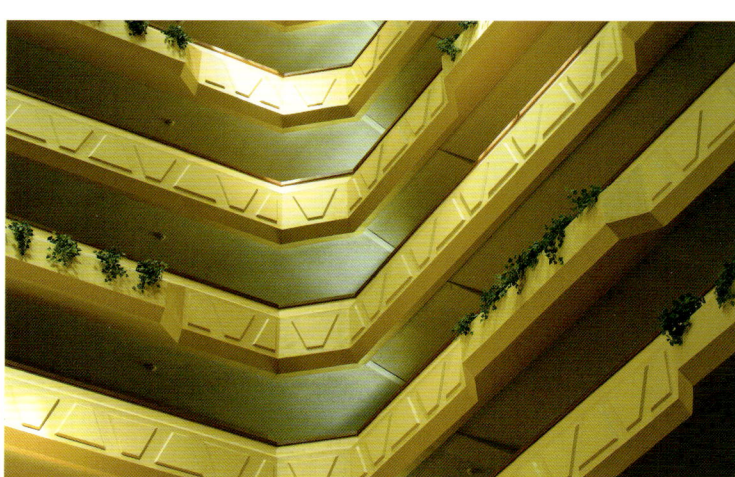

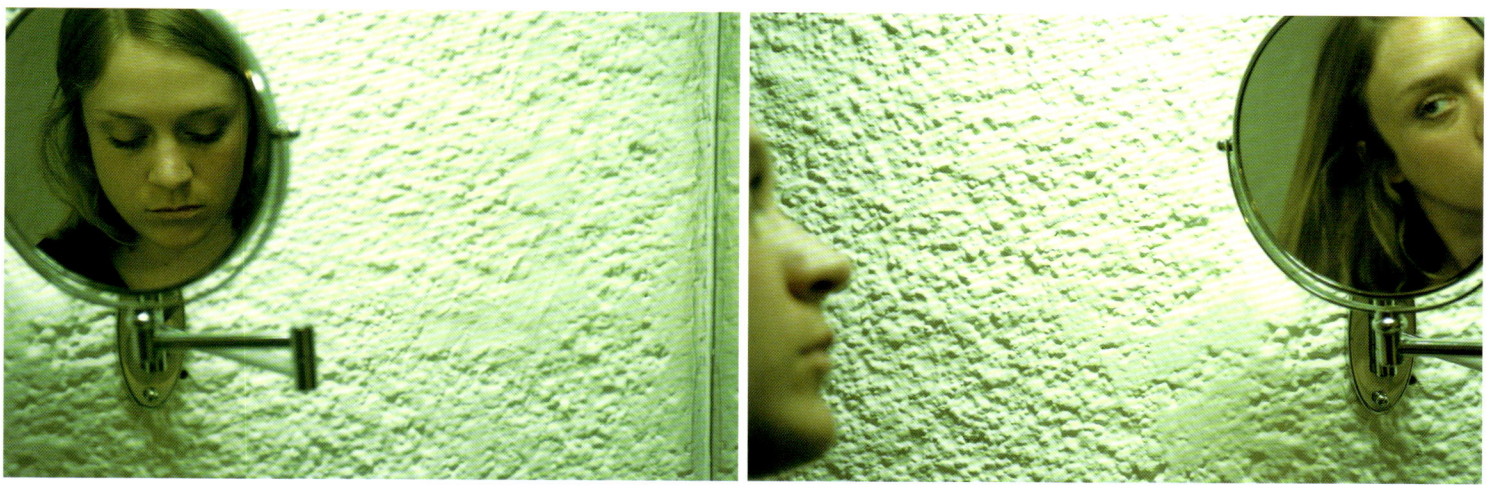

    Black Mirror is another attempt to represent such a state of forced wanderlust throughout the world. It is at once an installation and a performance, a film and a theater play, a stage and a screen. The performance took place on a large industrial barge off the island of Hydra in 2011. On the barge, a stage reconstituting an anonymous motel room is surrounded by four giant video screens. In the room we see the actress Chloë Sevigny on the phone, listing places she might have been to or places she might be going.[4] At times she is interrupted, accompanied by drummers, pole dancers, a whip cracker, a tap dancer. The drum, the whip, and the tap dance all impose a clear rhythmic anchor, a tempo against which she paces through places and time. Her words are about the acceleration of traveling far and restlessly: "Check in, check out. Exchange, connect, and move on. Customs, security, delay. Motel 6, Miami, never stagnate, never stop." Time and space are melancholically compressed.

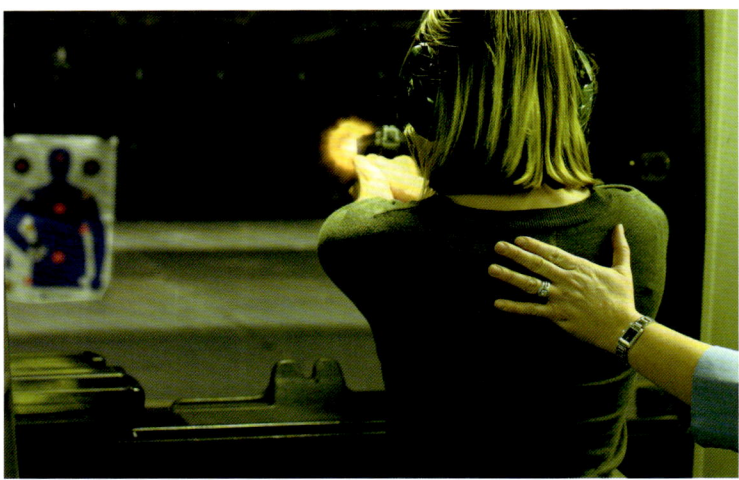 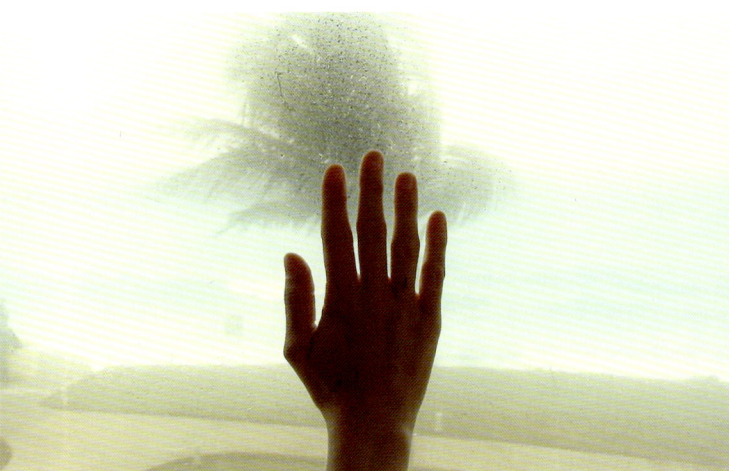

In the video installation of *Black Mirror*, Sevigny travels from the Very Large Array radio-telescope facility in New Mexico to hotel rooms, a shooting range—she is on the move, as if these systematic displacements and aimless trips were her condition. She is coldly disengaged and disconnected from the places and spaces that exist simultaneously. The fragmentation of her words and sentences suggests that storytelling has come to an end and that boredom has become a response to the world. She is doing nothing, feeling a yearning without knowing for what. Her present seems to depend on her next move; she exists in a monotonous state, where objects, places, movements, people, and emotions are fused. The continuum of the world does not need her acquiescence; it is in a perfect loop, very much like *La invención de Morel* (1940),[5] in which a fugitive discovers a recording machine that captures people's actions and replays them

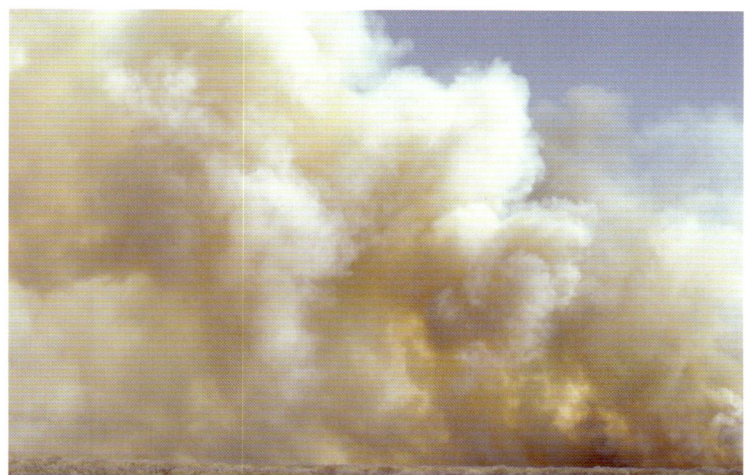 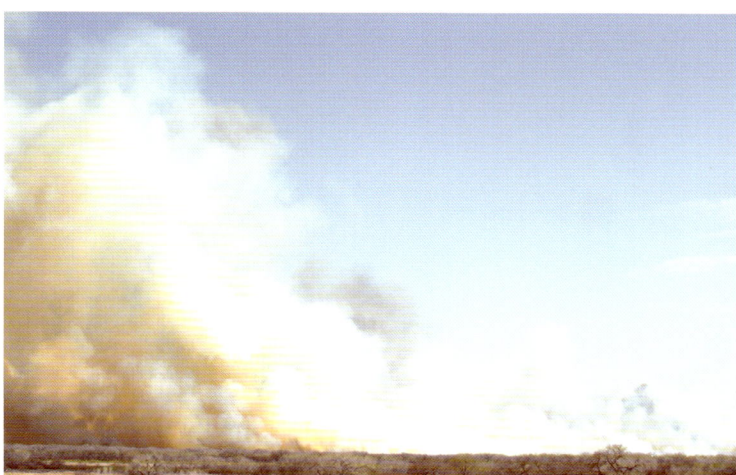

endlessly in real spaces, looping their lives forever and capturing their souls under a two-moon sky, where the real and the artificial are endlessly confounded. Someone, something, the network will connect the dots while her life is lived through the screen of her cell phone. Her experience is one of absolute fragmentation, physical and psychological. Her room is fragmented. Her image is fragmented. In the installation, which followed the performance, visitors enter a black, mirrored hall in which the images, described above, are themselves multiplied and divided on several screens, accentuating the fragmented nature of the narrative, of a life that is maybe yearning to be lived free of the grid. The life of a migrant managing the subtle and bewildering balance of maintaining, hanging onto a sense of familiarity with the reality of endlessly being confronted with unfamiliar, alien situations, cultures, and people.

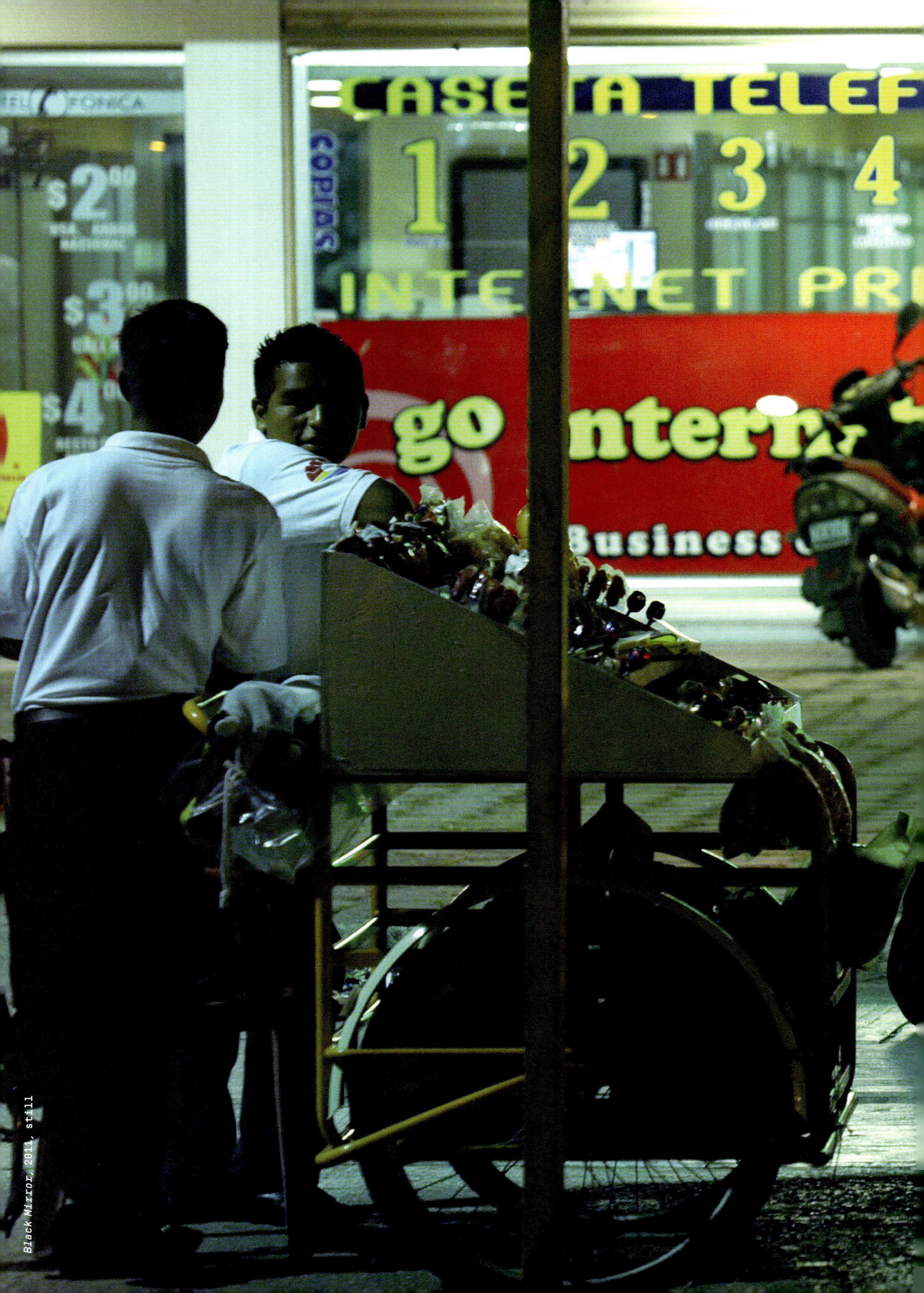

Black Mirror, 2011, still

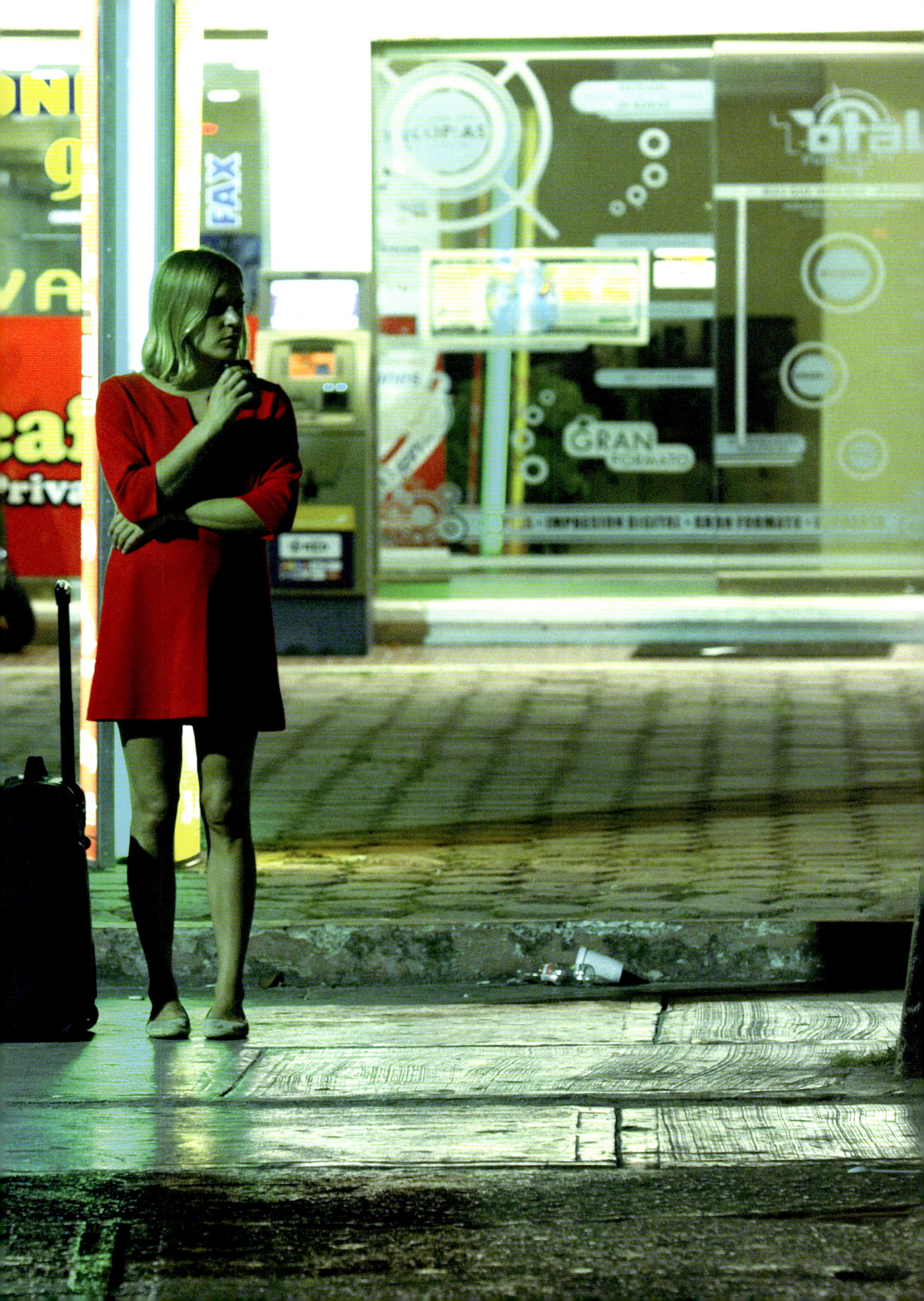

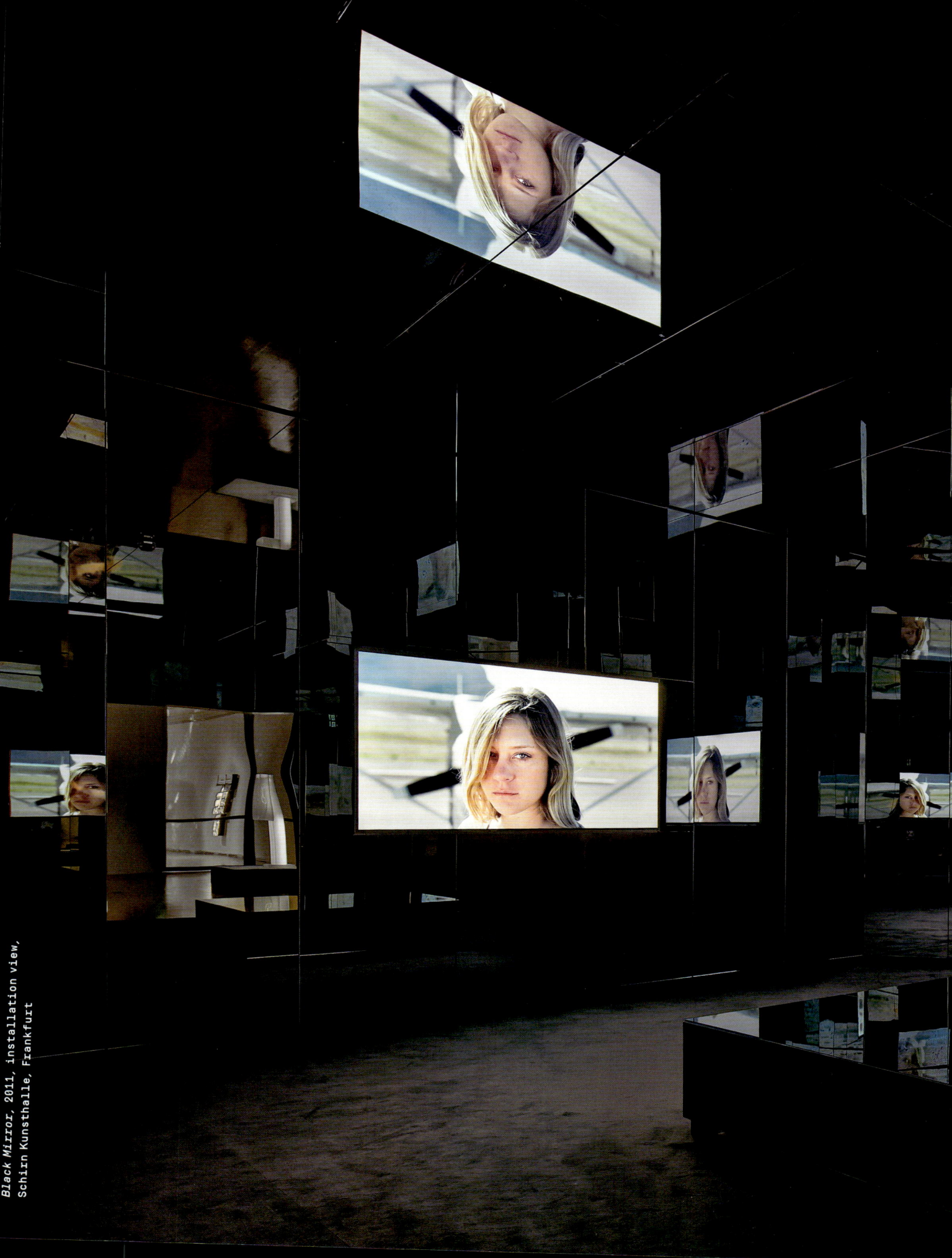

Black Mirror, 2011, installation view, Schirn Kunsthalle, Frankfurt

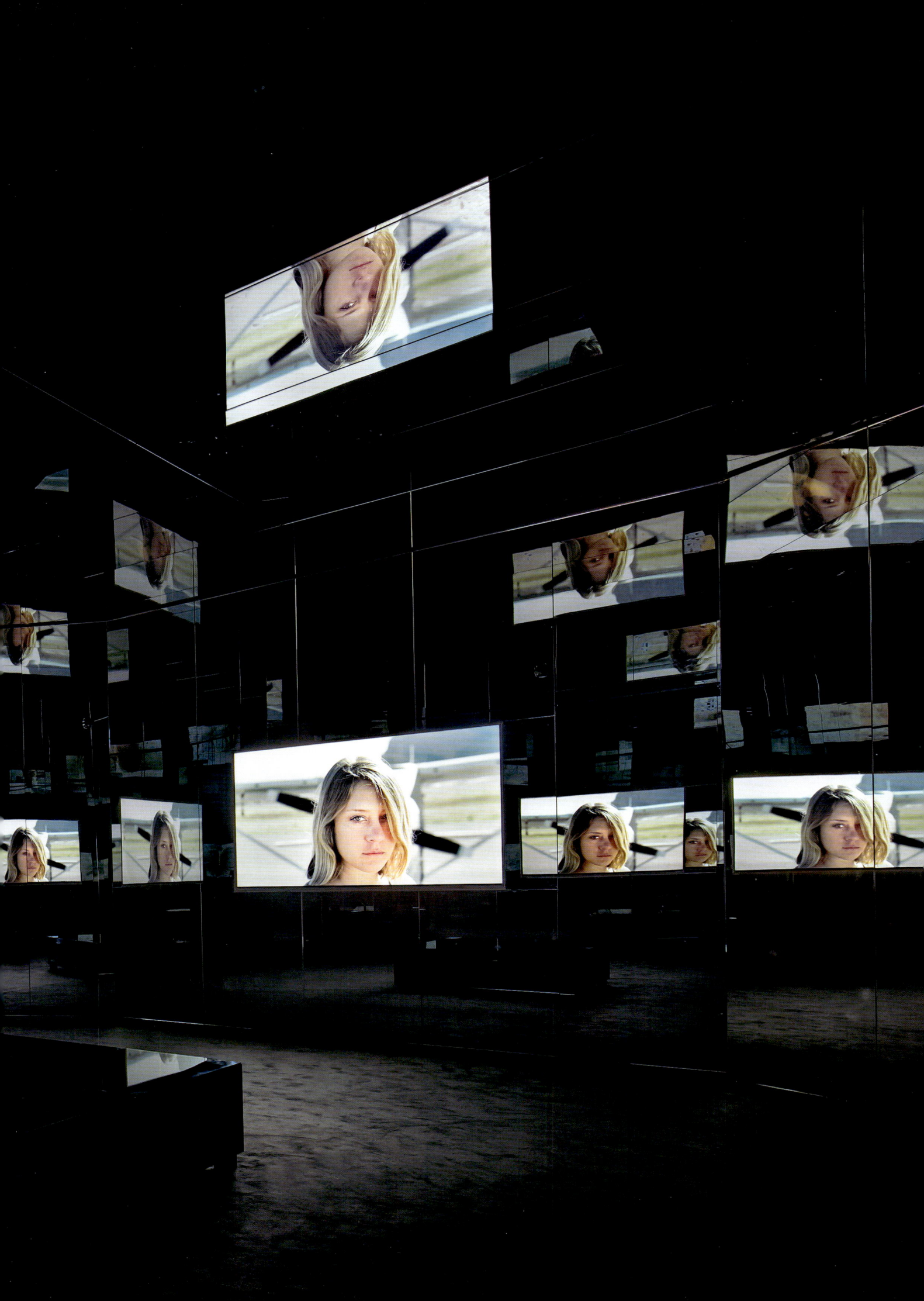

migration [empire], 2008, still

MIGRATION [EMPIRE]

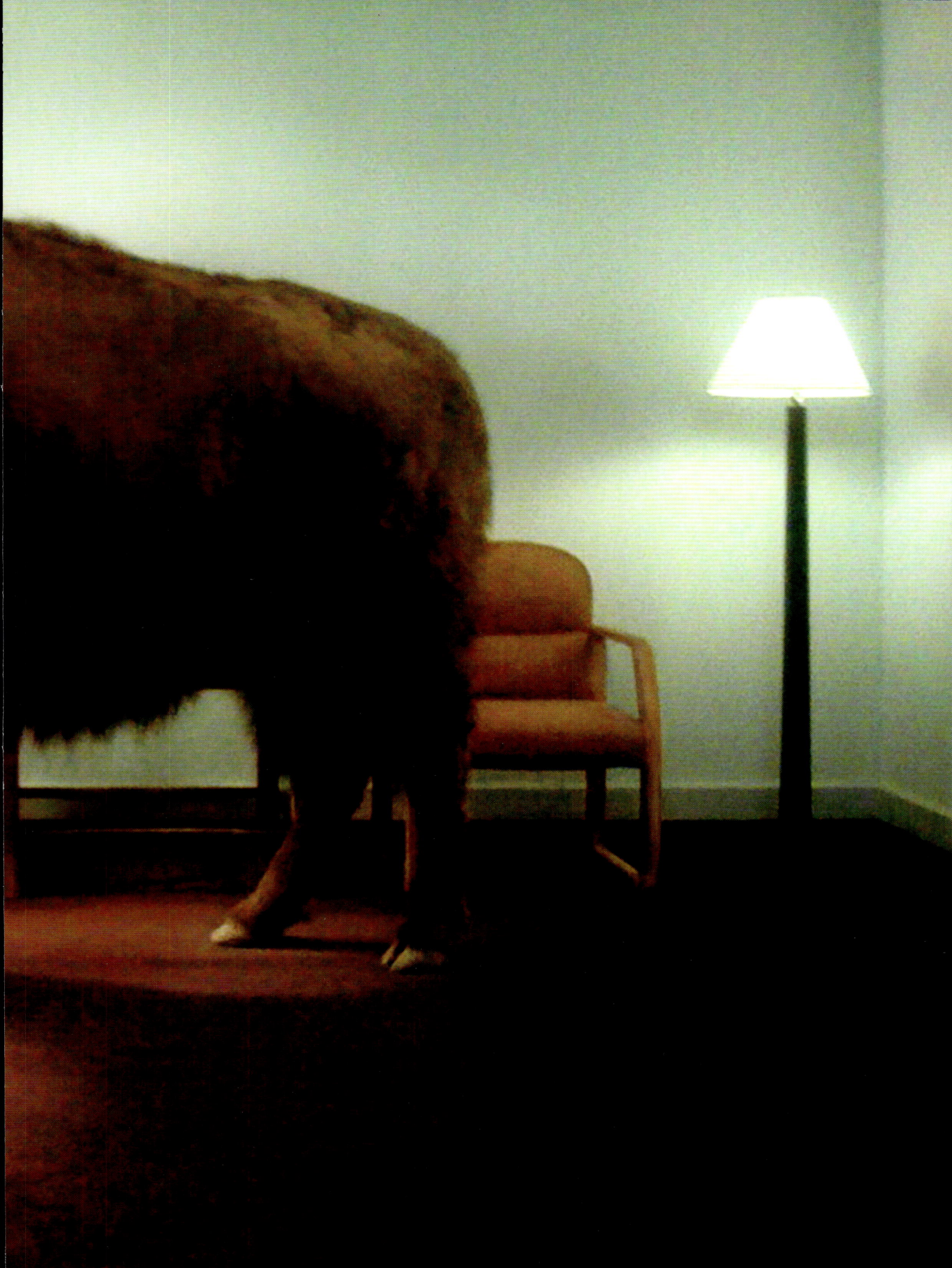

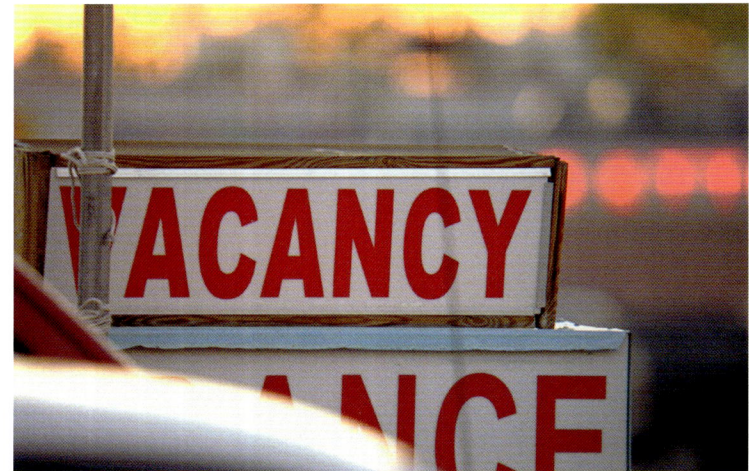
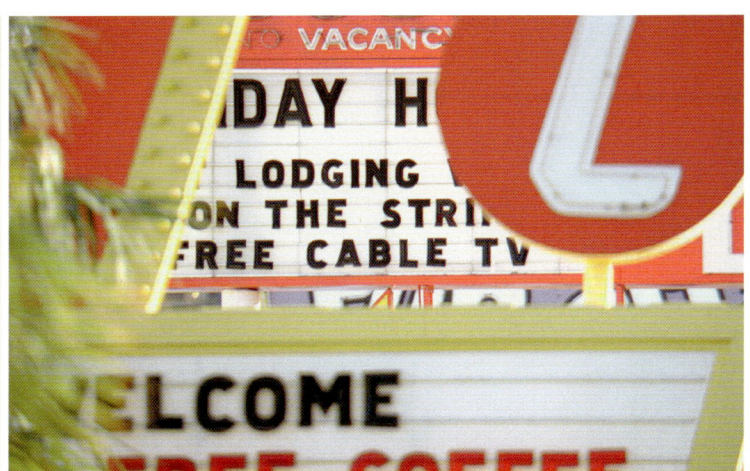

migration [empire], 2008, stills

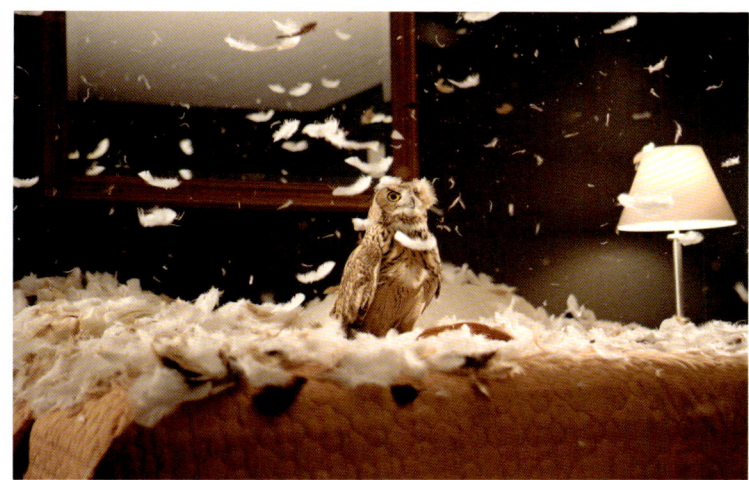
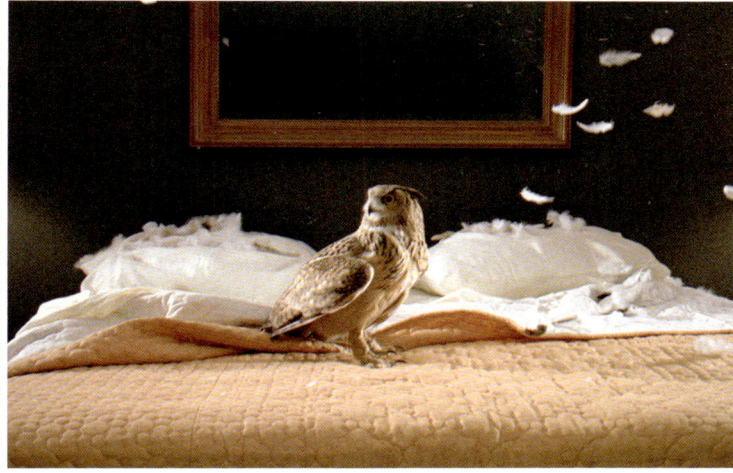

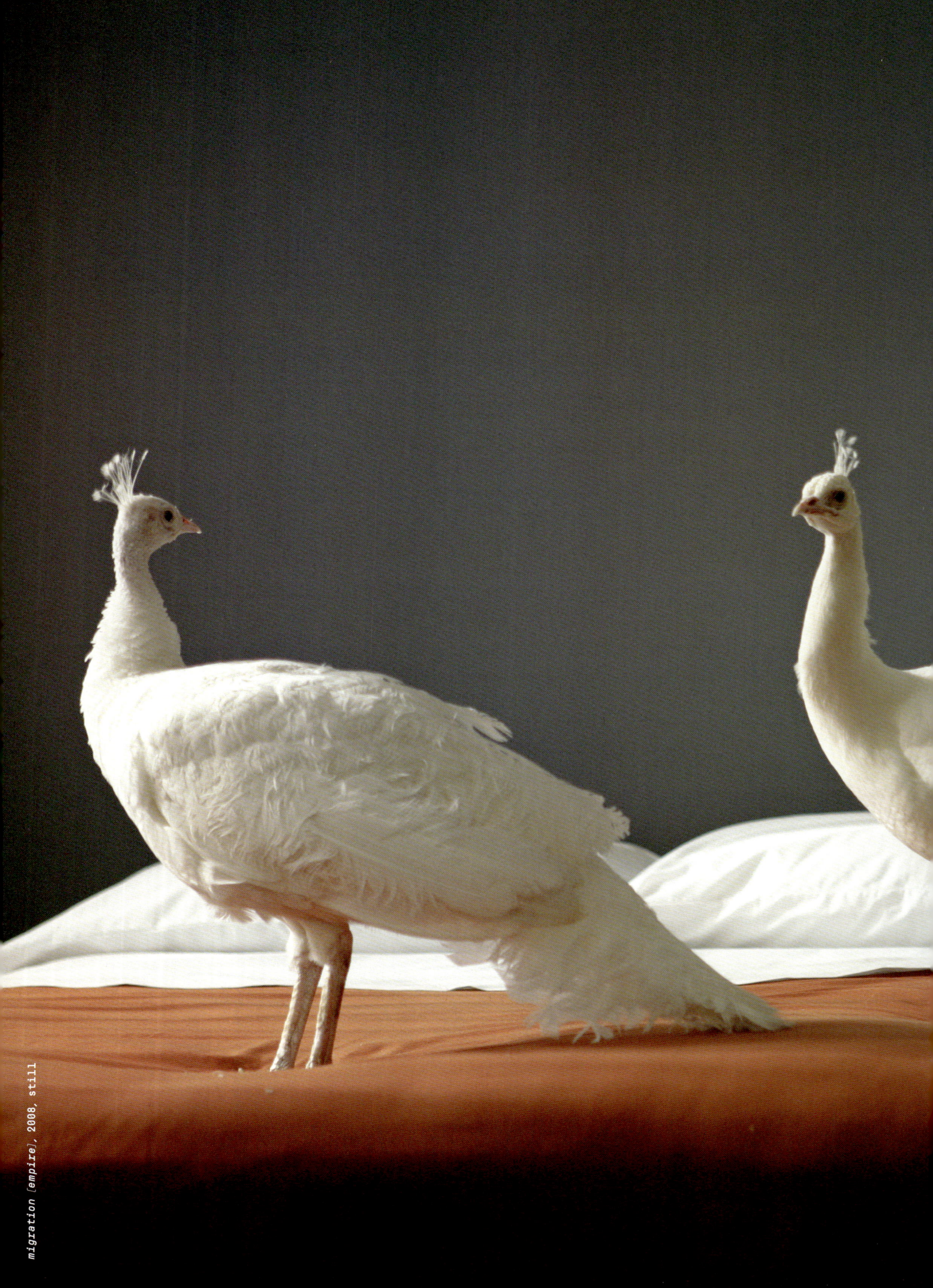

migration [empire] 2008, still

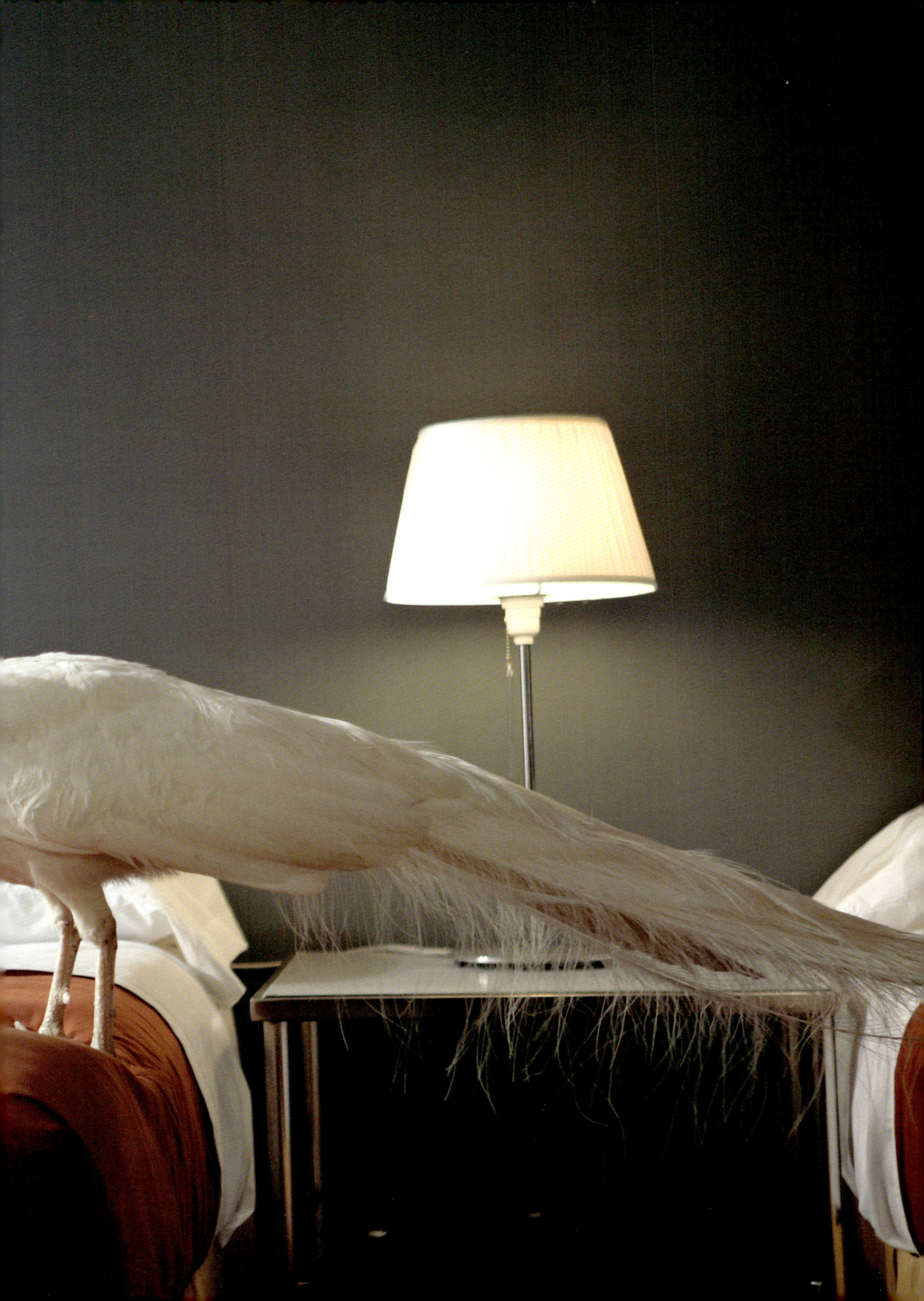

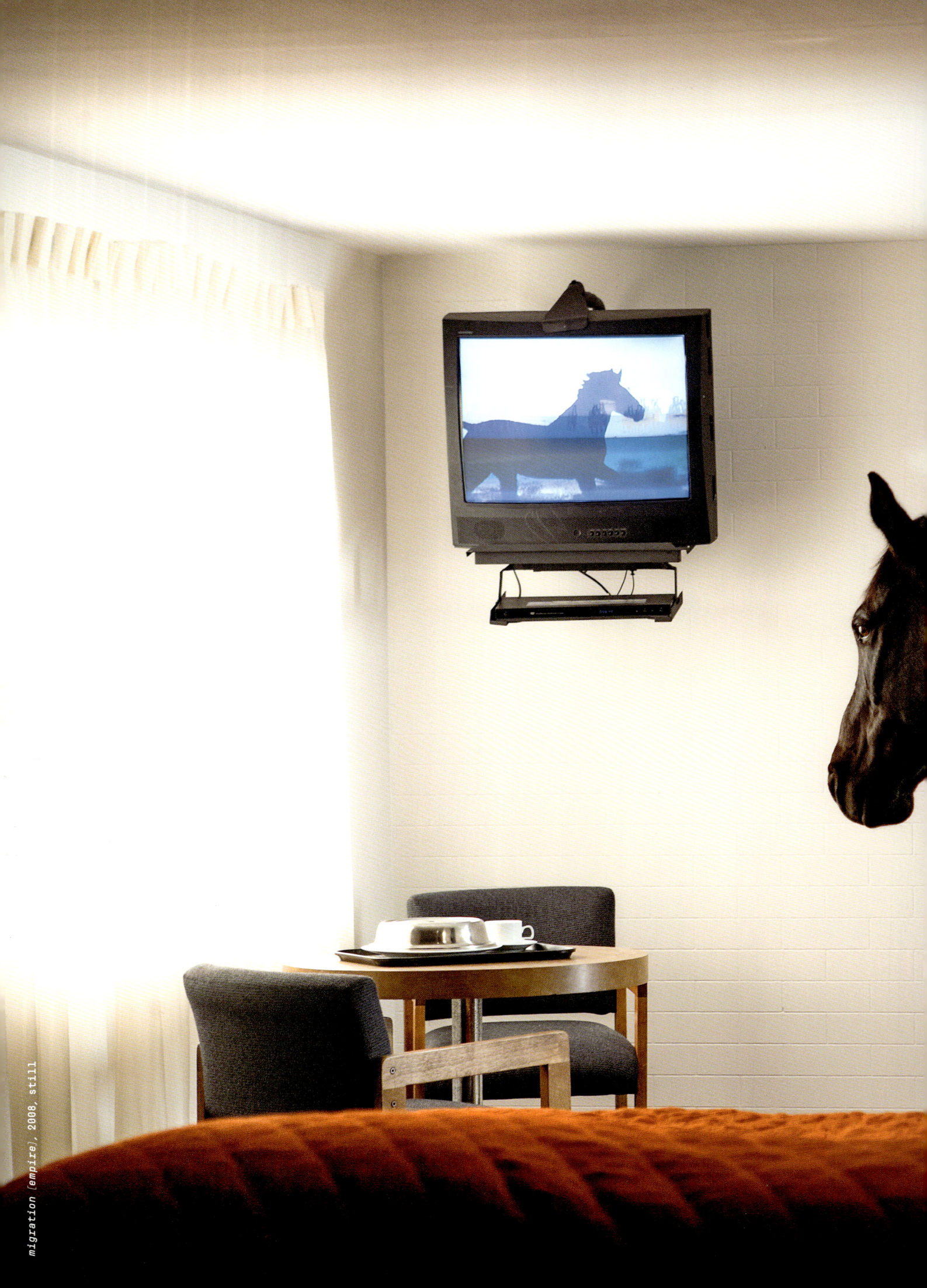
migration (empire), 2008, still

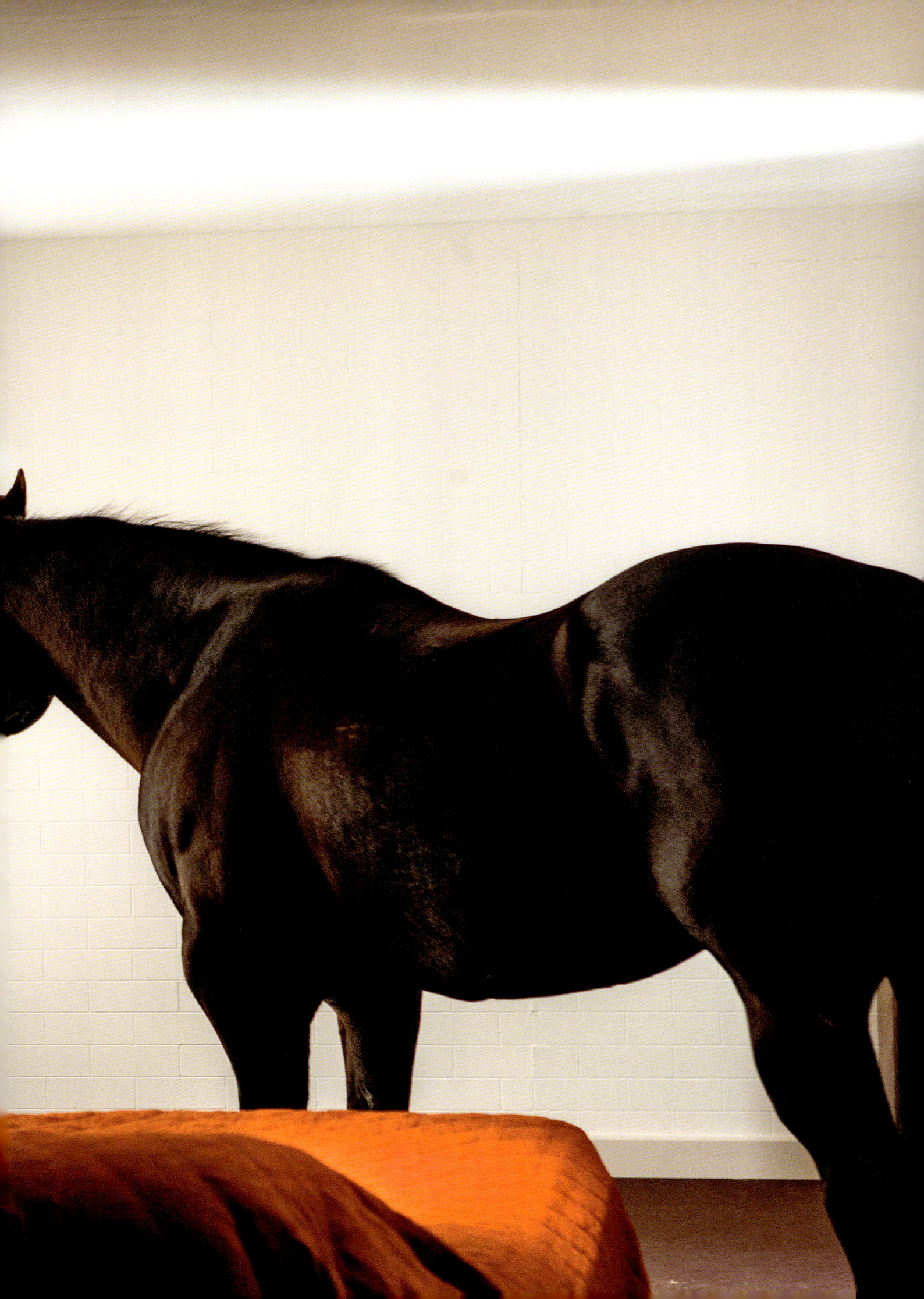

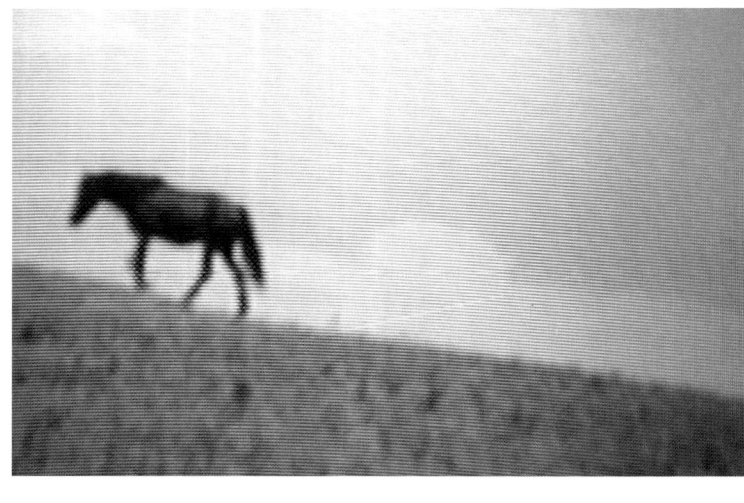 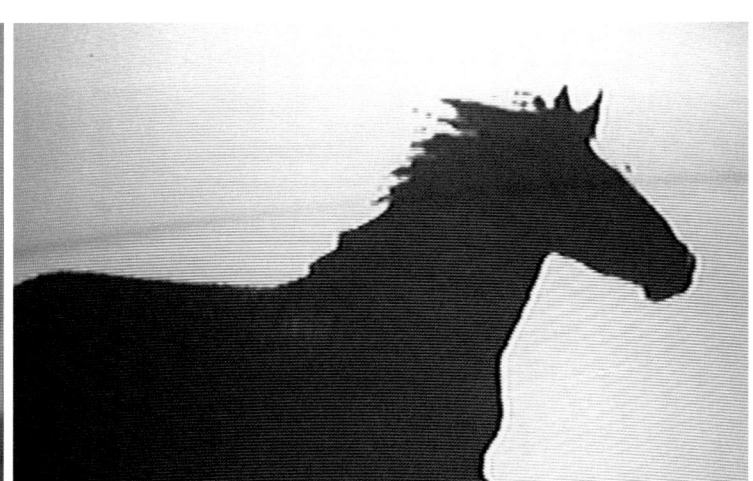

migration [empire], 2008, stills

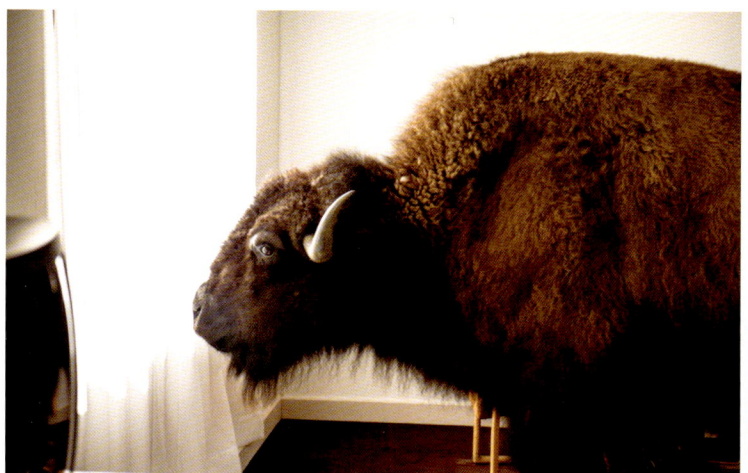 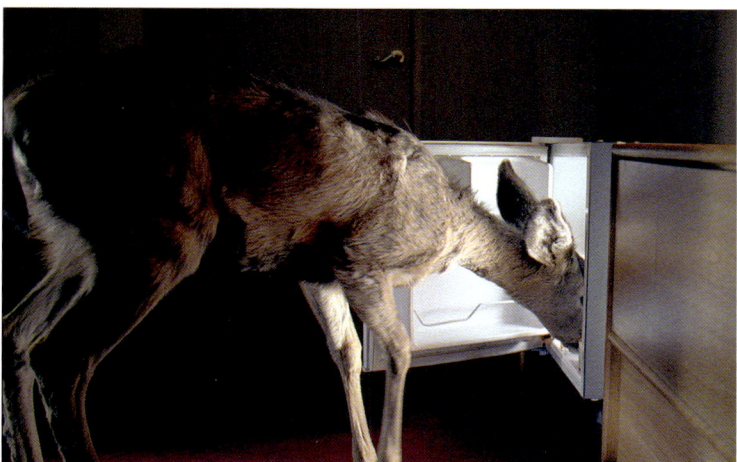

Aitken's *migration (empire)* is an installation of three large outdoor billboards featuring oversized video screens inside an architectural environment. Their sculptural presence, out of place, like a migrant, out of scale, accentuates the ever-dominating and inescapable ubiquity of these billboards in our daily urban and suburban lives. They are always speaking to us, and we cannot turn them off. They belong to our increasingly privatized public spaces. The mesmerizing images of animals: a horse, beaver, owl, lion, buffalo, deer, fox, all of which are worlds away from their natural habitats, like migrants in a world unprepared to welcome them and offer proper shelter. But devoid of human presence, it is a world that they might be slowly reclaiming as their own. As writer Alan Weisman has so precisely and disquietingly described in his book, this indeed is "the world without us."[6] Weisman paints a picture of how quickly nature would take over if the human species simply vanished. Massive infrastructures would collapse, the subway system flood, oil refineries explode, buildings crumble, and animals move in, while bronze sculptures, plastic, and radio waves would become our longest-lasting gifts to the universe. In Aitken's video, we witness the day after this human vanishing. The world is serene, and the television is still aglow, broadcasting.

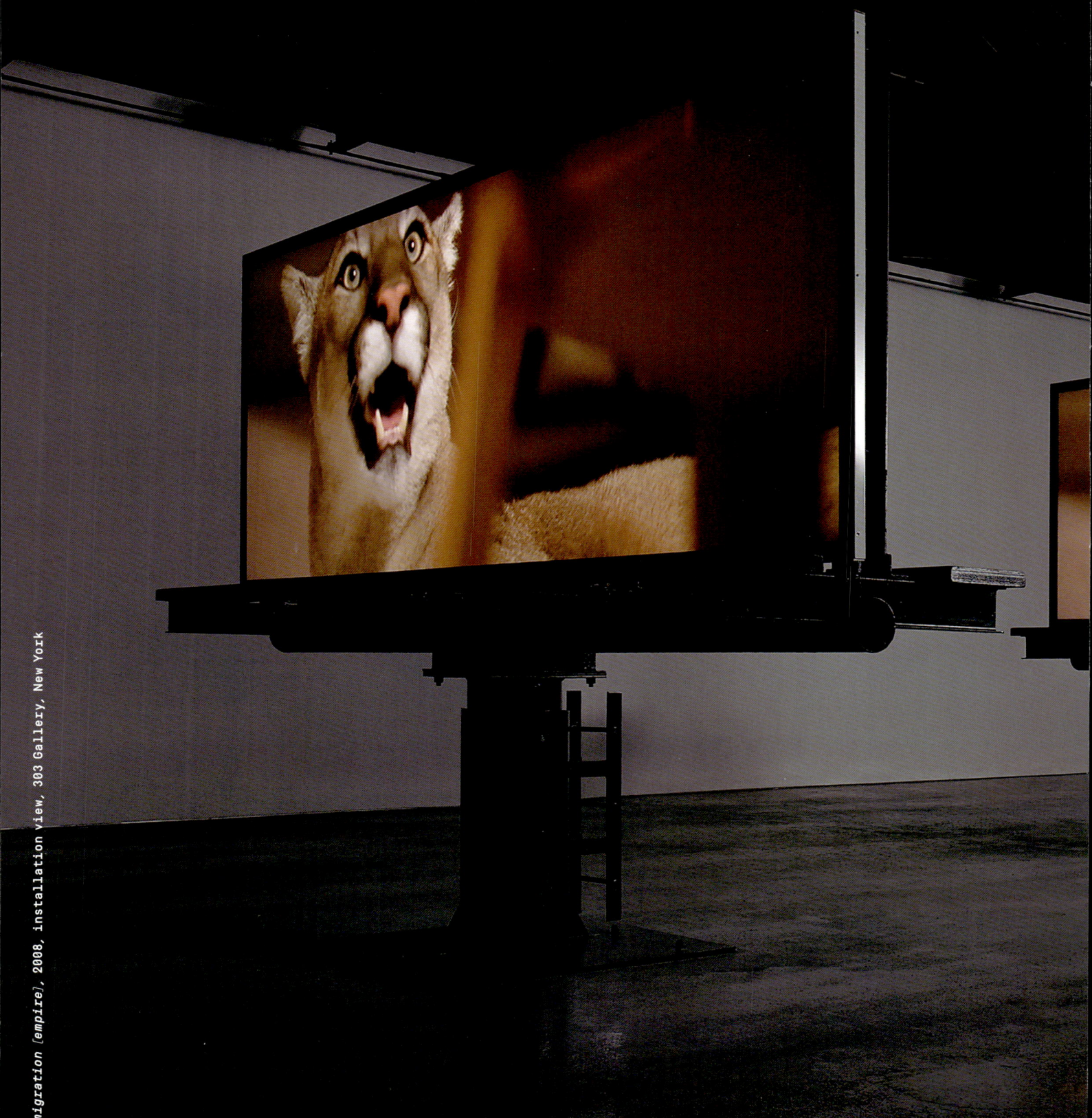

migration (empire), 2008, installation view, 303 Gallery, New York

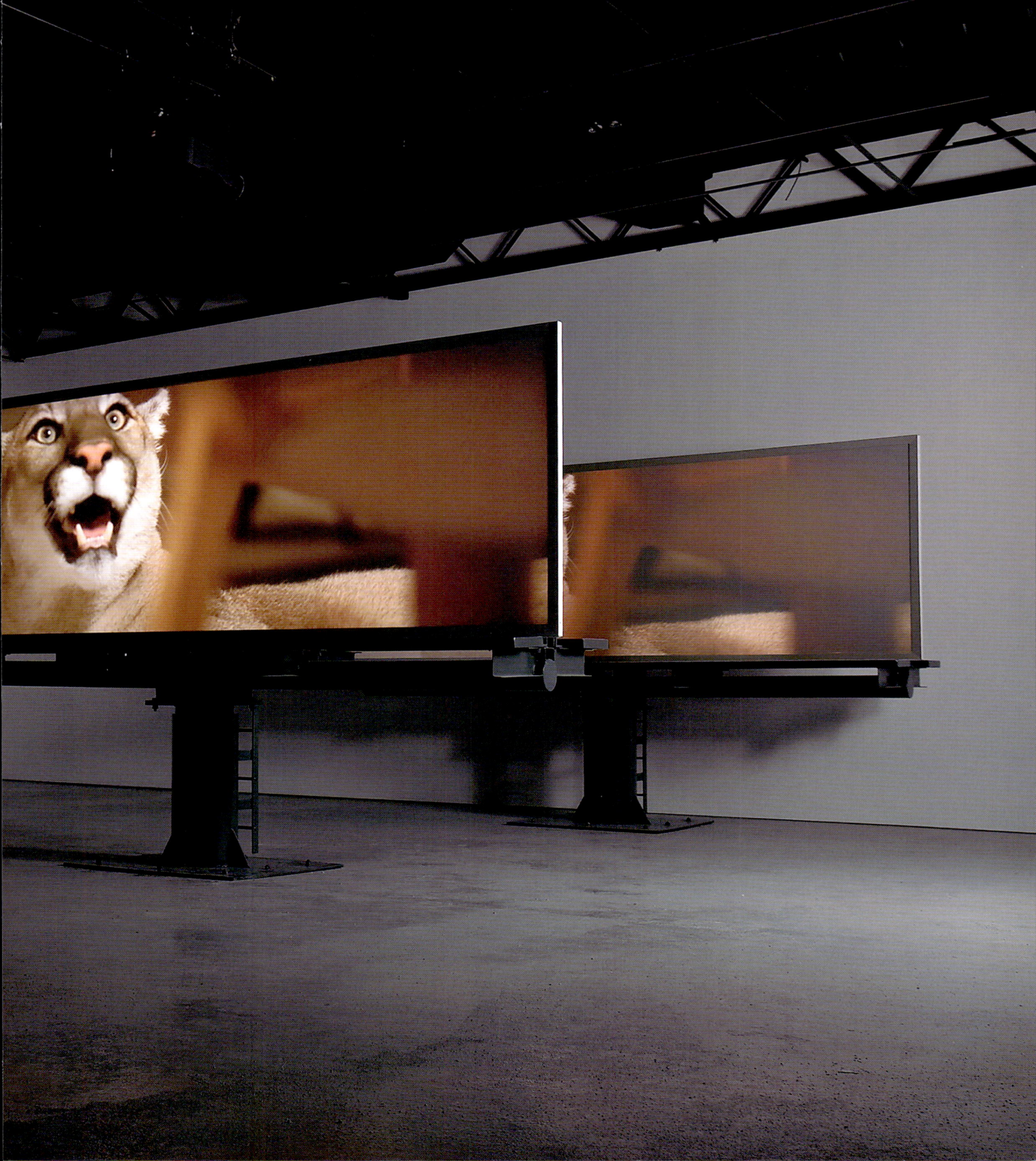

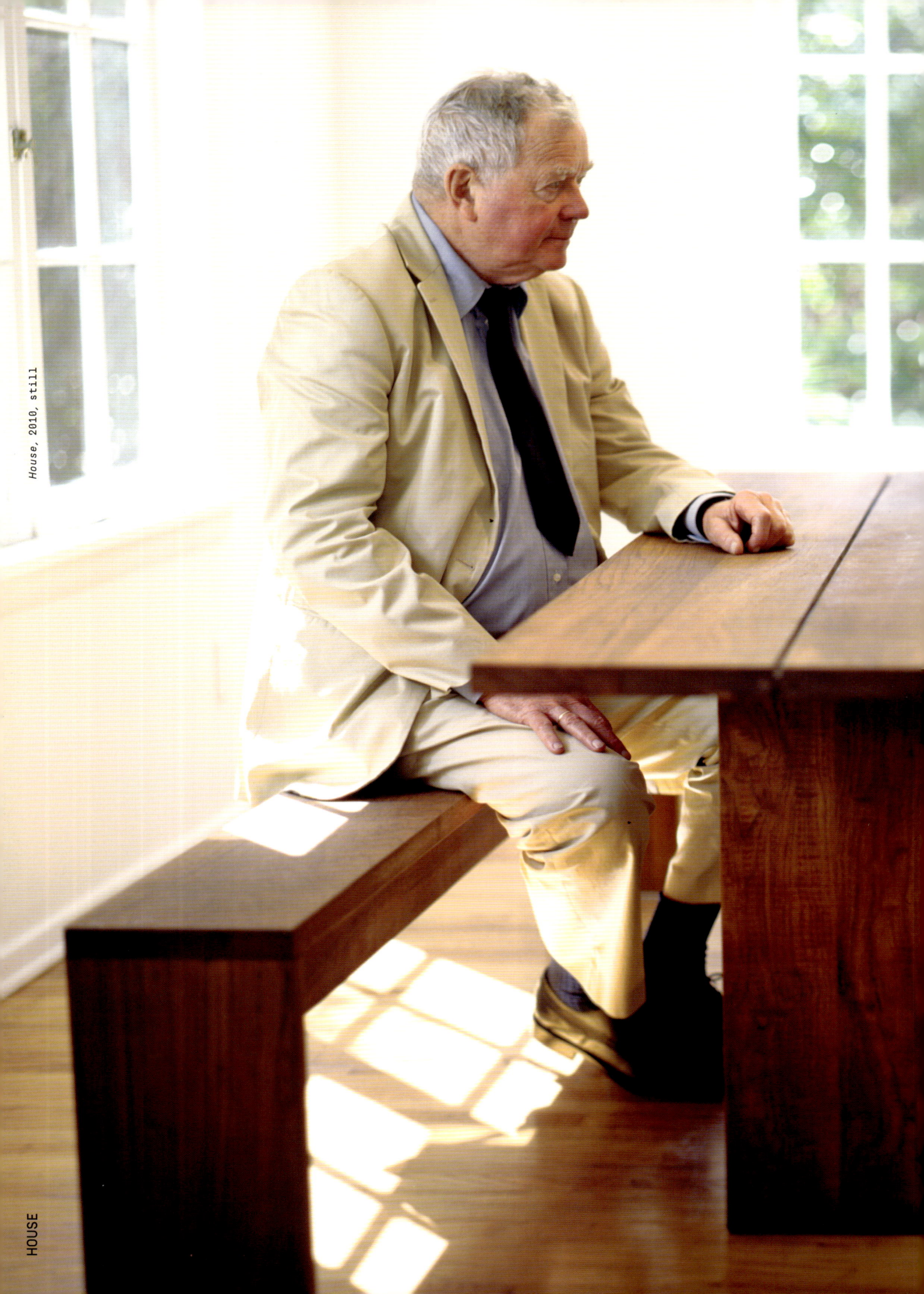

House, 2010, still

HOUSE

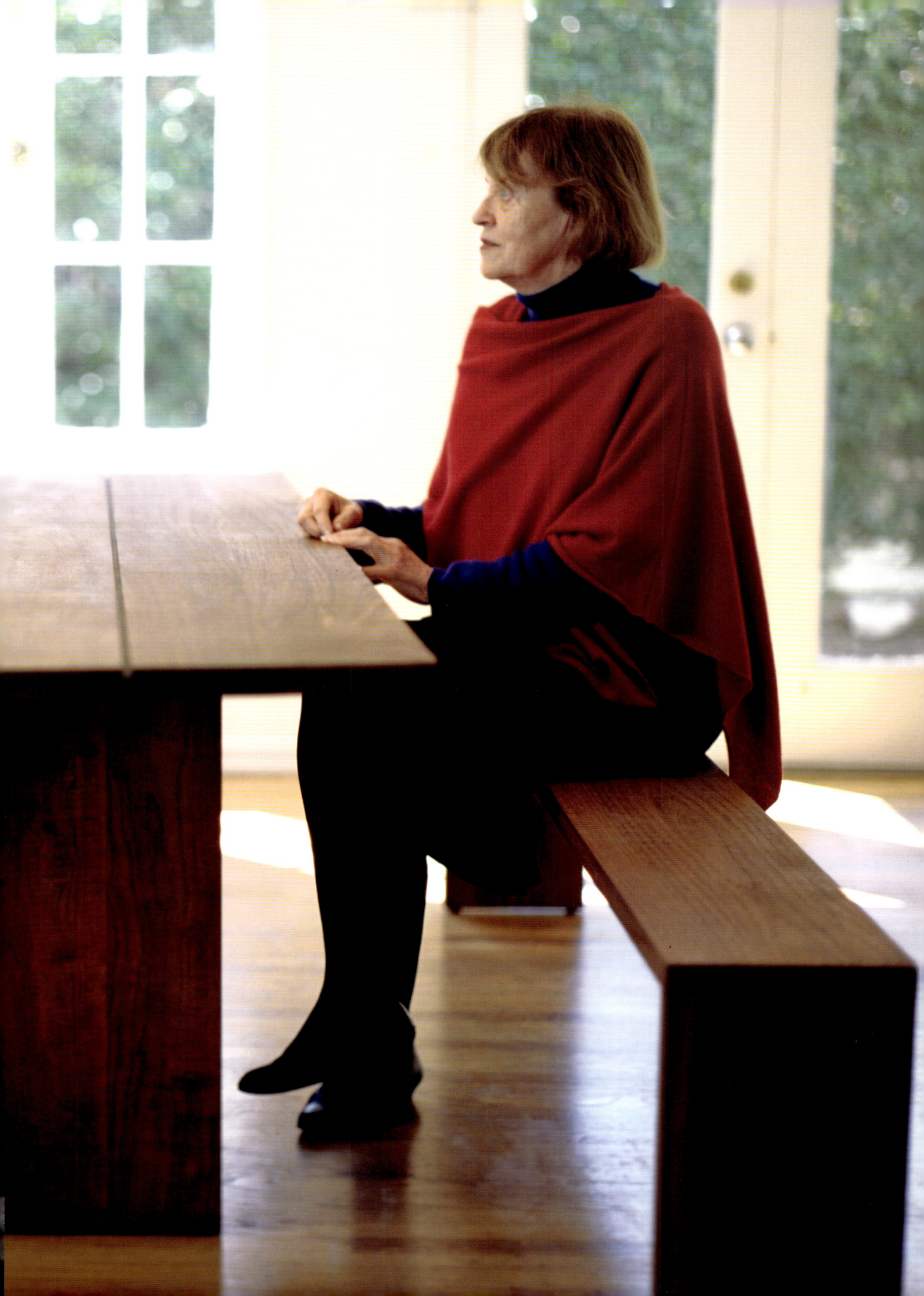

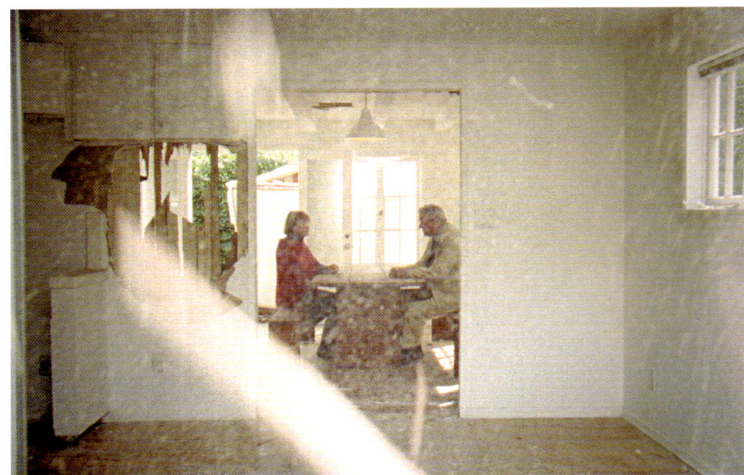
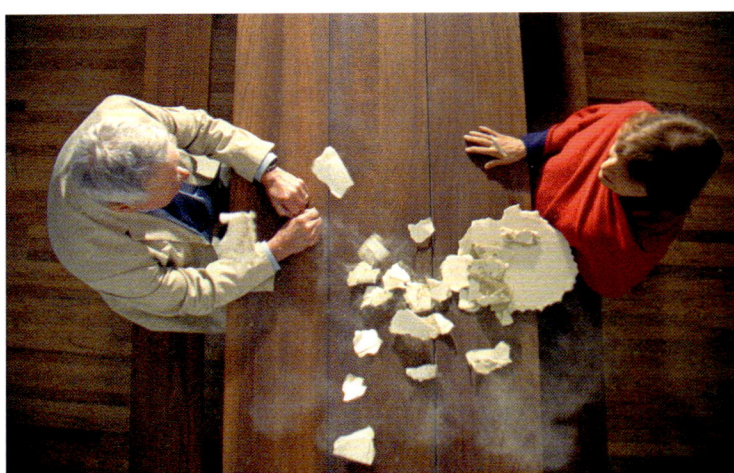

House, 2010, stills

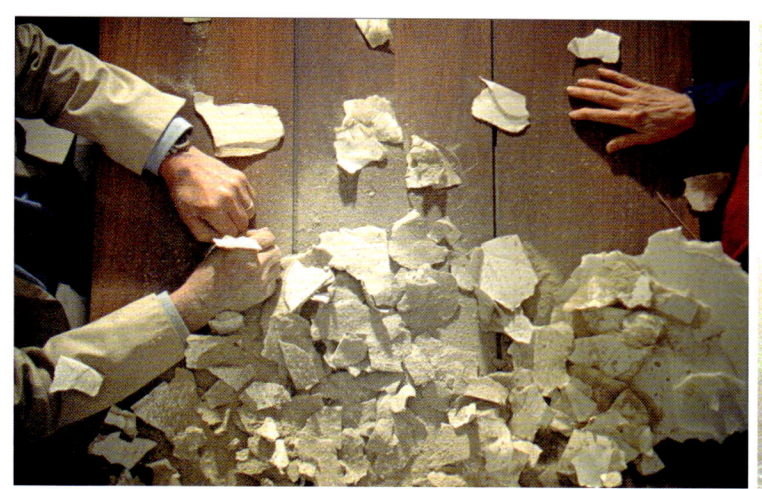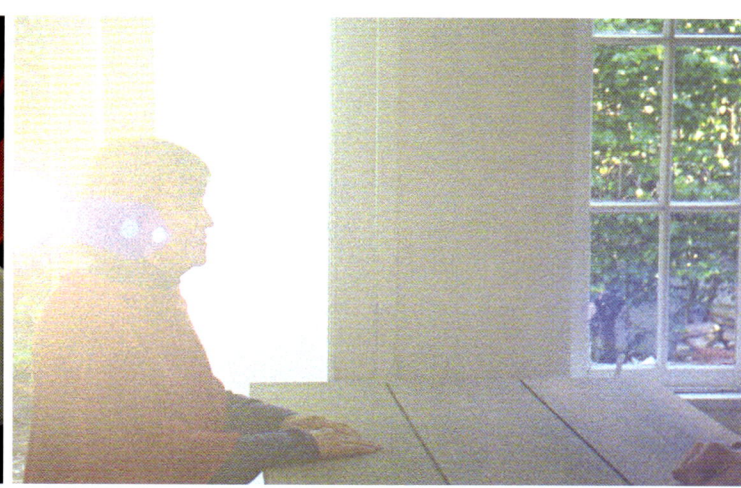

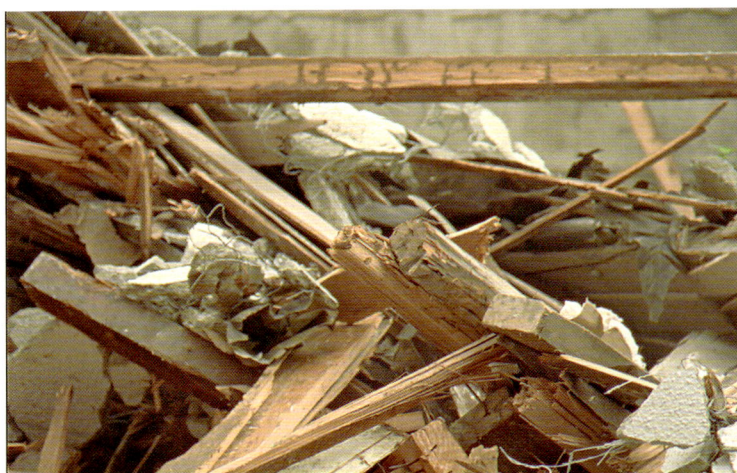
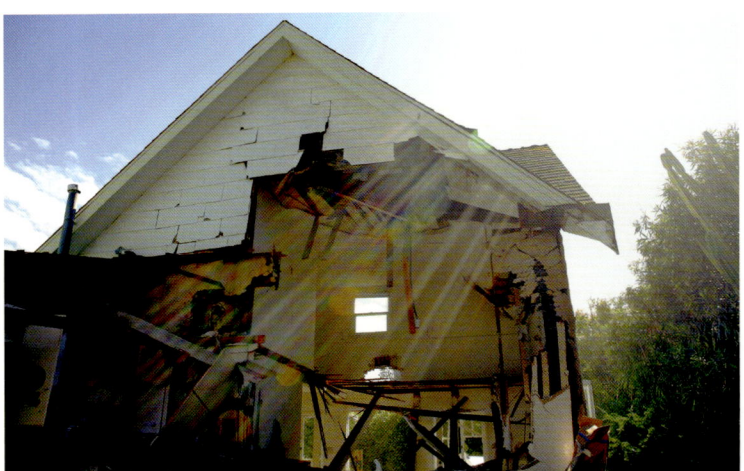

House, 2010, stills

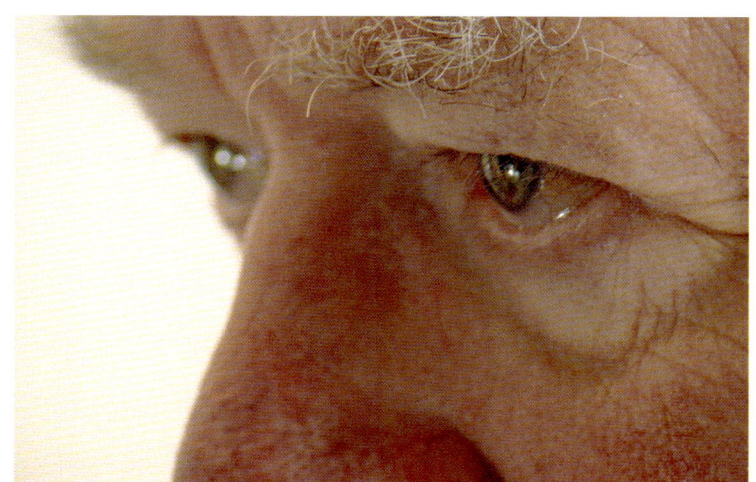 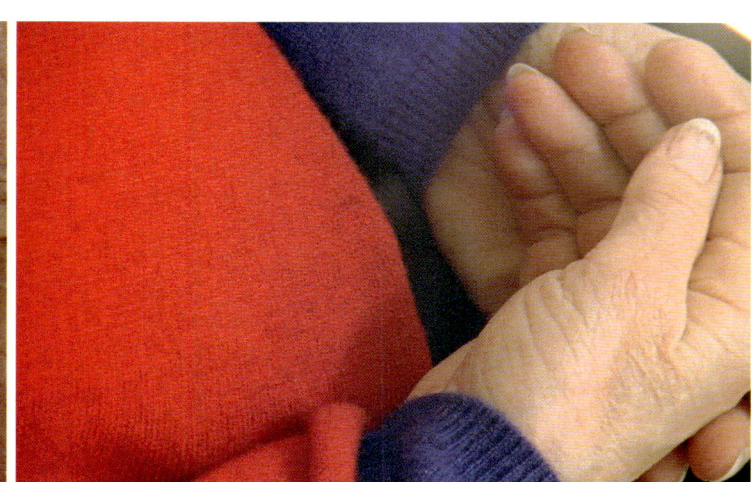

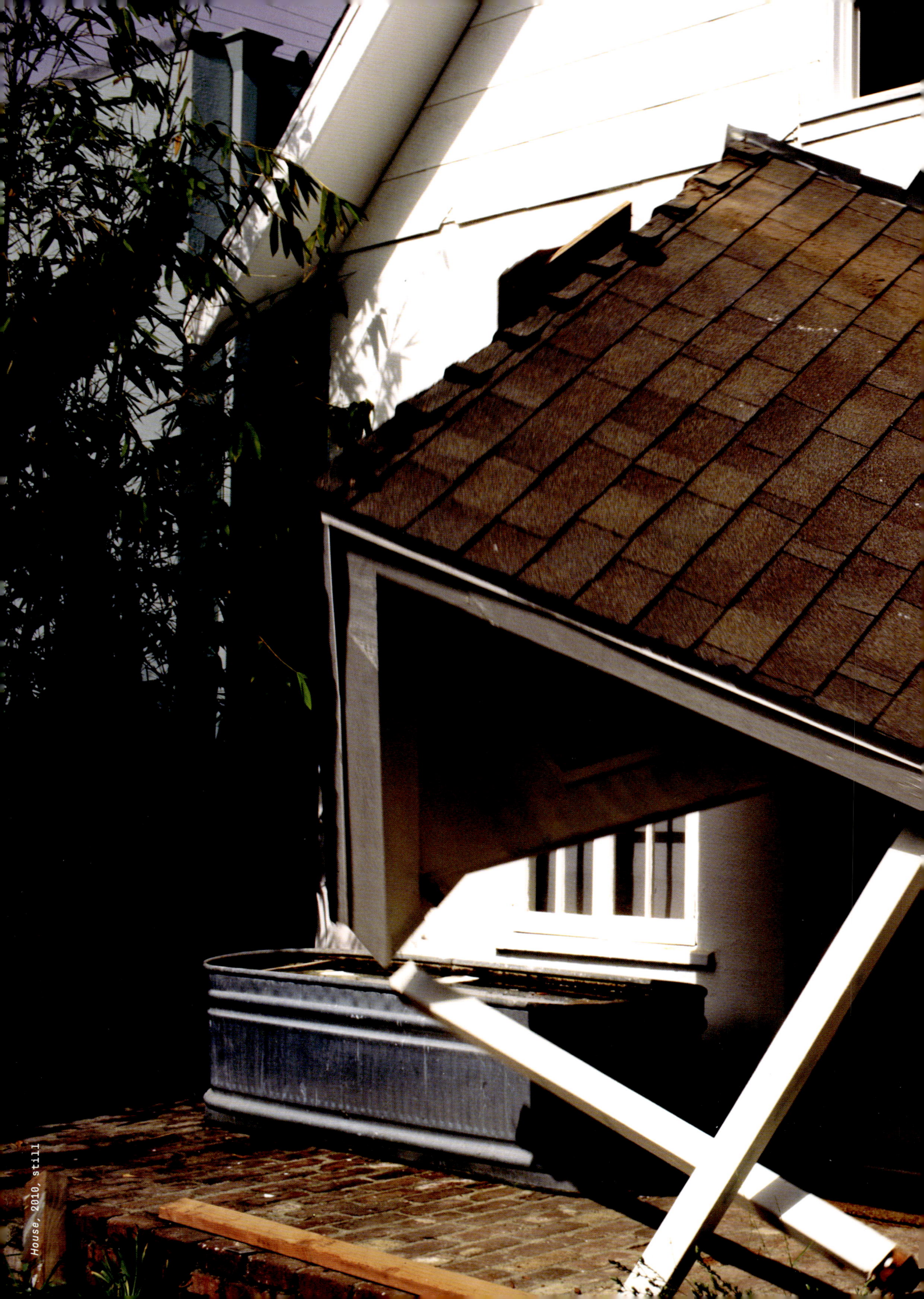

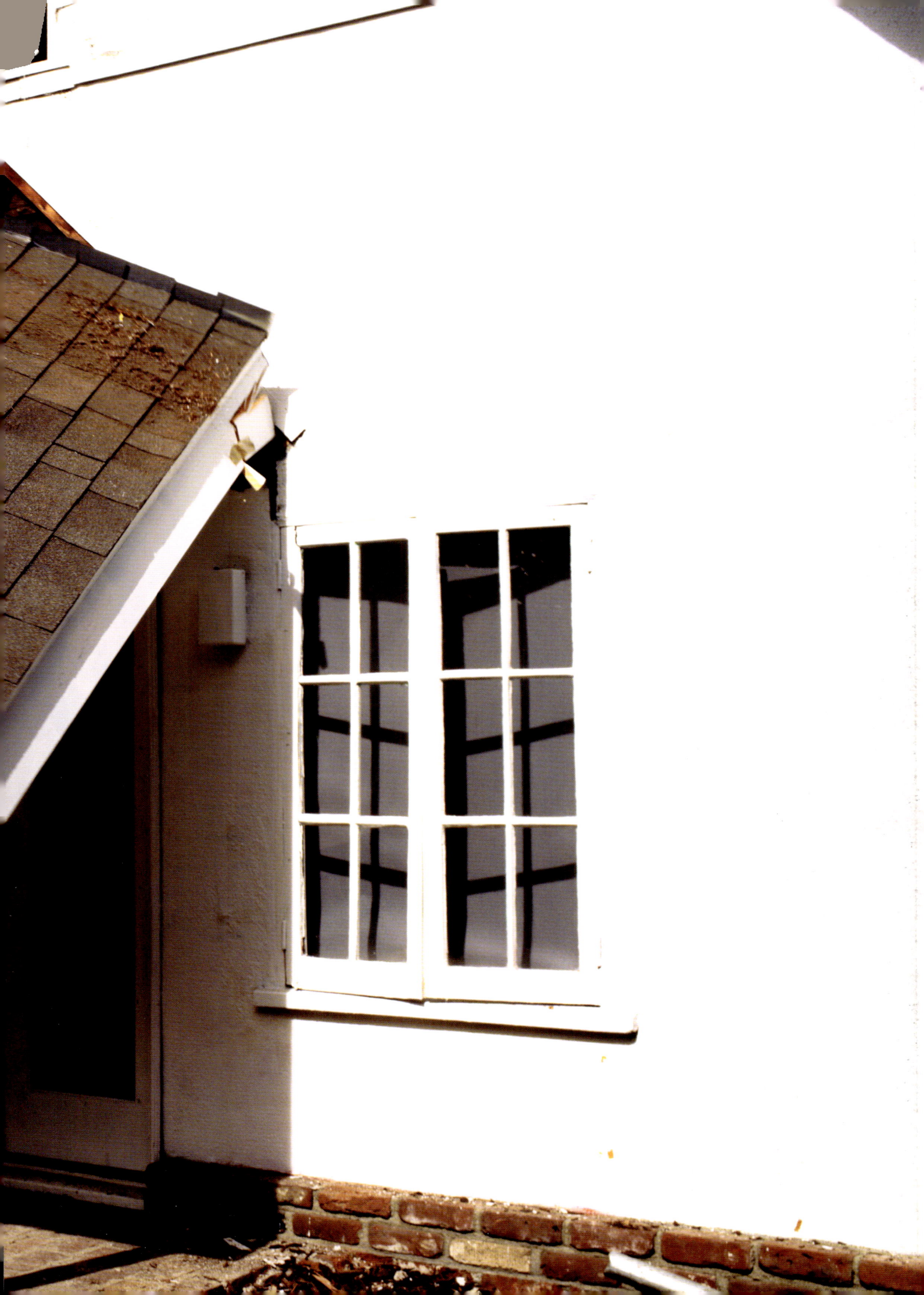

House (2010; pages 156–163, 165) is a counterpoint to *migration (empire)*. It is a sedentary work: a dining table with a TV set at its center. On the screen a couple in their sixties (Aitken's parents) are sitting facing each other on opposite sides of a similar table, inside a house. Around them, little by little and as they remain stoic, the house—their shelter, their shared place—is progressively destroyed, exposing them without their world, under conditions that will no longer protect them. Paradoxically, they appear serene, unscathed, as if their own company suffices. And the television is still on, broadcasting. They only have eyes for each other, expressing, without a word: you are here and so am I.

I only have eyes for you... These, of course, are the lyrics and the title of the song famously recorded by the Flamingos in 1959, and part of the soundtrack of Aitken's architectural work and installation *SONG 1* (2012; pages 166–167). A video-based work, it was projected on the 360-degree facade of the Hirshhorn Museum and Sculpture Garden in Washington, DC, a cylindrical edifice designed by Gordon Bunshaft in 1974. The building is a loop, with no beginning, middle, or end. It is a "museum in the round," simultaneously horizontal and vertical. *SONG 1* rendered the building as an antenna, projecting around itself as well as absorbing viewers' gazes. Beginning with an image of an old-fashioned audiotape, the video unfolds with images of all types of people singing "I Only Have Eyes for You"—anonymous people in empty lots, in factories filled with assembly lines, people in cafés, and known people such as Tilda Swinton and Devendra Banhart—all delivering their own renditions of the song. At times, they are interrupted by abstractions: a myriad of digital snow, a constellation of agitated electromagnetic particles. It is a true heterophony, or a soundscape where everyone has an equal voice. This audible version of radical democracy is located at the center of the American capital, on the Mall, where people come to celebrate their participation in democracy, come to protest and stand for their rights—the theater of democracy, the agora.

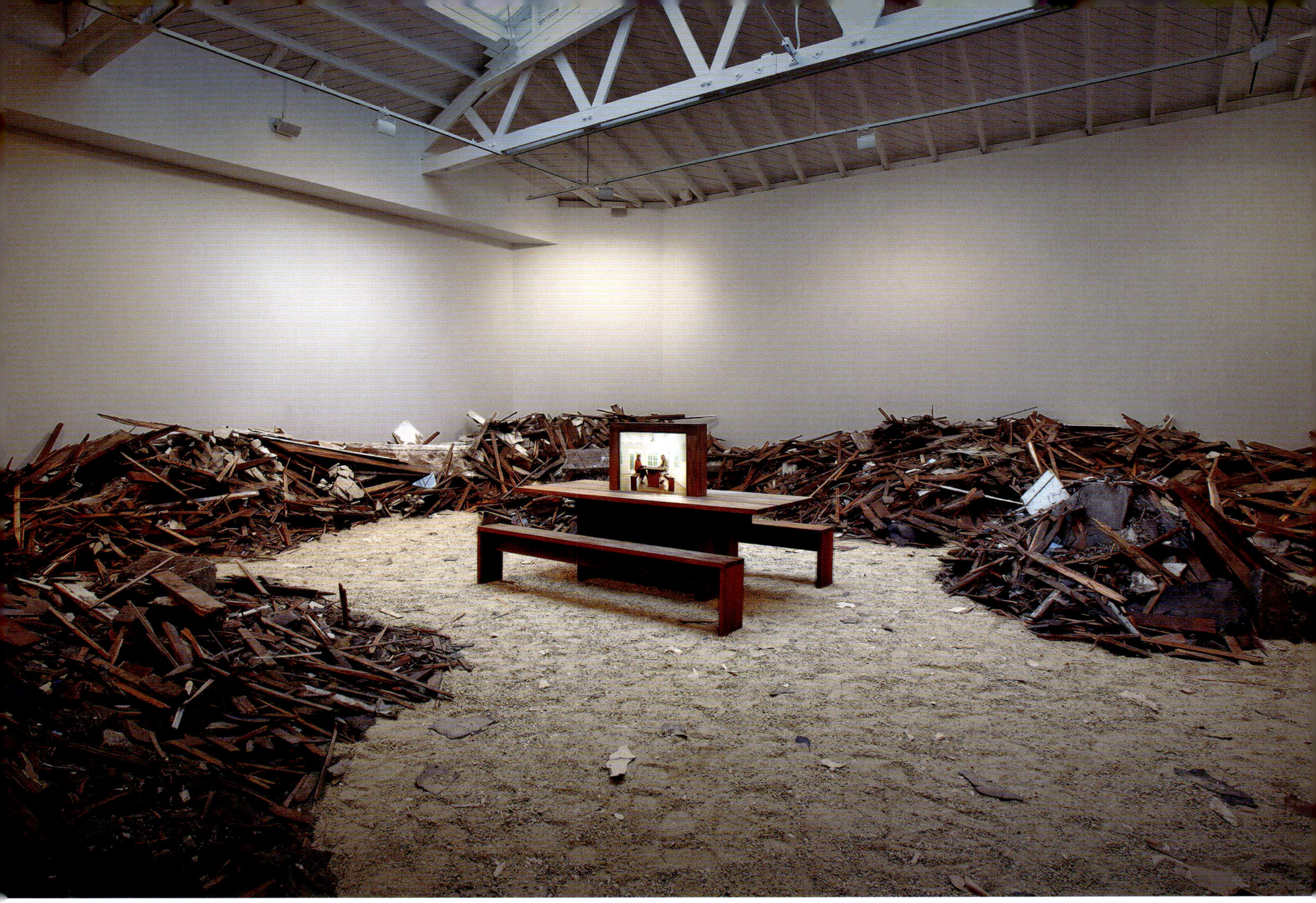

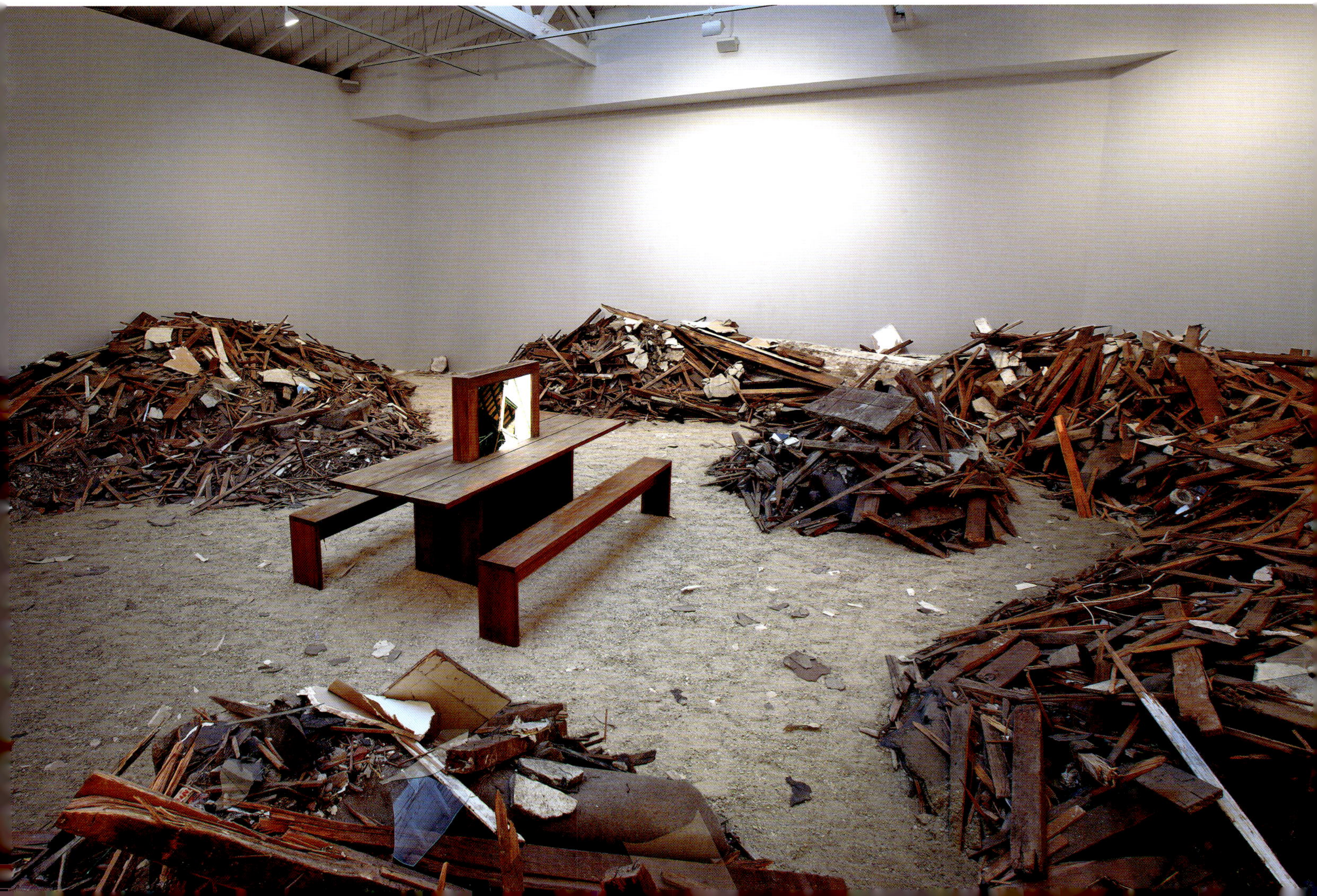

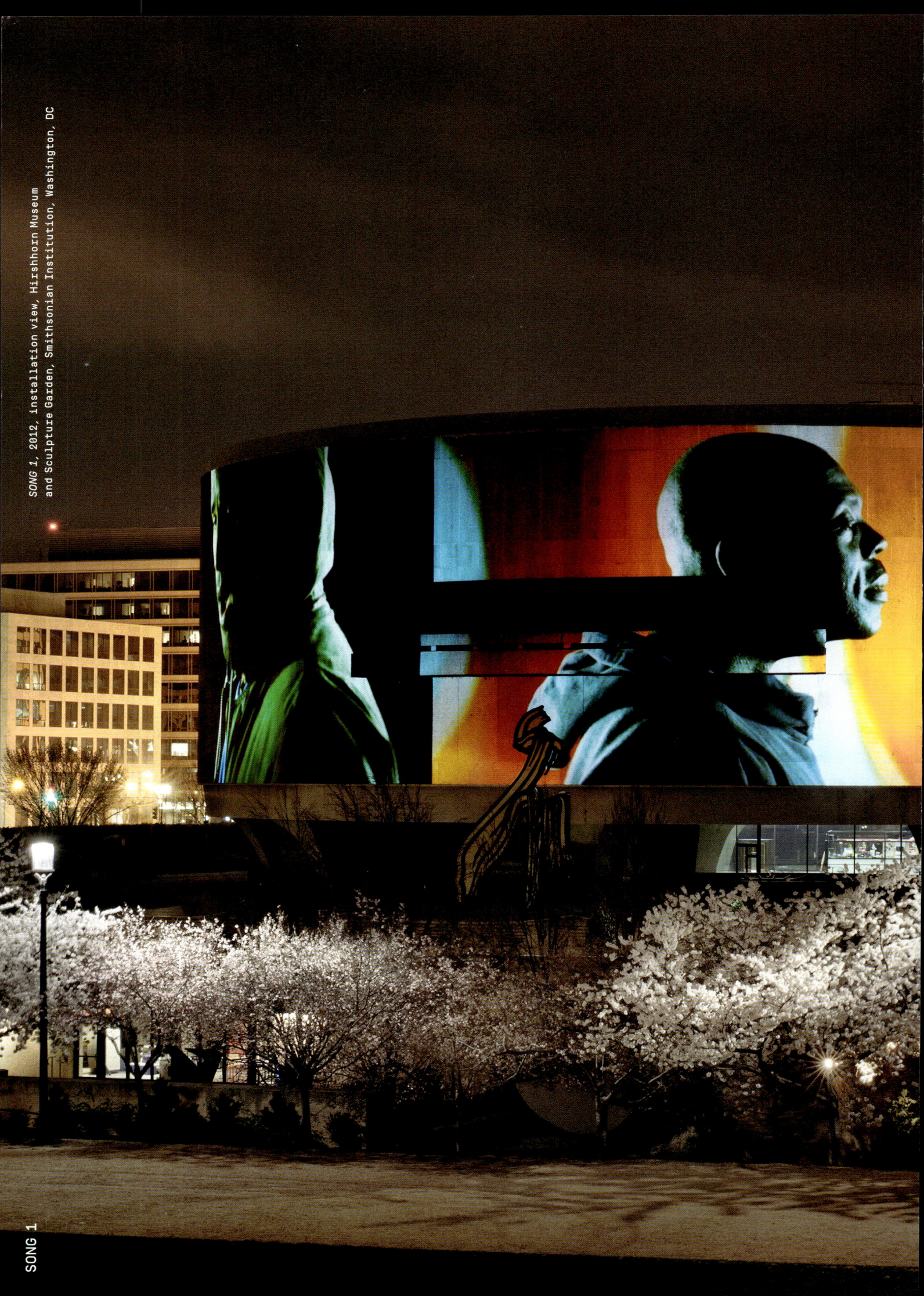
SONG 1, 2012, installation view, Hirshhorn Museum and Sculpture Garden, Smithsonian Institution, Washington, DC

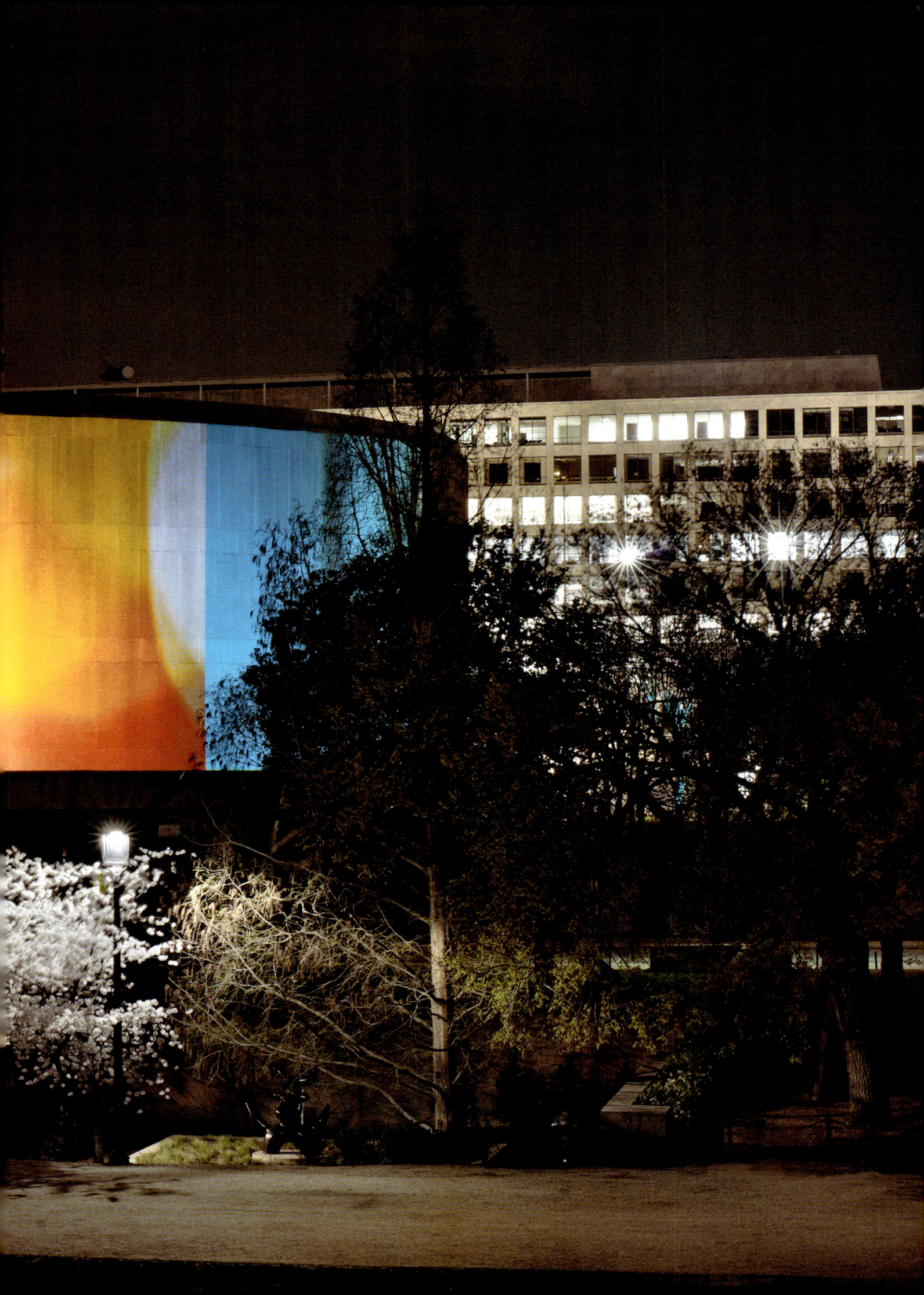

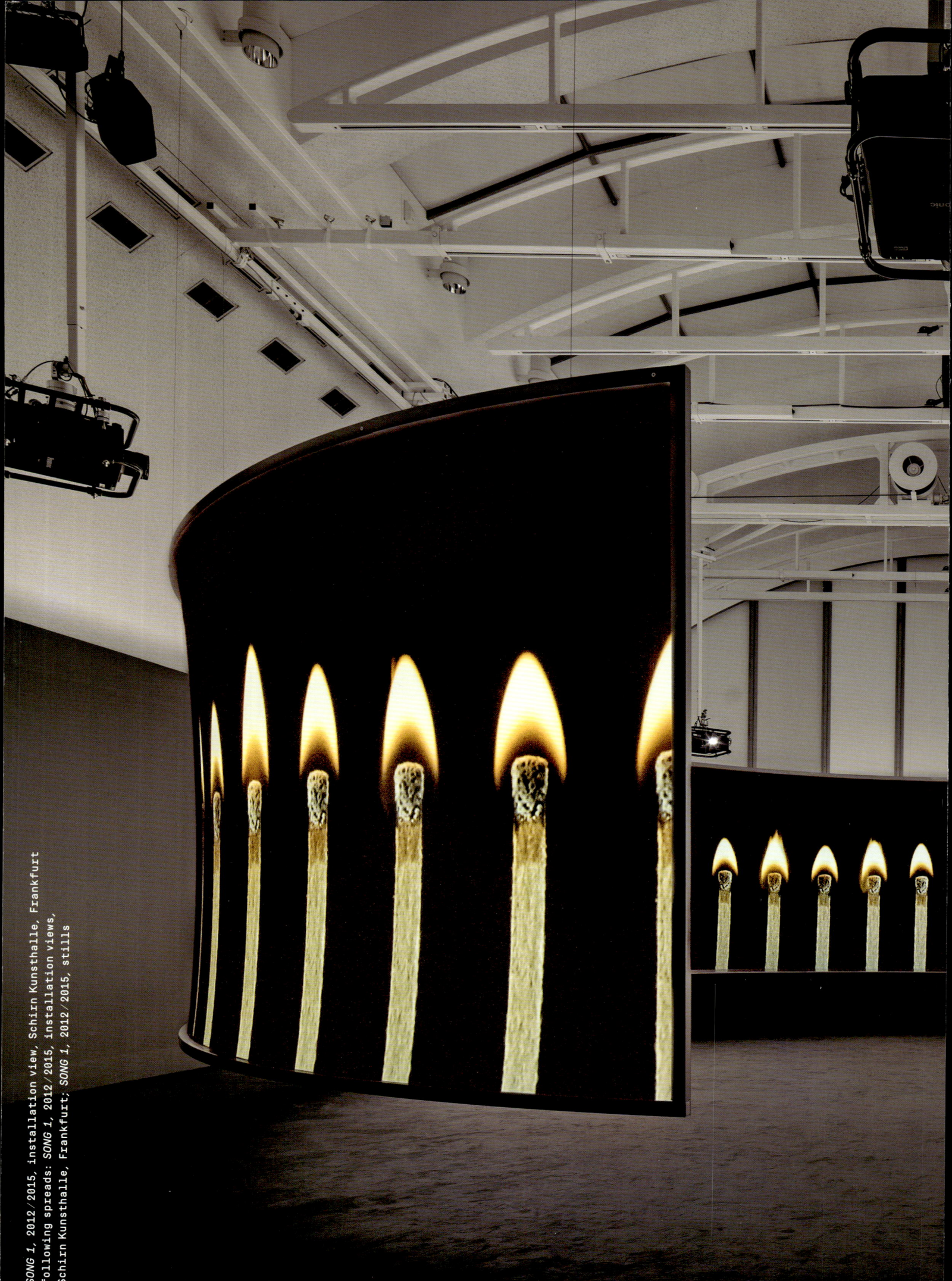

SONG 1, 2012/2015, installation view, Schirn Kunsthalle, Frankfurt
following spreads: SONG 1, 2012/2015, installation views,
Schirn Kunsthalle, Frankfurt; SONG 1, 2012/2015, stills

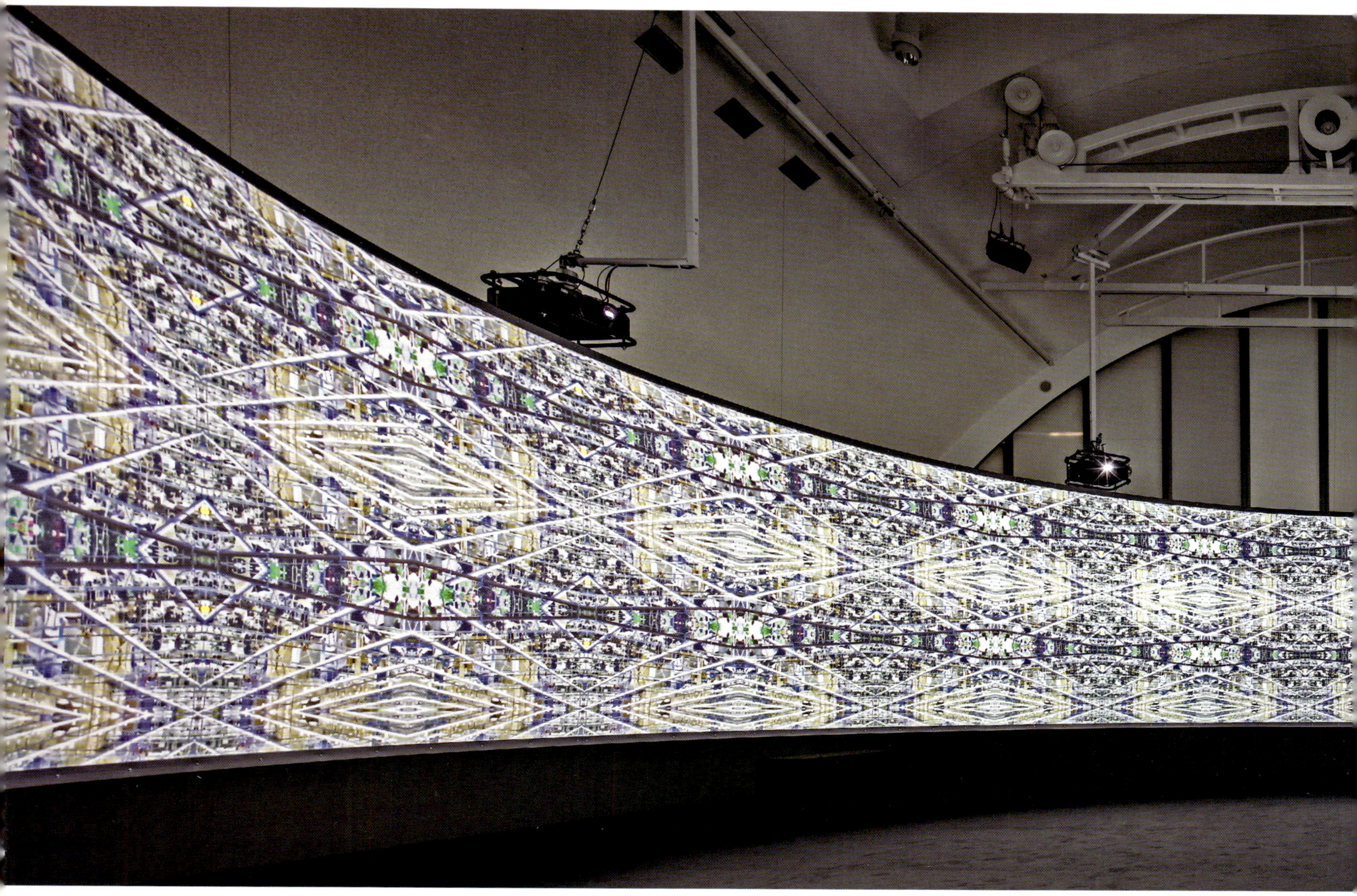

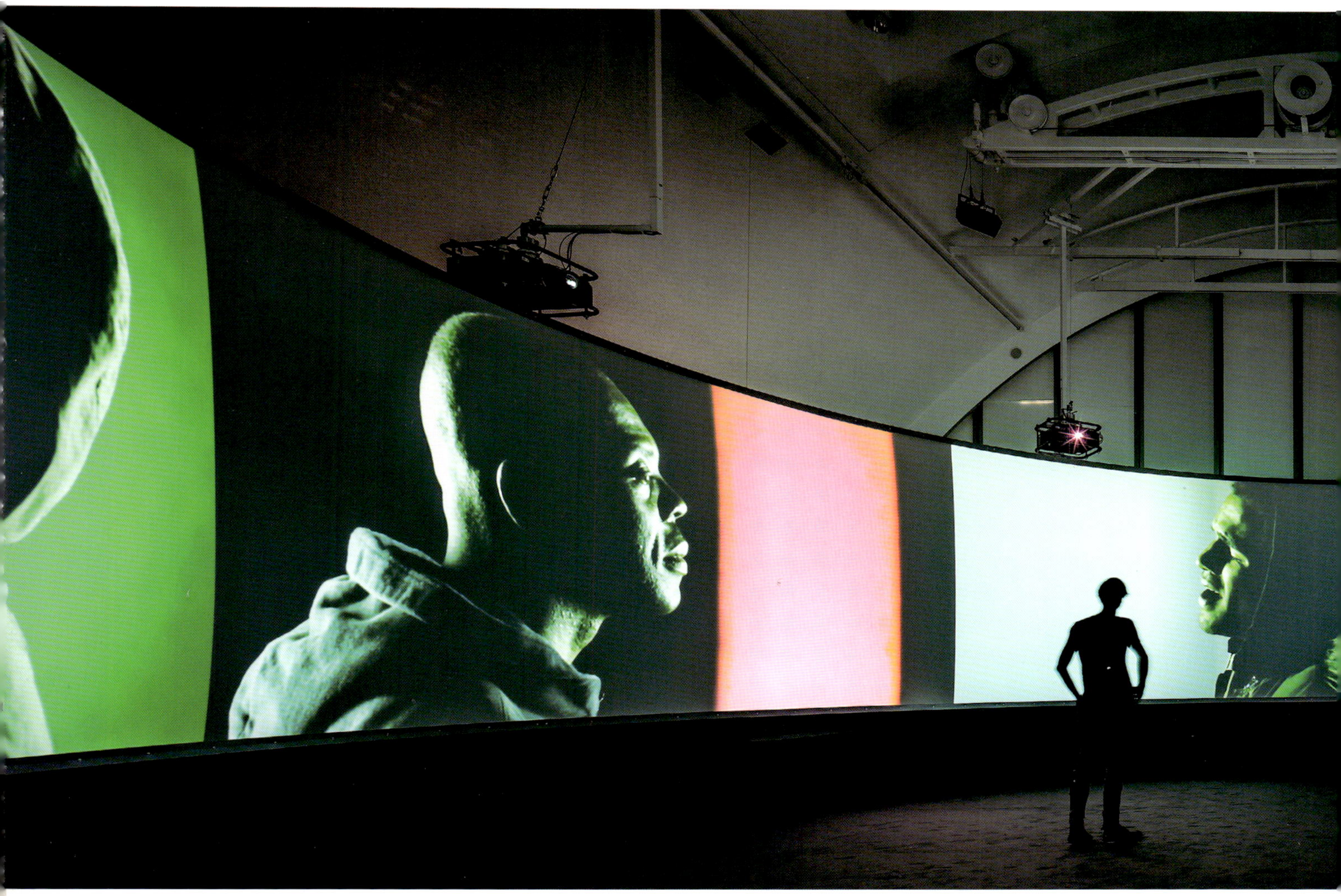

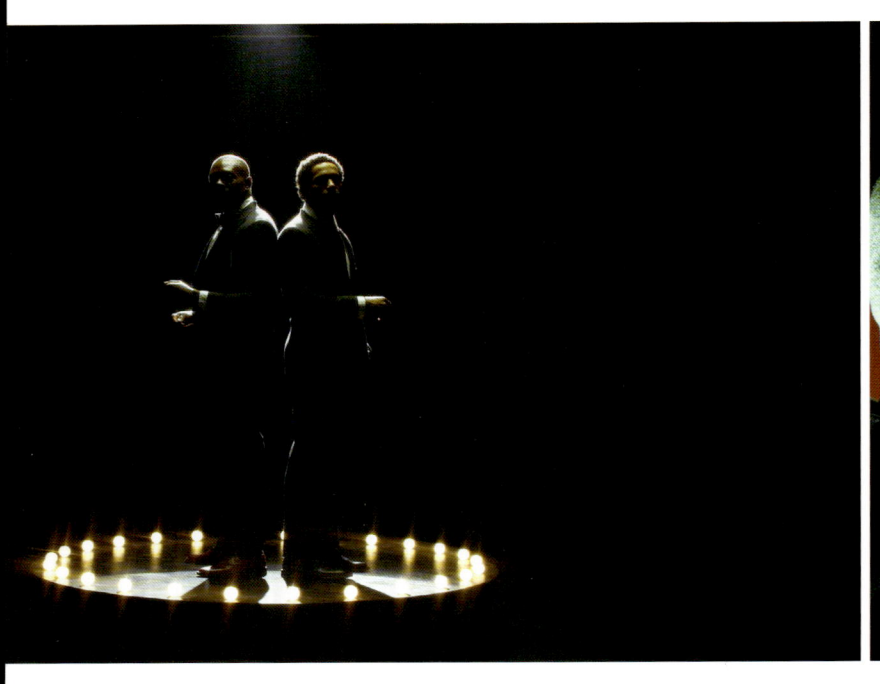
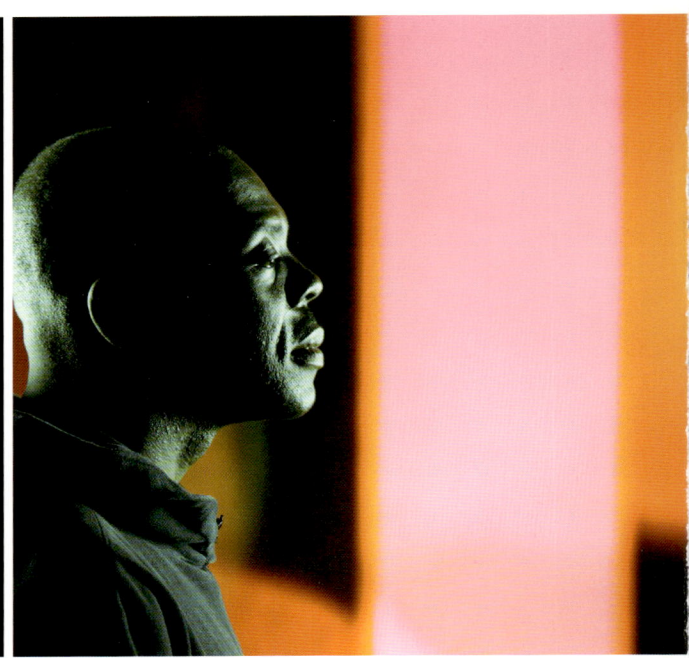
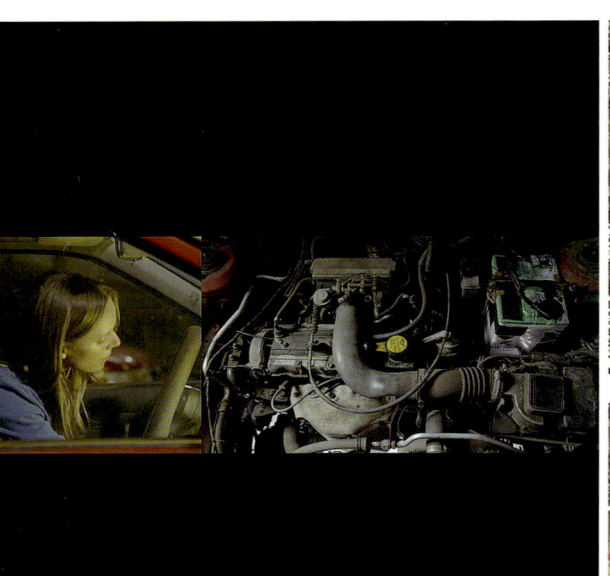
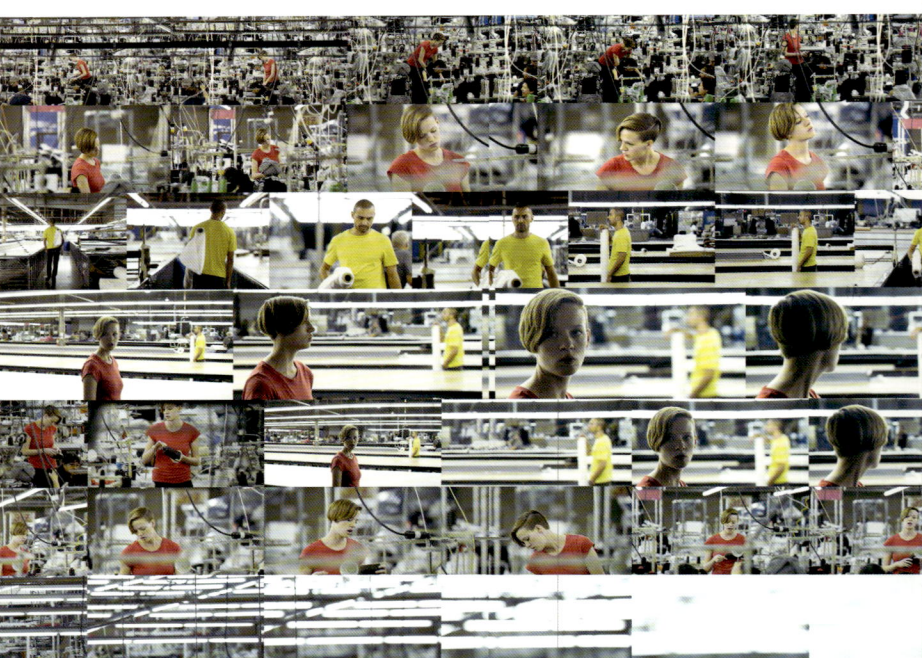
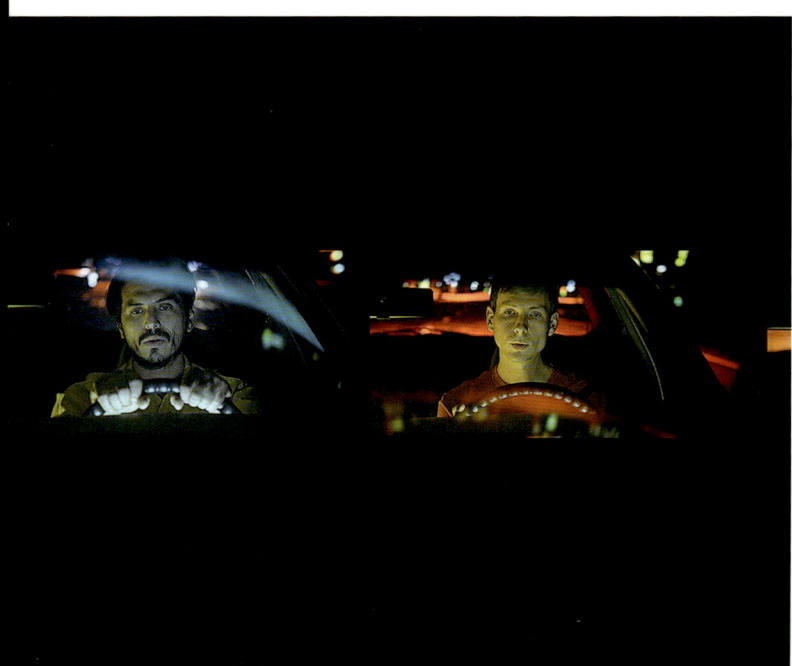
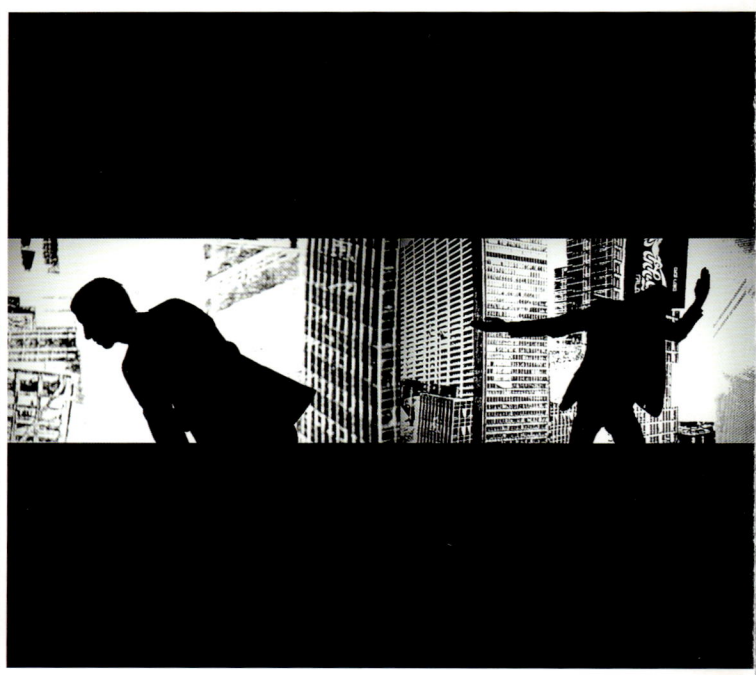

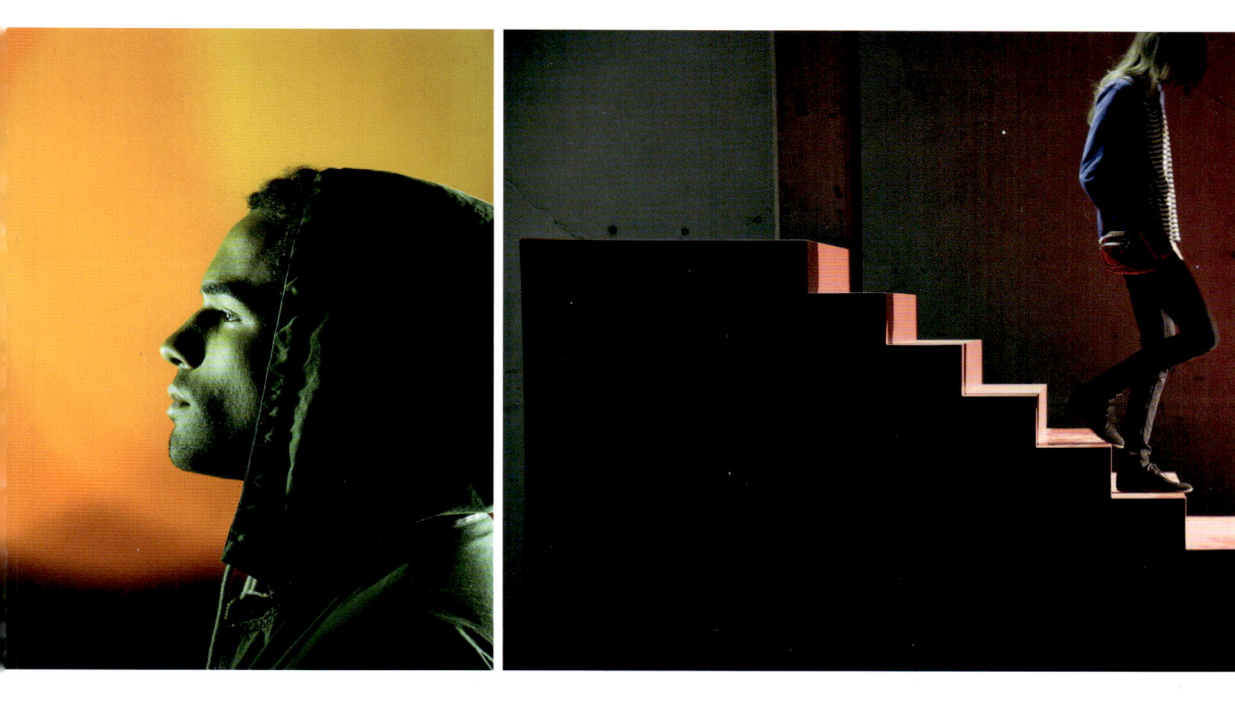
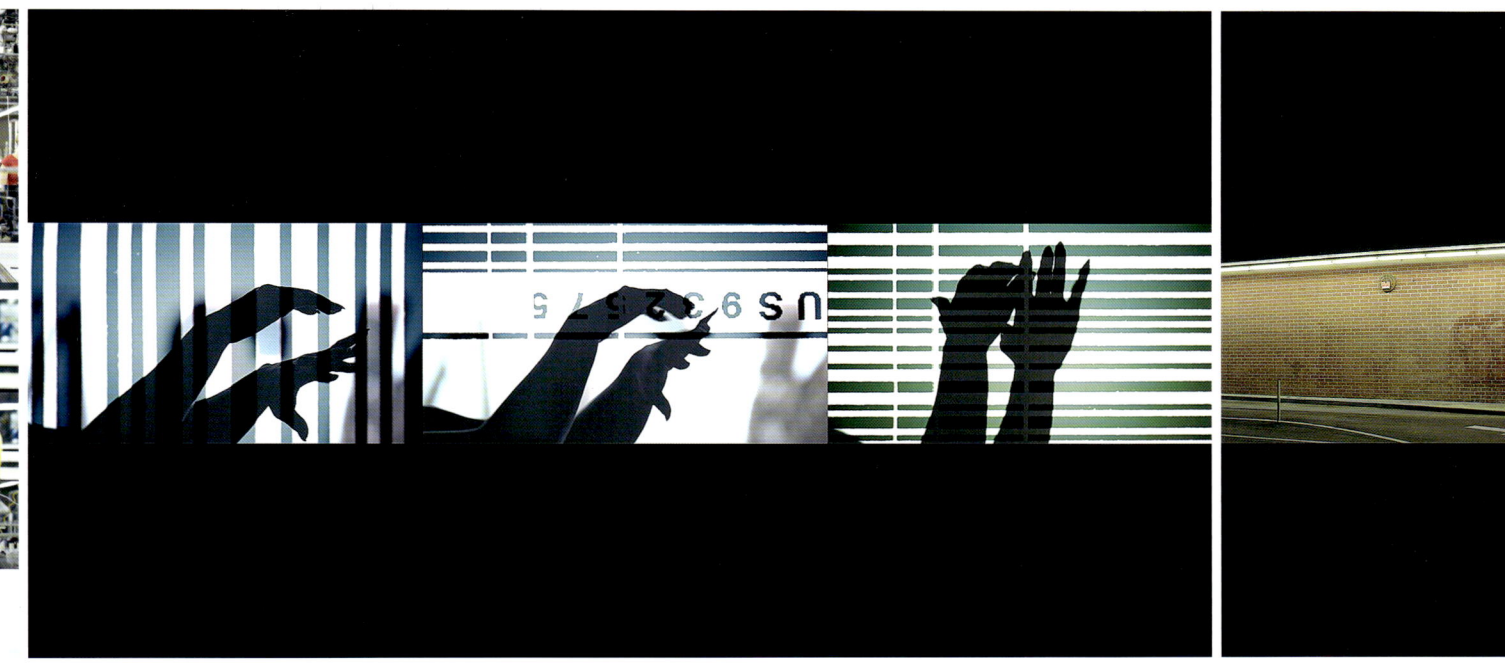
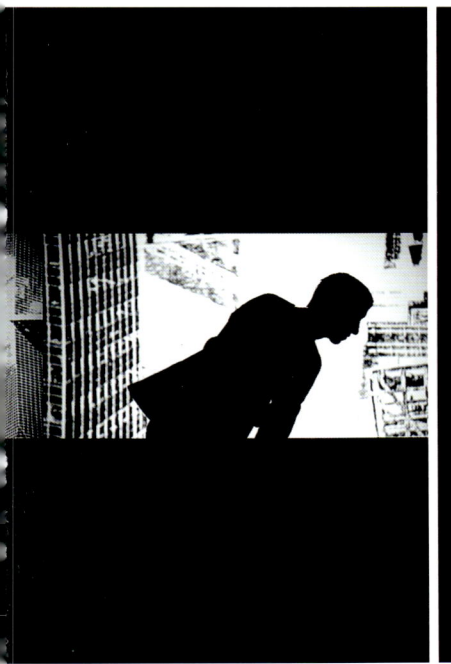
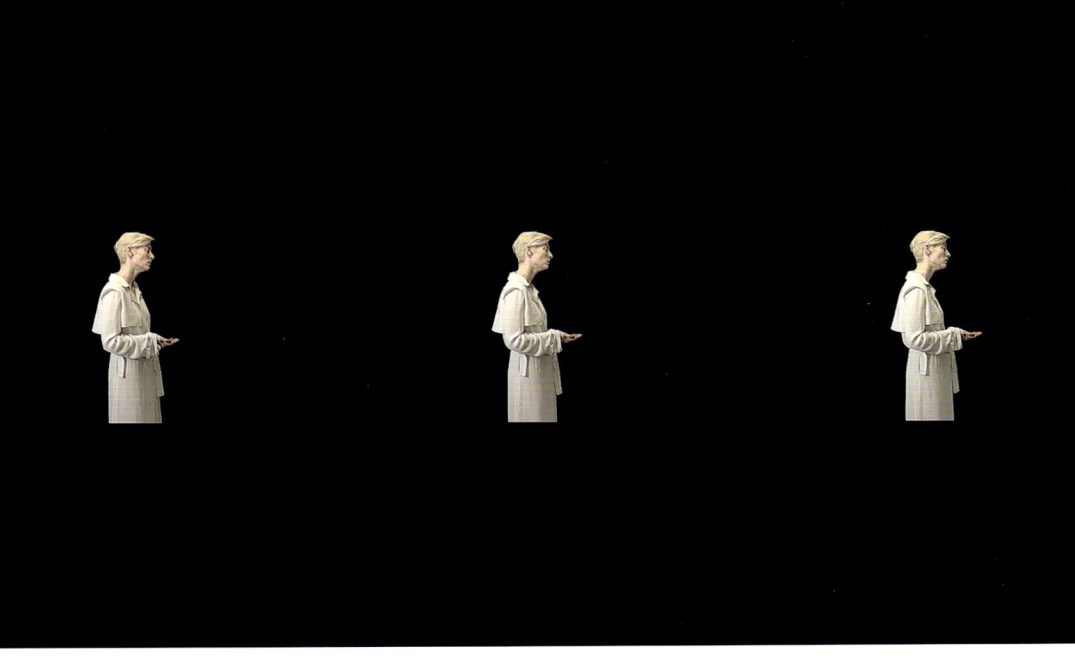

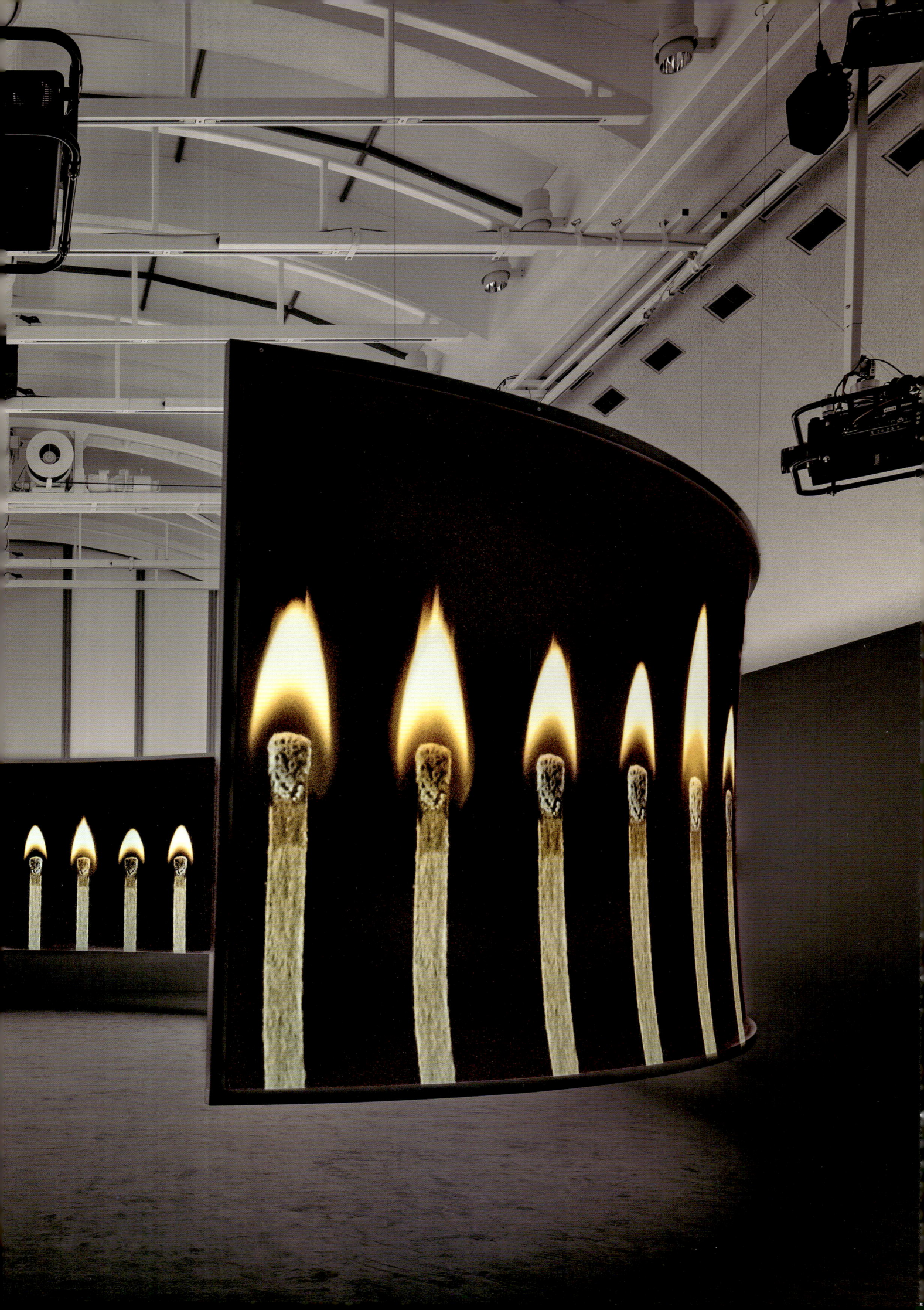

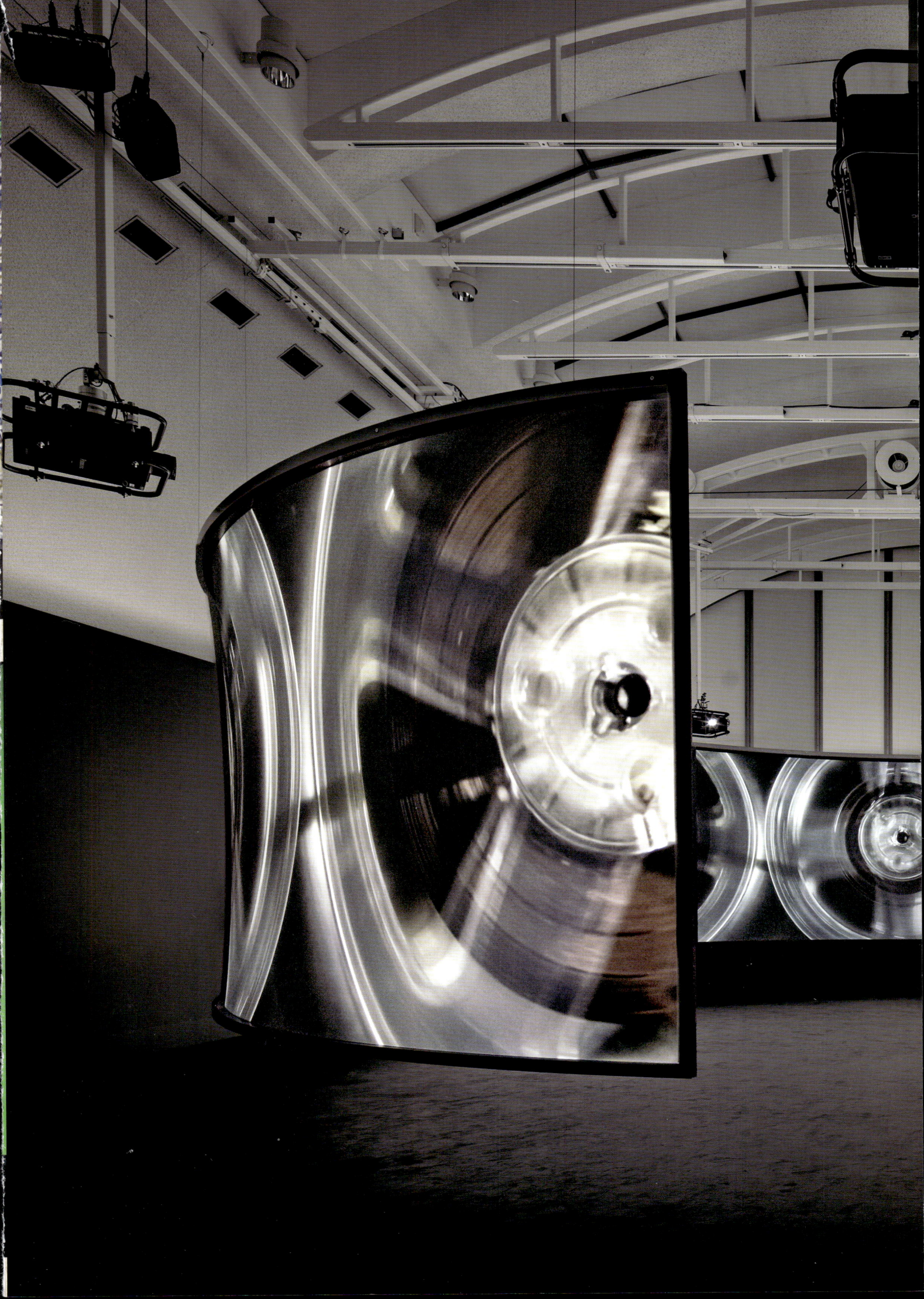

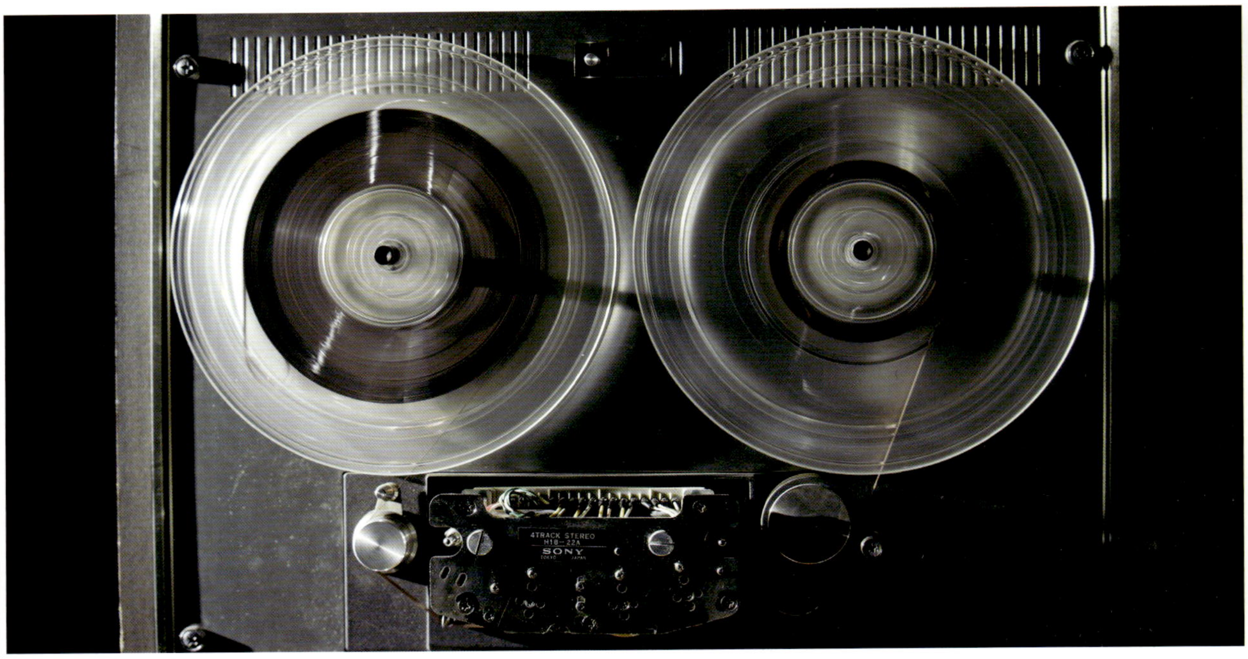

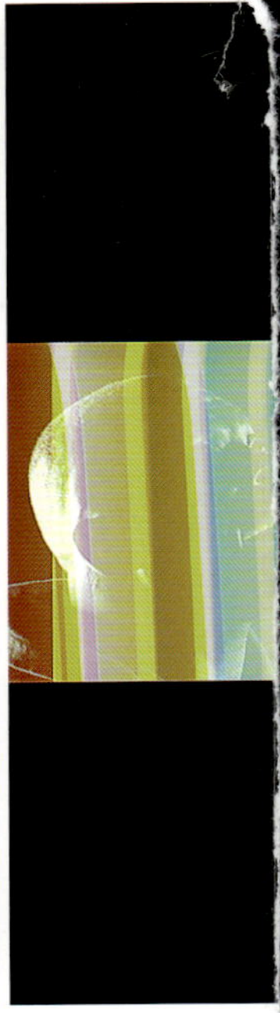

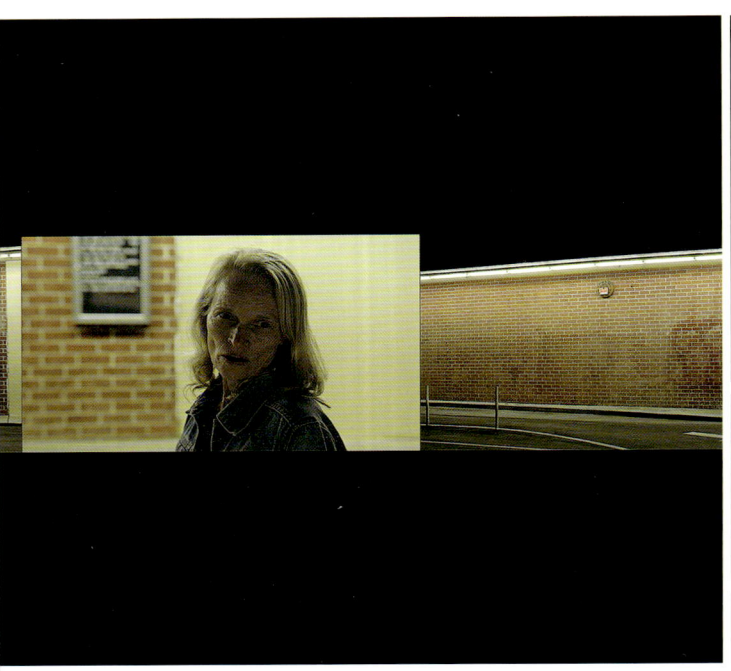
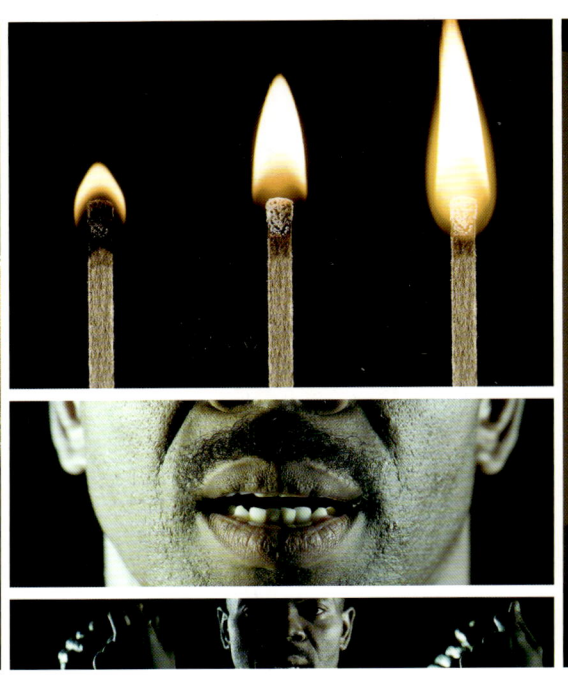

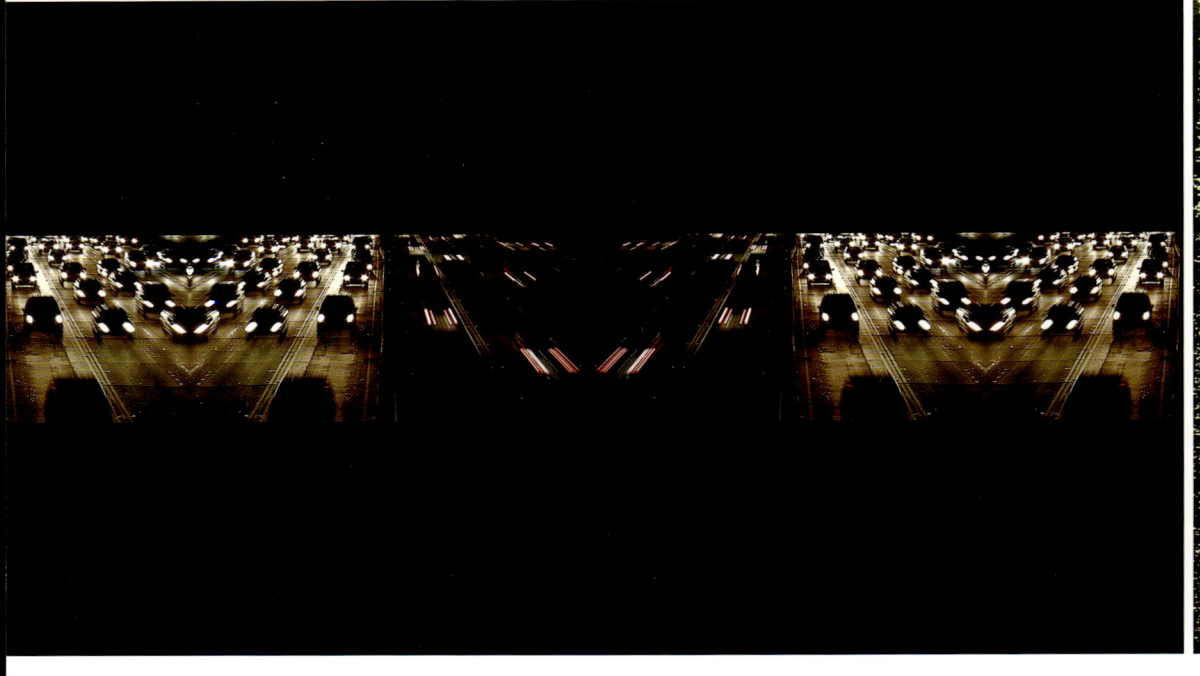
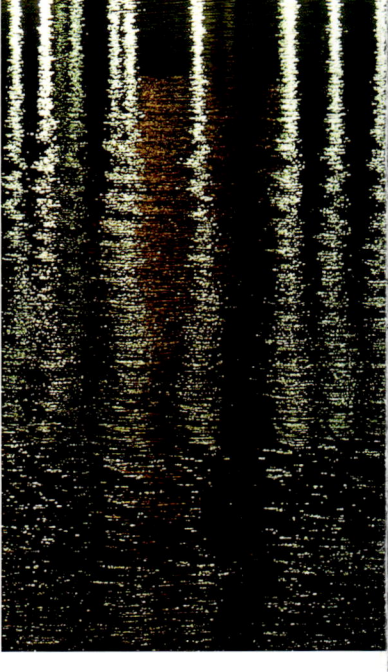

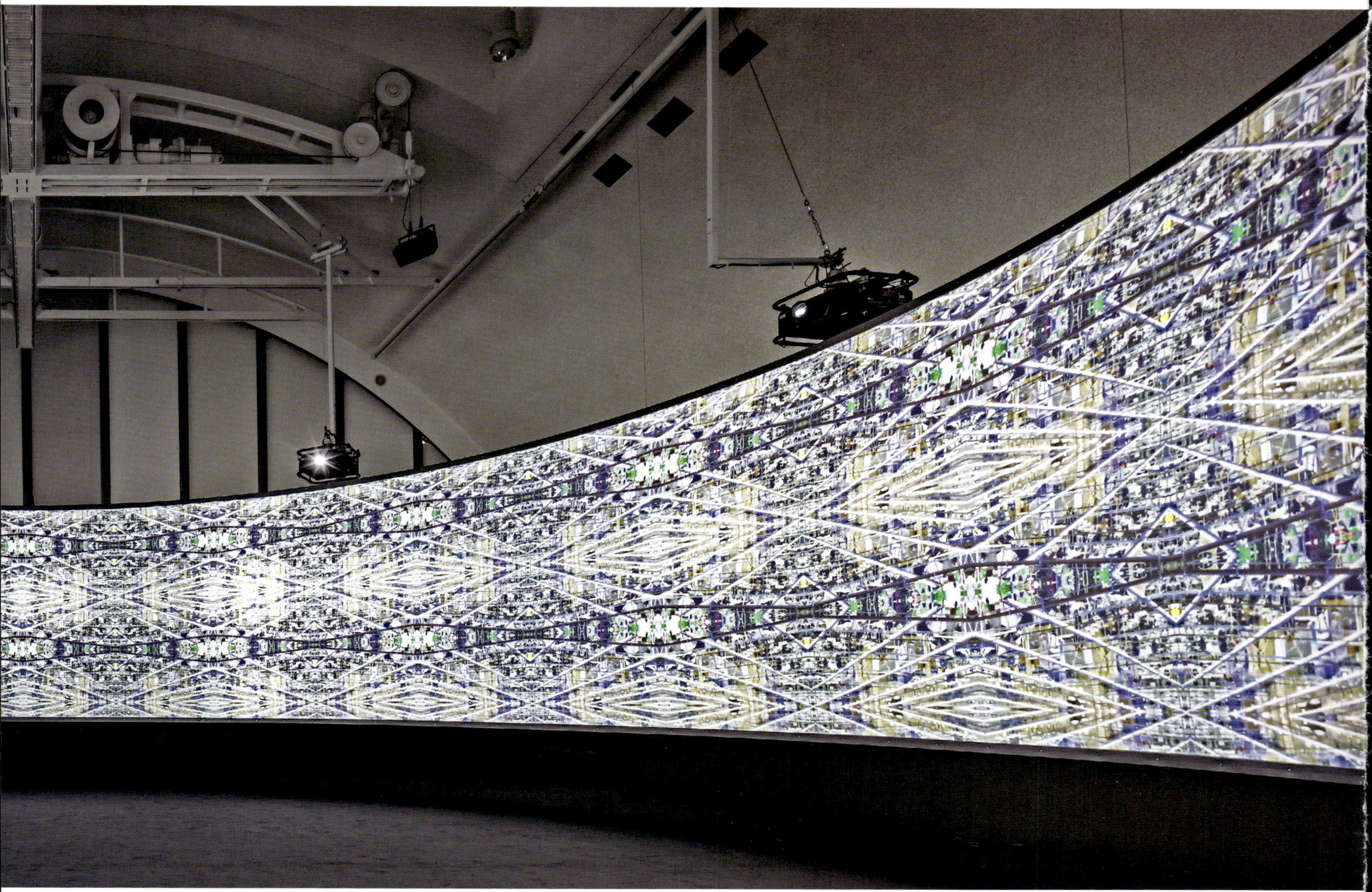

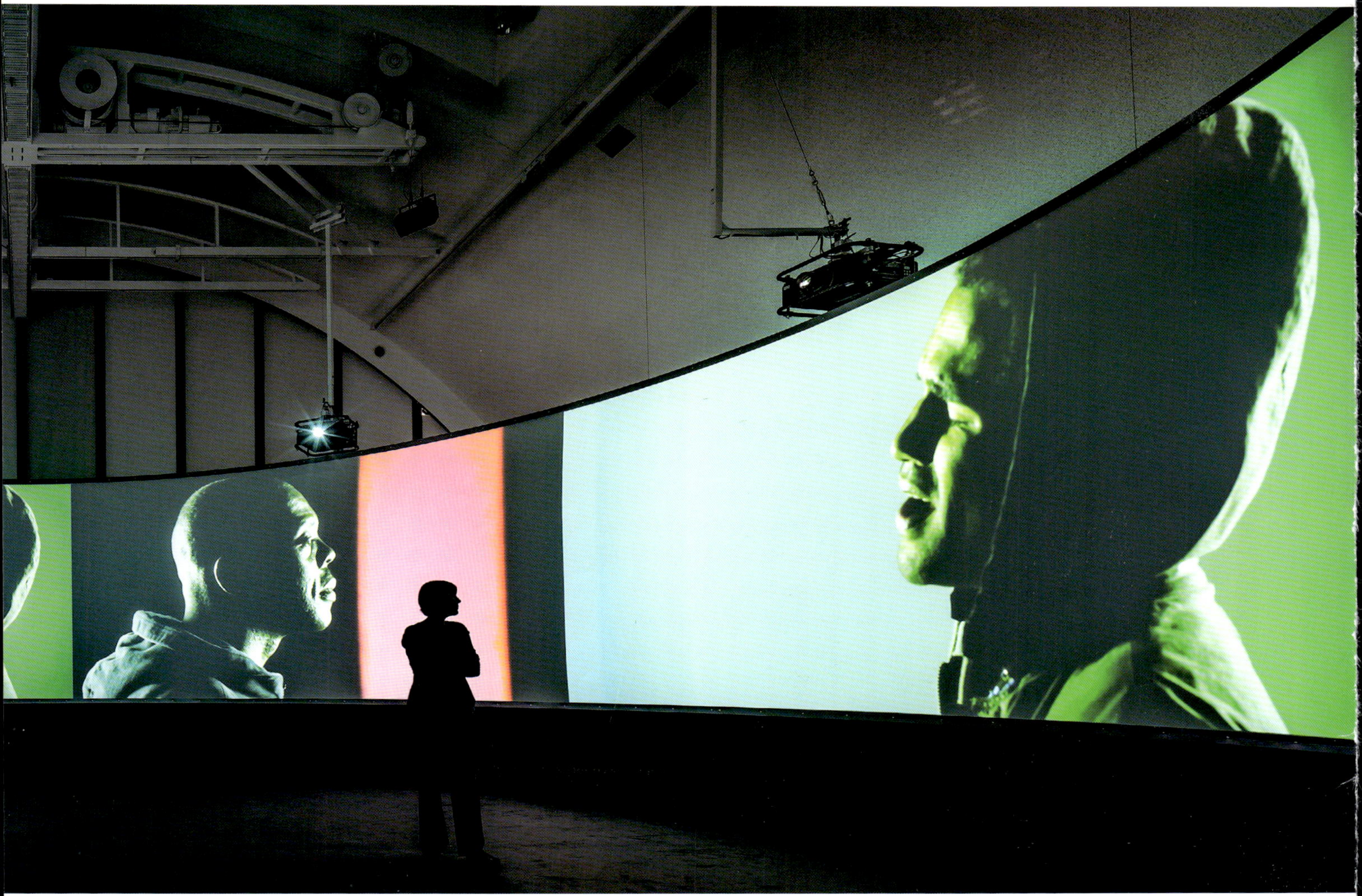

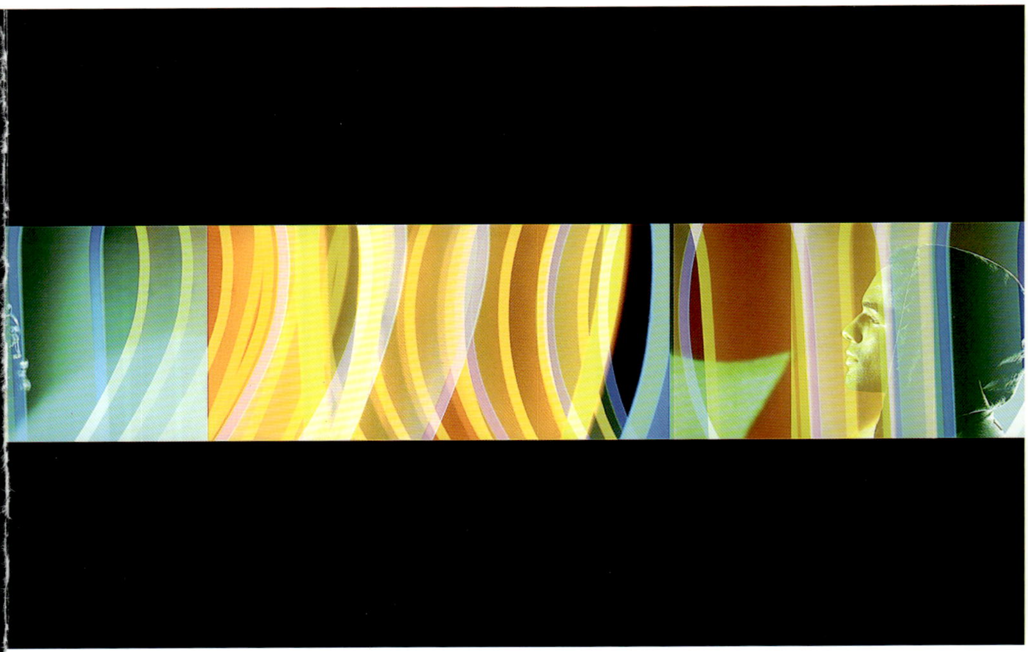

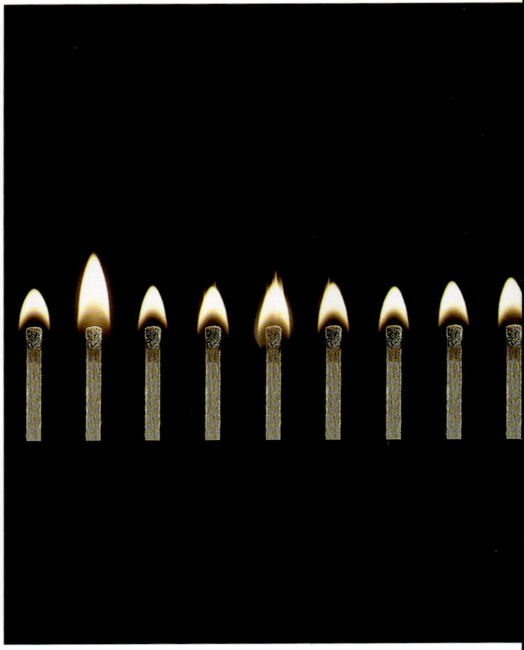

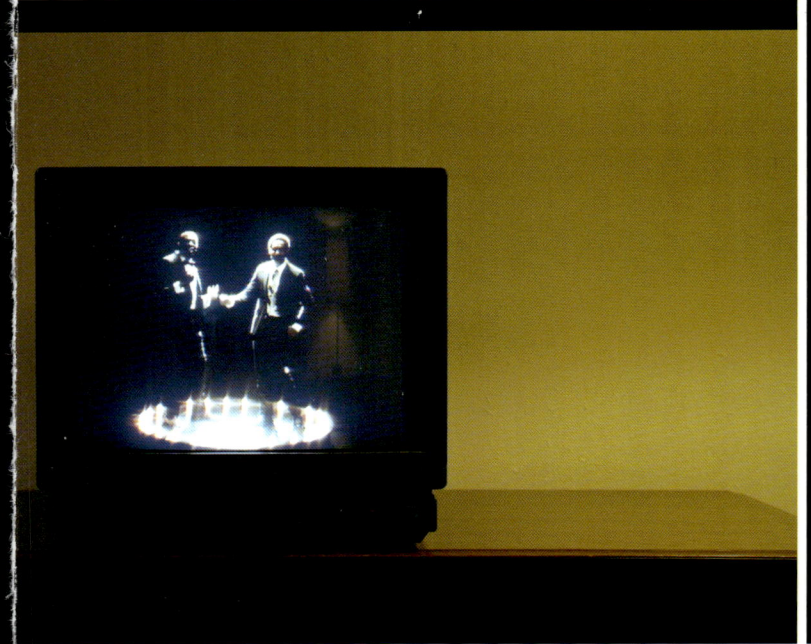
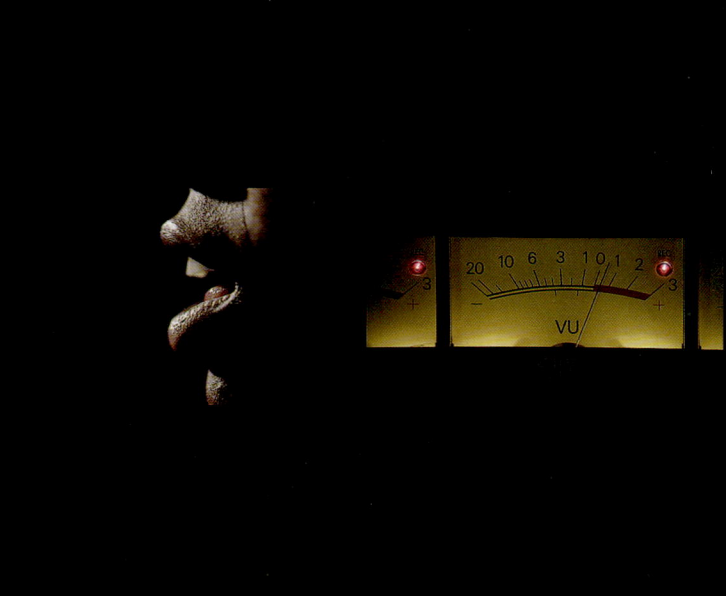
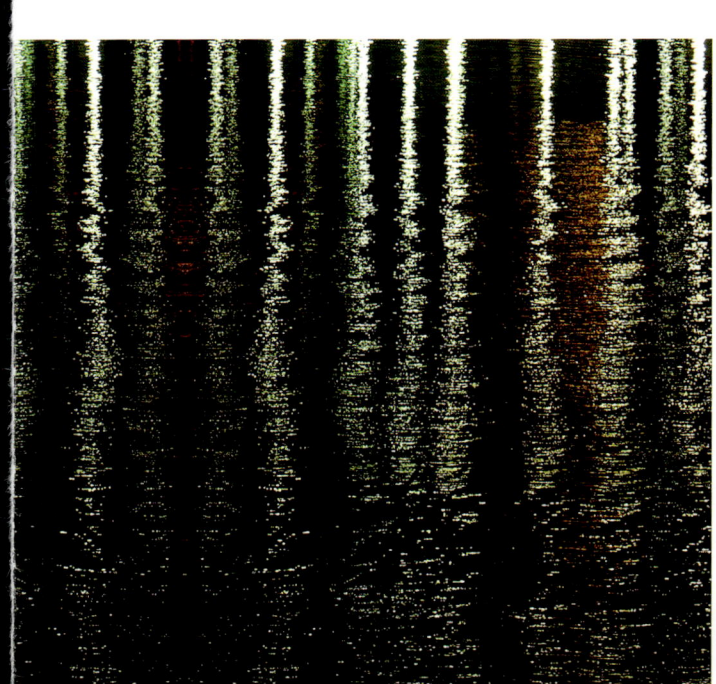
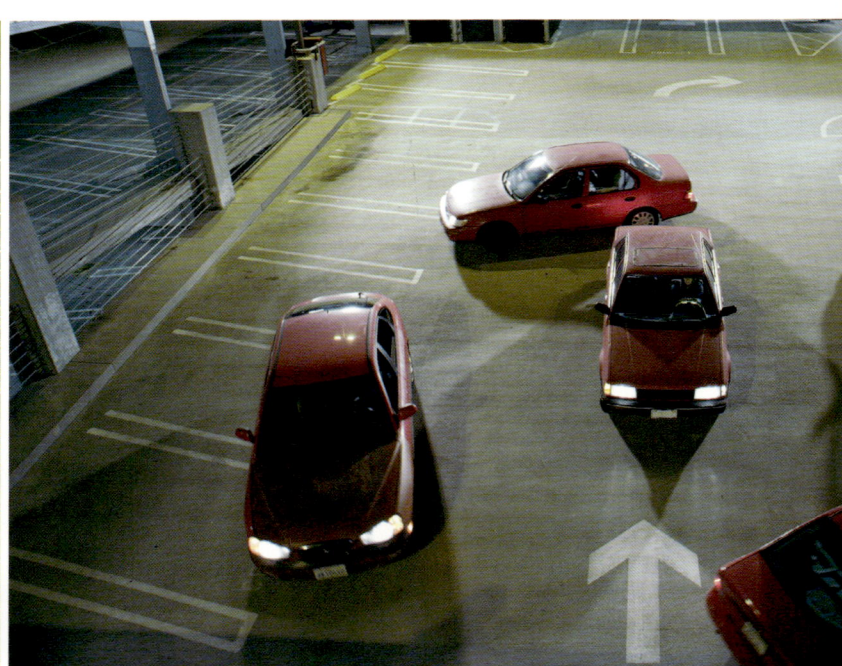

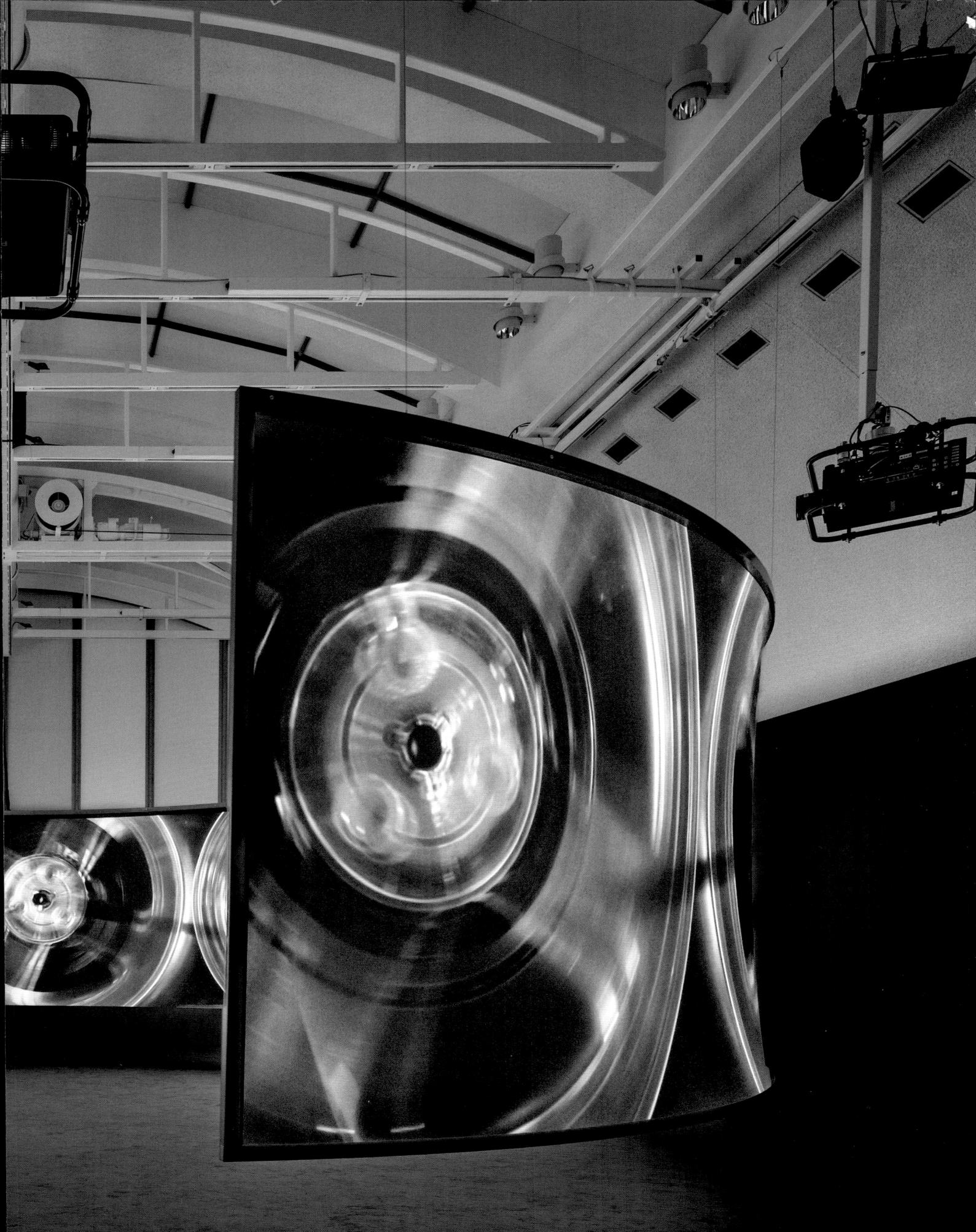

In so many ways, *SONG 1* crystallizes many aspects of Aitken's aesthetic program. The installation version of the work is a hanging circular screen on which the images and the song can be experienced from its center or from the periphery—in it and around it, as people elect to congregate according to their social patterns and desires. *SONG 1* is the architecture of an icon, an iconic song—one you only have ears for. Therefore it constitutes a space where the personal meets the collective and reveals what truly interests Aitken: the space between us, the space we share, the space that is common to many. Throughout his career, he has used his interests in a lineage of experimentations—visual, auditory, scientific, and aesthetic—to carve out this space, where sculpture expands into an architecture to share. And if his aesthetic pulls dry minimalist universality toward perceptual experience defined by the phenomenological model of mass communication, he does so with a resurgence of flower children and the counterculture's ethos. This is clearly visible in his graphic design, applied to his artist's books, posters, and other printed materials, all of which carry the graphic language and DNA of underground design and illustration, an aesthetic of psychedelia, and a familiarity with counterculture ideals and aesthetic movements, and which convey in his work the utopian spirit that fed Antonioni's water-obsessed *Zabriskie Point* (fig. 5).

But Aitken and his work are not subject to nostalgia, and his aesthetic program is also aware that the surface of our ultra-digital-communication world is not homogeneous but is made up of fragments and fractures, as is his. Aitken's forms live between languages, one expressive, one critical; one emancipatory, one as suave as the advertising persuasion; one constrained and ordered, one open; one reductivist, one porous to the natural sensuality of bodies and landscapes—porous to promiscuity, for which sensuality is a promise of something else, an escape from a growing, controlling uniformity and the morphology of mass communication. From this tension emerges an emancipatory and creative space with no walls; a place common to many, to come and contemplate the world, off the grid, where one can say to another, eye to eye: "you are here and so am I."

Notes and Figures

1   In his books, *The Gutenberg Galaxy: The Making of Typographic Man* (1962) and *Understanding Media* (1964), the Canadian professor and philosopher Marshall McLuhan (1911–1980) asserts his idea of a "global village," the notion that our planet and its people are interconnected by a "central nervous system" of communications networks.

2   Douglas Kahn, *Noise Water Meat: A History of Sound in the Arts* (Cambridge, MA: MIT Press, 1999).

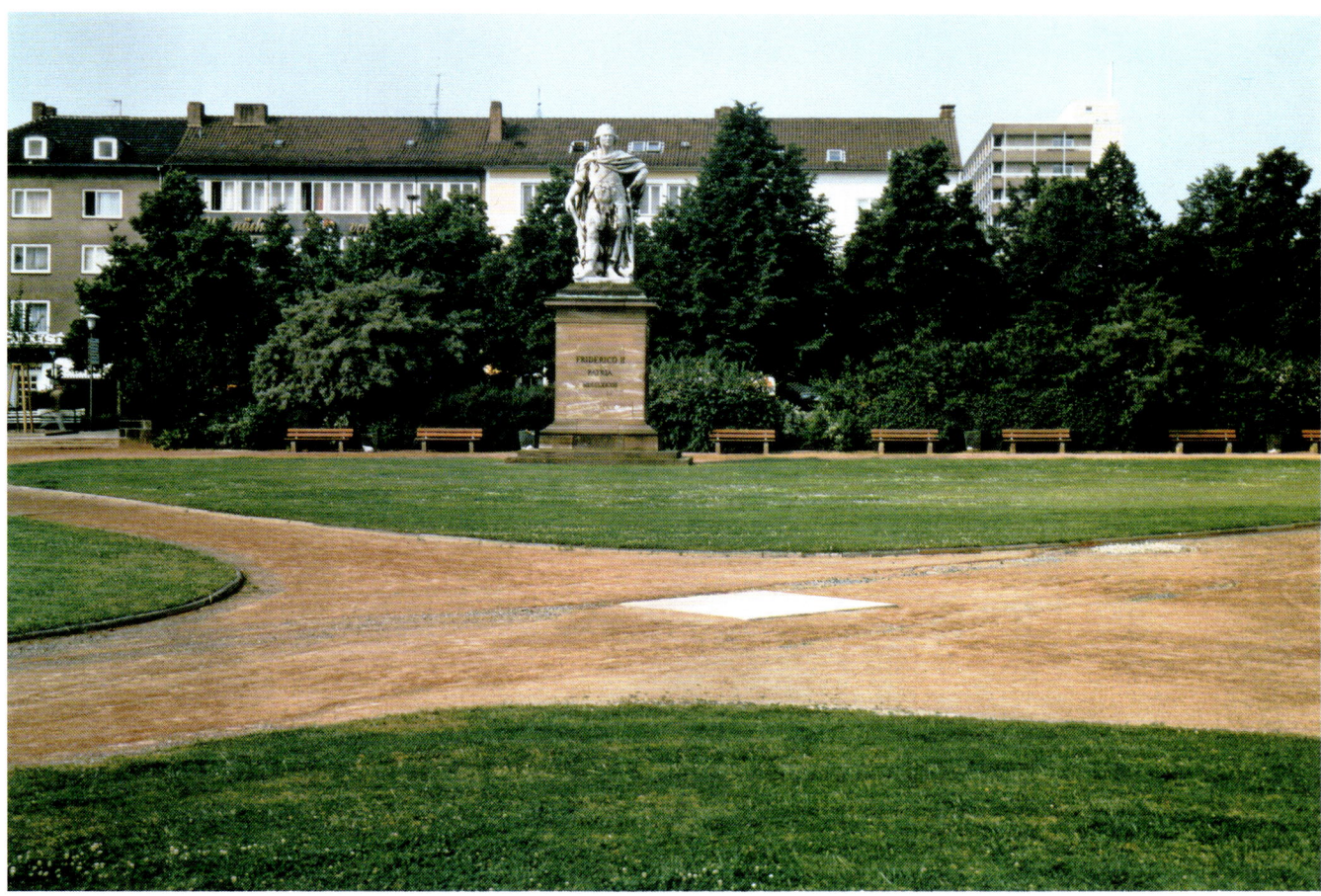

Fig. 1
Walter De Maria
The Vertical Earth Kilometer, 1977
Long-term installation,
Friedrichsplatz Park, Kassel, Germany
Dia Art Foundation
© 2016 The Estate of Walter De Maria
Photo: Nic Tenwiggenhorn.
Courtesy Dia Art Foundation, New York

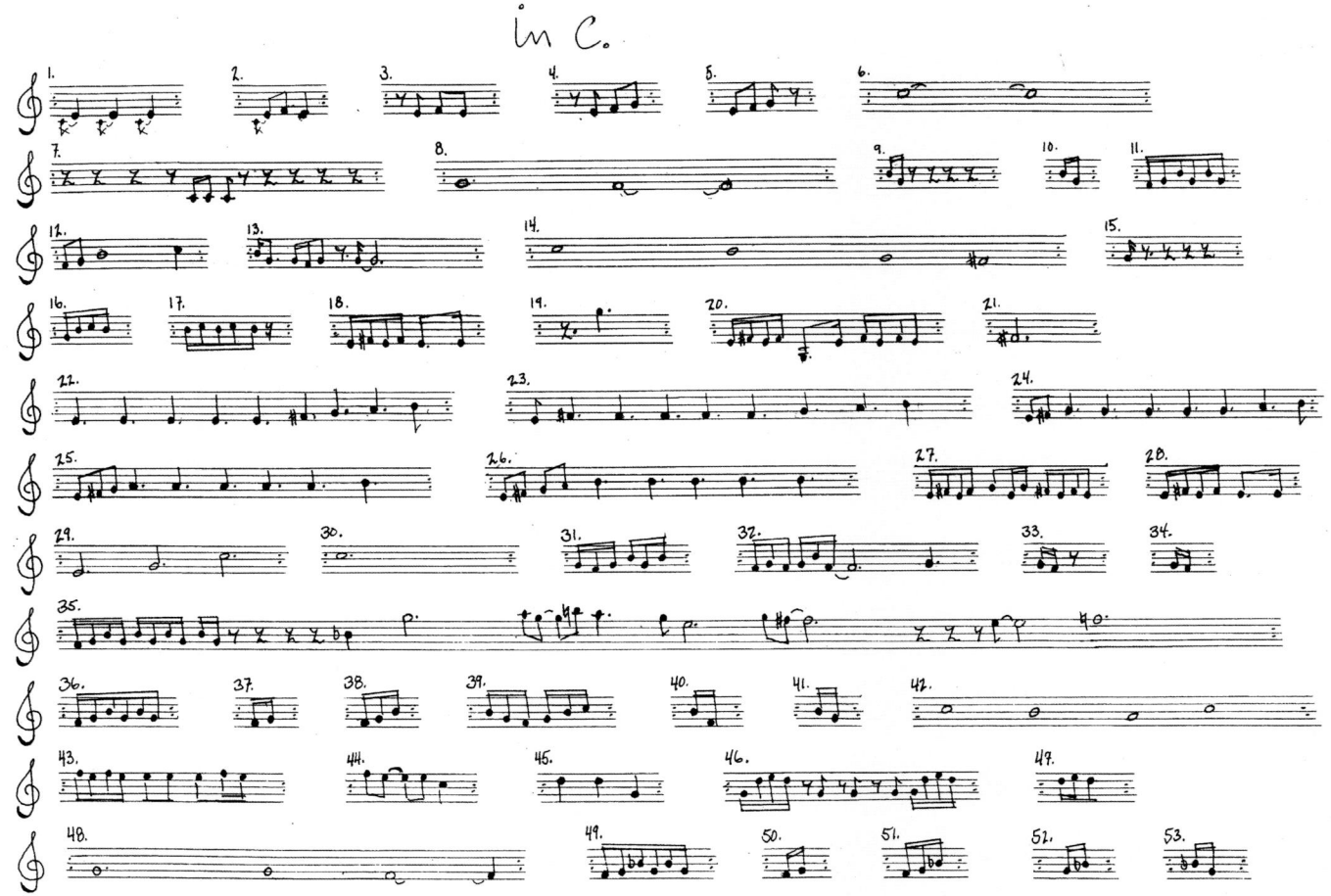

Fig. 2
Terry Riley
Score of *In C,* 1964
© Associated Museum Publishers Inc. [BMI]
International Copyright Secured.
All rights reserved
Reprinted by permission

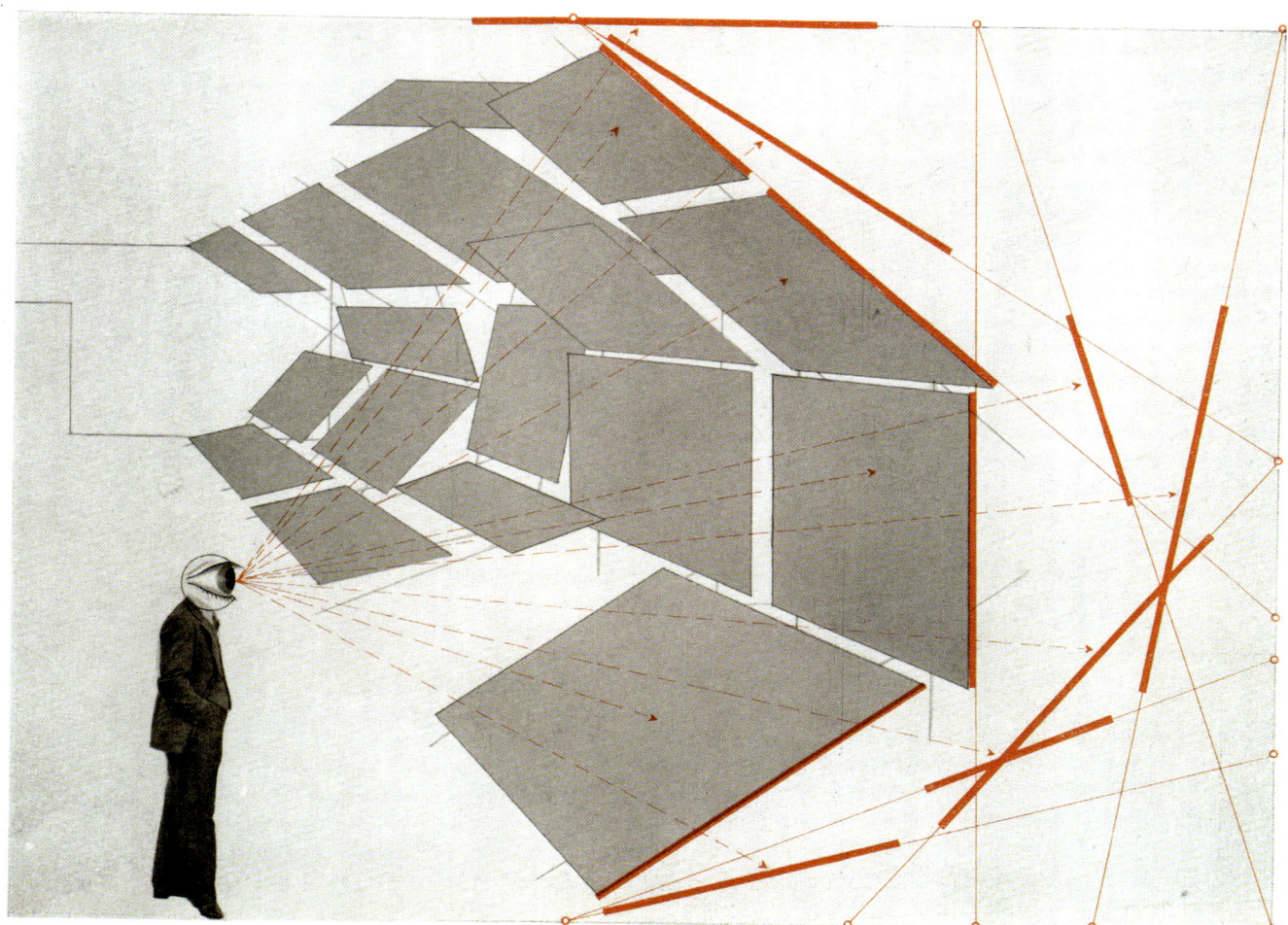

Fig. 3
Herbert Bayer
Diagram of the Field of Vision, c. 1930
Werkbund exhibition Paris,
German Section, Hall 5,
for Werkbundausstellung Paris 1930,
Bauhaus-Archiv Berlin, Inv.nr.: 8712/43
© Herbert Bayer, Artist Rights Society/New York
Photo: Courtesy of the Bauhaus-Archiv Berlin

3   The use of water as an instrument or composition device nevertheless does not begin with Cage, nor does it end with him: Erik Satie suggests the use of the "water chute" in *Sports et Divertissements* (1914) and later in *Parade* (1918). Satie also used a series of tuned bottles hanging from a rack known as a *bouteillophone*. Kurt Schwitters planned for a "water pipe that drips with uninhibited monotony" for his Merz Theater. Marcel Duchamp formulated a "libidinal plumbing" for his *The Bride Stripped Bare by Her Bachelors, Even (The Large Glass)* (1915–23). All of these myriad humid-to-wet investigations, superbly described in Douglas Kahn's *Noise Water Meat*, opened the doors—if not the floodgates—for the Fluxus movement, in which water was at the center of so many events, from George Brecht's *Drip Music* (1959–62) to Robert Whitman's *Water* (1963) and Max Neuhaus's *Water Whistle* (1971).

4   Aitken has worked and collaborated with publicly known figures: actors, musicians, and artists such as Chloë Sevigny, Tilda Swinton, Donald Sutherland, Cat Power, and Ed Ruscha. Doing so invites suspicion of attracting attention via self-serving motives, though I would argue that "working with" celebrities constitutes the deployment of known elements of our collective visual vocabulary. Faces, whether familiar or iconic, suggest backgrounds, histories, and gravitas in Warholian ways that words can neither express nor enumerate. Stars forge potentially illicit alliances, connections, and attachments, and for Aitken, this can resonate as a use of them as "medium." When we recognize, identify with, and relate to stars, we form an aspirational community with the shared culture, temporally saturated with all of its inherent vicissitudes, expectations, and desires.

5   See Adolfo Bioy Casares, *The Invention of Morel*, trans. Ruth L. C. Simms (New York: New York Review Books Classics, 2003).

6   See Alan Weisman, *The World Without Us* (London: Picador, 2008).

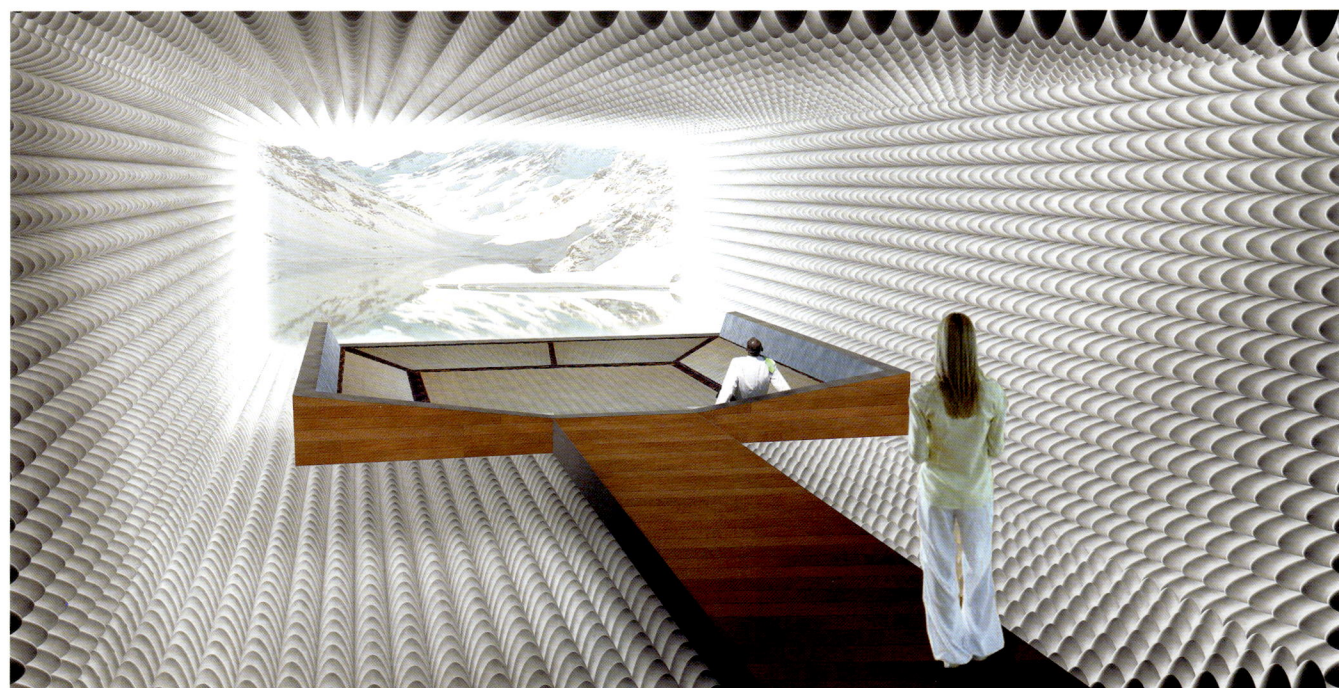

Fig. 4
Doug Aitken
silent pavilion, 2008
Modular, anechoic chamber
architectural installation
[not yet realized]
Dimensions variable
Courtesy of the artist

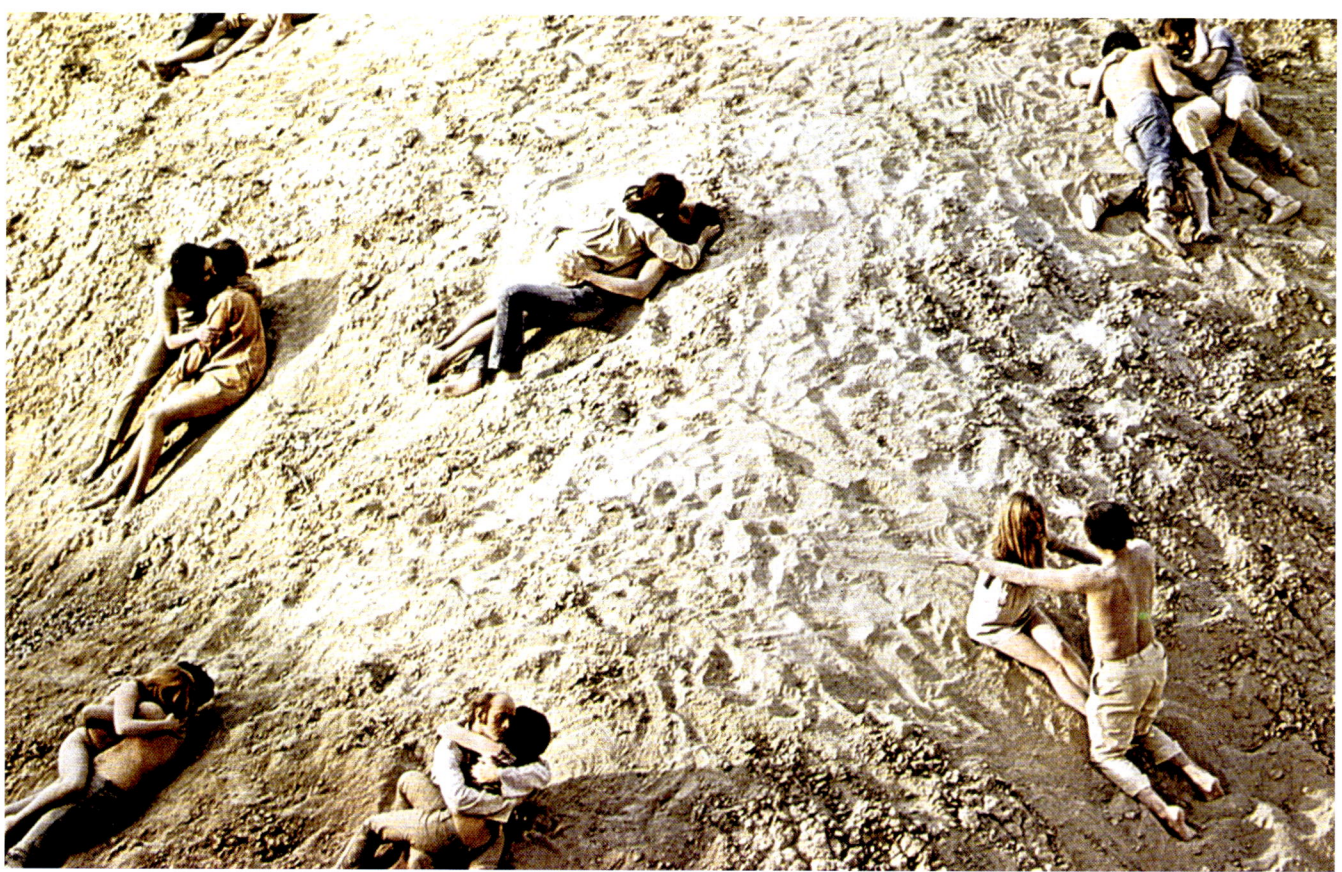

Fig. 5
Michelangelo Antonioni
Still from *Zabriskie Point,* 1969
MGM Studio/SNAP
Photo: © Zuma Press Inc./
Alamy Stock Photo

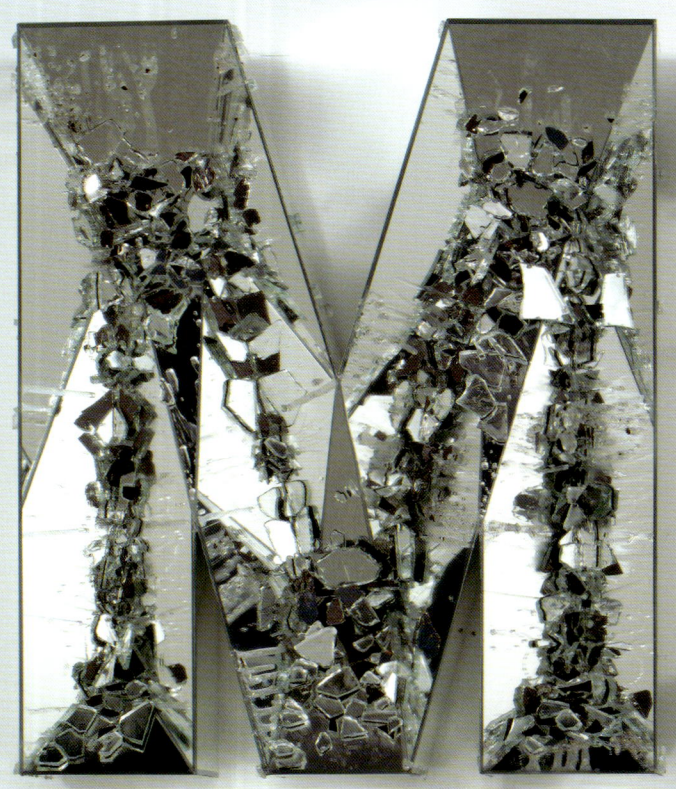
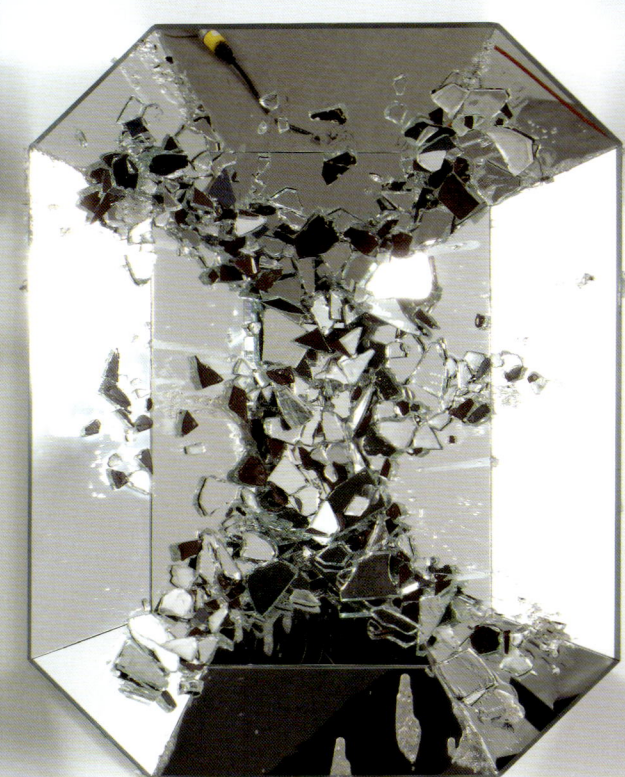
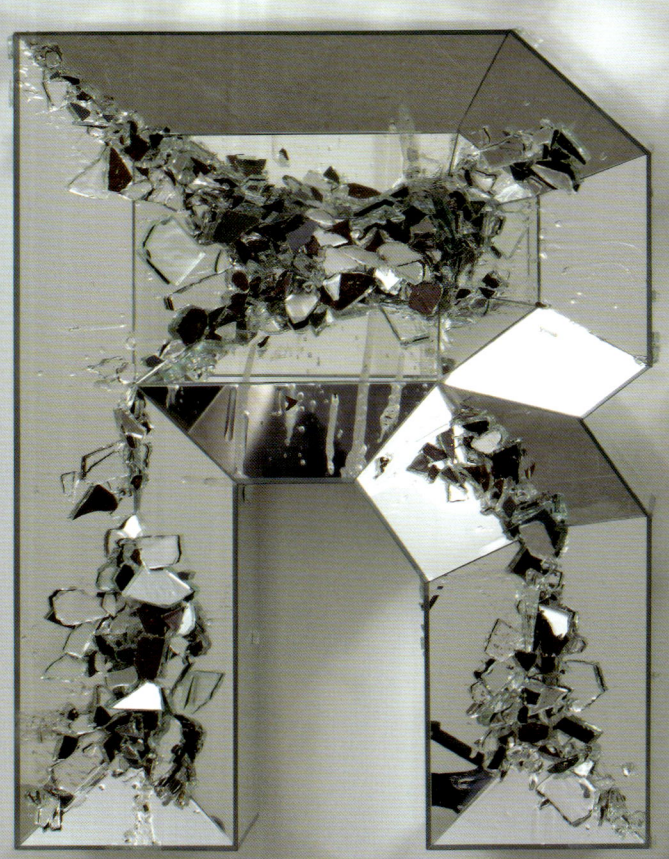
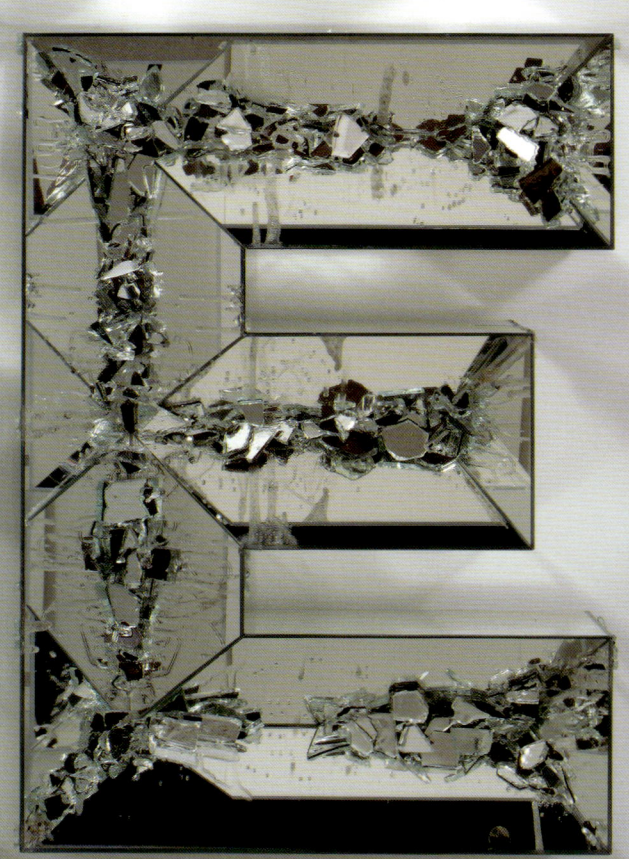

MORE [shattered pour], 2013

Doug Aitken, Mapmaker

Anna Katz

Three wall-hung pairs of letterforms make up Doug Aitken's *Sunset [black]* [2012; pages 58-59]: from left to right, a doubled *S*, an *E* that kisses the bottom of a *U*, and an *N* and a *T* melded edge to edge. The rounded contours of the foam sculpture are clear and precise. At more than six feet wide, the work is hefty and imposing, but scaled to the viewer's body. And as it is addressed to the viewer frontally, as three-dimensional text with planar surfaces, *Sunset [black]* is quite literally legible, self-evident, even. These are its plain, factual qualities.

The term "sunset" also reads as an imperative, a command, directed at the sun, to set, and it is in this mood that the sculpture opens onto ambiguity. As with the majority of Aitken's text sculptures, begun in 2006 with the lightbox work *disappear*, *Sunset [black]* draws on the basic discovery of Saussurean semiotics as it plumbs the arbitrary relationship between signified, the immaterial concept of a sunset, and signifier, a material form that always burns bright [or, in the case of *disappear*, a sculpture whose very presence contravenes its own instruction]. The setting of the sun is the paradigmatic marker of the passage of time. However, stasis and duration are structural features of Aitken's sculpture: the object's backside is outfitted with LEDs that bounce white light off the wall and generate an auratic field of "sunshine," meaning that this sun never sets, never fades. *Sunset [black]* hints that Aitken's sculptures are extracted from a landscape in which the normal rules of time and space, of demarcation and recurrence, do not apply. It is all horizon, all day.

"I like the idea of a word becoming a picture, almost leaving its body, then coming back and becoming a word again," Ed Ruscha has said.[1] In enigmatic word paintings such as *OOF* [1962; reworked 1963] and *Lisp* [1968; fig. 1], Ruscha contaminates long-observed categories of the linguistic and the aesthetic.[2] Like Ruscha, Aitken gives language the commercial-art treatment: isolated, succinct, sleek, designed for maximal visual impact, primed for a hard sell. But both artists do so only to twist these codes of communication. As Yve-Alain Bois has argued, in Ruscha's work typography, rhyme, material [e.g., caviar and axle grease used as paint], and the like may be considered "visual noise"—that is, everything that does not convey information, all that cannot be differentiated as message and recedes into a formless background comprised by the size and scale of letters, phonetic flutter, alliterations, and so on. Bois writes, "No information can ever exist that does not have to rise above an ocean of noise," and Ruscha retrieves that noise, making it palpable, as does Aitken, by endowing language with texture, depth, size, font, color, and imagery of no clear, and sometimes contradictory, relation to the ostensible "information."[3] For instance, the mottled, lava-rock-like surface of *Sunset [black]* evokes the pocked ground of the moon more than the light of the sun, and the black-and-white palette is at odds with the spectrum of colors the sunset scatters across the sky.

In a 2004 conversation between Aitken and Ruscha, the former remarks, "I've been really interested in the idea that we need to find a different way to navigate through information and experience. Maybe we need to find a way that is more dematerialized—lighter, looser and more nomadic. We should be making our own structures that take into account acceleration, and the experience

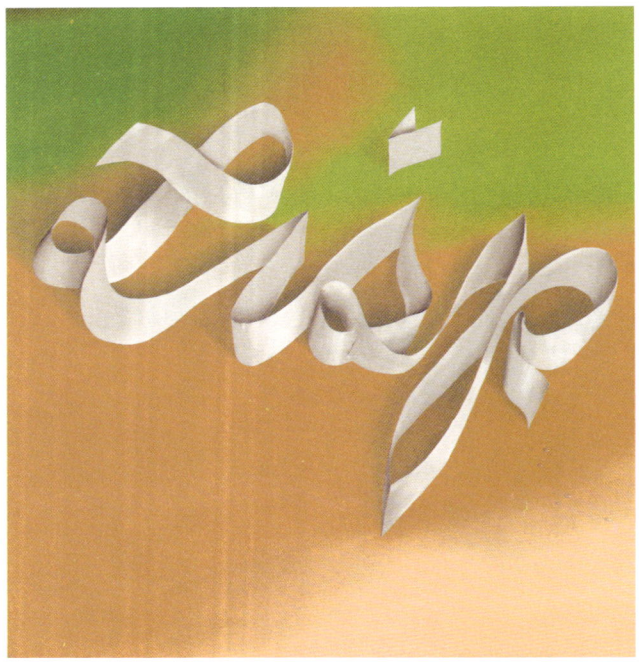

Fig. 1
Ed Ruscha
Lisp, 1968
Oil on canvas
59¼ × 54¾ inches [150.2 × 139.1 cm]
National Gallery of Art, Washington, DC
Gift of the Collectors Committee
2001.56.1
© Ed Ruscha
Photo: Courtesy National Gallery of Art, Washington, DC

of time being more fragmentary."[4] This petition is something of a refrain in Aitken's discussion of his work.[5] "Dematerialized," "fragmented" [or "nonlinear"] time, and "accelerated" are his watchwords, and my essay takes seriously his metaphor of navigation. He frequently asserts that it is incumbent on us to map our relationship to the "landscape of information"[6] that surrounds us: "This digital world is as much a landscape as the physical world, but, in a sense, it still exists completely outside the act of traditional mapping... We're in the process of redefining what landscape is and how to map it."[7] Urgency motivates Aitken's inquiry: "How do we evolve perceptually to sustain and thrive in it [the 'landscape of information']?"[8]

Aitken's text sculptures are signs; their semiotic plays announce as much. I propose that we also think of them as *signposts*, like buoys. In a 2010 article on the navigational, rather than mimetic, interpretation of maps, spurred by the advent of digital navigation, Eduardo Camacho-Hübner, Bruno Latour, and Valérie November contend that the grip of the "base map," which inscribes only the most material, physical reality, must be loosened.[9] We are advised to recollect Borges's lesson that the territory is not the map when Camacho-Hübner, Latour, and November clarify that the navigator inside the cabin of a yacht is not looking for a relation of resemblance between map and territory [or between words and worlds]; rather, the relationship between map and territory is one of detection of relevant cues that allow her to go through heterogeneous sets of data points [a "maze of data"] from one signpost to the next.[10] Considered as signposts, Aitken's sculptures equip us to navigate territories at once physical, informational, and social, to locate simultaneously material and immaterial sites—juxtaposed sites that are decidedly, meaningfully incompatible—and to find our way through new conceptions of spatiality and temporality.[11]

It must be said, to submit that sculpture of all mediums—solid, stationary, museum bound—furnishes "a different way to navigate through information and experience" is counterintuitive, especially given that "liquidity" amounts to a maxim for Aitken, and perhaps betrays the artist's adamant disregard for medium boundaries.[12] In fact, it is precisely the curiousness of sculpture as a response to Aitken's appeal that quickens me. "Dematerialized," "light," and "nomadic" are key attributes of sculpture, after all. One simply has to recall Clement Greenberg on David Smith's weightless "drawings in space,"[13] and the high-modernist protocols of mass sublated into syntax and of incorporeal materials that yield to the virtual; or Rosalind Krauss's canonical 1979 essay, "Sculpture in the Expanded Field," in which she diagnoses the condition of modernist sculpture as essentially nomadic, siteless or homeless, and operating in relation to an absolute loss of place.[14] Further, it is exactly the attempt to represent information, or content, as a solid, a thing, an object—nay, a sculpture—that makes this body of work so compelling. For in the "landscape of information that surrounds us," word and image alike are transmitted, coded, and received as so much data. As Aitken describes it, "language is reduced to electronic pulses; experiences are boiled down to single images; and human exchanges are often short, fleeting messages."[15] Yet in their very objecthood, Aitken's sculptures defy the presumption that information is purely immaterial or free.[16]

Buoys are to be steered clear of. Here again, the comparison to Ruscha is fruitful. Both Ruscha's and Aitken's chosen words possess a generic, nonspecific quality. Aitken's lexicon includes: "more," "sunset," "disappear," "yes," "west," "utopia," "bad," "riot," "sex," "now," "art," and "end," expressionless terms that would seem to provoke associations too broad to be ascribed to any one place and time, much less to the artist's private feelings or personal preoccupations. In Ruscha's vocabulary we discover commonality in a shared folk vernacular based on brand names and corporate logos and on the found language of jokes and clichés.[17] While Ruscha's words belong to everyone and may be held in common, Aitken's pack, like a loaded gun, the implication that we belong to them, that we are held by them. Take, for example, Aitken's MORE [shattered pour] [2013; page 184], a mirror-clad sculpture that cuts the word "more" like a gem and smashes it along the letterforms' faceted edges. Just as the reflective surfaces ensnare us, "more" takes us hostage, since the demand that "more" levies is insatiable. In principle, the desire of "more" cannot be slaked, and so we sense ourselves to be the thrall of "more." There is, as another of Aitken's sculptures drums, "not enough time in the day" for "more." Sunset [black] and MORE [shattered pour] are connected conceptually to NOT ENOUGH TIME IN THE DAY [2013; fig. 2], a flat white panel in which the doubling of raised linear black text suggests the blurred vision of extreme fatigue or the unfocused vacancy of the "machine zone," and a flash of light, scrolling from top to bottom, evokes the incessant, blasé signal emitted by an unplayed slot machine or arcade game.[18] As signposts, all three works mark the reformatting of time by a social and economic landscape digitized, technologically rationalized, and financialized to an extent still only quite recently unimaginable.[19]

In his bracing polemic, 24/7: Late Capitalism and the Ends of Sleep, Jonathan Crary characterizes the round-the-clock world of global capitalism as illuminated without shadows. Markets and informational networks do not rest, and human subjects are made to coincide with "a global infrastructure for continuous work and consumption."[20] Nonstop processes of production and consumption are eroding our relation to the "rhythmic and periodic textures of human life," Crary remonstrates.[21] He contends that capitalism steals our time from us, even and particularly sleep—sleep, which is essential as respite and a radical, if partial, interruption of "the unsparing weight of our global present."[22] Sleep, he insists, is our last unleveraged activity and thus our last hope for dreaming up alternative futures.

In a particularly devastating passage, Crary briefly glosses the machine-based designation of "sleep mode," as built into smartphones and other wirelessly connected electronic devices, proposing that "the notion of an apparatus in a state of low-power readiness remakes the larger sense of sleep into simply a deferred or diminished condition of operationality and access." "Continuous functioning" (another of Crary's terms) shores up my meaning when I write that we are beholden to Aitken's words. Continuous functioning is the waking nightmare of *Sunset [black]*, *MORE [shattered pour]*, and *NOT ENOUGH TIME IN THE DAY*, for sleep mode jettisons the logic of on/off and ensures that nothing (or no one) is ever fundamentally off.[23] The sculptural trio calibrates time bereaved of an actual state of rest—time without night, the never-endingness of more, the requirements of productivity and efficiency that squeeze more and more out of us.

As many readers will recognize, when Crary submits that a 24/7 environment must be distinguished from the empty, homogenous time of modernity, and instead that "what is new is the sweeping abandonment of the pretense that time is coupled to any long-term undertakings, even to fantasies of 'progress' or development," he is implying an argument that has been cultivated across the social sciences and humanities for some time now.[24] Roughly, this argument postulates the end of linear time, and its attendant promise of a progressive, teleological, or evolutionary unfolding of world events, and inaugurates the so-called spatial turn. There is no dearth of scholarship on the displacement of temporality as the organizing principle of economic, cultural, and social relations by an apprehension of the spatiality of our epoch, its cognates being, variously, late capitalism, globalism, and postmodernism. Whether we recall Jean Baudrillard's theorization of postmodern hyperspace, Jean-François Lyotard's death announcement for grand or master narratives, Doreen Massey's concept of power geometries, or Edward Soja's pronouncements on the end of historicism, it is not unreasonable to say that spatialization has replaced linearity with peripheries, geographies, relative positionalities, and multiplicities.[25] This clarifies another important function of sculpture in navigating fragmented experiences of time, for it is the medium whose primary dispensation is space, and in contemporary thought, space implicates nonlinearity.[26]

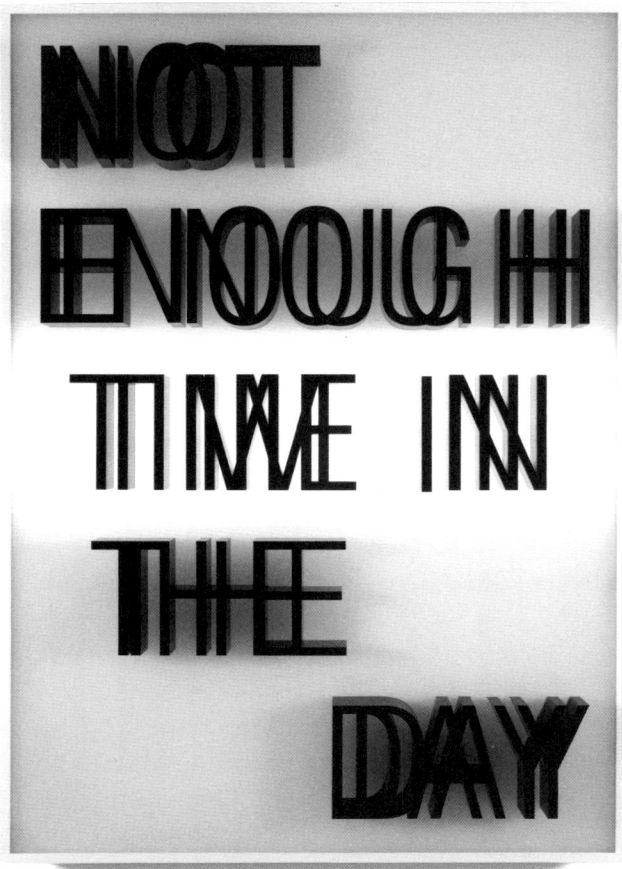

Fig. 2
Doug Aitken
NOT ENOUGH TIME IN THE DAY, 2013
Aluminum and acrylic lightbox, LEDs, acrylic letters
96¼ × 67¼ × 10 inches (245.1 × 170.8 × 25.4 cm)
Photo: John Berens, courtesy of the artist

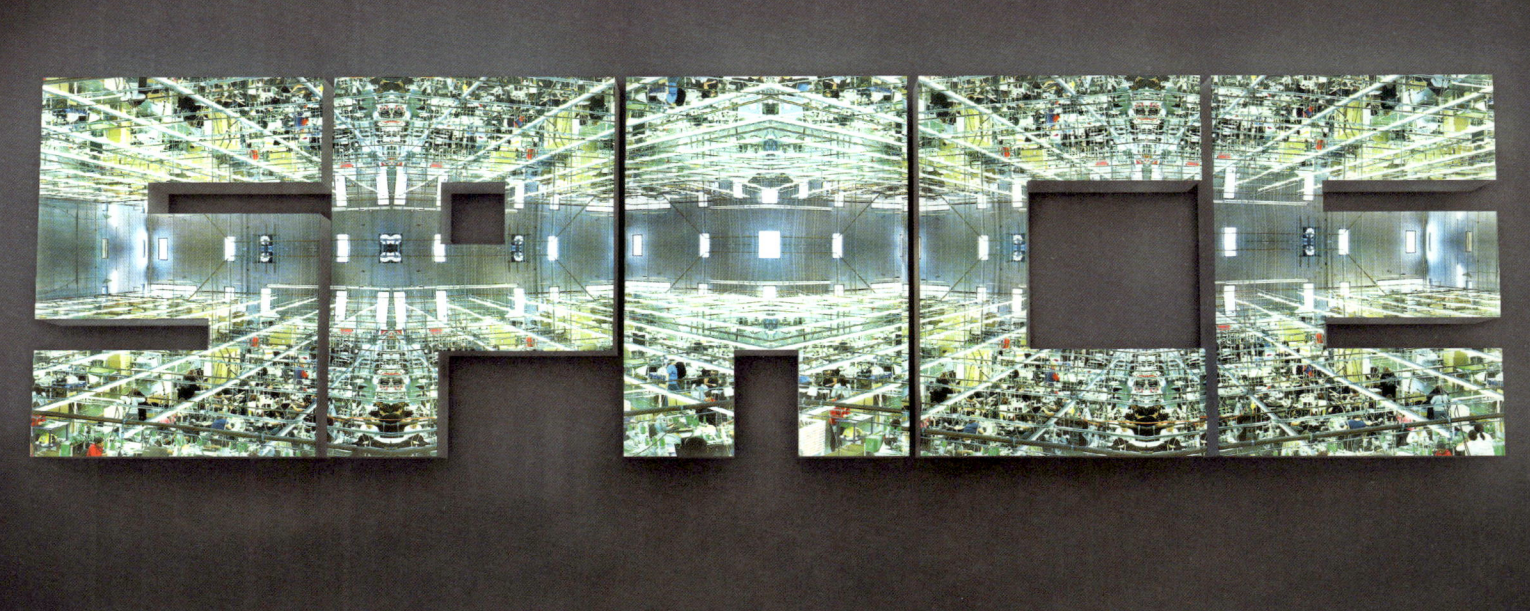

Of course, the sticky wicket (the razor's edge that Aitken's work walks) is that simultaneity and instantaneity, as opposed to temporality and history, are the alpha and omega of late capitalism's hallucination of an abstract global space of frictionless flows of information, capital, goods, and people. Unfettered mobility and "free trade" are the guiding lights of the neoliberal sublime—an image of a single, fully interconnected global present (think Francis Fukuyama or Thomas Friedman).[27] It hardly requires explication that the ethos of global mobility is well and good until, as Doreen Massey puts it, an asylum seeker crosses a boundary and the reality of border discipline makes abundantly clear that borderlessness is the privilege of capital, the rich, and the skilled, who move about the world as investment, trade, and tourism.[28]

Aitken makes us acutely aware of these terms, perhaps never more so than with his lightbox sculpture SPACE (2012; fig. 3). It consists of five wall-mounted units, all hard right angles and perfectly perpendicular and parallel lines. The glowing surface, a photographic transparency illuminated by LEDs, provides a kaleidoscopic view of an industrial interior, a textile factory in which converging lines of fluorescent lights hang above rows of workstations, tangled coils of electrical cables, and bolts of green fabric. The image multiplies symmetrically across horizontal and vertical axes. Thus, the structure of repetition subtending the image mimics the principle of the capitalist mode of production— the repetitive labor of the assembly line. The fact that it at first looks like a circuit board redoubles the fantasy of networked

Fig. 3
Doug Aitken
SPACE, 2012
Chromogenic transparency on acrylic in aluminum lightbox with LEDs
34¼ × 126¾ × 7½ inches (87 × 321.9 × 19.1 cm)
Photo: Stefan Altenburger, courtesy of the artist

labor. As an image of interchangeability across a single homogeneous plane that, theoretically, could be elaborated infinitely, *SPACE* pictures the ideology of instantaneous spatiality.

Yet as a sculpture, *SPACE* is rather more peculiar and ambiguous. First, like *Sunset [black]* and Ruscha's word paintings, it is visually "noisy," thwarting the communication of "pure information" by saddling the word with color, font, size, imagery—with excess, with friction. And second, as with all of Aitken's text sculptures, *SPACE* scrambles deeply entrenched art-historical codes. For centuries, word and image have been figured agonistically, and aligned with time and space, respectively. This is the insistence of Lessing's 1766 *Laocoön* essay, a founding document of the modernist belief in the irreducible difference of each discipline and its method of self-criticism. Lessing reasons that since painting and sculpture use different signs thanW poetry—figures and colors in space for painting and sculpture, articulated sounds in time for poetry—it follows that signs that coexist can only express objects that coexist, and signs that follow one another can only express objects that are consecutive. Since the eighteenth century, painting and sculpture have been located along a static, spatial axis of atemporal simultaneity, while poetry and the discursive arts have been located along a dynamic axis of temporal succession.[29] By crossing these wires, sending mixed signals—here, making space verbal and a word dimensional—Aitken plots impossible, but vital, coordinates of spatiality without instantaneity, temporality without linearity.

"We're living in a new topography," Aitken has commented. "Is it possible to be everywhere and nowhere?"[30] The quandary that Aitken's mirror-clad sculptures stage pertains to the experience of being here and elsewhere, whether that be everywhere or nowhere. The large scale and hard edges of *NOW [Blue Mirror]* [2014; pages 72-73] lend it an assertive, commanding presence. But the term "now" is slippery and unstable, as the moment it indexes immediately, inevitably becomes the just-past and is replaced by a newer, transient "now." This is not strictly a linguistic problem of the category of the shifter but a question of hypermediation, too. One thinks of another work grappling with the constraints on "now," Lynda Benglis's video *Now* [1973; fig. 4], in which she tries to conform physically in the present time of the video to recorded images of her own face in close-up, treating the monitor as a mirror. The two Benglises attempt to direct and obey each other—to communicate to and be present for the other—uttering the commands "Now!" and "Start recording!" The now of the meeting is never achieved. Benglis's *Now* takes to task video's claims of immediacy and authenticity. The anxiety plaguing Benglis is whether "directness of vision" and presence can survive translation and reproduction by "technological media," and with Aitken, added to that is self-contained, decentralized communication and a schizophrenic attention span imposed by unprecedented degrees of saturating technological mediation.[31]

I regard *1968 [broken]* [2011; pages 88-89] as a pendant to *NOW [Blue Mirror]*. The year it identifies functions as shorthand for the

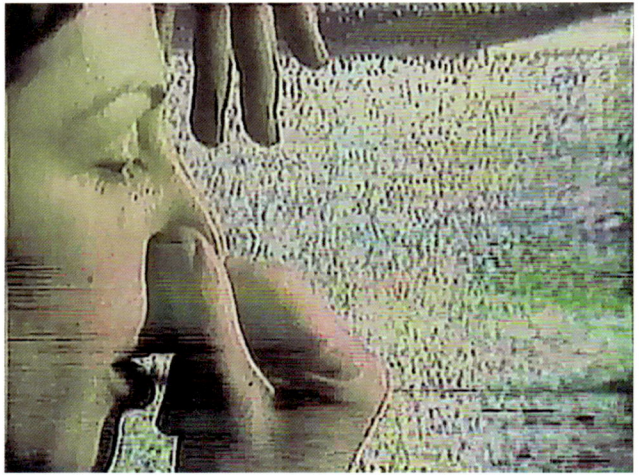

radical, utopian uprisings of the 1960s (it is Aitken's year of birth, as well). 1968 is also a cipher for the investigations of advanced art during that period—vesting the spatiotemporal phenomenological present, tethering artwork to a specific site, putting the gallery under scrutiny—and *1968 (broken)* digests them. Most notably, with its shattered surface and its mirrors positioned to multiply reflections, it summons Robert Smithson, who pointedly deployed mirrors, as with *Mirage No. 1* (1967; fig. 5), to refract and diffract the viewer's vision, dispersing it across a disjunctive temporal and spatial field and producing perceptual confusion and cognitive hiccups in order to instantiate the decentering, fragmenting effects of entropy. For Smithson, the mirror, like language, was a displacement, a nonsite.

Michel Foucault analyzes mirrors as nonsites (his term is "counter-sites") with great insight in his beloved, if short, essay "Of Other Spaces": "In the mirror, I see myself there where I am not, in an unreal virtual space that opens up behind the surface: I am over there, there where I am not, a sort of shadow that gives my own visibility to myself, that enables me to see myself there where I am absent." Such is the utopia of the mirror, Foucault tells us. He typologizes two kinds of spaces that are linked with other kinds of spaces, yet still contradict those other sites: utopias and heterotopias. While utopias are sites with no real place, possessing a relationship of direct or inverted analogy with the real space of society, or "unreal spaces," heterotopias are counter-sites, in which all the real sites that can be found within the culture are "simultaneously represented, contested, and inverted." He deems them heterotopias on the basis of their difference from all the other sites that they reflect and speak about.[32] Thus, a mirror is both a utopia and a heterotopia in Foucault's analysis, for the mirror exists in reality, "where it exerts a sort of counteraction on the position that I occupy": "It makes this place that I occupy at the moment when I look at myself in the glass at once absolutely real, connected with all the space that surrounds it, and absolutely unreal, since in order to be perceived it has to pass through this virtual point which is over there."[33]

There are heterotopias in every culture, in every civilization, but what occasions Foucault's discussion is the definition of the "epoch of space" in which we live— the epoch of "simultaneity," "juxtaposition,"

Fig. 4
Lynda Benglis
Now, 1973
Video (color, sound)
Running time: 12 min.
© Lynda Benglis/Licensed by VAGA, New York
Photo: Courtesy of the Video Data Bank

"the near and far," "the side-by-side," "the dispersed." Rather than conceive of our experience of the world in linear terms, like a "long life developing through time," Foucault describes a "network that connects points and intersects with its own skein."[34] The mirror is a heterotopia, and so is the museum, for in it time "never stops building up and topping its own summit." The museum demonstrates a will to "enclose in one place all times, all epochs, all forms, all tastes."[35] What matters about heterotopias—what matters about museums, mirrors, words—is that they are capable of juxtaposing in a single real place several spaces, several sites that are themselves incompatible. Spaces of otherness, they can contest the spaces in which we live.[36]

Aitken's text sculptures heterotopically link the counter-site of the museum to sites of information, to the abstract "depthless instantaneity"[37] of 24/7 techno-global capitalism, and, of course, to the commercial landscape, that forest of signs. Again, I want to say, following Camacho-Hübner, Latour, and November, that Aitken's buoy-like sculptures provide clues for the navigator making her way through heterogeneous data and territories, from one signpost to the next. For example, the neon sculpture *99c dreams* [2007; pages 102-103] operates like a commercial sign, of the order one encounters in every sector of private-interest-held public space, from strip malls to boulevards. But it advertises no good or service, peddling only a quizzical, almost oracular, and surrealist-inflected idea, a dream of sleep. In this, Aitken's word-based sculptures have an affinity with Jack Pierson's arrangements of appropriated movie-marquee and storefront lettering, such as *You are Allowed to Touch Things* [1991; fig. 6], which betrays a deep sense of yearning and loneliness. *You are Allowed to Touch Things* is triply oriented toward the commercial landscape, toward the artist's social context at the time of its making— the height of the HIV/AIDS epidemic in New York, when many members of Pierson's gay community were ostracized by the unfounded fear that the virus was transmissible through everyday human contact—and toward the environment of art in which it is seen, as it irreverently invites viewers to violate a sanctified rule and touch art. Similarly, Aitken's tondo lightbox work WHAT WE DID WAS

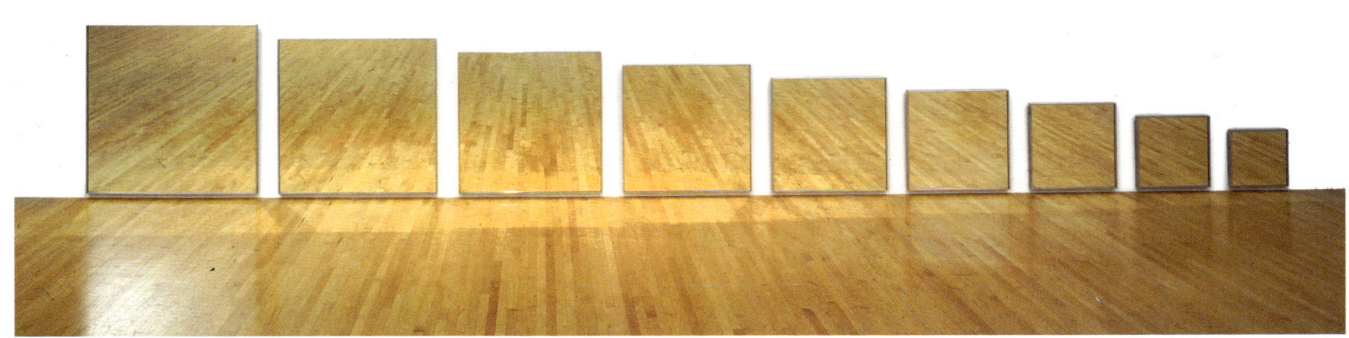

Fig. 5
Robert Smithson
Mirage No. 1, 1967
Nine units of mirrored glass
Overall 36¼ × 253¼ × 1 inches [92.4 × 343.26 × 2.54 cm]
The Museum of Contemporary Art, Los Angeles
Purchased with funds provided by the Collectors Committee
© Holt-Smithson Foundation/Licensed by VAGA, New York
Photo: The Museum of Contemporary Art, Los Angeles

STAND AROUND AND WAIT FOR SOMETHING TO HAPPEN [2011; pages 90–91] mimics the most basic image-with-text layout strategies from print advertising, but only to ventriloquize the viewer's encounter with the selfsame work of art, locating her both here in the museum and in an incompatibly other place: some very real—but inverted, contested—airport corridor, bus shelter, or urban facade, once again encroached on by an advertisement.

In the closing lines of "Of Other Spaces," Foucault proclaims the ship to be the heterotopia par excellence. It is not only the great instrument of economic development—the ship is also simultaneously "the greatest reserve of the imagination." The famous, fecund last sentence of Foucault's essay reads: "In civilizations without boats, dreams dry up, espionage takes the place of adventure, and the police take the place of pirates."[38] This is why I think of Aitken as a pirate of the "ocean of noise," taking what is not rightfully his [advertising and commerce, information, 24/7 time], in order to claim it for poetry, for sculpture, for the museum, for the public.

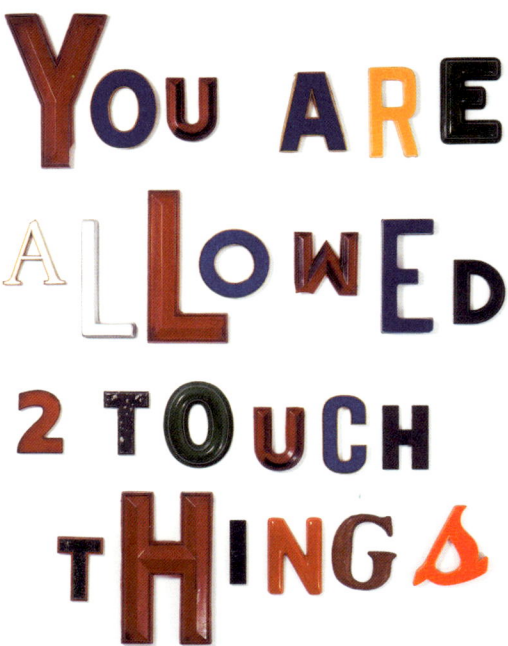

Fig. 6
Jack Pierson
You are Allowed to Touch Things, 1991
Plastic, wood, and metal
89 × 77 × 2 inches [226.1 × 195.6 × 5.1 cm]
The Museum of Contemporary Art, Los Angeles
Gift of Alan N. Kleinman from the Estate of Marsha Kleinman
© Courtesy of Cheim & Read, New York
Photo: The Museum of Contemporary Art, Los Angeles

Notes

1   Ed Ruscha, quoted in Hal Foster, *The First Pop Age: Painting and Subjectivity in the Art of Hamilton, Lichtenstein, Warhol, Richter, and Ruscha* (Princeton, NJ: Princeton University Press, 2012), 219.

2   Yve-Alain Bois, "Thermometers Should Last Forever," *October* 111 (Winter 2005): 62.

3   Ibid.

4   Ed Ruscha, "Earth Is the Alien Planet: Doug Aitken Talks to Ed Ruscha," interview by Doug Aitken, *Frieze* 84 (June-August 2004): 105. A version of this interview is published in Aitken's artist's book *Broken Screen: Expanding the Image, Breaking the Narrative: 26 Conversations with Doug Aitken,* ed. Noel Daniel (New York: D.A.P./Distributed Art Publishers, 2006).

5   As just two examples:
"I want viewers to feel that they can follow different roads simultaneously. This is what I find intriguing: the idea of no longer being on one highway, but on a journey of many roads"; see Doug Aitken, "In Conversation with Hans Ulrich Obrist," interview by Hans Ulrich Obrist, *Doug Aitken: 100 YRS,* ed. Karen Marta (New York: Rizzoli, 2013), n.p.
"I think that we do find ourselves increasingly in flux, we do find our lives uprooted. We find ourselves in contact with larger and larger degrees of information and within these changing levels of perception we also have to come up with new patterns of how to deal with it, how to survive"; see Anders Kold, "Doug Aitken—Art at the Edge of the World," *Doug Aitken: RISE* exhibition catalogue (Humlebæk, Denmark: Louisiana Museum of Art, 2002), 22.

6   Doug Aitken, quoted in Pierre Huyghe, "Pierre Huyghe," interview by Doug Aitken, *BOMB* 89 (Fall 2004): http://bombmagazine.org/article/2669/pierre-huyghe.

7   Aitken, "In Conversation with Hans Ulrich Obrist."

8   Aitken, quoted in Huyghe, "Pierre Huyghe."

9   Eduardo Camacho-Hübner, Bruno Latour, and Valérie November, "Entering a Risky Territory: Space in the Age of Digital Navigation," *Environment and Planning D: Society and Space* 28 (2010): 581-82. In an interview between Aitken and curator Hans Ulrich Obrist, the latter cites Camacho-Hübner, Latour, and November's essay; see Aitken, "In Conversation with Hans Ulrich Obrist."

10   Camacho-Hübner, Latour, and November, "Entering a Risky Territory," 585-86.

11   I am also compelled by the metaphor of navigation because in this same conversation with Ruscha, Aitken recounts a two-day trip he had recently taken in which he traveled up the Los Angeles River in a small boat, saying, "Even though it's a joke of a river, [I felt] I would understand the narrative of the land a little bit better"; see Ruscha, "Earth Is the Alien Planet," 105.

12   While Aitken has not spoken widely about his sculptures, he articulates the thinking behind his mirror-based sculptures in a recent catalogue essay. According to the artist, the aim of conventional cinema is to "create an engagement with narrative," drawing viewers in so that they "lose time, finding themselves inside the story." The novel approach of the mirrored works is to accomplish this directly, cutting out the middleman, so to speak: "I thought, if I extend the notion of reflectivity that plays out in my films and apply it to sculpture, the viewer becomes *the* subject. The mirrored sculptures enact an economy whereby the intermediary is taken out of the equation and the viewer becomes *the film.*" The viewer is repositioned as a filmic protagonist. See Joseph Akel, "A Sign of the Times," *Doug Aitken* exhibition catalogue (Frankfurt: Schirn Kunsthalle Frankfurt; Vienna: Verlag für moderne Kunst, 2015), 108.

13   Clement Greenberg, "The Pasted-Paper Revolution" (1958), in *The Collected Essays and Criticism,* vol. 4: *Modernism with a Vengeance, 1957-1969,* ed. John O'Brian (Chicago: University of Chicago Press, 1993), 64-65; see also Alex Potts, *The Sculptural Imagination: Figurative, Modernist, Minimalist* (2000; repr., New Haven: Yale University Press, 2009), esp. 145-77.

14   Rosalind Krauss, "Sculpture in the Expanded Field" (1979), in *The Anti-Aesthetic: Essays on Postmodern Culture,* ed. Hal Foster (Port Townsend, WA: Bay Press, 1983).

15   Aitken, "In Conversation with Hans Ulrich Obrist."

16   I mean to invoke both senses of "free" here—*gratis* and *libre,* or free beer and free speech—and I have in mind both the massive data centers, copper wires, and fiber-optic cables on which the cloud depends (and through which the cloud uses about thirty billion watts of electricity worldwide, equivalent to the output of thirty nuclear power plants) and technologies of surveillance, tracking, and targeting. I direct the reader to James Glanz, "Power, Pollution and the Internet," *New York Times,* September 22, 2012, http://nytimes.com/2012/09/23/technology/data-centers-waste-vast-amounts-of-energy-belying-industry-image.html; Metahaven, "Captives of the Cloud: Part II," *e-flux* 38 (October 2012): http://e-flux.com/journal/captives-of-the-cloud-part-ii; and Hito Steyerl, "The Spam of the Earth: Withdrawal from Representation," *e-flux* 32 (February 2012): http://e-flux.com/journal/the-spam-of-the-earth.

17   See Foster, *The First Pop Age*, esp. 210–47.

18   The "machine zone" is anthropologist Natasha Schüll's term for the extreme form of zone that players of slot machines enter: hypnotized, entranced, one's sense of time, space, and even self are annihilated; see Alexis C. Madrigal, "The Machine Zone: This Is Where You Go When You Just Can't Stop Looking at Pictures on Facebook," *Atlantic*, July 31, 2013, http://theatlantic.com/technology/archive/2013/07/the-machine-zone-this-is-where-you-go-when-you-just-cant-stop-looking-at-pictures-on-facebook/278185.

19   All three were shown in Aitken's *Gesamtkunstwerk*-like exhibition *100 YRS* at 303 Gallery, New York, from February 1 to March 30, 2013.

20   Jonathan Crary, *24/7: Late Capitalism and the Ends of Sleep* (London: Verso, 2013), 3.

21   Ibid., 9.

22   Ibid., 128.

23   Ibid., 8, 13.

24   Ibid., 9.

25   Doreen Massey, *For Space* (London: Sage Publications, 2005), 62.

26   It has long struck me that in Arthur Danto's lightning rod of an essay on the end of art—really, the end of a continuous art history, framed in Hegelian terms—it is sculpture (Andy Warhol's *Brillo Boxes*) that tolls the death knell of "the master narrative of the history of art." "The End of Art," first published in 1984, is revised and expanded in Arthur C. Danto, *After the End of Art: Contemporary Art and the Pale of History* (Princeton, NJ: Princeton University Press, 1997).

27   Massey, *For Space*, 76.

28   Ibid., 85–86.

29   See Gotthold Ephraim Lessing, *Laocoön: An Essay on the Limits of Painting and Poetry*, trans. Edward Allen McCormick (Baltimore: Johns Hopkins University Press, 1984). Diderot, too, maintained, though less programmatically, in his *Salon of 1767*, that "ut pictura poesis non erit" (poetry will not be like painting) is closer to the truth than Horace's dictum from *Ars Poetica*, "ut pictura poesis erit" (poetry will be like painting). What works well in painting will always work well in poetry, but, he insists, this is not a reciprocal relation; see Denis Diderot, *Diderot on Art*, vol. 2, *The Salon of 1767*, ed. and trans. John Goodman (New Haven: Yale University Press, 1995), 65. Perhaps the most significant art-historical writing about the ways in which postmodernism disturbs these codes is Craig Owens, "Earthwords," a review of *The Writings of Robert Smithson: Essays with Illustrations*, in *October* 10 (Autumn 1979): 120–30.

30   Aitken, quoted in Clive Thompson, "Vision Quest: This Man Has a Train, an Army of Artists, and an Entire Nation for a Gallery," *Wired*, August 19, 2013, http://wired.com/aitken-station-to-station.

31   This is the incisive argument developed in Anne M. Wagner, "Performance, Video, and the Rhetoric of Presence," *October* 91 (Winter 2000): 59–80.

32   Michel Foucault, "Of Other Spaces," trans. Jay Miskowiec, *diacritics* 16, no. 1 (Spring 1986): 24. The text was published in the French journal *Architecture-Mouvement-Continuité* in October 1984 and was based on a lecture given by Foucault in 1967, entitled "Des Espaces Autres." Foucault briefly mentions heterotopias in the preface to his 1966 book, *Les mots et les choses*, published in English in 1970 as *The Order of Things: An Archaeology of the Human Sciences*.

33   Ibid.

34   Ibid., 22.

35   Ibid., 26. Fascinatingly, Foucault identifies a range of heterotopias that have also served as sites in Aitken's most ambitious projects: motels, festivals, trains, and boats.

36   Ibid., 25.

37   Massey, *For Space*, 61.

38   Foucault, "Of Other Spaces," 27.

From *sleepwalkers* to *Station to Station:*
Inverting the Museum

Glenn D. Lowry

Doug Aitken is an unlikely radical. Tall and lanky, with an easy smile and a laid-back personality, he comes across as a heliotropic idealist full of almost impossible-to-imagine projects, rather than someone intent on rethinking how we tell stories and challenging how we conceive of the space of the museum. But behind his apparent nonchalance is a keen and questioning mind, and a driven artist whose work has been breaking down barriers for more than two decades. Among the issues that Aitken has been exploring from the outset of his career is how to take his work beyond the limits of a given space, whether a gallery, a private house, or a museum. His work *sleepwalkers* [fig. 1; pages 200–201, 234], commissioned by Creative Time and The Museum of Modern Art in 2007, reflects many of his ideas about time and space, architecture and the city, museums and their place in the larger cultural landscape, and the liquidity of art. Originally conceived as a seven-channel projection on the facades of The Museum of Modern Art, *sleepwalkers* was later remastered into a single-channel projection.

It built on several of Aitken's long-standing interests, including the idea of an expanded cinema, the nocturnal life of the so-called city that never sleeps, and what might be called the dematerialized museum, whose hermetically sealed walls give way to the freedom of the street. Like many of his projects, it brought together a highly talented group of artists, musicians, and performers, reflecting Aitken's uncanny ability to persuade people to participate.

Aitken worked in New York for several years at the beginning of his career and became fascinated with the way the city comes to life at night. The video installation *sleepwalkers* is the result of his ruminations on the people who inhabit the city when most of us are turning off the lights and heading to bed. It is also a kind of investigation of the various systems—from the subway to the electrical grid—that create the urban fabric of the city. Five characters—an office clerk (Tilda Swinton), a businessman (Donald Sutherland), a FedEx clerk (Chan Marshall), a bicycle messenger (Ryan Donowho), and an electrician (Seu Jorge)—act as surrogates, or, maybe even better, archetypes, for the nocturnal denizens of the city. We follow them as they wake, dress, prepare for the evening, travel to work, and unwind at the end of their day.

Aitken tells their stories through a series of fragmented images, or what he has called the "broken screen." By disrupting the linear progression of a traditional narrative with a seemingly endless flow of

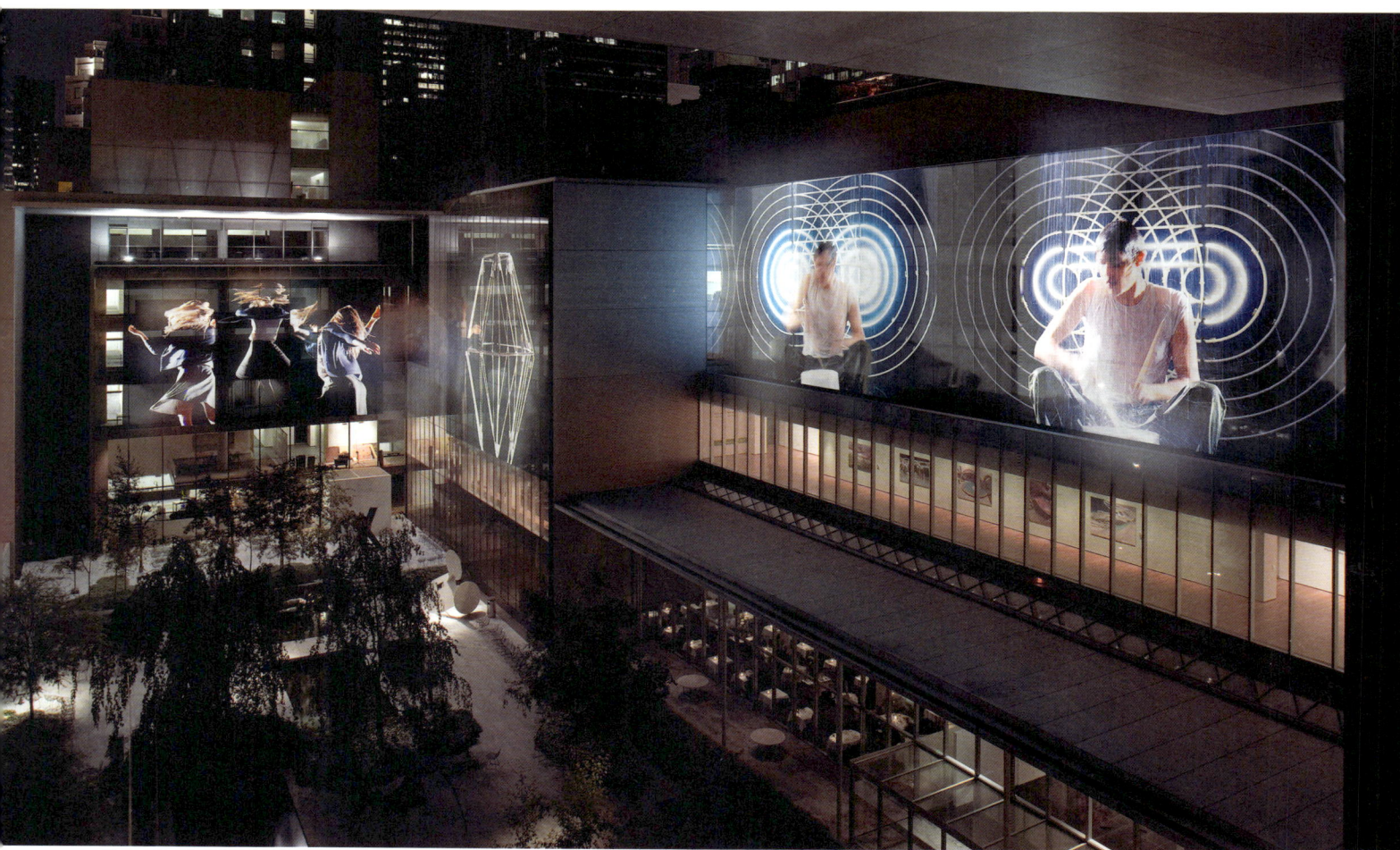

Fig. 1
Doug Aitken
sleepwalkers, 2007
Outdoor video installation on facade of The Museum of Modern Art, six channels of video (color, silent), eight projections forming seven screens
12:57 minutes/loop
Courtesy of the artist

intersecting images that combine and recombine in unexpected ways, he both alters the notion of time as a simple, continuous stream of sequential events and opens up the story to an almost infinite number of interpretations. He has said of this technique:

In some works there is a very aggressive cutting and pasting of time. For example in interiors *I wanted to tell a series of stories all set in different locations throughout the world, from scenes in Tokyo high-rises to vast helicopter factories or ghetto streets. In each location we follow an individual, each person very disparate and isolated in their separate environments, but at a certain fleeting moment their stories begin to collide into a single collective synchronicity. Sound and image suddenly lock and merge, generating a momentary sense of order in the chaos. Through polyrhythmic moments the stories merge as one unified fast moving amplified "pop" moment. They then collide just as quickly and break apart again in their separate paths.*[1]

Sleepwalkers follows a similar structure. Each of the characters in the story is presented as a solitary figure, wrapped up in his or her own thoughts and actions, oblivious to the world around them. Their stories are linked, at first only by the repetition of an image: a head resting in sleep, a hand dangling from the bed, an eye caught in the mirror, a character showering, someone slipping on shoes for the day—small, quotidian gestures that establish common connections between the characters. The seven screens at the museum operated in a syncopated rhythm, moving back and forth between each figure, collaging fragmentary bits of their lives together, emphasizing the similarity of their routines despite their vastly different socioeconomic backgrounds.

Aitken further interrupts the flow of their routines with a series of highly abstracted, visually lush images of various objects: wheels spinning that evoke futurist paintings or Russian avant-garde photographs, lightbulbs rapidly flashing that recall the setting sun that begins and ends the workday, color grids that echo Gerhard Richter's color charts, or spirals spinning into orbs, first in red and then in green, that have an almost psychedelic quality to them. These interruptions act as visual and emotional elisions, allowing different parts of the story to collide or break apart, establishing alternate narratives and possibilities that are as much about a meditation on various modern and contemporary artistic practices as they are about the characters themselves. Aitken often thinks of the history of twentieth-century art as a sequence of movements in pursuit of ever-greater degrees of formalism and abstraction, and his references to earlier traditions in *sleepwalkers* are both a nod to the past and an effort to move beyond it.[2]

This sense of the work as a dynamic progression, evolving as it developed, was amplified by a complicated algorithm that ensured that every possible combination of sequences between the screens occurred so that no loop was ever identical. This

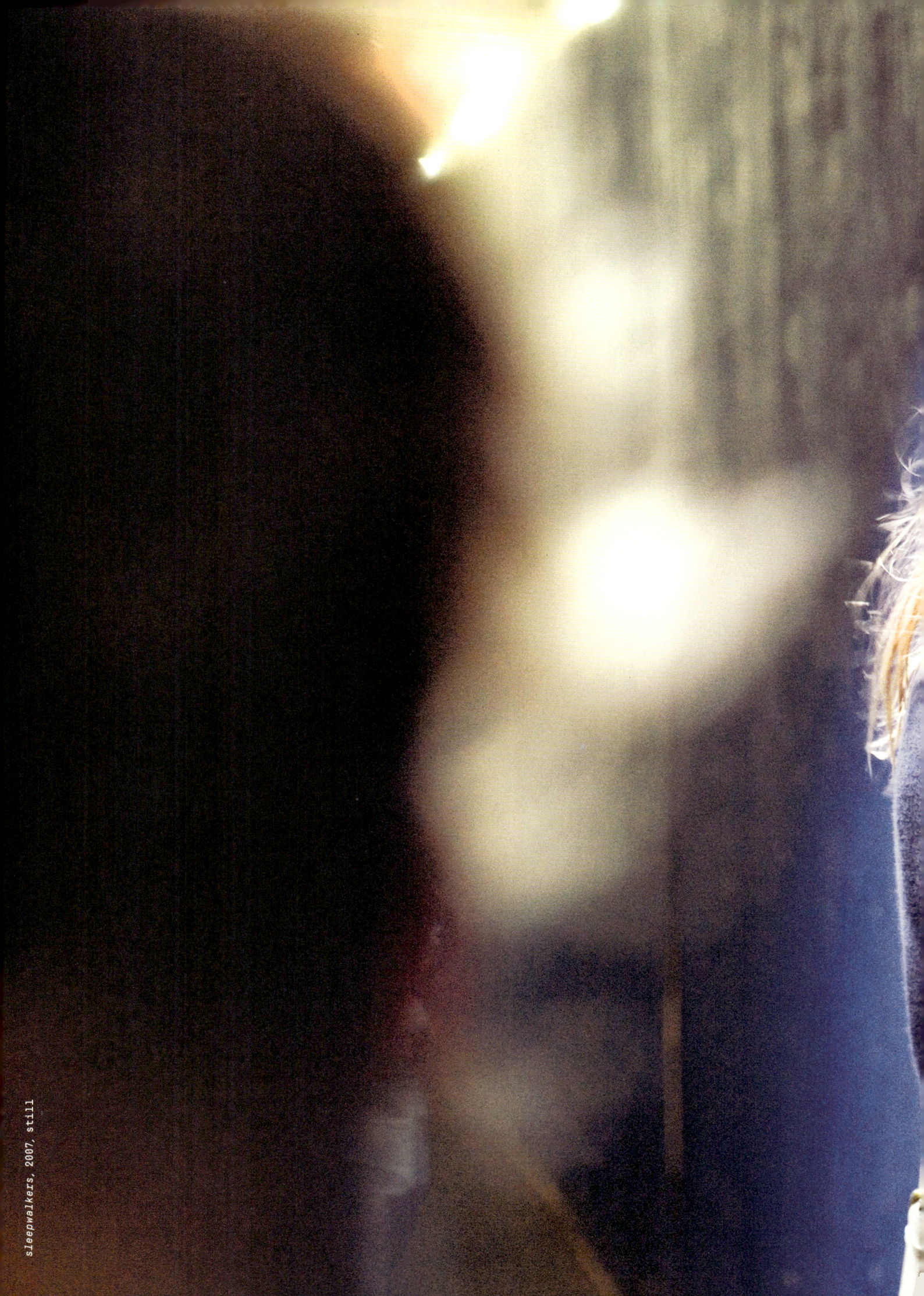

sleepwalkers, 2007, still

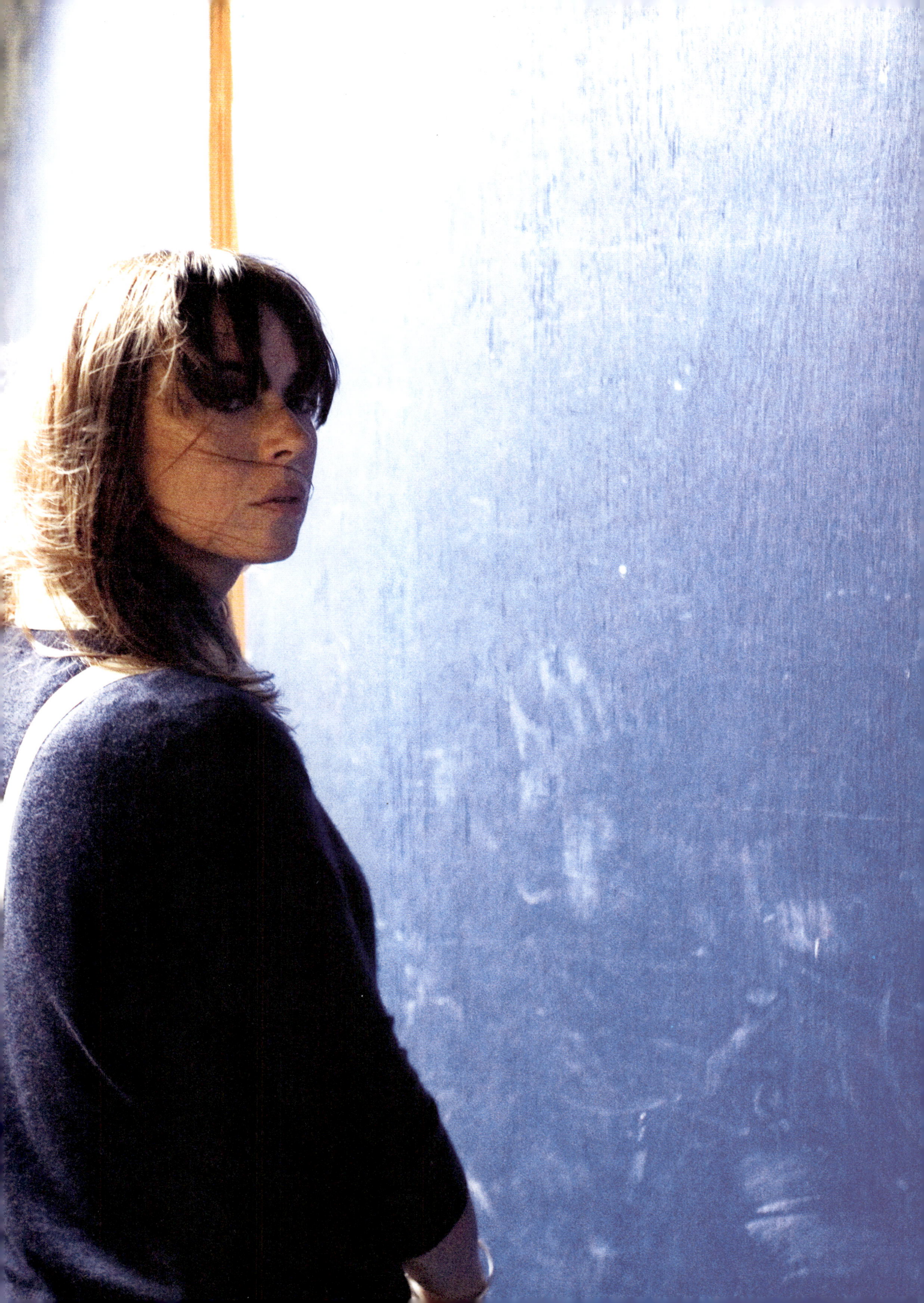

created a constantly changing story that was like a living organism, fluid and evolving, where traditional works of art are solid and stable. What Aitken wanted to achieve in *sleepwalkers* was an architecture of ideas that could develop on its own, independently of anything that had happened before.[3] This conceptual conceit was echoed in the fast-paced imagery of architectural details and buildings that punctuated the seven screens of the installation. As one image dissolved into another, as the urban fabric of the city slipped by in ever more complicated patterns, the architecture of the city, with its myriad elements, became liquid-like. As the hard forms of the background—windows, walls, doorways, streets—gave way to a flowing stream of imagery, the city seemed to become malleable and expansive, to in effect almost dematerialize before our eyes.

What is most striking about *sleepwalkers* is how, despite the visual intensity of the images and the carefully realized settings in which the characters work and move, they always remain self-absorbed, caught in their private thoughts and reveries. As solitary as they may be, Aitken treats them with a tenderness, even a compassion, that underscores their humanity. As he has said:

> *I think I am very interested in the placement of the individual and how we situate ourselves in the world. A world where we are at times harmonizing with the time we are moving through, and at other times in conflict. But I think in many ways we do move through life as solitary vehicles. We're self-contained although we try to reach out to others, but the act of perception is a very solitary experience.*[4]

In one of the most telling moments in *sleepwalkers*, each of the characters reaches out to touch a glass window with their hand, tentative and gentle at first, and then more forceful, the soulful sound of a trumpet playing in the background. It is a gesture charged with meaning—an assertion of each figure's presence in the world, as if they were marking their place in the city, but it is also a gesture of yearning and wanting to connect with their surroundings, and by association with one another, to be part of something larger than their individual existence. Moments later, as Donowho passes a wall scarred by graffiti, we make out the words "Don't Disappear," adding a poignant but emphatic marker to their spectral presence.

Although Aitken's interest lies in how we as individuals experience the city, and his figures always seem to be enveloped in themselves, *sleepwalkers* ultimately is about how we connect to one another. Toward the end of the projection the solitariness of the characters gives way to their interaction with other people and by implication with one another. Sutherland is upended by a taxi as he is crossing the street and lies motionless for a moment on the hood of the car. In the background we hear the steadily escalating beat of Donowho's drumming. Then, slowly, Sutherland begins to move and eventually starts tap-dancing on the hood of the car while Donowho's drumming intensifies. As the camera follows Donowho, we catch glimpses of a second drummer. Meanwhile Marshall starts to dance, spinning ever faster in a kind of ecstatic trance, and Jorge slowly pulls a cable from a manhole and then takes a strand and twirls it like a lasso, and Swinton starts to play her violin along with several other musicians. Scenes of streets, buildings, and windows are cut in between these images, amplifying the sense of urban life, as the music takes on an ever-faster beat. Eventually a group of people dance around the taxi on which Sutherland is tapping away as everything starts to gyrate at ever-greater speed, the camera creating a syncopated rhythm between the figures, winding them together in a centrifugal vortex.

Peter Eleey, who co-curated the presentation of *sleepwalkers* at The Museum of Modern Art, links it to a history of films that have dealt with modern urban life, and Charles and Ray Eames's 1959 *Glimpses of the USA* in particular.[5] And there is an aspect of *sleepwalkers*, with its saturated images and colors, crisp details, and almost futuristic sense of time and space, that consciously evokes a utopian America of the 1950s with all of its then potential, though Aitken tempers this with an awareness of the grittiness of New York today. The mass of tangled wires that Jorge contends with, for instance, easily becomes a metaphor for an overburdened system gone awry, just as the graffiti on walls reminds us that not all of the city is gentrified.

The presentation of *sleepwalkers* as an open-air experience associated it with an older American tradition of drive-in movies. Like drive-ins, *sleepwalkers* combined the dreamlike inward experience of film—usually experienced in the darkness of the cinema—with cars, parking, the outdoor air, and a crowd invested with what Eleey has called "the dynamic potential of mobility."[6] But as much as *sleepwalkers* evoked drive-ins of the past, it also built on the idea of multiplex cinemas. Where the drive-in was a destination, *sleepwalkers* was designed to surprise and engage people who would be walking along Fifty-Third or Fifty-Fourth Street at night not expecting to see anything. And where the drive-in required its viewers to remain stationary in their cars, nestled together, *sleepwalkers* encouraged viewers to circulate around the museum, encountering different projections and one another. Like multiplexes, *sleepwalkers* offered its viewers multiple stories and screens to choose from. By having to circulate around the block where the museum is located in order to fully understand *sleepwalkers*, viewers were required to "reenact" the process of moving through the city, creating chance encounters and random associations as they gave up their own sense of privacy or solitude to participate in a larger collective urban experience. To see *sleepwalkers* was to become a Benjamin-like flaneur[7] as we moved about the work as well as the city itself. In doing so, *sleepwalkers* altered the relationship between transmitter and receiver as viewers became participants in the work and exchanged their own experience with others in the crowd who moved about from screen to screen, at times together and at other times independently. The work invited us to engage in a prolonged meditation on what it means to be part of the city and how we define ourselves within this nocturnal landscape.

The tension in *sleepwalkers* between individual and collective experiences mirrors the tensions Aitken develops between projected images and the means by which we encounter them, and extends Aitken's own commitment to developing new formats for engaging with art. His use of multiple projections in earlier works such as *electric earth* [1999; pages 120-131] and *interiors* [2002; page 235] established his interest in an expanded notion of cinematic experience and engaging the viewer in an almost performative way to fully experience his projects. Many of these ideas are explored in detail in the 2006 publication *Broken Screen: Expanding the Image, Breaking the Narrative*, whose subtitle is *26 Conversations with Doug Aitken*. In discussion with artists like Pipilotti Rist, Matthew Barney, and Bruce Conner, filmmakers like Robert Altman, Werner Herzog, and Alejandro Jodorowsky, and architects like Rem Koolhaas and Greg Lynn, among others, Aitken elicits a robust discussion about unpacking the notion of linear time and experience and nontraditional ways of presenting art. He concludes with a diagram of nonlinear film that is both a history of works that have challenged traditional notions of time and space and an outline for many of the strategies he favors, including the manipulation of structure and story line [interweaving plots and timelines], immersion [overtaking the environment with image and sound], structural manipulation [subverting linear story lines through technical experimentation], and the broken image [challenging content through image fragmentation].

Like many of Aitken's earlier works, *sleepwalkers* used all of these techniques but was even more radical in its approach. This is not only because of its scale—almost a full city block—but also because of its ambition: to create a multilayered story across seven distinct but interconnected projection screens that transformed the space of the museum from a dark and controlled container where you have to pay admission to see art into a luminescent screen where art was experienced unexpectedly, and for free, by anyone who happened to walk on Fifty-Third or Fifty-Fourth Street at night. By inverting the space of the museum, Aitken offered us a very different idea of what a museum can be. In doing so he joined a long list of artists who have looked, often critically, at the museum, from Hubert Robert, who saw the Louvre as a classical ruin in postrevolutionary France, to Ed Ruscha, who imagined the Los Angeles County Museum of Art as a site of conflagration during the height of the Vietnam War, to Hans Haacke, and more recently, Andrea Fraser, who have critiqued it as a place of power, conservative politics, and the reification of the establishment.[8]

Aitken's remaking of the museum into an open-air multiplex was less overtly political than many artists' approach to the museum, but it was at least as radical, if not more so. Where other artists only imagined the museum in a different way, Aitken actually altered it in real time and in real space, challenging almost all of its operating principles. Admission was free rather than paid, the action took place outside rather than inside, it occurred at night rather than during the day, and there was no fixed point of entry or departure. Seen in this way, Aitken reframed the institution's administrative and curatorial perspectives by taking control of the museum and creating— albeit for a limited period—its exact opposite. The museum itself, of course, was complicit in this process, and that is one of the keys to Aitken's success: his ability to persuade institutions to change their practices and modes of operation, if only briefly, in order to enable new kinds of artist-centric experiences to occur.

Aitken added to this sense of inhabiting the museum by presenting a series of happenings, carefully curated evenings, that overlapped with the showing of *sleepwalkers*. These included performances by Cat Power, Donowho, Hisham Bharoocha, Melissa Plaut, and others, and provided an alternative to programmed exhibitions at the museum. Thus, *sleepwalkers* became a catalyst that turned the museum into a kind of cultural hub enabling a wide array of artists, and nonartists, who might not otherwise have engaged with the institution, to become part of its life. Where an earlier notion of the museum might have seen it as a treasure house, defined by a set of objects and the ideas of its curators, Aitken suggested a more fluid and open institution, an incubator more than a repository. This "museum" recognized that art and culture today are produced and experienced in and out of walls, in and out of institutions, in and out of urban environments, and that the museum need not be thought of as a place fixed in time and space.

Seen this way, *sleepwalkers* becomes a precursor to *Station to Station* [2013; pages 42-49], a nine-car train that traveled from the Atlantic to the Pacific over twenty-three days, stopping in ten cities, bringing together artists, musicians, performers, and a coterie of Aitken's friends and acquaintances to form a rolling museum, or cultural laboratory, that passed through the vast American landscape. Like *sleepwalkers*, it took the idea of the museum as a place to encounter art and altered one of its fundamental principles—that of being a stationary building located in a fixed place— in order to expand on its potential. For Aitken this is part of an ongoing experiment to dematerialize the museum, by which he means turning it into an idea rather than a place; but it is also about relocation, not just of the space of the museum but of how it is used and experienced. The train's progression across the country meant that the audience was constantly changing, just as what was happening on the train was never the same as some artists left and others joined.

Aitken's project is not so much about replacing the museum as it is about reinventing it for the twenty-first century as an artist-inspired idea that can be used and reused in new and unforeseen ways. In an era in which digital platforms challenge the need for physical places like the museum,

Aitken actually underscores their importance as gathering places in real time for those interested in creating and experiencing art.

There is something almost utopian in Aitken's belief that culture and creativity are everywhere and that if you bring together an interesting array of highly talented people from a broad range of backgrounds—artists, auctioneers, musicians, architects, filmmakers, even cowboys—you will produce something unexpected and moving. The result is an ongoing investigation into the creative process in which nothing is fixed and everything is possible, and where "the museum" stands for an idea rather than a place. If *sleepwalkers* dematerialized the walls of the institution to embrace the street and the city, *Station to Station* took the entire idea and put it on the road—the museum as a transcontinental show, always moving, always changing.

Notes

1   Doug Aitken, in conversation with Russell Ferguson, *Doug Aitken: A-Z Book [Fractals]*, ed. Marion Boulton Stroud, Beatrix Ruf, and Russell Ferguson [Stuttgart: Hatje Cantz, 2003], n.p.

2   Doug Aitken, in conversation with the author, August 16, 2015.

3   Ibid.

4   Anders Kold, "Doug Aitken—Art at the Edge of the World," *Doug Aitken: RISE* exhibition catalogue [Humlebæk, Denmark: Louisiana Museum of Art, 2002], 21.

5   Peter Eleey, "The Exploded Drive-in," *Doug Aitken: Sleepwalkers* exhibition catalogue [New York: Museum of Modern Art, 2007], 98.

6   Ibid., 99–100.

7   Ibid., 100.

8   In an interesting prefiguration of a work to come for Aitken, *Station to Station,* Ruscha described the structure of the Los Angeles County Museum of Art as on fire, with its lower-right-hand to upper-left-hand direction creating the sense of a transitional shot of somebody traveling on a train followed by a shot of a train coming out of nowhere in the right-hand corner that pretty soon fills up the frame. See Doug Aitken, *Broken Screen: Expanding the Image, Breaking the Narrative: 26 Conversations with Doug Aitken*, ed. Noel Daniel [New York: D.A.P./Distributed Art Publishers, 2006].

An Architecture for the Now

Joseph Grima

In the opening scene of the memorable BBC documentary *Reyner Banham Loves Los Angeles*, aired on British TV in 1972, the viewer is shown the eminent bewhiskered historian—at the time a professor of the history of architecture at University College London—emerging from the arrivals terminal at LAX. "You might wonder," muses Banham in voice-over as, animated by visible excitement, he climbs into his rental car, "what I'm doing in Los Angeles, a city that makes nonsense of history and breaks all the rules. Well, I love the place with a passion that goes beyond all sense or reason!"[1]

Over the following hour, sedate British television audiences, presumably in a state of mounting shock, are treated to a passionate panegyric of the city, articulated into detailed investigations of what Banham describes as the "four ecologies": Surfurbia, Foothills, The Plains of Id, and Autopia (or, more prosaically, beach, basin, foothills, freeways).[2] Banham, whose vehicle of choice was until then the trusty Moulton F-frame folding bicycle, claimed that like earlier generations of English intellectuals who taught themselves Italian in order to read Dante in the original, he had learned to drive in order to read Los Angeles in the original.

Despite his choice of platform, the true target of this provocation was not the somnolent occupant of the British TV armchair. Banham's Californian antics amounted to a conceptual missile fired from within the European architectural establishment and directed squarely at his own encampment. Throughout the film, Banham is at pains to regularly contrast LA's creative swagger and exuberance with the drab monotony of his quaint hometown, Norwich, a bastion of traditional Britishness. At the core of Banham's perceived blasphemy was the very suggestion that something could be learned from Los Angeles in the realms of "serious" disciplines such as urban planning—that it was in some way the embodiment of human achievement in the second half of the twentieth century, not just as the global capital of media and entertainment but as a visionary and pioneering experiment in architecture and planning. As a historian of architecture, to take Los Angeles seriously was in itself a form of heresy, but how else to shake the establishment out of its complacent faith in the absolute value of history and preordained order? Banham's argument, articulated from the backseat of his drop-top Cadillac over sundaes with Ed Ruscha and through extended voice-over monologues while drifting through spaghetti junctions [fig. 1], is for a sort of urbanistic relativism according to which the form of the city and the language of art are inextricably entangled with each other. It is no coincidence that Ruscha's 1963 artist's book *Twentysix Gasoline Stations*, a publication now considered seminal in the history of the artist's book, makes an appearance: in many ways it captures the unstated essence of Banham's argument that not only is Los Angeles a praiseworthy paradigm of efficiency for the late twentieth century but, despite its bluster and grittiness—or perhaps because of it— its landscape captures the *esprit du temps* to the point of becoming legible as *art*.

For Banham, whose perspective is quintessentially European, the expedition to Los Angeles is an exercise in reverse Orientalism, in which the study of the physical and cultural landscape is both a guilty intellectual pleasure and an act of defiance toward the scholarly conservatism of his birthplace. At the precise moment in which Banham tours Venice Beach, farther east the demolition of Pruitt-Igoe is ushering in the era of postmodernism in architecture; in a state of media shock, the world looks to the past to find a direction for the future. In LA, Banham embraces California's transgressive ideology of a permanent present: drifting along the freeways, studiously dodging the city's architects [Frank Gehry is already active in the city, but makes no appearance], he delineates the contours of a Californian ideal of temporality and antimonumentalism—an ideal of beauty that treats artistic practice, public space, pop culture, and architecture as an indivisible whole.

California's predilection for the "thinness" of the present may seem like a disadvantageous point of departure to argue that Doug Aitken's work is defined by a deeply architectural understanding of space and the city. Architects, whose vision tends to be skewed by the fact that even their most modest creations will likely outlive them, like to think of themselves as the foot soldiers of history—manufacturers of a condition of permanence that is frequently used to justify a propensity toward mystification and earnestness that would be unlikely to be tolerated in many other domains. Architecture is often equated to what Paolo Portoghesi once described as "the presence of the past" in the landscape,³ and over the centuries this has led to a concept—particularly in Western culture—of permanence in built form as an absolute prerequisite for something to be considered architectural. Yet I would argue that this equivalency is false, and that there are several ways in which Aitken's work can be read and understood in architectural terms, if we observe it with the open-mindedness Banham reserved for Los Angeles throughout his *dérives* of 1972.

The Hirshhorn Museum and Sculpture Garden [fig. 2] is situated exactly halfway between the Washington Monument and the US Capitol, anchoring the southernmost end of the L'Enfant axis. Concentric in plan, it measures 231 feet in diameter and is surfaced with precast concrete aggregate of pink Swenson granite. Its architect, Gordon Bunshaft, whose long career included only one single-family home [the Travertine House, built for his own family in 1963, and later purchased by Martha Stewart and subsequently demolished], was not famous for the creation of amiable urban presences, and the Hirshhorn was no exception. As Ada Louise Huxtable summed it up in her 1974 *New York Times* review, "[The building] is known around Washington as the bunker or gas tank, lacking only gun emplacements or an Exxon sign...It totally lacks the essential factors of esthetic strength and provocative vitality that make genuine 'brutalism' a positive and rewarding style. This is

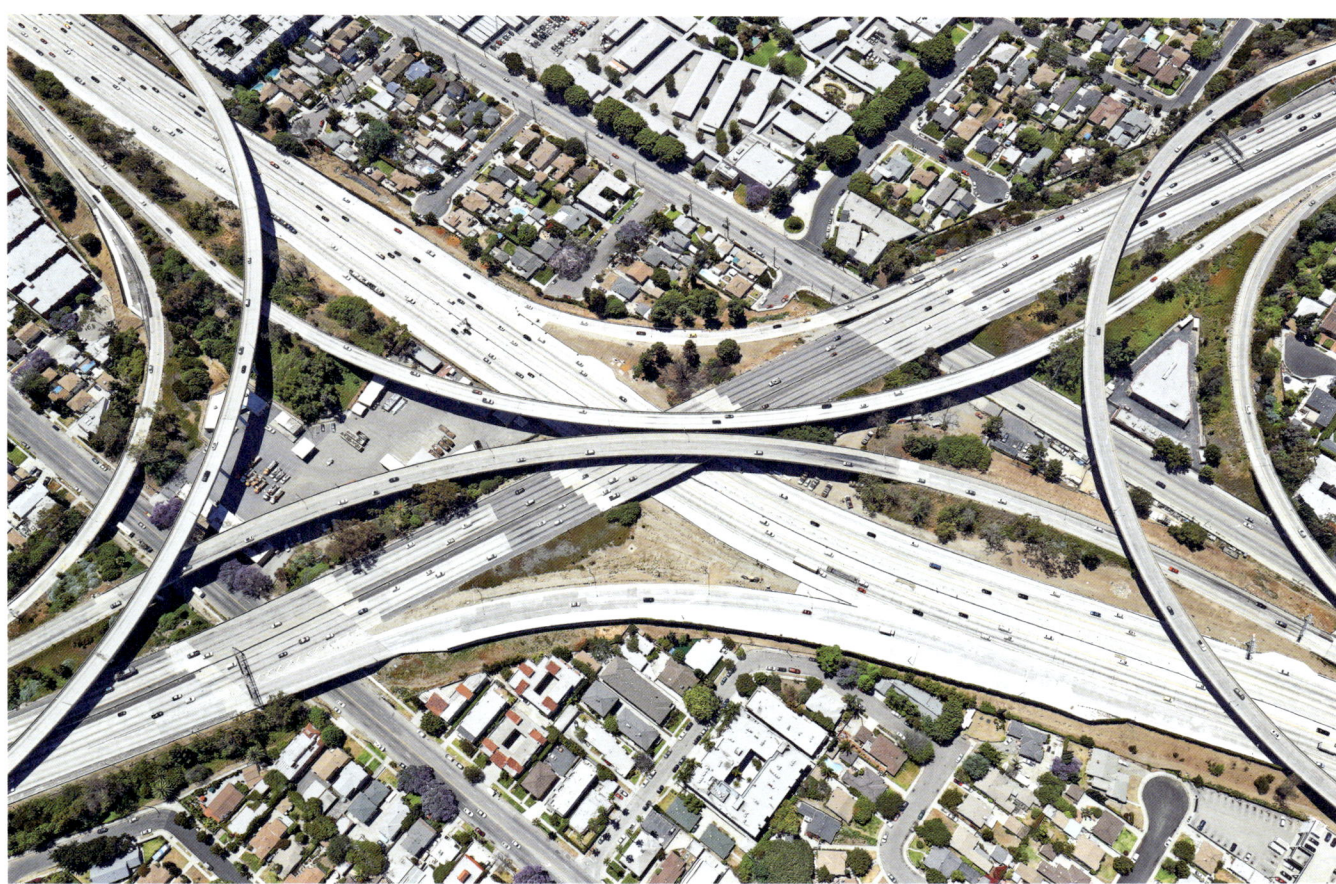

Fig. 1
1-405/I-10 Interchange, Los Angeles, 2014
Photo: © Peter Andrew Lustyk

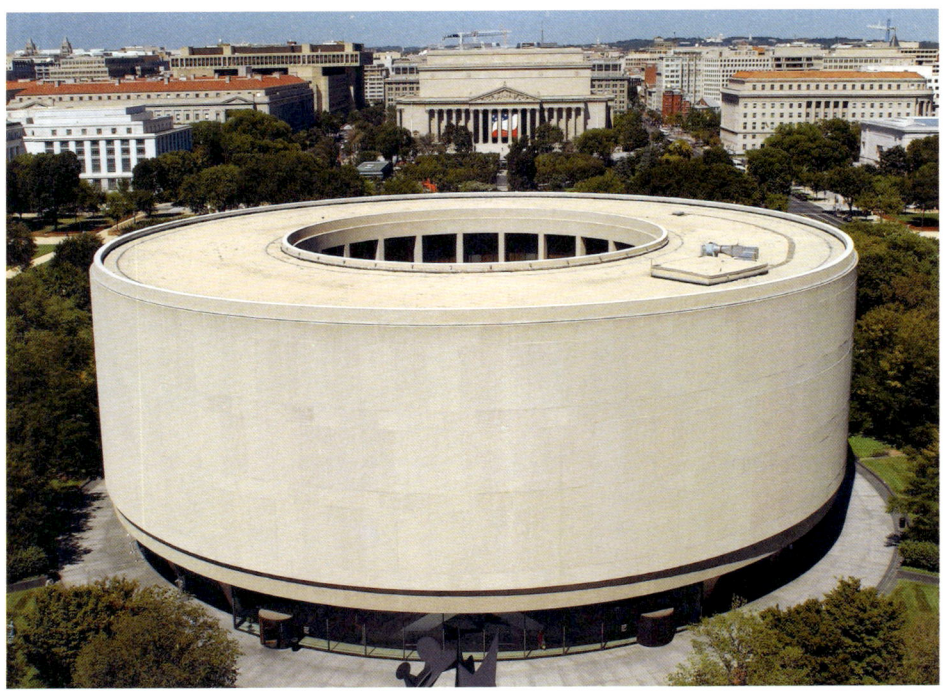

born-dead, neo-penitentiary modern. Its mass is not so much aggressive or overpowering as merely leaden."[4]

Although each critic read her or his own meaning into the building's form [Paul Goldberger, for instance, argued that "the fortress quality of the Hirshhorn suggests some rather obvious thoughts about the nature of housing art in our time"[5]], it is interesting to note that Bunshaft himself considered the Hirshhorn Museum "a large piece of functional sculpture,"[6] implying that through a feat of architectural prowess he had not only produced an urban presence imbued with the qualities of an artwork but even succeeded in giving it civic purpose. Despite these artistic aspirations— or perhaps because of them—the building's effect is to "museumify" the mall, allying itself with its peers in the neighborhood to recast the mall as an open-air sculpture museum of Brobdingnagian proportions. The value—or even the existence—of a human presence is negated through the building's impassive blankness. Paradoxically, the museum comes across as both obsessed with being urban and utterly uninterested in the elementary particle of urbanity— human life.

When Aitken was invited to produce a major site-specific piece for the museum, his fundamental intuition was that the museum's urban presence, imposing and aloof though it may be, could become its key asset, and the result of his engagement with the Hirshhorn, SONG 1 [2012; pages 166–167], could be described as a work of urban alchemy. At first it comes across as a somewhat

Fig. 2
Hirshhorn Museum and Sculpture Garden, Smithsonian Institution, Washington DC
Photo: Lee Stalsworth, courtesy of the Hirshhorn Museum and Sculpture Garden

enigmatic piece—a panoramic video projection that wraps the museum's cylindrical shell, set to the tune of "I Only Have Eyes for You," the eminently catchy number. On the face of it, it is more the stuff of Californian bonhomie than serious art—a lighthearted and humorous piece, which instead of denouncing the building that hosts it for its indifference, plays with its geometry. The visual structure is underpinned by a series of studies of the circle as a form permeating everyday life, returning frequently to close-ups of revolving spools, spinning wheels, and other circular forms. Most of all though, SONG 1 is a celebration of precisely that which the building appears to ignore. With a characteristically Californian spirit of irreverence that would have been sure to delight Banham, Aitken tears Bunshaft's Hirshhorn off its pedestal of unsentimental indifference, persuading it to finally engage with the city around it by making it into a beacon that broadcasts fragments of metropolitan life. The invisible grid underpinning the song is projected onto the tangible grid of the city, and in doing so, it also redefines the museum's definition of itself and of its audience, reaching out to hundreds of thousands—transforming the city into a museum of itself. Parking garages, diners, factories, corner shops, access ramps—like a mirror held up to the city, SONG 1 transposes the building's introversion, and through an exaggeration of humanity on an architectural scale to compensate for the museum's deficit of humanity, it finally completes the architect's original intention.

Although SONG 1 and other pieces such as sleepwalkers [2007; pages 200–201, 234], a similarly urban piece projected onto the walls of The Museum of Modern Art in 2007, clearly speak of Aitken's ongoing interest in the architectural, and the themes he touches on are in many instances identical, it is interesting to observe how his attitude toward the space of the city is from the perspective of an architect. There is a passage from Rem Koolhaas's watershed 2001 essay "Junkspace" that could almost be read as a description of Aitken's work:

> *Superstrings of graphics, transplanted emblems of franchise and sparkling infrastructures of light, LEDs and video describe an authorless world beyond anyone's claim, always unique, utterly unpredictable, yet intensely familiar.*[7]

Like SONG 1, "Junkspace" is a poetic meandering through the spaces of modernity—hotels, department stores, airports, nightclubs, escalators, casinos, theme parks, highways. Yet where Aitken finds poetry and structure, Koolhaas perceives chaos and death:

> *Junkspace is what remains after modernization has run its course; or more precisely, what coagulates while modernization is in progress, its fallout. Modernization had a rational program: to share the blessings of science, universally. Junkspace is its apotheosis, or meltdown....Junkspace thrives on design, but design dies in junkspace.*[8]

Aitken's work is grounded in an attitude toward the present less jaded than that of his contemporaries in architecture, more reminiscent of an earlier generation that didn't regard pop culture with despair and valued performativity over permanence. At the very moment Koolhaas was lamenting the fact that "we do not leave pyramids," his mentor, the iconoclastic architect Cedric Price, was advocating the demolition of York Minster cathedral on the grounds that the building, originally built for worship, no longer served its purpose. Aitken's work could be described as "architectural" according to Price's understanding of the word, which famously entreated architects to not think of buildings as the default solution to architectural problems. Undoubtedly one of the most challenging figures in the field of architecture in Britain during the second half of the twentieth century, Price struggled vehemently against what he perceived as the authoritarian nature of architecture, and dedicated much of his career to the search for a flexibility that could embrace rather than preclude unexpected future uses. The utilitarian spaces of industry and logistics were an inspiration to him not only aesthetically but also conceptually: Price found them to possess an energy and dynamism absent in conventional architecture. Many of his projects were audacious experiments in the architectural revisitation of key social services such as the museum [with the 1961 *Fun Palace,* a building-as-happening later cited by Renzo Piano and Richard Rogers as an inspiration for their winning Centre Pompidou competition entry], challenging the assumption that they needed to be housed in buildings in the first place.

Price's most audacious experiment in this sense was *Potteries Thinkbelt* [1964-66; fig. 3], a project that tested the possibility of reconstructing a university environment across a distributed system of rail carriages and interchange points in Staffordshire. *Potteries Thinkbelt* remained on paper, but the principles that inspired it are the same as those underlying Aitken's project *Station to Station* [2013; pages 42-49]. Like *Thinkbelt, Station*

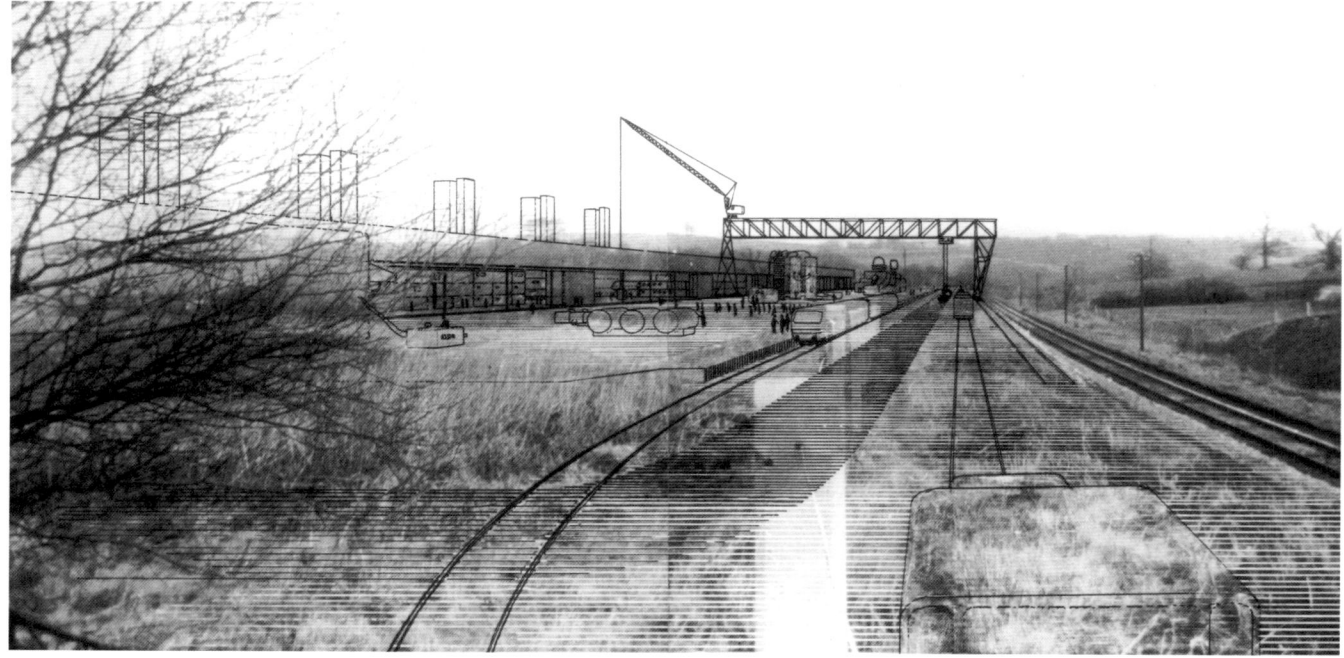

Fig. 3
Cedric Price
Potteries Thinkbelt, North Staffordshire, England
Perspective sketch of transfer area, 1966
Gelatin silver print of photomontage
Cedric Price fonds,
Collection Centre Canadien d'Architecture/
Canadian Centre for Architecture, Montreal DR2006:0019
© Cedric Price Archive/
Canadian Centre for Architecture

to Station substitutes a building with a train as a venue for a happening, which sounds very much like the kind of thing Price envisaged taking place in the Fun Palace. Aitken describes the project, which unfolded as a "nomadic happening" based around a convoy of nine train carriages traveling from the Atlantic Ocean to the Pacific, as a living project exploring modern creativity, a "kinetic light sculpture" on the move. Just as the Fun Palace would have done had it been realized, the train housed a recording studio where musicians could record tracks, art-making space and studios [in a sleeping car], and spaces for retreat, encounter, and socialization. Moreover, the train itself served as a work of art signaling its passage through the landscape with flanks pulsating with LEDs. At night, the train would transform into a moving light show.

One of Price's favorite aphorisms was that no one should be interested in the design of bridges, they should be concerned with how to get to the other side. Price's struggle was to reframe architecture as the practice not of making buildings but of structuring the relationships between people in space. By dematerializing the university building, Price was pointing out that by renouncing architecture in the conventional sense, a new universe of possibilities could be opened up. His interest was in the dynamics of a lecture in a moving rail carriage and how it might bring staff and students into contact in a way that is all too easily avoided in the stratified space of the campus. For Price, every work of architecture should also be a happening.

It is in precisely this way that Aitken's work is architectural. It casts us back to another, more open-minded era in architecture, less preoccupied with questions of permanence and form. When he rebuilt his own home in Venice, California, *Acid Modernism* [2012; page 259], Aitken set five seismic sensors in the foundations and hooked them up to his home stereo, as if to point out that even the mundane act of dwelling in one's home can become an opportunity to produce deep, unearthly music. Had Banham traveled to Venice Beach forty years later than he did, one can clearly picture him roaming through in delight.

Notes

1   *Reyner Banham Loves Los Angeles,* BBC Television, 1972.

2   Reyner Banham, *Los Angeles: The Architecture of Four Ecologies* [New York: Harper and Row, 1971].

3   *Presence of the Past: Venice Biennale '80* is the title of the publication for the First International Biennial of Architecture, directed by Paolo Portoghesi.

4   Ada Louise Huxtable, *New York Times,* October 6, 1974.

5   Paul Goldberger, "A Fortress of a Building That Works as a Museum," *New York Times,* October 2, 1974.

6   Hirshhorn Museum and Sculpture Garden site: http://hirshhorn.si.edu/collection/history-of-the-hirshhorn/#detail=/bio/the-architect/&collection=history-of-the-hirshhorn.

7   Rem Koolhaas, "Junkspace," in *Harvard Design School Guide to Shopping,* ed. Chuihua Judy Chung, Jeffrey Inaba, Rem Koolhaas, and Sze Tsung Leong [Cologne: Taschen, 2001], 408–21.

8   Ibid.

A Granular History of Space:
Doug Aitken

Norman M. Klein

Within Doug Aitken's installations, there is a history of a cultural transformation, toward what I call feudalistic pluralism. To explain, as a historical context for his use of space, I begin with a quotation from Aitken in 2001:

> All information is caught up in a state of flux, graceful and weightless but at the same time violent... There is chaos until finally nothing is visible. Everything is white noise... As the debris falls back as it was, we realize no human presence is left...[1]

He is saying that white noise is sensory debris: data in chaos. It is a granular effect: debris floats, like crystals, inside an immersive space—perhaps a museum or a street, wherever information traffics as time and space. The crystals are microscopic bytes of what is not directly remembered: collective forgetting. The crystalline effects are generally unseen but sensed by viewers and by artists, by their praxis.

But why are they "unseen," hidden? Michel Foucault would have called these ruptures—the historical cues that must be evaded [collectively sublimated]. They are symptoms of political chaos that must be ignored, or radical changes in technology, or risky capitalist manipulation. They almost seem alive, like one-celled animals, a smart dust. They are noisy whispers across the room.

Vibrations and Hubbub

For centuries, "noise" referred to vibrations more than sounds. And vibrations were social as much as aural. Often the French expression was used—*bruit*—to suggest a noisy rumor. In medieval Latin, the slang was *boare*: a shrill, invasive noise, like the braying of a donkey. By the seventeenth century, when a noise had *bruit*, it often announced that you were popular far and wide. In 1677, the philosopher Leibniz, in his job as master librarian, advised Duke Johann Ferdinand of Auersberg on books that have *bruit*—that make "noise . . . in the world."[2]

White noise is a product of late twentieth-century antilogic. It means a noise that barely registers, like elevator music, or sublimated anomie in Don DeLillo's novel *White Noise* [1985]. It is explosive monotony; the subterranean, the buzz of capitalism; what DeLillo calls "the radiance in dailiness."[3] I am particularly fascinated by Aitken's *Sonic Pavilion* [2009; pages 2-3, 233]; its narrative suggests white noise as tectonic—the sound of tectonic plates recovered from hundreds of feet below.

White noise is indeed the sound of tectonic forgetting, like a faint ringing in the ears—like a vertigo induced by global capitalism. Writer and critic Martin Herbert compares Aitken's soundscapes to "a sonic analogue for global capital's glide, all soft metronomic pulse and murmur, superficially comforting but bleak underneath."[4] Like Luc Boltanski and Eve Chiapello's book *The New Spirit of Capitalism*, Aitken takes us through "networked, precarious, post-Fordist, steel-in-a-velvet glove" forms.[5] Or in Aitken's *these restless minds* [1998; pages 92-99, 101], where an auctioneer blusters through his routine, at lightning speed, a white noise about data and commodity; a scene in which sound becomes a commodity, in a space where nothing is on auction [except perhaps the ritual of the art market]. Indeed, in our data-centered world, flash trading is very much like those auctioneers—an industrialization of forgetting.

These are soundscapes about industrial noise severing boundaries, like the quotation from Paul Virilio's *Speed and Politics*, featured in Aitken's artist's book *I Am a Bullet: Scenes from an Accelerating Culture* [2000]:

> *Here, once again, we must look at the Speedometer of the racing engine. The combat racecar: an existential measure of the warrior's being, the dizzying flow of time, a rapidity tax on the covered meter that ruins the earthly inhabitant, but simultaneously destroys the substance of its conqueror and measures the survivor's remaining hours.*[6]

Noise was very much a political art in the nineties, for West Coast hip-hop, for noise hop in the UK, for postpunk uses of experimental, atonal, and dissonant musical forms. But since the nineties, the big-market auctioneers have taken over—but not only there. By 2016, the term is widely in use throughout the Internet—as a kind of software—generally defined as a dissonant transmission algorithm. White noise overcompresses so many frequencies all at once that it can lead to annoying buzzes [as in radio transmissions]. Or it may add contour and ambience.

The term has found a nest in other fields as well. In social media, hubbub and chatter are called white noise. Among writers, onomatopoeic words are now white noise, like the graphics of pow, sizzle, and buzz. For ad companies, these effects can be violent somehow—invasive like the boots of marching soldiers, or as silky as a snare drum. Dozens of white-noise apps are free over the counter. When used properly, white noise will deaden loud and obnoxious sounds. It helps with selective memory. White noise generators [widely for sale online] will help you sleep. In the sound installation *Sonic Fountain* [2013; pages 30-32, 34-35], Aitken treats white noise as naturally fake, by amplifying the sound of dripping water.

Dissolving Noise

We begin with *diamond sea* in 1997 [pages 74-85], an odyssey across the Namib Desert in Africa, where mines are operated without people, with a few abandoned structures as the only human "noise." Aitken's installations are very much time capsules about the sensory dissolve brought on by the melting of late industrial-capitalist forms. By that I mean the melting of the postwar rules set up by the Bretton Woods agreements of 1944, which were dissolved by President Nixon in 1971— a move that would usher in globalism after the economic shocks of 1973. Aitken enters this chaotic story at the time of the Asian financial crisis of 1997. His installations are a highly organized homage to political dissonance—a kind of *Gesamtkunstwerk*. Their phantasmagoric power echoes the transmigration of capital across cities and media.

In Aitken's poetics, two elements repeat and trade off constantly. First, there is noise [sculptural or aural] that migrates outward; it perforates boundaries. Second, there is inward compression, like a moth inside a narrative theatrical frame. These opposites are like spatial language about the radical changes in our physical life over the past twenty years. Since 1997, the world economy has been hit by one crash after another; by never-ending civil wars; by terrorist paranoia; by meltdowns in the labor markets. These, in turn, have affected various culture industries, and they are reflected in the allegories within Aitken's installation spaces.

Of course, white noise is our comic tragedy. It is raucous with Berlusconis and Trumps. In the noise, so many comic fictions pass for facts. This story must be told in a subjunctive mood. Allow me a few pages to explain that, by way of prologue. That takes us briefly to 1969. This will help, when we return to 1997-2016.

Ten Thousand Scratchy Prologues

Behind the visible façade of the system, one posits the rich uncertainty of disorder.
—Michel Foucault,
The Archaeology of Knowledge [1969][7]

Foucault rewrote *The Archaeology of Knowledge* [still in manuscript] after witnessing the travesties of May 1968. He restructured it as an archaeology of the dicey present, of how he and others were caught off guard. He offers splendid tools for excavation on discourse and cultural rupture. These match the spirit of his earlier books. The present always takes place before it happens— for example, in his first book *Madness and Civilization: A History of Insanity in the*

Age of Reason [1960] about bourgeois madhouses in France before the French Revolution. His subject was always power embedding itself before the fact. History was asynchronous, but readable—its noise, let us say, was highly structured. All you need to do is slow down your vision.

In that sense, Foucault was a master researcher of white noise. For example, he admired the historians of the Annales school, particularly Marc Bloch and Fernand Braudel. After the fall of France in 1940, both Bloch and Braudel were prisoners of war. While in POW camps, they each rewrote histories about the distant past: Bloch about feudalism, Braudel about the sixteenth-century Mediterranean world. These seemingly objective chronicles [in their syntax, at least] were histories of white noise in the everyday. They sound objective, but there are noisy intrusions, like unconscious memoir. Bloch called these "devolutions" and "disintegration at the edges."

White noise showed them [and Foucault] how power relies on local blackmail—that it always grasps blindly for control. Authoritarianism for Foucault, and for Bloch and Braudel, was achieved in the everyday. Outwardly, the events seem tiny. Accumulated white noise reveals the larger historical processes. Power sublimates through white noise—perverse changes in local customs, in local transactions, and in the way cities and resources are manipulated.

2016

To get that subjunctive irony, white noise comments on the present—on unseen but deeply felt ruptures. The present is always cluttered. As Foucault wrote in *The Archaeology of Knowledge,* the present is "a space of multiple dissensions."[8] Art captures these dissensions, even humanizes them. Art is filled with reveals that are white noise. This is not its primary goal, merely an unavoidable gift. If something is taboo, it will show up nakedly in art; as a moment of forgetting. Of course, the artist is not an economist, but the economy is embedded in the artist.

Now we turn to Aitken's installations and sculptures from another perspective: a different kind of noise. Altogether, Aitken's dozens of installations are a scripted journey about the shifting relationship between the viewer and the collective [coming from the Internet, economic inequality, urban planning, consumer marketing]. They are indeed time capsules, as soundscapes, as sculpture embedded with media memory, as multiscreen immersive spaces.

Cities: The Centrifugal Versus Compression

Here is a binary for understanding the changes captured by "white noise": Aitken often refers to the "nomadic" in his pieces centering on the city, as in his atlas-like, diaristic photo series *99¢ dreams* [2008; pages 104–109]. "Nomadic" implies mobile cityscapes that push out from the center—centrifugal, borderless, postsuburban. However, over the past decade [for reasons I will explain later], cities have shifted toward compressed, more theatrical narrative spaces. With that, the rhythm of the street, and of human sociality, has shifted as well: how we touch and are touched. The granular noise within cities has changed—I mean the sensorium of urban life itself. For example, Aitken's *electric earth* [1999; pages 120–131] is an updated sensorium of the new metropolis, where data overflows into brick and mortar.

The borderless stage of the 1990s has risen, emerging from a cocoon. During the early nineties, greater Los Angeles was at the highest point of its suburban expansion. Like other great cities, it was measured by the extent of its centrifugal sprawl. Today, densification has revived much of the inner city. Instead of a borderless LA region, we find an imperialist city-state: very arterial, not borderless.

The great cities are now layered kingdoms that choreograph our financial madness. Real estate and financial capital have cross-embedded, along with social networks and cityscapes. Also, the inequalities have hardened. The gated communities of the nineties have matured into more than simply suburban enclaves. They are now the model for urban control, even of greenscape planning. The crash of 2008 was frightening, the end of the world. Now we see that it wasn't the end; it was a transition. We may not like organized greedy chaos, but one looks for hopeful signs—perhaps in the new city-state.

That is why Aitken's newer installations use compression much more than earlier works, rely more on the nomadic as infrastructure, as if a new legibility were in place. This cautious optimism is most evident in Aitken's *Station to Station* [2013; pages 42–49], his cross-country tribute to our "nomadic hothouse." He takes us on a twenty-three-day familial montage by train: a variety theater about our mood since the crash. He finds a certain grace in our confusion. Nine cars roll along; performances are recorded minute by minute. It is a compressed narrative more than a multimedia sprawl. Each format operates as a component part, within a train [which is symbolically a nineteenth-century compression of media]. Among these components, *Station to Station* exists as a film, was "performed" for thirty days at the Barbican Centre in the summer of 2015, has been published in book form, and lives on in videos and photographs on Instagram.

Station to Station compresses the history of the train as media. So often, Aitken has reused icons about speed and our gothic fascination with industrial decay. The train was both in America: the symbol of machine culture—from the 1850s metropolis to the birth of cinema; from armored trains during the First World War to the simultaneity of collage [watching the rails intersect when you pulled into a train yard]; and then, by 1997, as a symbol of collapsing infrastructure.

But in 2016, the train suggests something much dreamier, more like synesthesia. Travel by rail is futuristic again. We don't hear the screech of the rails anymore. Trains let our anxieties roar in a synchronous way; their noise is engineered; leaving us almost medicated, drifting as though traveling through time. The soundproof windows help us settle into our nervous breakdown somehow. The trains are data interfaces now— immersive, cutting across the landscape, yet on a parallel track.

FRED: A Global One-Celled Animal

In September 2015, Doug Aitken and I chatted about disasters. We joked that our new political madness needs a new kind of mascot, a symbol of our collective stupidities. What if global parasitic madness were a living creature, in a biopolitical sense? What chimera would it look like?

Back in 2005, I had imagined this subjunctive madness as a place, rather than the "blur between fact and fiction." It was a floating city, organized for business. "The steel prow is held together electronically, no rivets only data... It sails uncontested... a translocal nowhere, a not-to-be-found government. It can pierce anything solid, go straight through concrete."⁹

But today, this noisy madness is surely a creature, with DNA. Aitken asked me to introduce this creature within my essay. This took some research.

I asked the Department of Plasmic Geology at UCLA for advice: were there any animals that resembled, say, flash trading on Wall Street? They said yes, there was one; but it could never be found on Google [too risky]. Over the past twenty years, they have been following the growth of a creature by the noise it makes. They call this thing a Fossilized Reticulated Engineered Digi-organism. The acronym is FRED.

FRED resembles a gigantic yellowish tapeworm. It lives, and reproduces, under the floorboards of every house — even below the skin of every gravelly and muddy spot on earth. As far as the scientists can tell, FRED is blind and hermaphroditic — but most dangerous of all, FRED is a one-celled animal. Sometimes, they found exposed slabs of FRED's protein mass. But clearly, they are only part of FRED; it has no hide, is as naked as a glass-bottomed boat.

The plasmic geologists were nervous about these slabs, because they seemed abnormal. Perhaps FRED had an ulcer. That would threaten all of the world's financial data, which apparently moves inside FRED's arteries. They really tried to fix what bumps they found, but could never be sure.

Since FRED is happy to whistle along at the speed of light, it clearly has no interest in whether we live or die. To say FRED has a plan for us would be presumptuous. That left a hard pill to swallow: like a stupid god, humans had created FRED, by merging software into living infrastructure. However, FRED clearly does not remember a thing. To be honest, FRED doesn't remember much at all, not the way we do.

Visually, according to laser video, FRED is the color of an infected toenail, like an earthworm perhaps. To the touch, FRED's surface is slug-like. Its protein muscles will cringe, even moan, if you poke at them. Zoologically speaking, FRED is closest to a supernatural jellyfish.

FRED only talks to itself and only thinks in commands [never asks questions]. When an idea is needed, FRED makes new proteins that move along transfer fluids. At its center, FRED has a spiky brain that is highly plastic. We don't know what may happen when FRED runs out of floorboard, in about ten years. It will probably add a second layer, maybe ten thousand layers, like grasses. FRED likes to feel botanical.

We sometimes hear FRED investigating us, in the form of a migraine, or a case of vertigo. But I can't pursue all that. What, cosmically speaking, FRED may "be" is too theological for a short essay. We'll just stay on track: FRED is very much a creature of 2016, where the boundaryless and the horizontal have become a new civilization based on white noise. It is actor-network theory run amok. But it is also a historical structural shift toward what I have been calling "feudalistic pluralism," a term that Aitken and I discussed a lot.

Noise and Feudalistic Pluralism

In the 1880s, during America's industrial takeoff, a plutocratic class arose like medieval princes. For the first time in the United States, there were endless complaints about serfdom. And indeed, as a condition, more than a system, an American feudalism does emerge between 1880 and 1929.

This American feudalism was not medieval, though all forms of colonization are feudal in some respects. There are simply many different species of feudalism—from fourth-century Greece, to seventeenth-century Japan, to nineteenth-century Egypt, to feudal Indonesia, China, Poland, Russia, the Ottoman Empire, the Moorish caliphate in North Africa and Spain...

Our feudalism probably resembles sixteenth-century Brazil more than eleventh-century France. Simply put, every country has a unique feudal condition waiting in the wings. It is oligarchic. It favors indentured labor. It tends to rely on financial blackmail. It cannot master-plan easily. It requires a very weak central government.

Our 2016 version of feudalism resembles early modern Europe from 1600 to 1800 more than the Middle Ages. That means feudalism is the ancestor of capitalism.[10] In Europe, feudalism incubated democracy, fascism of all kinds, communism, capitalism of all kinds, mercantilism, industrialism, much of the Renaissance, and the foundations of the modern city.

Many of these are like brood parasites. They cripple their host. What results is feudalistic pluralism. For example, digital banking is a parasite. It was incubated by its host, the federal government. At first, in the eighties, the new speed of "free trade" promised an effortless and borderless utopia, an alternative to the Cold War. Now we see the mature version. Digital banking is FRED. It has left the federal government crippled. Without federal laws, we cannot master-plan. Our national infrastructure, the pride of the American century, will probably not be upgraded in time: the roads, schools, power grids, waterways—and, most of all, our job economy.

I often compare feudalistic pluralism to a tattered sweater. Moths leave holes that cannot be repaired. These become voids that incubate oligarchies (pirates) of all kinds. The holes also liberate regional authority, especially in coastal megacities. With each financial crisis since 1997, oligarchy has become more entrenched, more the law of the land. Oligarchic finaglings are deregulated, made legal. Tax havens legalize piracy through offshore businesses. And cities have achieved a strange new splendor.

In the artist's book for his happening for the 2010 Museum of Contemporary Art, Los Angeles gala, *The Idea of the West* (2010)—one thousand interviews about the West—Aitken looks through a hotel window to "the modern re-gentrified downtown (LA)," where "city lines intersect and penetrate one another creating a vast grid seemingly without an entry point."[11] This is a shift in narrative method surely. It suggests more compression, where boundaryless flow is now a civilization, a map—a system built (as a grid) around noise. In *Station to Station*, this narrative compression is even more apparent. Indeed, the space inside the train reenacts the buzz and blur of a great one-celled animal—but one with an exoskeleton, on rails, with stops along the way.

Aitken's *sleepwalkers* (2007; pages 200-201, 234) is another curious example. Through outdoor projections, he clearly meant to convert the pulse of midtown Manhattan (via the exterior of The Museum of Modern Art) into a kind of one-celled biomass. He writes:

"The city becomes a living breathing body merging with the diverse and constantly changing individuals who make up the city."[12]

In the cinematic poem and installation *Black Mirror* [2011; figs. 1, 2, pages 132-143], we find edited videos built around the noises of machinery in a woman's life. Finally, the pulse is compressed into a small arena around a bed, where actress Chloë Sevigny repeats the line "Exchange, connect, and move on," rather like Aitken comparing the pulse of rock music to "an implosion."[13]

Today, as part of the Internet of things, "noise" is a workhorse with many practical uses. It is a mode of data transmission. It is a tradition coming out of ambient drone music, "an acoustic foundation from which other sounds emerged, and to which all sounds eventually return."[14] It is advanced baroque[15] immersion [the clatter of the new gig economy].

The nineties in America were notable for baroque immersion, but it was seen mostly in themed spaces. That language has since found its way to China and the Middle East—as infrastructure. Instead of malls and theme parks, immersion is now the hardwired regime of city-states—highly integrated urban regions, especially on the coasts. Los Angeles has been thoroughly redesigned structurally since 1997. It is now an arterial economy, thoroughly networked from its harbors. It is increasingly a crossroads city, a region of eighteen million people

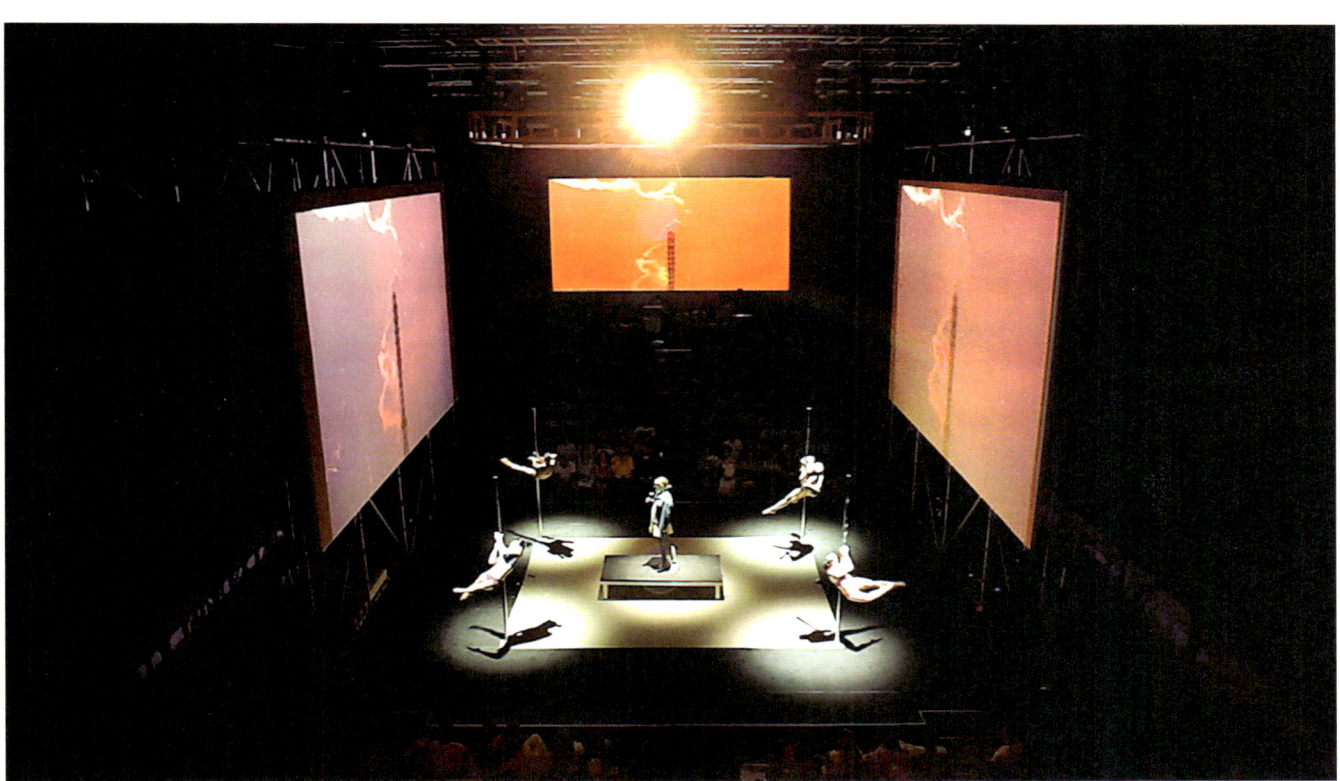

Fig. 1
Black Mirror, 2011
Documentation still from Hydra, Greece, performance
Courtesy of the artist; DESTE Foundation
for Contemporary Art; Hellenic Festival;
Burger Collection; 303 Gallery, New York;
and Galerie Eva Presenhuber, Zurich

linked [hardwired] to three continents, ethnographically, economically, and culturally—station to station. We have not seen urban kingdoms on this scale—or as arterial—since the fifteenth century. And there are dozens of them throughout the world. Los Angeles is simply Aitken's sculptural hyperspace.

On the seas, container ships are neofeudalist white noise. The ships themselves parallel Aitken's immersive spaces, where the crisis of labor—the loss of the human, the loss of agency—are materialized. What in the 1990s looked more like the adventure of flow [of no boundary] has evolved into a world of fiercer boundaries, but not without options [again, *Black Mirror*].

Consider the strange comeback of American freight lines lately and the public's renewed fascination with trolleys. We are retro moderns imagining a smaller carbon footprint. Like Aitken's soundscapes and multichannel engines, we live in a granular modernity, more like 1896 than 1996. Everything seems to be incubating at once, from new forms of authoritarianism to new modes of socialist revolt—expanded democracy and inequality at the same time. We identify FRED with climate change, with the withering of the nation-state, with growing inequality, with oligarchic stupidities that grow more bizarre year by year. That is what I see in Aitken's art, a genealogy of the senses in a world that accelerates sideways, under the new conditions of feudalistic pluralism.

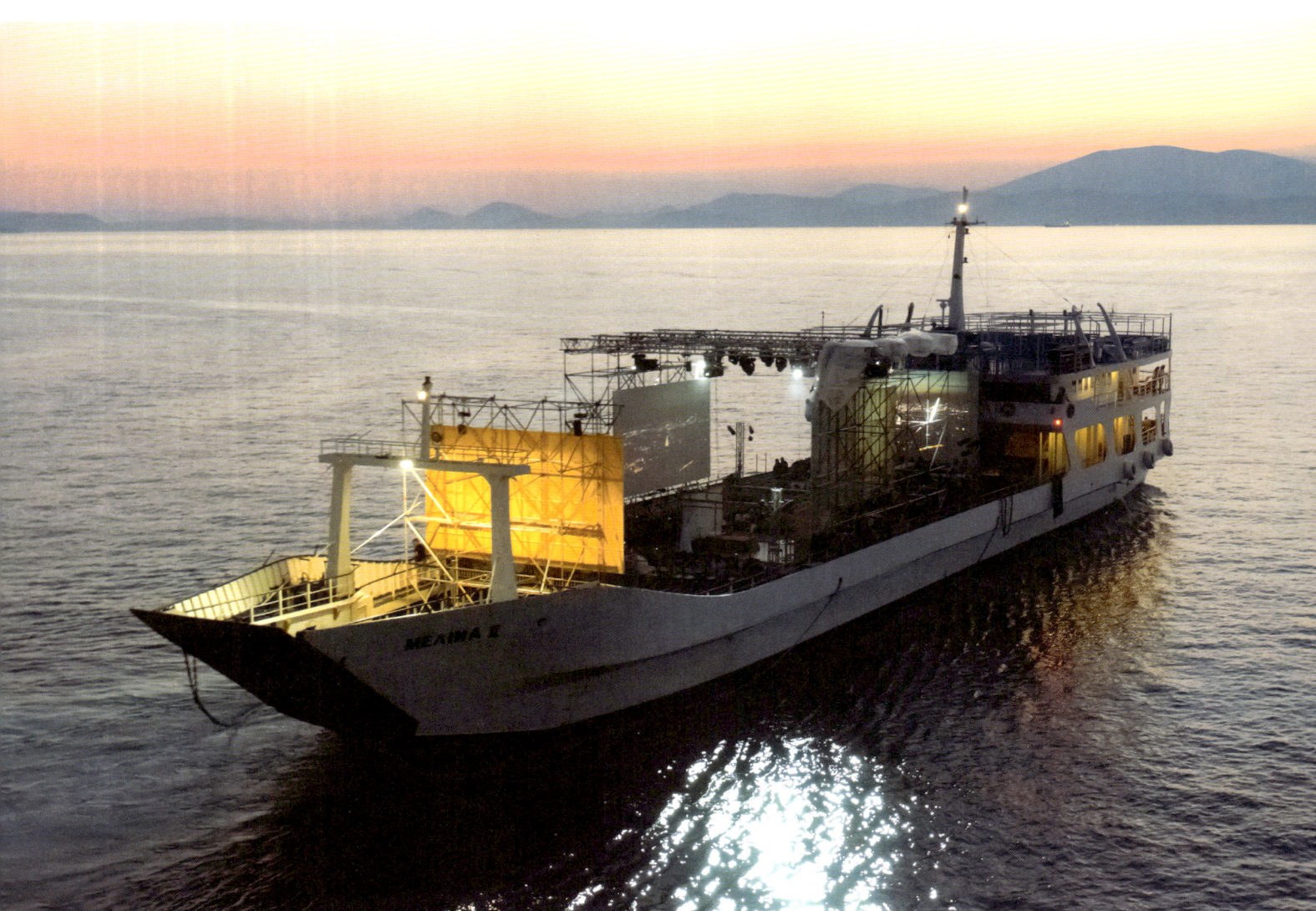

Notes

1 Doug Aitken, quoted in "Amanda Sharp in Conversation with Doug Aitken," *Doug Aitken* (London: Phaidon, 2001), 29.

2 William Clark, *Academic Charisma and the Origins of the Research University* (Chicago: University of Chicago Press, 2006), 374.

3 Anthony Curtis, "An Outsider in This Society: An Interview with Don DeLillo," in *Introducing Don DeLillo*, ed. Frank Lentricchia (Durham, NC: Duke University Press, 1991), 63.

4 Martin Herbert, "Vanishing Point: On *Black Mirror*," *Doug Aitken* exhibition catalogue (Frankfurt: Schirn Kunsthalle Frankfurt; Vienna: Verlag für moderne Kunst, 2015), 79.

5 Ibid.

6 Paul Virilio, quoted in Dean Kuipers and Doug Aitken, *I Am a Bullet: Scenes from an Accelerating Culture* (New York: Crown Publishers, 2000), 105.

7 Michel Foucault, *The Archaeology of Knowledge and the Discourse on Language* (1971), trans. A. M. Sheridan Smith (New York: Vintage Books, 2010), 76.

8 Ibid., 155.

9 Norman M. Klein, *Freud in Coney Island and Other Tales* (Los Angeles: Otis Books, 2006), 39.

10 Feudalism is usually identified with manorialism, or an autarkic (thoroughly inbred) version of vassalage and manorial life. Very early on, embedded in this system was a money economy, to make all the fees and dues viable.

11 Doug Aitken, *The Idea of the West* (New York: DAP; Los Angeles: MOCA; Zurich: JRP|Ringer, 2010), 128.

12 Doug Aitken, quoted in Klaus Biesenbach, "Building Images," *Doug Aitken: Sleepwalkers* exhibition catalogue (New York: The Museum of Modern Art, 2007), 6.

13 Aitken, quoted in Clive Thompson, "Vision Quest: This Man Has a Train, an Army of Artists, and an Entire Nation for a Gallery," *Wired*, August 19, 2013, http://www.wired.com/aitken-station-to-station.

14 Joanna Demers, *Drone and Apocalypse: An Exhibit Catalog for the End of the World* (Portland, OR: Zero Books, 2014), 9.

15 When I discuss the baroque, I emphasize that it flourished during the centuries when feudalistic pluralism was at its peak in Europe: 1600–1780. We find the mercantilist bourgeoisie and the old feudal monarchs as the two most dangerous factions in this era. Although feuding themselves, like gangsters, they had a common enemy: the feudal nobility. What resulted, amid countless gruesome disasters, was an unsteady alliance between the two. This alliance created endless frictions. And from this friction, there emerged architectural noise. We see it in baroque palaces—intricately suggested by the flamboyant stucco and layers of domed illusion. The raw deal is even more apparent in baroque theater design, so *raffiné*, but thoroughly corrupted by noise, perhaps from a disdainful aristocrat, seated in a box directly onstage. Then came the thrum of expensive effects. What does this noisy, immersive baroque setting tell us—then and now—this flutter of special effects, in 1650 very nautical, like sails in a shipwreck, throwaway details in the corners and underneath, overhead? The noise is filled with morbid and comical, but expert, uses of the new business software (mathematical and nautical perspective), but on behalf of—in promotion of—the king. Neither side trusted the other, any more than global capital trusts the nation-state today.

There lies the heart of the baroque, then and now: no matter how internalized a space may seem, it cannot be a formalism. It is, instead, always a concatenation, a contrapuntal (almost unconscious, subjunctive) attempt at narrativizing the shipwrecks that threaten the unsteady alliances between capital and the state.

As a result, baroque forms of immersion have always been an epic story about dissonance and tonality corrupted by spectacular noise (by chaos brought to heel). No doubt, this noise is inescapably political, whatever its expressionist and magic realist thrills—its aesthetic remove. It is always filled with the sound of evasions, secrets, and political scoundrels. The language of the space is indeed in the air.

Fig. 2
Black Mirror, 2011
Documentation still from Hydra, Greece performance.
Dimensions variable
Courtesy of the artist; DESTE Foundation for Contemporary Art; Hellenic Festival; Burger Collection; 303 Gallery, New York; and Galerie Eva Presenhuber, Zurich

Exhibition Checklist

Unless otherwise noted, all works are courtesy of the artist; 303 Gallery, New York; Galerie Eva Presenhuber, Zurich; Victoria Miro Gallery, London; and Regen Projects, Los Angeles.

Acid Modernism, 2012
Video documentation
4:30 minutes
Courtesy of the artist

Black Mirror, 2011
Video installation with three channels of video [color, sound], three monitors, freestanding room, mirrors
13:20 minutes/loop
Installation dimensions variable
Edition 2 of 4

conspiracy, 1998
Chromogenic print mounted on acrylic
48 × 48 inches [121.9 × 121.9 cm]
Edition 6 of 10

desire [chemical spills], 2009
Chromogenic print with MSG [monosodium glutamate], fluoxetine [Prozac], and chlorine bleach mounted on aluminum
56¾ × 47 inches [144.1 × 119.4 cm]
Collection of Cristina and Thomas Bechtler

diamond sea, 1997
Video installation with three channels of video [color, sound], three projections, monitor, chromogenic transparency mounted on acrylic in aluminum lightbox with LEDs
11:50 minutes/loop
Installation dimensions variable
Edition 1 of 3
Exhibition copy
La Colección Jumex, México

don't think twice II, 2006
Neon on lacquered wood panel with electronic controls
84 × 114 × 9 inches [213.4 × 289.6 × 22.9 cm]
Edition 4 of 4
Collection of Allison and Warren B. Kanders

electric earth, 1999
Video installation with eight channels of video [color, sound], eight projections, four-room architectural environment
9:50 minutes/loop
Installation dimensions variable
Edition 3 of 4
The Museum of Contemporary Art, Los Angeles
Partial and promised gift of David Teiger in honor of Jeremy Strick

END [mirror], 2014
Mirrored glass, resin, concrete
44¼ × 47 × 11¼ inches
[112.7 × 119.4 × 28.6 cm]
Variation 1 of 4
Marciano Art Collection

eraser, 1998
Single-channel video [color, sound]
17:35 minutes
Edition 1 of 5
Partial and promised Gift of Pamela and C. Richard Kramlich to the New Art Trust to benefit the San Francisco Museum of Modern Art, The Museum of Modern Art, New York, and Tate, United Kingdom

Frontier, 2009
Single-channel video [color, sound]
17:40 minutes
Edition 2 of 6
Kadist Art Foundation

the handle comes up, the hammer comes down, 2009
Video documentation
5:33 minutes
Courtesy of the artist

House, 2010
Video installation with one channel of video [color, sound], two monitors, wood table
8:36 minutes/loop
Edition 1 of 2

i am in you, 2000
Single-channel video [color, sound]
11:17 minutes
Edition 1 of 4
Exhibition copy
Sammlung Goetz, München

i'd die for you, 1993
Single-channel video [color, sound]
10:58 minutes
Edition 1 of 5

inflection, 1992
Single-channel video [color, silent]
14:02 minutes
Edition 1 of 5

interiors, 2002
Single-channel video [color, sound]
7:04 minutes
Edition 1 of 6

lighthouse, 2012
Video documentation
5:10 minutes
Courtesy of the artist

migration [empire], 2008
Video installation with three channels of video [color, sound], three projections, three steel and PVC screen billboard sculptures
24:28 minutes/loop
Installation dimensions variable

the mirror #11 [rise], 1998
Chromogenic print mounted on acrylic
30 × 35 inches [76.2 × 88.9 cm]
Exhibition copy

the moment, 2005
Single-channel video [color, sound]
6:42 minutes
Edition 4 of 4
Collection of Gustavo Mana

monsoon, 1995
Single-channel video [color, sound]
6:43 minutes
Edition 1 of 5
The Art Institute of Chicago,
Gift of Donna and Howard Stone

MORE [shattered pour], 2013
High-density foam, wood, mirror
63 × 48½ × 7½ inches [160 × 121.9 × 19.1 cm]
Variation 4 of 4
Collection of Jenny Emerson

new shelter II, 2001/2016
Chromogenic transparency
mounted on acrylic in aluminum
lightbox with LEDs
90 × 120 × 7 inches [228.6 × 304.8 × 17.8 cm]

1968 [broken], 2011
High-density foam, wood, mirror
36 × 80 × 8½ inches [91.4 × 203.2 × 21.6 cm]
Variation 3 of 4
Anthony and Jeanne Pritzker
Collection

99c dreams, 2007
Neon
35¼ × 54¼ × ½ inches [89.5 × 137.6 × 1.3 cm]
Edition 3 of 4
Private collection

99c dreams, 2008
216 chromogenic prints
18 × 23 inches [45.7 × 58.4 cm] each
Edition 3 of 4
Collection of Maja Hoffmann

NOW [Blue Mirror], 2014
Wood, mirror, glass
48¼ × 108½ × 18 inches
[122.6 × 275.6 × 45.7 cm]
Variation 4 of 4
Private collection

ONE, 2011
Chromogenic transparency
mounted on acrylic in aluminum lightbox
with LEDs
30 × 84 × 7½ inches [76.2 × 213.4 × 19.1 cm]
Edition 4 of 4

100 YRS [part 2], 2013
Video documentation
2:25 minutes
Courtesy of the artist
and 303 Gallery, New York

100 YRS [neon], 2014
Hand-carved foam, acrylic, neon
64 × 88 × 10¼ inches [162.6 × 223.5 × 26 cm]
Variation 2 of 4

open door [chemical series], 2007
Chromogenic print with codeine
and nitric acid mounted on aluminum
60 × 48 inches [152.4 × 121.9 cm]

passenger, 1997
Chromogenic print mounted
on acrylic
38¾ × 47¾ inches [98.4 × 121.3 cm]
AP 2 of 2

Please, 2016
Chromogenic transparency mounted
on acrylic in aluminum lightbox
with LEDs
45½ × 45½ × 7 inches
[115.6 × 115.6 × 17.8 cm]
Edition 2 of 4

points of transition [chemical series], 2007
Chromogenic print with hydrochloric
acid and fluoxetine [Prozac]
mounted on aluminum
60 × 48 inches [152.4 × 121.9 cm]

sleeper [chemical series], 2007
Chromogenic print with sulfuric
acid, melatonin, zolpidem [Ambien],
and tryptamine mounted on aluminum
60 × 48 inches [152.4 × 121.9 cm]

sleepwalkers, 2007
Single-channel video [color, sound]
16:18 minutes
Edition 2 of 6
Collection of Allison
and Warren B. Kanders

SONG 1, 2012/2015
Video installation with seven-
channel composite video
[color, sound], seven blended
projections, 360-degree aluminum
and PVC screen
34:44 minutes/loop
Installation dimensions variable
Edition 1 of 4
Hirshhorn Museum and Sculpture
Garden, Smithsonian Institution,
Washington, DC, Joseph H.
Hirshhorn Bequest Fund and
Anonymous Gift, 2012, dedicated in
honor of Kerry Brougher's service
to the Hirshhorn Museum and
Sculpture Garden [2000–2014], 2014

Sonic Fountain II, 2013/2015
Live sound installation
with computer-controlled nine-
valve fountain, tinted water,
basin, nine underwater microphones,
speakers
Installation dimensions variable
Variation 2 of 4

Sonic Pavilion, 2009
Video documentation
5:15 minutes
Courtesy of the artist

Station to Station, 2015
Documentary feature film
with 62 one-minute segments
70 minutes

station to station [chemical series], 2007
Chromogenic print with sulfuric
acid, fluoxetine [Prozac],
and zolpidem [Ambien] mounted
on aluminum
60 × 48 inches [152.4 × 121.9 cm]
Collection of Tom and Mila Tuttle

Station to Station [Volume], 2013
Earth, acrylic, steel
60 × 12 × 12 inches [152.4 × 30.5 × 30.5 cm]
Edition 2 of 10

Station to Station [Volume], 2013
Earth, acrylic, steel
60 × 12 × 12 inches [152.4 × 30.5 × 30.5 cm]
Edition 5 of 10
Kramlich Collection

Station to Station [Volume], 2013
Earth, acrylic, steel
60 × 12 × 12 inches [152.4 × 30.5 × 30.5 cm]
Edition 6 of 10
Collection of Ruth and William True

*Sun Sinking into the Santa
Monica Bay,* 2010
Mixed-media collage
19¼ × 15¼ inches [48.9 × 38.7 cm], framed

Sunset [black], 2012
Hand-carved foam, epoxy, LEDs,
hand-silkscreened acrylic
63½ × 78½ × 8 inches
[161.3 × 198.8 × 20.3 cm]
Variation 2 of 4
Collection of Ellen Pompeo

these restless minds, 1998
Video installation with three
channels of video [color, sound],
three monitors, plywood platform
and benches
8:03 minutes/loop
Installation dimensions variable
Edition 2 of 4
The Dallas Museum of Art,
Lay Family Acquisition Fund

twilight, 2014
Cast resin, acrylic, responsive LEDs
71¾ × 54¼ × 54¼ inches
[182.2 × 137.8 × 137.8 cm]
Edition 2 of 4
The Broad Art Foundation

twilight [triptych], 2016
Cast resin, acrylic, responsive LEDs
30¾ × 79½ × 9½ inches
[78.1 × 201.9 × 24.1 cm]
Edition 1 of 4

ultraworld A, 2005
Mixed-media collage
19¾ × 15¾ inches
[49.8 × 39.7 cm], framed
The Museum of Modern Art, New York,
Judith Rothschild Foundation
Contemporary Drawings Collection

ultraworld B, 2005
Mixed-media collage
15¾ × 19¾ inches [39.7 × 49.8 cm], framed
The Museum of Modern Art, New York,
Judith Rothschild Foundation
Contemporary Drawings Collection

ultraworld C, 2005
Mixed-media collage
15¾ × 19¾ inches
[39.7 × 49.8 cm], framed
The Museum of Modern Art, New York,
Judith Rothschild Foundation
Contemporary Drawings Collection

ultraworld I, 2007
Mixed-media collage
17¾ × 13 inches [45.1 × 33 cm], framed
Kravis Collection

ultraworld K, 2007
Mixed-media collage
12¾ × 17½ inches [32.1 × 44.5 cm],
framed
Kravis Collection

ultraworld L, 2007
Mixed-media collage
25¾ × 19¾ inches [65.4 × 50.2 cm],
framed
Kravis Collection

ultraworld M, 2007
Mixed-media collage
17¾ × 13 inches [45.4 × 33 cm], framed
Kravis Collection

ultraworld N, 2007
Mixed-media collage
17¾ × 13½ inches [44.8 × 34.3 cm],
framed
Kravis Collection

ultraworld Q, 2007
Mixed-media collage
25¾ × 19¾ inches [65.4 × 50.2 cm],
framed
Kravis Collection

ultraworld R, 2007
Mixed-media collage
19 × 14 inches [48.3 × 35.6 cm], framed
Kravis Collection

ultraworld T-W, 2006–2008
Four mixed-media collages
19 × 15 inches [48.3 × 38.1 cm] each,
framed
Kravis Collection

Untitled, 2005–2010
Mixed-media collage
19¼ × 15¼ inches [48.9 × 38.7 cm],
framed
Collection of Tracey Jacobs

Untitled, 2005–2010
Mixed-media collage
32 × 24 inches [81.3 × 61 cm], framed

*untitled [Santa Barbara Offshore
Platforms] I*, 1998
Chromogenic print mounted
on acrylic
40 × 51¾ inches [101.6 × 131.4 cm]
Edition 1 of 5

*WHAT WE DID WAS STAND AROUND AND
WAIT FOR SOMETHING TO HAPPEN*, 2011
Chromogenic transparency
on acrylic in aluminum lightbox
with LEDs
45½ × 45½ × 7 inches
[115.6 × 115.6 × 17.8 cm]
Edition 3 of 4
Collection of Gelila
and Wolfgang Puck

WILD JUSTICE, 2014
Chromogenic transparency
on acrylic in aluminum lightbox
with LEDs
46 × 46 × 5 inches [116.8 × 116.8 × 12.7 cm]
Edition 4 of 4
Collection of Janet Friesen

Image Captions

Acid Modernism, 2012
Architectural and audio environment of private residence in Venice, CA; house, sound, microphones, lighting, objects, and mirrors
p. 259

Black Mirror, 2011
Video installation with three channels of video [color, sound], three monitors, freestanding room, mirrors
13:20 minutes/loop
pp. 132–143

conspiracy, 1998
Chromogenic print mounted on acrylic
48 × 48 inches [121.9 × 121.9 cm]
pp. 114–115

desire [chemical spills], 2009
Chromogenic print with MSG [monosodium glutamate], fluoxetine [Prozac], and chlorine bleach mounted on aluminum
56¾ × 47 inches [144.1 × 119.4 cm]
p. 6

diamond sea, 1997
Video installation with three channels of video [color, sound], three projections, monitor, chromogenic transparency mounted on acrylic in aluminum lightbox with LEDs
11:50 minutes/loop
88 × 197 × 12 inches
[224 × 500 × 30 cm] [lightbox]
pp. 74–85

don't think twice II, 2006
Neon on lacquered wood panel with electronic controls
84 × 114 × 9 inches [213.4 × 289.6 × 22.9 cm]
pp. 10–11

electric earth, 1999
Video installation with eight channels of video [color, sound], eight projections, four-room architectural environment
9:50 minutes/loop
pp. 120–127, 130–131

END [mirror], 2014
Mirrored glass, resin, concrete
44¾ × 47 × 11¼ inches
[112.7 × 119.4 × 28.6 cm]
pp. 62–63

eraser, 1998
Single-channel video [color, sound]
17:35 minutes
p. 237

Frontier, 2009
Single-channel video [color, sound]
17:40 minutes
p. 234

the handle comes up, the hammer comes down, 2009
Performance with auctioneers
Part of *Il Tempo del Postino*, Basel, Switzerland
p. 246

House, 2010
Video installation with one channel of video [color, sound], two monitors, wood table, debris
8:36 minutes/loop
pp. 156–163, 165

i am in you, 2000
Single-channel video [color, sound]
11:17 minutes
p. 236

i'd die for you, 1993
Single-channel video [color, sound]
10:58 minutes
p. 238

inflection, 1992
Single-channel video [color, silent]
14:02 minutes
p. 238

interiors, 2002
Single-channel video [color, sound]
7:04 minutes
p. 235

landscape signs [sign happening], 2014
Performance, Los Angeles, CA
p. 54

lighthouse, 2012
Outdoor video installation wrapping house exterior with moving images of surrounding landscape, six channels of video [color, silent], seven projections forming five screens
Jill and Peter Kraus residence, Dutchess County, NY
41:43 minutes/loop
p. 232

migration [empire], 2008
Video installation with three channels of video [color, sound], three projections, three steel and PVC screen billboard sculptures
24:28 minutes/loop
121 × 184 × 45 inches [307 × 467 × 116 cm];
119 × 184 × 45 inches [302 × 467 × 116 cm];
116 × 184 × 45 inches [295 × 467 × 116 cm]
pp. 144–155

the mirror #9, 1998
Chromogenic print mounted on acrylic
30 × 35 inches [76.2 × 88.9 cm]
pp. 38–39

the mirror #11 [rise], 1998
Chromogenic print mounted on acrylic
30 × 35 inches [76.2 × 88.9 cm]
pp. 40–41

the moment, 2005
Single-channel video [color, sound]
6:42 minutes
p. 235

monsoon, 1995
Single-channel video [color, sound]
6:43 minutes/loop
p. 237

MORE [shattered pour], 2013
High-density foam, wood, mirror
63 × 48½ × 7½ inches [160 × 121.9 × 19.1 cm]
p. 184

new shelter II, 2001/2016
Chromogenic transparency mounted on acrylic in aluminum lightbox with LEDs
90 × 120 × 7 inches [228.6 × 304.8 × 17.7 cm]
pp. 86–87

1968 [broken], 2011
High-density foam, wood, mirror
36 × 80 × 8½ inches [91.4 × 203.2 × 21.6 cm]
pp. 88–89

99c dreams, 2007
Neon
35¼ × 54¼ × ½ inches
[89.5 × 137.6 × 1.3 cm]
pp. 102–103

99c dreams, 2008
216 chromogenic prints
18 × 23 inches [45.7 × 58.4 cm] each
pp. 104–109

no history, 2005
Stainless steel mirrors,
electric motors
94 × 186 × 340 inches [240 × 472 × 864 cm]
pp. 60-61

Nomadic Light Sculpture, 2013
Sensor-controlled LEDs on train
for *Station to Station*,
New York to San Francisco
pp. 262-263

NOW (Blue Mirror), 2014
Wood, mirror, glass
48¼ × 108½ × 18 inches
[122.6 × 275.6 × 45.7 cm]
pp. 72-73

ONE, 2011
Chromogenic transparency
on acrylic in aluminum lightbox
with LEDs
30 × 84 × 7½ inches [76.2 × 213.4 × 19.1 cm]
pp. 230-231

100 YRS (part 2), 2013
Performance with elevator operator
and three percussionists/
destructors at 303 Gallery,
New York
Five days
pp. 31-32, 244

open door (chemical series), 2007
Chromogenic print with codeine
and nitric acid mounted
on aluminum
60 × 48 inches [152.4 × 121.9 cm]
p. 116

passenger, 1997
Chromogenic print mounted
on acrylic
38¼ × 47¼ inches [98.4 × 121.3 cm]
pp. 110-111

*points of transition (chemical
series)*, 2007
Chromogenic print with hydrochloric
acid and fluoxetine [Prozac]
mounted on aluminum
60 × 48 inches [152.4 × 121.9 cm]
p. 117

sleeper (chemical series), 2007
Chromogenic print with sulfuric
acid, melatonin, zolpidem
[Ambien], and tryptamine mounted
on aluminum
60 × 48 inches [152.4 × 121.9 cm]
p. 118

sleepwalkers, 2007
Single-channel video [color, sound]
16:18 minutes
pp. 200-201, 234

SONG 1, 2012
Outdoor video installation
on 360-degree facade of Hirshhorn
Museum and Sculpture Garden,
Smithsonian Institution,
Washington, DC, seven-channel
composite video [color, sound],
eleven projections forming
one screen
34:44 minutes/loop
50 × 725 feet circumference
[15.2 × 220.9 m circumference] [screen]
Commissioned, with generous
production support, by the
Hirshhorn Museum and Sculpture
Garden, Smithsonian Institution
pp. 166-167

SONG 1, 2012/2015
Video installation with seven-
channel composite video [color,
sound], seven blended projections,
360-degree aluminum and PVC screen
34:44 minutes/loop
Commissioned, with generous
production support, by the
Hirshhorn Museum and Sculpture
Garden, Smithsonian Institution
pp. 168-177

Sonic Fountain, 2013
Live sound installation
with computer-controlled five-valve
fountain, tinted water, basin,
five underwater microphones,
speakers
pp. 30-32, 34-35

Sonic Pavilion, 2009
Architecture and sound installation, Centro de Arte Contemporânea
Inhotim, Brumadinho, Brazil.
At the pavilion's center is a hole
bored 700 feet into the earth;
microphones capture the earth's
sounds and tectonic plates
shifting, which are heard inside
the pavilion.
46 feet diameter × 13.8 feet
above grade [14 m diameter × 4.2 m
above grade]
pp. 2-3, 233

Station to Station, 2013
A kinetic light sculpture in
the form of a train traveled from
New York City to San Francisco
making ten stops along the way for
a series of site-specific happen-
ings in New York, Pittsburgh,
St. Paul, Chicago, Kansas City, MO,
Lamy, NM, Winslow, AZ, Barstow,
CA, Los Angeles, and Oakland, CA;
September 6-28, 2013
pp. 44-47

Station to Station, 2015
Documentary feature film
with 62 one-minute segments
70 minutes
pp. 42-44

*station to station (chemical
series)*, 2007
Chromogenic print with sulfuric
acid, fluoxetine [Prozac],
and zolpidem [Ambien] mounted
on aluminum
60 × 48 inches [152.4 × 121.9 cm]
p. 119

Station to Station (Volume), 2013
Earth, acrylic, steel
60 × 12 × 12 inches [152.4 × 30.5 × 30.5 cm]
pp. 48-49

THE SOURCE [evolving], 2012–ongoing
Video installation with six channels of color video and six channels of stereo sound, six projections, featuring twenty-three conversations in an architectural pavilion. Additional conversations may be added over time. *THE SOURCE* Pavilion, designed by Adjaye Associates, collaboration with Doug Aitken.
60 minutes/loop
Pavilion: 57 feet 2 inches diameter × 19 feet 2 inches height
[17.4 m diameter × 5.8 m height]
Screens [six]: 87.5 × 155 inches
[222 × 394 cm]
Made possible by a generous contribution from The Maurice Marciano Family Foundation
pp. 50–57

Sun Sinking into the Santa Monica Bay, 2010
Mixed-media collage
19¼ × 15¼ inches [48.9 × 38.7 cm]
p. 24

Sunset [black], 2012
Hand-carved foam, epoxy, LEDs, hand-silkscreened acrylic
63½ × 78¼ × 8 inches
[161.3 × 198.8 × 20.3 cm]
pp. 58–59

these restless minds, 1998
Video installation with three channels of video [color, sound], three monitors, plywood platform and benches
8:03 minutes/loop
pp. 92–99, 101

twilight, 2014
Cast resin, acrylic, responsive LEDs
71¾ × 54¼ × 54¼ inches
[182.2 × 137.8 × 137.8 cm]
pp. 66–71

ultraworld A, 2005
Mixed-media collage
19⅝ × 15⅝ inches [49.8 × 39.7 cm], framed
p. 22

ultraworld B, 2005
Mixed-media collage
15⅝ × 19⅝ inches [39.7 × 49.8 cm], framed
p. 23

ultraworld C, 2005
Mixed-media collage
15⅝ × 19⅝ inches [39.7 × 49.8 cm], framed
p. 23

ultraworld I, 2007
Mixed-media collage
17¾ × 13 inches [45.1 × 33 cm], framed
p. 27

ultraworld K, 2007
Mixed-media collage
12⅝ × 17½ inches [32.1 × 44.5 cm], framed
p. 16

ultraworld L, 2007
Mixed-media collage
25¾ × 19¾ inches [65.4 × 50.2 cm], framed
p. 19

ultraworld M, 2007
Mixed-media collage
17⅞ × 13 inches [45.4 × 33 cm], framed
p. 17

ultraworld N, 2007
Mixed-media collage
17⅝ × 13½ inches [44.8 × 34.3 cm], framed
p. 20

ultraworld Q, 2007
Mixed-media collage
25¾ × 19¾ inches [65.4 × 50.2 cm], framed
p. 18

ultraworld R, 2007
Mixed-media collage
19 × 14 inches [48.3 × 35.6 cm], framed
p. 4

ultraworld T from set *ultraworld T–W*, 2006–2008
Mixed-media collage
19 × 15 inches [48.3 × 38.1 cm], framed
p. 26

ultraworld U from set *ultraworld T–W*, 2006–2008
Mixed-media collage
19 × 15 inches [48.3 × 38.1 cm], framed
p. 26

ultraworld V from set *ultraworld T–W*, 2006–2008
Mixed-media collage
19 × 15 inches [48.3 × 38.1 cm], framed
p. 20

ultraworld W from set *ultraworld T–W*, 2006–2008
Mixed-media collage
19 × 15 inches [48.3 × 38.1 cm], framed
p. 24

Underwater Pavilions, 2016
Underwater geometric environments [three] with composite materials, mirror and live video feed
p. 245

Untitled, 2005–2010
Mixed-media collage
19¼ × 15¼ inches [48.9 × 38.7 cm], framed
p. 21

Untitled, 2005–2010
Mixed-media collage
32 × 24 inches [81.3 × 61 cm], framed
p. 25

Untitled [Santa Barbara Offshore Platforms] I, 1998
Chromogenic print mounted on acrylic
40 × 51¾ inches [101.6 × 131.4 cm]
pp. 112–113

Untitled [shopping cart], 2000
Chromogenic print mounted on acrylic
48 × 56 inches [121.9 × 142.2 cm]
pp. 128–129

WHAT WE DID WAS STAND AROUND AND WAIT FOR SOMETHING TO HAPPEN, 2011
Chromogenic transparency on acrylic in aluminum lightbox with LEDS
45½ × 45½ × 7 inches
[115.6 × 115.6 × 17.8 cm]
pp. 90–91

WILD JUSTICE, 2014
Chromogenic transparency on acrylic in aluminum lightbox with LEDs
46 × 46 × 5 inches [116.8 × 116.8 × 12.7 cm]
pp. 64–65

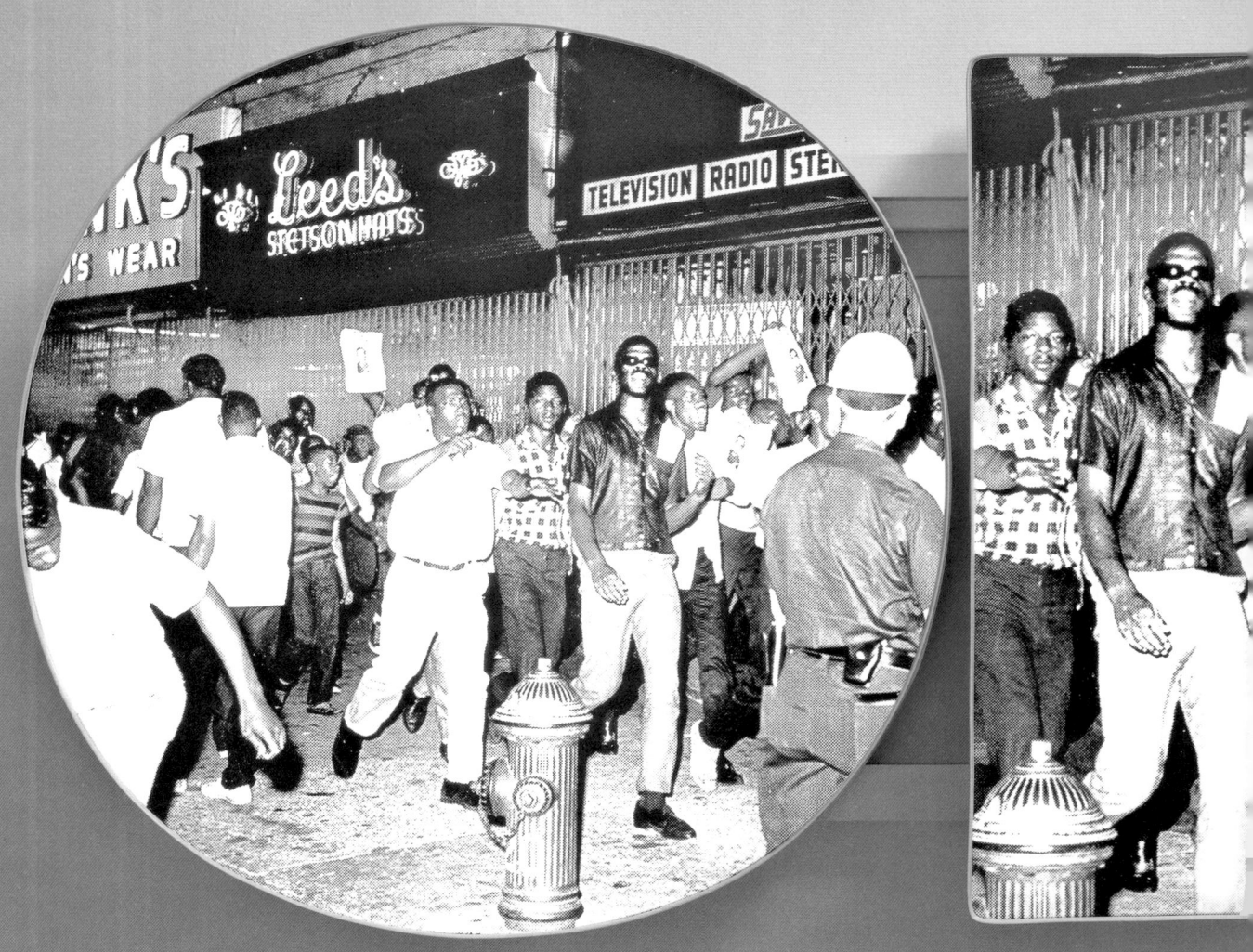

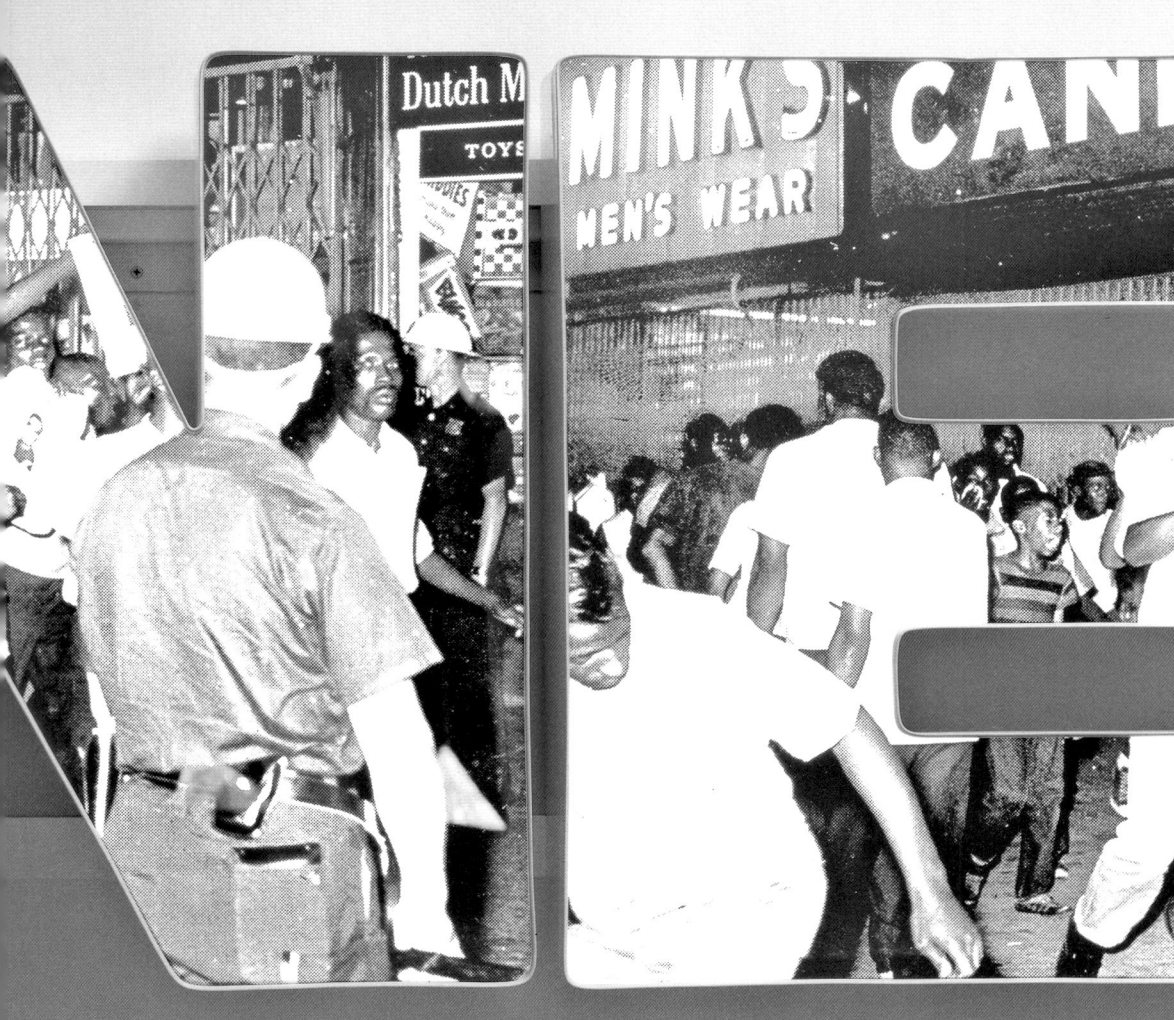

Doug Aitken

Born 1968 in Redondo Beach, CA

Education

1987–91 BFA, Art Center College of Design, Pasadena, CA
1986–87 Marymount College, Palos Verdes, CA

Installations, Videography, and Filmography

2015 SONG 1, video installation with seven-channel composite video [color, sound], seven blended projections, 360-degree aluminum and PVC screen; 34:44 minutes/loop
Sonic Fountain II, live sound installation with computer-controlled nine-valve fountain, tinted water, basin, nine underwater microphones, speakers; loop

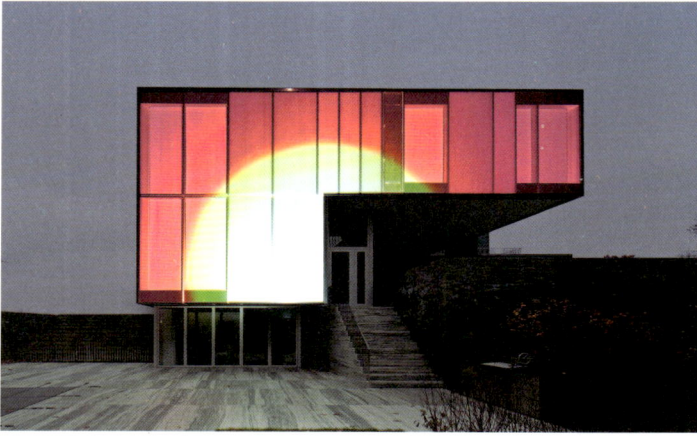

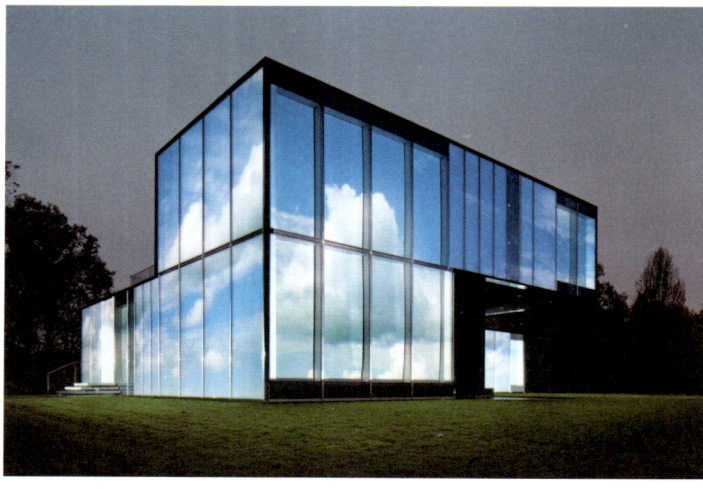

Station to Station, documentary feature film [color, sound] with 62 one-minute segments; 70 minutes

2013 MIRROR, custom software editor displaying responsive video [color, silent] on a site-specific architectural media facade; environmentally triggered continuous video recombination
Sonic Fountain, live sound installation with computer-controlled five-valve fountain, tinted water, basin, five underwater microphones, speakers; loop

2012 ALTERED EARTH, video installation with twelve channels of video [color, sound], multiple projections forming twelve screens; 49 minutes/loop
lighthouse, site-specific outdoor video installation wrapping house exterior with moving images of surrounding landscape, six channels of video [color, silent], seven projections forming five screens; 41:43 minutes/loop
SONG 1, outdoor video installation on 360-degree screen, with seven-channel composite video [color, sound], eleven projections forming one screen; 34:44 minutes/loop
SONG 1, single-channel video [color, sound]; 24:13 minutes
THE SOURCE [evolving], video installation with six channels of color video and six channels of stereo sound, six projections, featuring twenty-three conversations in an architectural pavilion. Additional conversations may be added over time. THE SOURCE Pavilion, designed by Adjaye Associates, collaboration with Doug Aitken; 60 minutes/loop

lighthouse, 2012

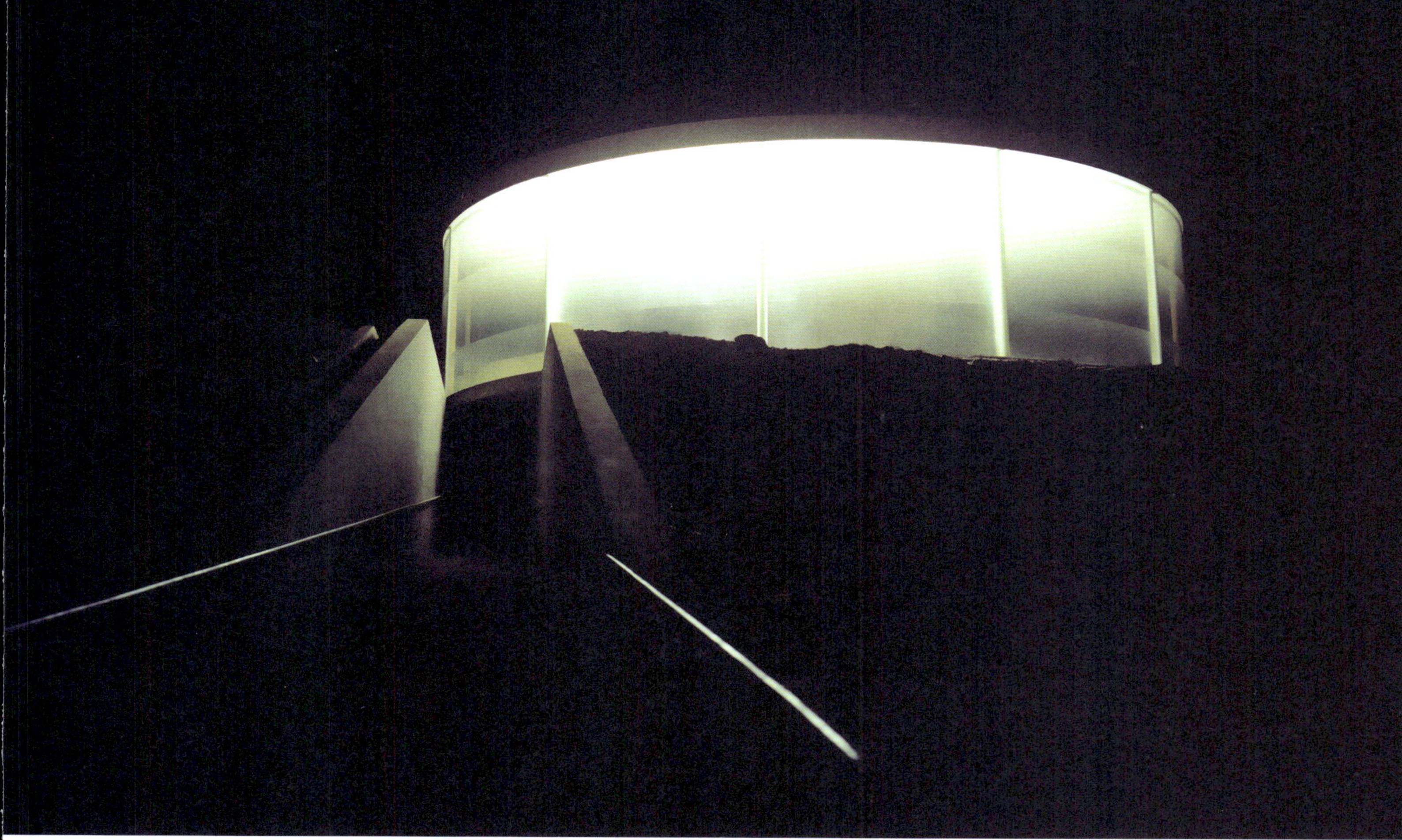

THE SOURCE, video installation with six channels of color video and six channels of stereo sound, six projections, featuring eighteen conversations in an architectural pavilion. THE SOURCE Pavilion, designed by Adjaye Associates, collaboration with Doug Aitken; 48 minutes/loop

wildlife, single-channel video [color, sound], custom monitor case; 8:09 minutes/loop

2011   Black Mirror, single-channel video [color, sound]; 13:20 minutes

Black Mirror, video installation with three channels of video [color, sound], multiple monitors, freestanding room, mirrors; 13:20 minutes/loop

2010   House, single-channel video [color, sound]; 8:36 minutes

House, video installation with one channel of video [color, sound], two monitors, wood table, debris; 8:36 minutes/loop

2009   Frontier, single-channel video [color, sound]; 17:40 minutes

Frontier, video installation with three channels of video [color, sound], six projections, site-specific structure; 17:40 minutes/loop

Sonic Pavilion, site-specific live sound installation in permanent architectural pavilion; at pavilion's center a 700-foot-deep hole contains microphones that capture the earth's sounds and tectonic plates shifting, which are heard inside the pavilion

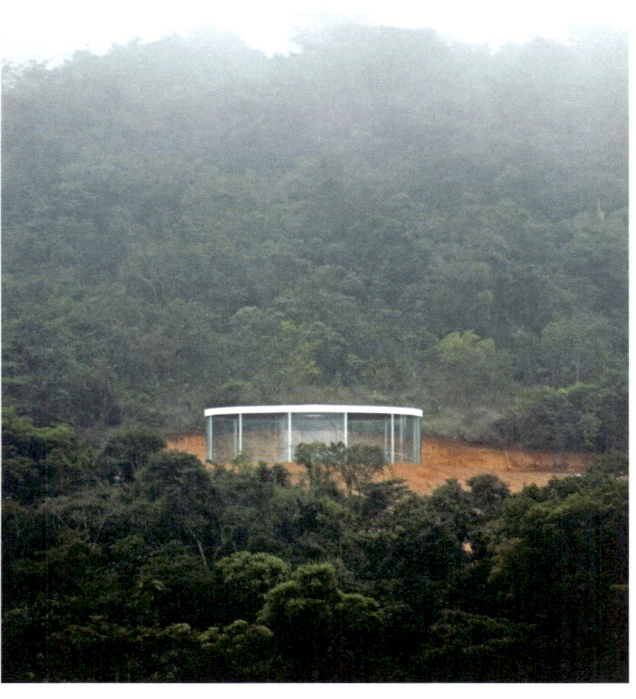

Sonic Pavilion, 2009

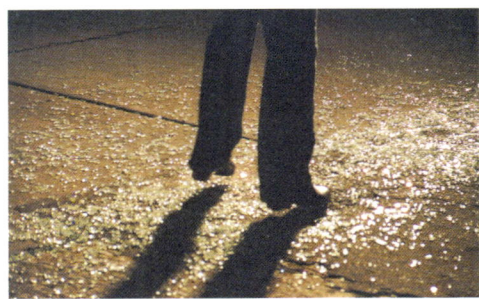 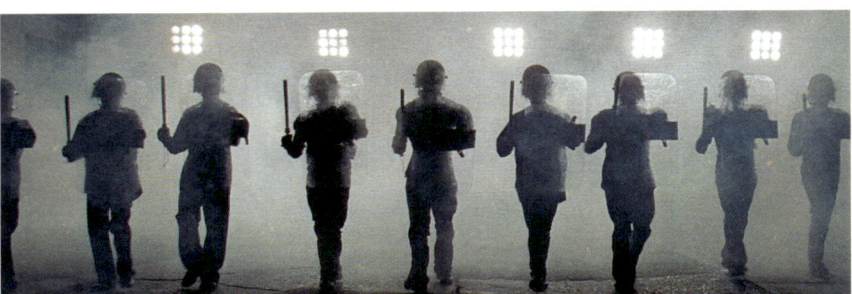

2008 *migration [empire]*, single-channel video
          [color, sound]; 24:28 minutes
       migration [empire], video installation
          with one channel of video [color, sound],
          one projection, steel and PVC screen billboard
          sculpture; 24:28 minutes/loop
       migration [empire], video installation with three
          channels of video [color, sound], three
          projections, three steel and PVC screen
          billboard sculptures; 24:28 minutes/loop
       sleepwalkers [miami], video installation
          with multiple channels of video [color, sound],
          outdoor projections or monitors;
          12:57 minutes/loop

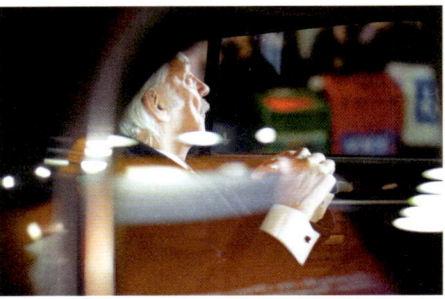
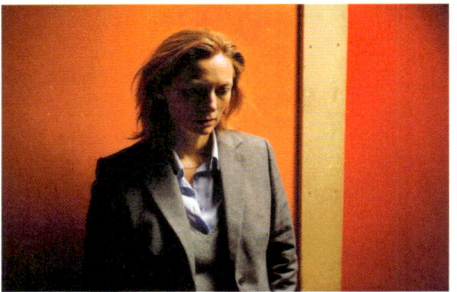
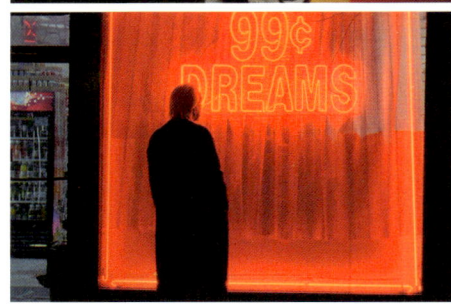

above: *Frontier*, 2009, stills
below: *sleepwalkers*, 2007, stills

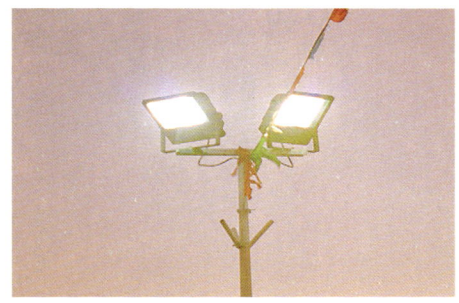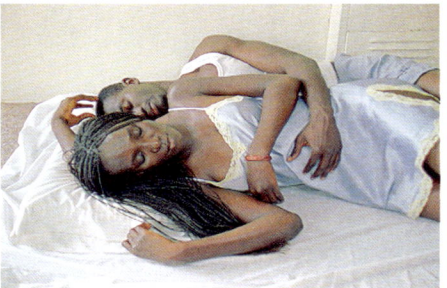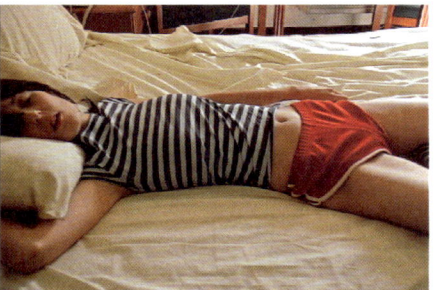

2007 *sleepwalkers*, single-channel video [color, sound]; 16:18 minutes
sleepwalkers, site-specific outdoor video installation, six channels of video [color, sound], multiple projections forming seven screens; 12:57 minutes/loop

2005 *glass era*, video installation with three channels of video [color, sound], three projections; 7:30 minutes/loop
lighttrain, video installation with five channels of video [color, sound], five monitors, custom aluminum monitor case; 8 minutes/loop
the moment, single-channel video [color, sound] with nine small screens on one channel; 6:42 minutes
the moment, video installation with eleven channels of video [color, sound], eleven monitors, custom monitor cases [aluminum, mirrors]; 6:26 minutes/loop

2004 *skyliner*, sound installation with 5.1 channels of audio, sonic mobile [aluminum, motors, directional speakers], carpet; 3:28 minutes/loop

2002 *interiors*, single-channel video [color, sound]; 7:04 minutes
interiors, video installation with three channels of video [color, sound], three projections, screen structure [aluminum, PVC, silk screen], circular bench; 13:50 minutes/loop
new skin, video installation with four channels of video [color, sound], four projections, elliptical X-shaped aluminum and PVC screen; 12 minutes/loop
on, video installation with one channel of video [color, sound], one projection, circular screen sculpture [wood, fabric, speaker]; 3:25 minutes/loop
on, video installation with three channels of video [color, sound], four projections, four circular screens, mirrored room; 11:37 minutes/loop
you exist/you think, sound installation with nine parabolic [or directional] speakers, plywood platforms; loop

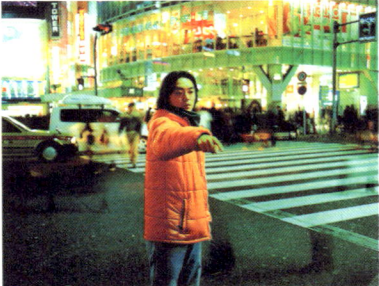
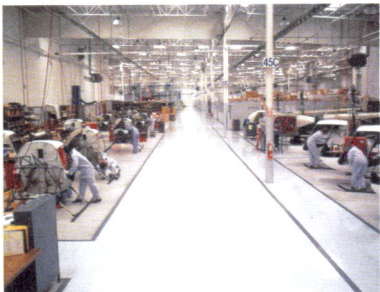
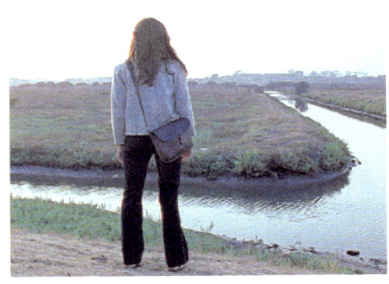

above: *the moment*, 2005, stills
below: *interiors*, 2002, stills

2001   *hysteria [breaths]*, sound installation with one
          channel of stereo audio, parabolic speaker,
          plywood platform; 8:42 minutes/loop
        New Ocean: 1 second expansion, video installation
          with one channel of video [color, sound],
          one projection, circular screen sculpture
          [wood, fabric, speaker]; 5:34 minutes/loop
        New Ocean: thaw, video installation with
          three channels of video [color, sound],
          three projections, screen; 4:10 minutes/loop
        New Ocean: new machines / new ocean floor,
          video installation with four channels of video
          [color, sound], eight projections,
          two X-shaped aluminum and PVC screens;
          10:18 minutes/loop
        New Ocean: new ocean cycle, video installation
          with four channels of video [color,
          sound], seven projections, 360-degree wall
          screen, circular aluminum and PVC screen;
          9:10 minutes/loop

2000   *blow debris*, single-channel video [color, sound];
          20:22 minutes
        blow debris, video installation with nine channels
          of video [color, sound], nine projections,
          three-room architectural environment;
          15:12 minutes/loop
        i am in you, single-channel video [color, sound];
          11:17 minutes
        i am in you, video installation with three channels
          of video [color, sound], five projections,
          five aluminum and PVC screens, architectural
          environment [plywood, felt]; 11 minutes/loop

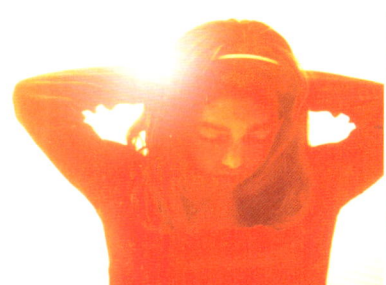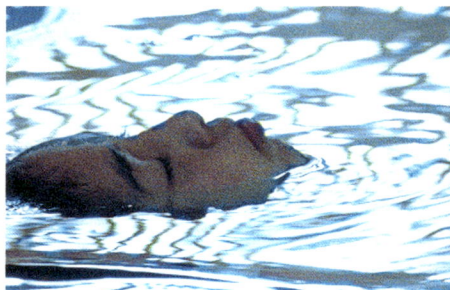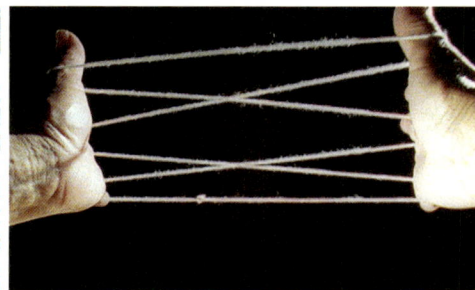

i am in you, 2000, stills

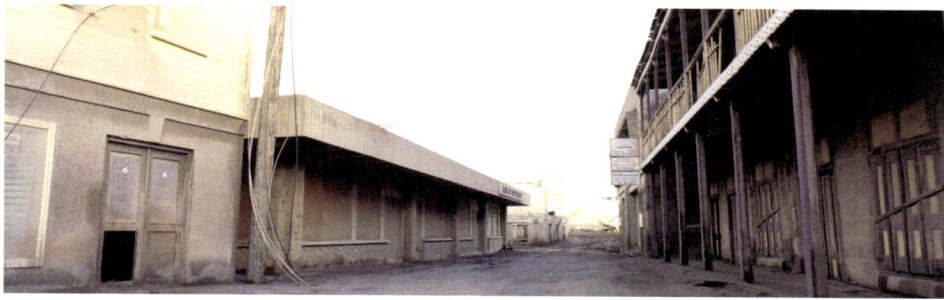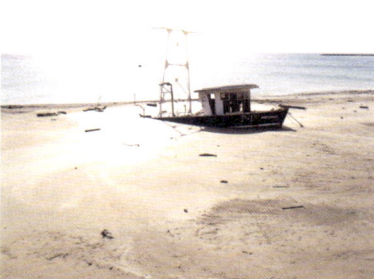

1999 *electric earth,* single-channel video [color, sound]; 14:51 minutes
      electric earth, video installation with eight channels of video [color, sound], eight projections, four-room architectural environment; 9:50 minutes/loop
      into the sun, single-channel video [color, sound]; 13:06 minutes
      into the sun, video installation with three channels of video [color, sound], four projections, canvas, earth; 11:44 minutes/loop

1998 *eraser,* single-channel video [color, sound]; 17:35 minutes
      eraser, video installation with seven channels of video [color, sound], seven projections, three-room architectural environment; 15:08 minutes/loop
      hysteria, single-channel video [color and black and white, sound]; 6:10 minutes
      hysteria, video installation with two channels of video [color and black and white, sound], four projections, X-shaped aluminum and PVC screen; 6:10 minutes/loop
      me amour, single-channel video [color, sound]; 3:25 minutes
      these restless minds, single-channel video [color, sound]; 8:03 minutes
      these restless minds, video installation with three channels of video [color, sound], three monitors, plywood platform and benches; 8:03 minutes/loop

1997 *cathouse,* video installation with three channels of video [color, sound], three monitors, architectural environment, carpet; 4 minutes/loop
      diamond sea, single-channel video [color, sound]; 17:05 minutes
      diamond sea, video installation with three channels of video [color, sound], three projections, monitor, chromogenic transparency mounted on acrylic in aluminum lightbox with LEDs; 11:50 minutes/loop
      moving, audio/light installation, synchronized airport runway lights, outdoor and/or architectural environment; loop

1996 *anchorage,* site-specific audio installation; loop
      bad animal, single-channel video [color, sound]; 6:40 minutes
      rise, video installation with one channel of video [color, sound], two monitors; 15:04 minutes/loop

1995 *monsoon,* single-channel video [color, sound]; 6:43 minutes/loop

above: *eraser,* 1998, stills
below: *monsoon,* 1995, stills

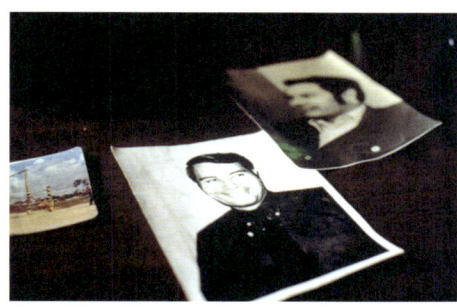
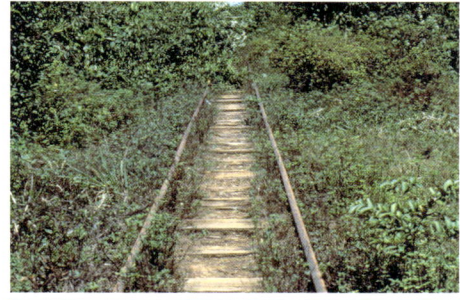
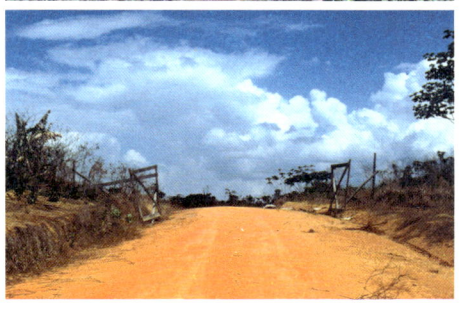

1994   *autumn,* single-channel video [color, sound];
            7:21 minutes
        dawn, single-channel video [color, sound];
            6 minutes
        fury eyes: american international, single-
            channel video [color, sound]; 7:30 minutes

1993   *i'd die for you,* single-channel video [color and
            black and white, sound]; 10:58 minutes
        superstar [development 3], single-channel video
            [color, sound]; 9:22 minutes

1992   *inflection,* single-channel video [color, silent];
            14:02 minutes

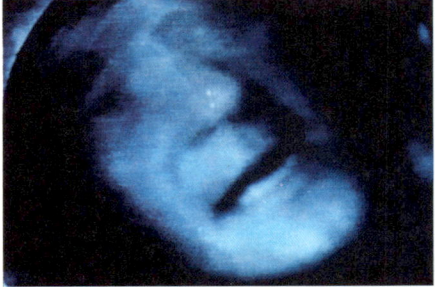
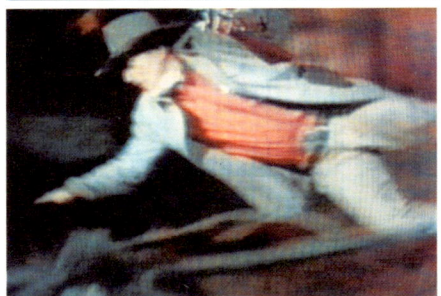
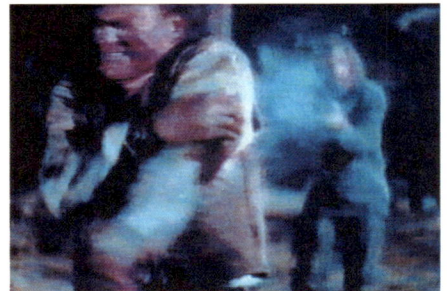

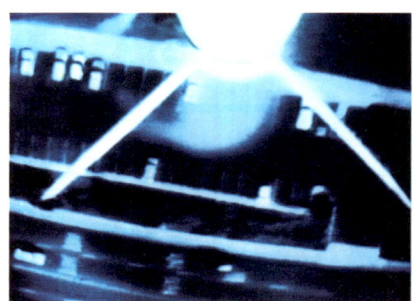
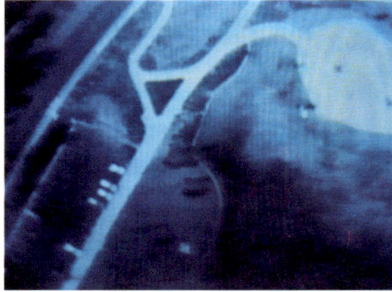
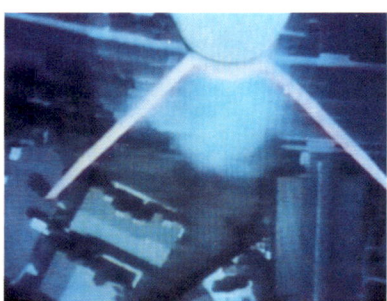

above: *i'd die for you,* 1993, stills
below: *inflection,* 1992, stills

Site-Specific Projects

2013   MIRROR, Seattle Art Museum, Seattle, WA [long-term installation]
        Nomadic Light Sculpture, New York, NY, to San Francisco, CA

2012   Acid Modernism, private residence, Venice, CA [long-term installation]
        lighthouse, Jill and Peter Kraus residence, Dutchess County, NY [long-term installation]

2009   Sonic Pavilion, Centro de Arte Contemporânea Inhotim, Brumadinho, Brazil [long-term installation]

Solo Exhibitions

2016   Doug Aitken: Electric Earth, The Museum of Contemporary Art, Los Angeles, Los Angeles, CA; travels to Modern Art Museum of Fort Worth, Fort Worth, TX
        Doug Aitken: twilight, Peder Lund, Oslo, Norway

2015   Galerie Eva Presenhuber, Zurich, Switzerland
        Schirn Kunsthalle, Frankfurt, Germany
        Victoria Miro Gallery, London, UK

2014   Still Life, Regen Projects, Los Angeles, CA

2013   electric earth, Nam June Paik Art Center, Yongin-si Gyeonggi-do, Korea
        100 YRS, 303 Gallery, New York, NY

2012   ALTERED EARTH: Arles, city of moving images, LUMA Foundation, Grande Halle, Parc des Ateliers, Arles, France
        Black Mirror, Galeria Helga de Alvear, Madrid, Spain
        Doug Aitken: THE SOURCE, Sky Arts Ignition series, Tate Liverpool, Liverpool, UK
        Galerie Eva Presenhuber, Zurich, Switzerland
        SONG 1, Hirshhorn Museum and Sculpture Garden, Smithsonian Institution, Washington, DC

2011   Black Mirror, DESTE Foundation Project Space, slaughterhouse and open-air barge, Hydra Island, Greece
        Victoria Miro Gallery, London, UK

2010   Doug Aitken: migration [empire], Princeton University Art Museum, Princeton, NJ
        electric earth, Cincinnati Art Museum, Cincinnati, OH
        House, Regen Projects, Los Angeles, CA
        migration [empire], Sammlung Goetz at Haus der Kunst, Munich, Germany
        the moment, Matadero Madrid, Madrid, Spain

2009   Frontier, Museum of Contemporary Art Roma/Enel Contemporanea, Tiber Island, Rome, Italy
        Los Angeles Public Domain/Art on the Outside, Los Angeles, CA
        migration [empire], St. Louis Art Museum, St. Louis, MO
        Regen Projects, Los Angeles, CA

2008   99c dreams, Galerie Eva Presenhuber, Zurich, Switzerland
        303 Gallery, New York, NY

2007   sleepwalkers, The Museum of Modern Art, New York/Creative Time, New York, NY
        303 Gallery, New York, NY

2006   A Photographic Survey, Aspen Art Museum, Aspen, CO

2005   interiors, Henry Art Gallery, University of Washington, Seattle, WA
        the moment, Regen Projects, Los Angeles, CA
        Sell yourself for nothing, Galerie Eva Presenhuber, Zurich, Switzerland
        ULTRAWORLD, Musée d'Art Moderne de la Ville de Paris, ARC, Couvent des Cordeliers, Paris, France

2004   Sammlung Goetz, Munich, Germany
        This Moment Is the Moment, Taka Ishii Gallery, Tokyo, Japan
        We're safe as long as everything is moving, La CaixaForum and Mies van der Rohe Pavilion, Barcelona, Spain; traveled to Sala Rekalde, Bilbao, Spain

2003   I don't exist, Victoria Miro Gallery, London, UK
        Kunsthalle Zurich, Zurich, Switzerland
        new ocean, Fondazione Sandretto Re Rebaudengo per l'Arte, Turin, Italy

2002   Interiors, Fabric Workshop and Museum, Philadelphia, PA
        Rise, Louisiana Museum for Moderne Kunst, Humlebæk, Denmark; traveled to Le Magasin, Centre National d'Art Contemporain de Grenoble, Grenoble, France
        303 Gallery, New York, NY
        new ocean, Kunsthaus Bregenz, Austria
        new ocean, Tokyo Opera City Art Gallery, Japan

2001   i am in you, Kunst Werke Berlin, Berlin, Germany
        Metallic Sleep, Kunstmuseum Wolfsburg, Wolfsburg, Germany
        new ocean, Serpentine Gallery, London, UK

2000   glass horizon, Vienna Secession, Vienna, Austria
        i am in you, Galerie Hauser & Wirth & Presenhuber, Zurich, Switzerland
        Matrix 185/Into the Sun, Berkeley Art Museum, Berkeley, CA
        Taka Ishii Gallery, Tokyo, Japan

1999   Concentrations 33: Doug Aitken, Diamond Sea, Dallas Museum of Art, Dallas, TX
        Diamond Sea, Lannan Foundation, Santa Fe, New Mexico
        Doug Lawing Gallery, Houston, TX
        Fondazione Pitti Discovery, Pitti Immagine, Florence, Italy
        into the sun, Victoria Miro Gallery, London, UK

1998   Diamond Sea, Jiri Svestka Gallery, Prague, Czech Republic
        Gallery Side 2, Tokyo, Japan
        Taka Ishii Gallery, Tokyo, Japan
        303 Gallery, New York, NY

1997   303 Gallery, New York, NY

1996   Taka Ishii Gallery, Tokyo, Japan

1994   303 Gallery, New York, NY

1993   AC Project Room, New York, NY

Selected Group Exhibitions

2016 *Daydreaming with Stanley Kubrick,* Somerset House, London, UK
Summer Exhibition 2016, Royal Academy of Arts, London, UK

2015 *Camera of Wonders,* Centro de la Imagen, Mexico City, Mexico
Come as You Are: Art of the 1990s, Montclair Art Museum, Montclair, NJ; traveled to Telfair Museum of Art, Savannah, GA; University of Michigan Museum of Art, Ann Arbor, MI; Blanton Museum of Art: University of Texas at Austin, Austin, TX
Works on Paper, Galerie Eva Presenhuber, Zurich, Switzerland

2014 *Common Ground: Earth,* Borusan Contemporary, Istanbul, Turkey
Damage Control: Art & Destruction Since 1950, Hirshhorn Museum and Sculpture Garden, Smithsonian Institution, Washington, DC; traveled to Musée d'Art Moderne Grand-Duc, Jean, Luxembourg City, Luxembourg; Kunsthaus Graz, Graz, Austria
High Performance. The Julia Stoschek Collection, Zentrum für Kunst und Medientechnologie, Karlsruhe, Germany
Melting Walls: Works from the Igal Ahouvi Art Collection, Genia Schreiber University Art Gallery, Tel Aviv University, Tel Aviv, Israel

2013 *El Cazador y la Fábrica,* Colección Jumex, Mexico City, Mexico
Collection Reinstallation for the 2013 Carnegie International, Carnegie Museum of Art, Pittsburgh, PA
DIALOGUES: Art/Architecture, Paris/Los Angeles, MAK Center for Art & Architecture and ForYourArt at 6020 Wilshire Blvd., Los Angeles, CA
Homebodies, Museum of Contemporary Art Chicago, Chicago, IL
Little Water, Dojima River Biennale, Osaka, Japan
Performing Architecture, Tate Britain, London, UK
A Sense of Place, Pier 24 Photography, San Francisco, CA
The Time Is Now, John Berggruen Gallery, San Francisco, CA
Turn off the Sun: Selections from la Colección Jumex, Arizona State University Art Museum, Tempe, AZ

2012 *Inaugural Exhibition by Gallery Artists,* Regen Projects, Los Angeles, CA
OC Collects, Orange County Museum of Art, Newport Beach, CA
The Perfect Show, 303 Gallery, New York, NY

2011 *Elgiz 10 Istanbul: A Decade of Commitment to Contemporary Art,* Elgiz Museum of Contemporary Art, Istanbul, Turkey
Expanded Cinema, Moscow Museum of Modern Art/Garage Center for Contemporary Culture, Moscow, Russia
In the Name of the Artists—American Contemporary Art from the Astrup Fearnley Collection, Ciccillo Matarazzo Pavilion, Parque do Ibirapuera, São Paulo Biennial, São Paulo, Brazil
Now: Obras de la Colección Jumex, Centro Cultural Hospicio Cabañas, Guadalajara, Mexico
Paradise Lost, Istanbul Museum of Modern Art, Istanbul, Turkey
Sculpture Now, Galerie Eva Presenhuber, Zurich, Switzerland
Why I Never Became a Dancer, Sammlung Goetz at Haus der Kunst, Munich, Germany

2010 *Ars Itineris: the journey in contemporary art,* Artium, Centro-Museo Vasco de Arte Contemporáneo de Vitoria-Gasteiz, Álava, Basque Country, Spain
Art Unlimited 2010, Art Basel, Basel, Switzerland
The Artist's Museum, The Museum of Contemporary Art, Los Angeles, Los Angeles, CA
Between Here and There: Passages in Contemporary Photography, Metropolitan Museum of Art, New York, NY
Contemplating the Void: Interventions in the Guggenheim Museum, Solomon R. Guggenheim Museum, New York, NY
Disquieted, Portland Art Museum, Portland, OR
Hard Targets, Wexner Center for the Arts, Ohio State University, Columbus, OH
I want to see how you see-Julia Stoschek Collection, Deichtorhallen Hamburg, Hamburg, Germany
Let's Dance, Musée d'Art Contemporain du Val-de-Marne, Vitry-sur-Seine, France
Neugierig? Kunst des 21. Jahrhunderts aus privaten Sammlungen, Kunst- und Ausstellungshalle der Bundesrepublik Deutschland, Bonn, Germany
Passages. Travels in Hyper-Space, LABoral Centro de Arte y Creación Industrial, Gijón, Spain
La trama se complica/The Plot Thickens, Museo de Arte Contemporáneo de Monterrey, Monterrey, Mexico
The Traveling Show, Galeria de Fundación/ Colección Jumex, Mexico City, Mexico
Until Now: Collecting the New [1960-2010], Minneapolis Institute of Arts, Minneapolis, MN

2009 *Life Patterns,* Savannah College of Art and Design, Lacoste, France
No Sound, Aspen Art Museum, Aspen, CO
Photography in the Abstract, Lora Reynolds Gallery, Austin, TX
Private Universes: Media Work, Dallas Museum of Art, Dallas, TX
Sites, Whitney Museum of American Art, New York, NY
Twenty-Six Gasoline Stations ed Altri Libri d'Artista—Una Collezioni, Museo Regionale di Messina, Messina, Italy
We Are Sun-Kissed and Snow-Blind, Galerie Patrick Seguin invites Galerie Eva Presenhuber, Paris, France
"Zwischen Zonen" La Colección Jumex, Mexico, Museum Moderner Kunst Stiftung Ludwig, Vienna, Austria

2008 *Elements and Unknowns,* The Museum of Modern Art, New York, NY
Falling Right into Place, Kunstmuseen Krefeld, Krefeld, Germany
Las implicaciones de la imagen/The Implications of the Image, Museo Universitario de Ciencias y Arte, Mexico City, Mexico
Life on Mars: 55th Carnegie International, Carnegie Museum of Art, Pittsburgh, PA
Mexico: Expected/Unexpected, La Maison Rouge, Paris; traveled to BPS22 Musée d'art de la Province de Hainaut, Charleroi, Belgium; American University Museum at the Katzen, Washington, DC
Moscow on the Move, Garage Center for Contemporary Culture, Moscow, Russia
El Mundo del Hielo, Expo 2008, Zaragoza, Spain
Rhine on the Dnipro: Julia Stoschek Collection/ Andreas Gursky, Pinchuk Art Centre, Kiev, Ukraine
Rock My Religion, DA2/Domus Artium 2002, Salamanca, Spain
St. Moritz Art Masters, St. Moritz, Switzerland
When It's a Photograph, Bolsky Gallery at Otis College for Art and Design, Los Angeles, CA

2007 *Brave New Year,* 303 Gallery, New York, NY
Ensemble, Institute of Contemporary Art at the University Of Pennsylvania, Philadelphia, PA
her[his]tory, Museum of Cycladic Art, Athens, Greece
Mapping the City, Stedelijk Museum, Amsterdam, the Netherlands
Martin Margulies Collection, Miami, FL
Mouth Open, Teeth Showing: Major Works from the True Collection, Henry Art Gallery, University of Washington, Seattle, WA
Number One: Destroy, She Said, Julia Stoschek Collection, Düsseldorf, Germany
Playback, Musée d'Art Moderne de la Ville de Paris, ARC, Paris, France
Power of Ten: Gifts in Honor of Miami Art Museum's Tenth Anniversary, Miami Art Museum, Miami, FL
The Shadow, Compton Verney Art Gallery, Warwickshire, UK
Silence. Listen to the Show, Fondazione Sandretto Re Rebaudengo, Turin, Italy
Uneasy Angel/Imagine Los Angeles, Sprüth Magers, Munich, Germany
Window | Interface, Kemper Art Museum, Washington University, St. Louis, MO

2006 *.all hawaii eNtrées/luNar reGGae,* Irish Museum of Modern Art, Dublin, Ireland
Beyond Cinema: The Art of Projection, Hamburger Bahnhof, Museum für Gegenwart, Berlin, Germany
Broad Art Foundation, Santa Monica, CA
Cosmic Wonder, Yerba Buena Center for the Arts, San Francisco, CA
Ecotopia: The Second ICP Triennial of Photography and Video, International Center of Photography, New York, NY
Fuori Pista, Fondazione Sandretto Re Rebaudengo, Capanna Mollino di Sauze d'Oulx, Piedmont, Italy

Red Eye: L.A. Artists from the Rubell Family Collection, Rubell Family Collection/ Contemporary Arts Foundation, Miami, FL
Surprise, Surprise, Institute of Contemporary Arts, London, UK
Touch My Shadows: New Media from the Goetz Collection in Munich, Centre for Contemporary Art, Ujazdów Castle, Warsaw, Poland

2005 *Art 36 Basel: Art Unlimited 2005,* Basel, Switzerland
Disorientation—New Ways of Storytelling, Rialto, Amsterdam, the Netherlands
Glasgow International Festival of Contemporary Visual Art, Glasgow, UK
Jump-Cut Nights: Choreographic Structures in Moving Images, part 3, "Time Images," Studio der SK Stiftung Kultur, Cologne, Germany
Now's the Time, Kunsthaus Graz, Graz, Austria
Second Guangzhou Triennial, Guandong Museum of Art, Guangzhou, China
Universal Experience: Art, Life, and the Tourist's Eye, Museum of Contemporary Art Chicago, Chicago, IL; traveled to Hayward Gallery, London, UK

2004 *Hard Light,* MoMA PS1, New York, NY
Kunstmuseum Wolfsburg, Wolfsburg, Germany
Landscape and Memory [Paisaje y Memoria], La Casa Encendida, Madrid, Spain; traveled to Centro Atlántico de Arte Moderno, Las Palmas de Gran Canaria, Canary Islands, Spain
Modus Operandi, Thyssen-Bornemisza Art Contemporary, Vienna, Austria
New in the Collection, two-person show, Museum Het Domein Sittard, Sittard, the Netherlands
Past, Present, Future: Contemporary Art 1950– Present, Art Institute of Chicago, Chicago, IL
3', Schirn Kunsthalle, Frankfurt, Germany
21st Century Museum of Contemporary Art, Kanazawa, Japan
The Uses of the Image: Photography, Film and Video in the Jumex Collection, Colección Costantini, in association with Espacio Fundación Telefónica, Museum of Latin American Art, Buenos Aires, Argentina

2003   *Audiolab 2,* collaboration with Steven Roden, Centre Pompidou, Paris, France
Breathing the Water, Galerie Hauser & Wirth & Eva Presenhuber, Zurich, Switzerland
Defying Gravity: Contemporary Art and Flight, North Carolina Museum of Art, Raleigh, NC
Edén, Colección Jumex, Museum of San Ildefonso, Mexico City, Mexico, and Luis Angel Arango Library, Central Bank, Bogotá, Colombia
fast forward, Zentrum für Kunst und Medientechnologie, Karlsruhe, Germany
Imperfect Innocence: The Dennis and Debra Scholl Collection, Contemporary Museum, Baltimore, MD
Liquid Sea, Museum of Contemporary Art, Sydney, Australia
The New Yorkers, collaboration with Bang on a Can, Brooklyn Academy of Music, New York, NY
Painting Pictures: Painting and Media in the Digital Age, Kunstmuseum Wolfsburg, Wolfsburg, Germany
Site Specific, Museum of Contemporary Art Chicago, Chicago, IL
Spiritus, Magasin 3, Stockholm, Sweden
Then all the world would be upside down, Tina Kim Fine Art, New York, NY
Within Hours We Would Be in the Middle of Nowhere, 303 Gallery, New York, NY
world rush_4 artists, National Gallery of Victoria, Melbourne, Australia

2002   "Society for Contemporary Art Annual Exhibition," Art Institute of Chicago, Chicago, IL
Doug Aitken & Sharon Lockhart, Galerie Jan Mot, Brussels, Belgium
French Collection, Musée d'art moderne et contemporain, Geneva, Switzerland
Remix: Contemporary Art and Pop, Tate Liverpool, Liverpool, UK
Screen Memories, Contemporary Art Gallery, Art Tower Mito, Mito, Japan
Sonic Process, Museu d'Art Contemporani de Barcelona, Barcelona, Spain; traveled to Centre Pompidou, Paris, France

2001   *ARS 01: Unfolding Perspectives,* Museum of Contemporary Art Kiasma, Helsinki, Finland
Colección Jumex, inaugural exhibition, Mexico City, Mexico
Collaborations with Parkett: 1984 to Now, The Museum of Modern Art, New York, NY
Form Follows Fiction, Castello di Rivoli Museo d'Arte Contemporanea, Turin, Italy
Media Connection: How the media have changed art, Palazzo delle Esposizioni, Rome, Italy
Moving Pictures: Photography and Film in Contemporary Art, 5th International Photo Triennial Esslingen, Villa Merkel, Esslingen, Germany
Urban Pornography, Artists Space, New York, NY

2000   *Flight Patterns,* The Museum of Contemporary Art, Los Angeles, Los Angeles, CA
Future Identities: Reflections from a Collection, Fondazione Sandretto Re Rebaudengo Collection, Sala de Exposiciones del Canal de Isabel II, Madrid, Spain
Hypermental: Rampant Reality 1950–2000, from Salvador Dalí to Jeff Koons, Kunsthaus Zurich, Zurich, Switzerland
Let's Entertain, Walker Art Center, Minneapolis, MN; traveled to Centre Pompidou, Paris, France; Kunstmuseum Wolfsburg, Wolfsburg, Germany; Miami Art Museum, Miami, FL; Portland Art Museum, Portland, OR
Raw, Victoria Miro Gallery, London, UK
Speed of Vision: On the Construction and Perception of Time in Video Art, Aldrich Museum of Contemporary Art, Ridgefield, CT; traveled to Pittsburgh Center for the Arts, Pittsburgh, PA
12th Biennale of Sydney, Museum of Contemporary Art, Sydney, Australia
2000 Whitney Biennial, Whitney Museum of American Art, New York, NY

1999   *Clues: An Open Scenario Exhibition,* MonteVideo, Amsterdam, the Netherlands
dAPERTutto, 48th Venice Biennale, Venice, Italy
From Film, Victoria Miro Gallery, London, UK
Natural Order, Art Gallery of Alberta, Alberta, Canada
Poor Man's Pudding; Rich Man's Crumbs, AC Project Room, New York, NY
Two Doors—True Value, Mai 36 Galerie, Zurich, Switzerland
video cult/ures, Zentrum für Kunst und Medientechnologie, Karlsruhe, Germany

1998 *L.A. Times: Arte da Los Angeles nella Collezione Sandretto Re Rebaudengo,* Palazzo Re Rebaudengo, Guarene d'Alba, Italy
I Love New York: Crossover of Contemporary Art, Museum Ludwig, Cologne, Germany
New Selections from the Permanent Collection, Walker Art Center, Minneapolis, MN
New Visions: video 1998, Long Beach Museum of Art, Long Beach, CA
Speed: Visions of an Accelerated Age, Photographers' Gallery, London, UK
Unfinished History, Walker Art Center, Minneapolis, MN
La Voie Lactée, organized by the Purple Institute, Alleged Gallery, New York, NY

1997 *Camera Oscura,* San Casciano dei Bagni, Italy
Doug Aitken, Alex Bag, Naotaka Hiro, Taka Ishii Gallery, Tokyo, Japan
Doug Aitken, Peter Gehrke, Index, Stockholm, Sweden
1997 Whitney Biennial, Whitney Museum of American Art, New York, NY
One Minute Scenario, Le Printemps de Cahors, Saint-Cloud, France
Portrait—Human Figure, Galerie Peter Kilchmann, Zurich, Switzerland
[re]Mediation: The Digital in Contemporary American Printmaking, 22nd International Ljubljana Biennial of Graphic Arts, Cankarjev dom Cultural and Congress Centre, Modern Gallery, and Tivoli Gallery, Ljubljana, Slovenia
We Gotta Get out of This Place, Cubitt Gallery, London, UK

1996 *a/drift: Scenes from the Penetrable Culture,* Center for Curatorial Studies and Art in Contemporary Culture, Annandale-on-Hudson, NY
Art in the Anchorage 1996, organized by Creative Time, Brooklyn Bridge Anchorage, New York, NY
Campo 6: Il Villaggio a Spirale, Galleria Civica d'Arte Moderna e Contemporanea, Turin, Italy; traveled to Bonnefanten Museum, Maastricht, the Netherlands
Doug Aitken, Mariko Mori, Ricardo Zulueta, Elga Wimmer Gallery, New York, NY
Intermission, Basilico Fine Arts, New York, NY
Show and Tell, Lauren Wittels Gallery, New York, NY
29' 0"/East, New York Kunsthalle, New York, NY; traveled to Kunstraum Vienna, Vienna, Austria

1995 *La Belle et la Bête,* Musée d'Art Moderne de la Ville de Paris, Paris, France
The Image and the Object: Art and Video in the United States, Museo Laboratorio di Arte Contemporanea, Università degli Studi di Roma, Rome, Italy

1994 *Audience 0.01,* Trevi Flash Art Museum, Trevi, Italy; traveled to Vera Vita Gioia, Naples, Italy
Beyond Belief, Lisson Gallery, London, UK
New York, New York, Mánes Gallery, Prague, Czech Republic
Not Here Neither There, Los Angeles Contemporary Exhibitions, Los Angeles, CA
Out West and Back East: New Work from Los Angeles and New York, Santa Monica Museum of Art, Santa Monica, CA
still, Espace Montjoie, Paris, France

1993 *Doug Aitken and Robin Lowe,* AC Project Room, New York, NY
Okay Behavior, 303 Gallery, New York, NY
Outside Possibilities, Rushmore Festival, Woodbury, NY
Underlay, 15 Renwick Street, New York, NY

1992 *The Art Mall: A Social Space,* New Museum of Contemporary Art, New York, NY
Invitational 92, Stux Gallery, New York, NY
Multiplicity, Christopher Middendorf Gallery, Washington, DC
Small, Medium, Large: Lifesize, Centro per l'Arte Contemporanea Luigi Pecci, Prato, Italy

1991 *Artworks/Artworkers,* AC Project Room, New York, NY

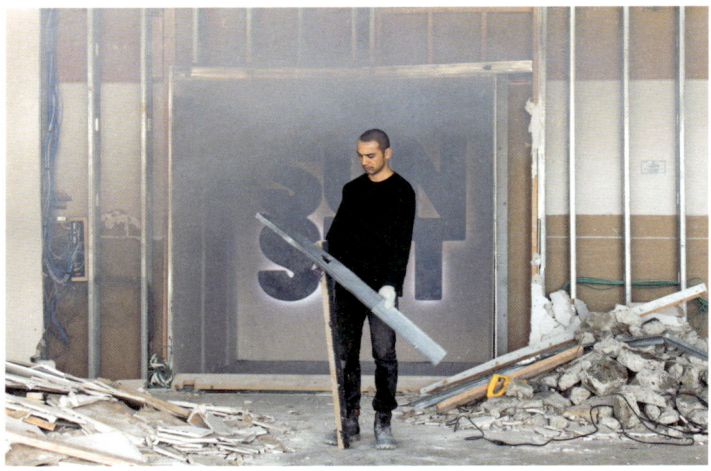

Happenings and Special Events

2015 *Doug Aitken: Special Happening & Performance*, Schirn Kunsthalle, Frankfurt, Germany; film screening, performances, and sound installation with the Junge Deutsche Philharmonie

Station to Station: A 30 Day Happening, Barbican Centre, London, UK; a continuously evolving "living exhibition" with more than one hundred free events by over one hundred artists, choreographers, filmmakers, musicians, and others, consisting of newly introduced and created works as part of a program of live rehearsals, performances, talks, interviews, and workshops

2014 *landscape signs [sign happening]*, Regen Projects, Los Angeles, CA; professional sign spinners performed with signs featuring subversive texts designed to create a "cultural ambush" along Santa Monica Blvd.

2013 *MIRROR*, Seattle Art Museum, Seattle, WA; Terry Riley performing *In C* with the Seattle Symphony Orchestra and Steve Reich's Clapping Music

100 YRS [part 2], 303 Gallery, New York, NY; five-day time-based destruction installation with an elevator operator and three-person percussionist performance

Station to Station, multiple locations across US; over three weeks in September, a train designed as a kinetic light sculpture traveled from New York City to San Francisco, making ten stops along the way for a series of site-specific happenings

2012 *ALTERED EARTH*, LUMA Foundation, Grande Halle, Parc des Ateliers, Arles, France; exhibition opening with musical accompaniment by Terry Riley, Gyan Riley, and Tracy Silverman

sleepwalkers box, MoMA PS1, New York, NY; *sleepwalkers* remixed with musical performances by the Hisham Bharoocha Trio and Jonathan Galkin

SONG 1, Hirshhorn Museum and Sculpture Garden, Smithsonian Institution, Washington, DC; musical accompaniment by Animal Collective's Geologist, Leo Gallo, High Places, Nicolas Jaar, Tim McAfee-Lewis, No Age, and Oneohtrix Point Never

2011 *ALTERED EARTH*, Serpentine Gallery, London, UK; interview with Hans Ulrich Obrist, for the *ALTERED EARTH* App

Black Mirror, Athens and Hydra, Greece; four-night event staged on a custom barge in conjunction with the Athens Theater Festival and the DESTE Foundation for Contemporary Art; performances by Leo Gallo, Tim McAfee-Lewis, No Age, Chloë Sevigny, and a professional whip cracker

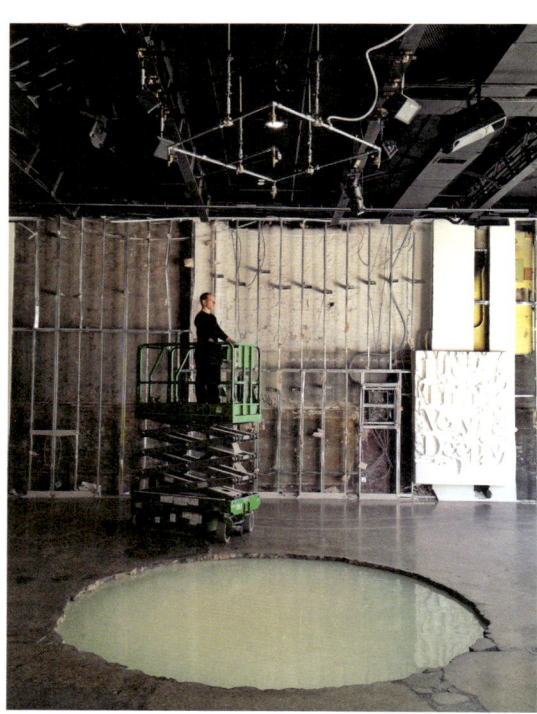

100 YRS [part 2], 2013

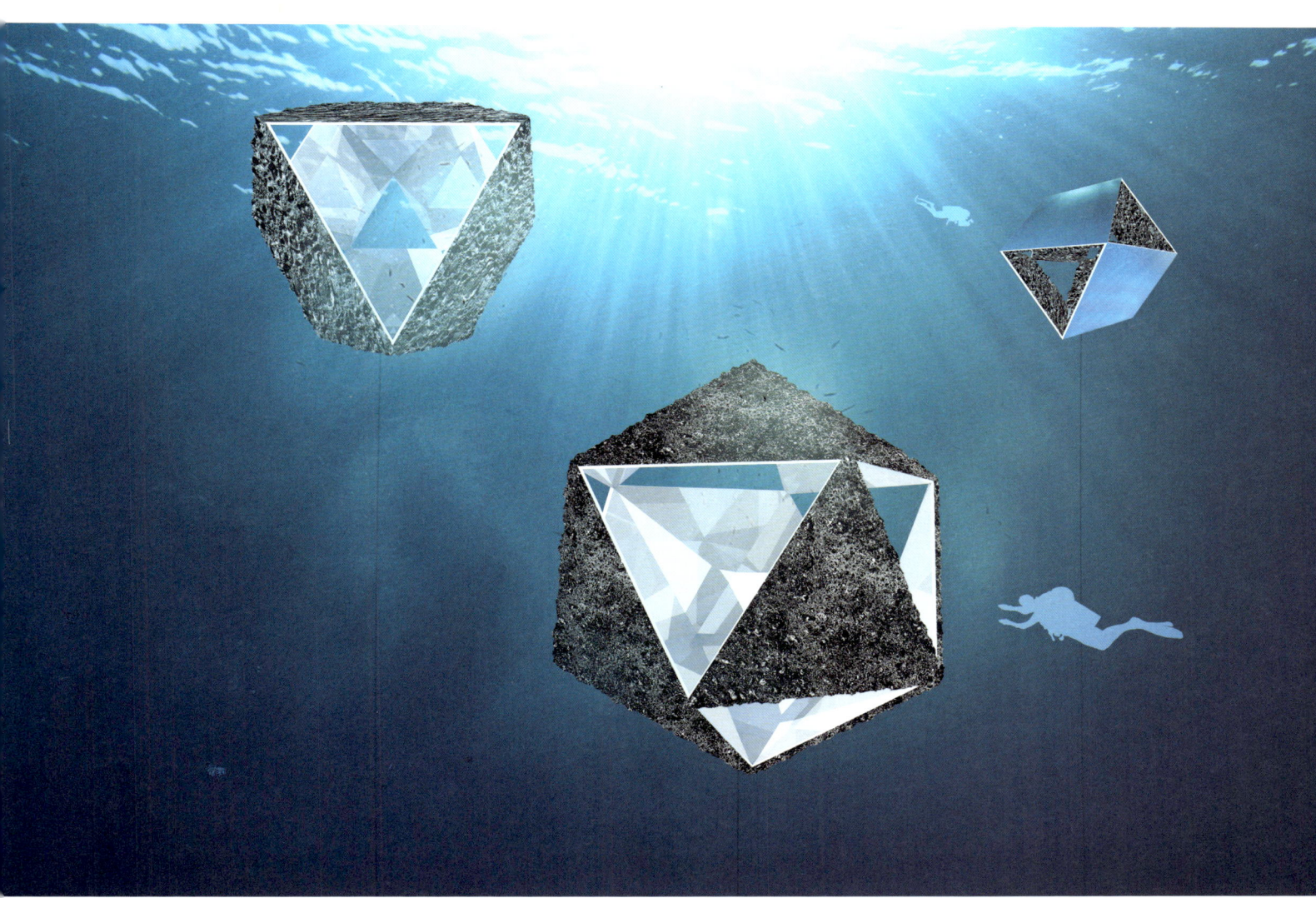

Underwater Pavilions, 2016

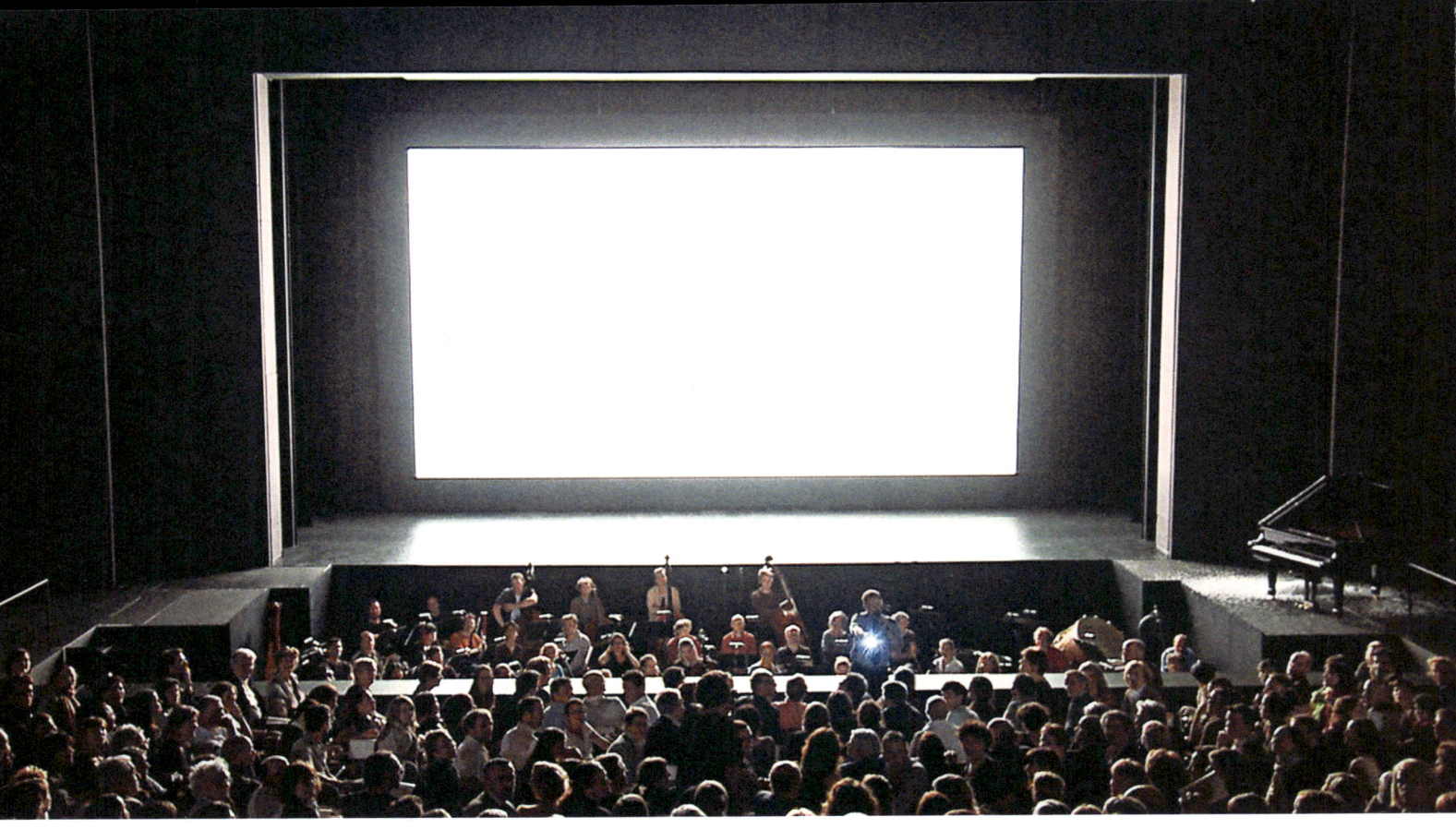

2010 *The Artist's Museum*, The Museum of Contemporary Art, Los Angeles, Los Angeles, CA; musical performances by Devendra Banhart, Beck, and Caetano Veloso, and performances by members of the Agape Choir, rural farm auctioneers, drummers, and a professional whip cracker; curated for MOCA's gala
migration, Princeton University Art Museum, Princeton, NJ; musical accompaniment by ARP, Lichens, and White Rainbow

2009 *Frontier*, Enel Contemporanea, Tiber Island, Rome, Italy; musical accompaniment by Lichens and performances by rural farm auctioneers, tap dancers, and a professional whip cracker, staged in a site-specific open-air architectural structure
the handle comes up, the hammer comes down, Theater Basel, Basel, Switzerland; performance with rural farm auctioneers, part of *Il Tempo del Postino*
migration, Regen Projects, Los Angeles, CA; musical performances by Lucky Dragons, Nudge, White Rainbow, Steve Roden, and the Urxed

2008 *migration*, 303 Gallery, New York, NY; musical accompaniment by ARP, Lichens, and White Rainbow
99¢ Dreams Happening, Westside Gentleman's Club, New York, NY; multiscreen projection with musical performances by Lissy Trullie and the Fibs and Justin Miller
Ocean, University of California, Santa Barbara, Santa Barbara, CA; multiscreen projection on beach at nighttime
Write-In Jerry Brown President, The Museum of Modern Art, New York, NY; featuring John Bowe, with musical performances by Pepi Ginsberg and Jeffrey Lewis

2007 *the handle comes up the, hammer comes down*, Opera House, Manchester, UK; performance with rural farm auctioneers, part of *Il Tempo del Postino*, the Manchester International Festival
sleepwalkers, The Museum of Modern Art, New York, NY; musical performances by Hisham Bharoocha, Ryan Donowho, and Cat Power, and reading by Melissa Plaut

2006 *Broken Screen*, Essex Street Market, New York, NY; featuring Vito Acconci, Black Dice, Adam Green, Miranda July, and Jeff Koons, with films by Acconci, Stan Brakhage, George Greenough, Alejandro Jodorowsky, Kelly Sears, and Superstudio
Broken Screen, Schindler House, MAK Center, Los Angeles, CA; featuring John Baldessari, Ariel Pink, Tim Sweeney, and Andrea Zittel, with films by Stan Brakhage, George Greenough, Alejandro Jodorowsky, Kelly Sears, and Ryan Trecartin
K-N-O-C-K-O-U-T, Parrish Art Museum, Southampton, NY; performance by Street Drum Corps

2005 *K-N-O-C-K-O-U-T*, Regen Projects, Los Angeles; performances by Street Drum Corps and rural farm auctioneers

the handle comes up, the hammer comes down,
Theater Basel, Basel, Switzerland, 2009

Selected Film Festivals and Screenings

2015 ACMI, Melbourne, Australia
Barbican Centre, London, UK
Festival do Rio, Rio de Janeiro, Brazil
Film Independent at LACMA, Los Angeles, CA
The Institute of Contemporary Art, Boston, MA
Nuart Theatre, Los Angeles, CA
Portland Art Museum Northwest Film Center, Portland, OR
SIFF Cinema, Seattle, WA
Sound + Vision, Film Society of Lincoln Center, New York, NY
Sundance Film Festival, New Frontier, Park City, UT
Teatrino di Palazzo Grassi, Venice, Italy
Walker Art Center, Minneapolis, MN

2014 Sundance Film Festival, New Frontier, Park City, UT

2010 67th Venice International Film Festival, Venice, Italy

2009 Aurora Picture Show, Houston, TX
Highlights from the KunstFilmBiennale, touring exhibition, KW Institute for Contemporary Art, Berlin, Germany; Museo Nacional Centro de Arte Reina Sofía, Madrid, Spain; and Centre Pompidou, Paris, France
KunstFilmBiennale, Cologne, Germany

2008 Locarno International Film Festival, Locarno, Switzerland
Sundance Film Festival, Park City, UT

2007 KunstFilmBiennale, Cologne, Germany

2005 Best of Festivals #2, Médiathèque José Cabanis, Toulouse, France
Locarno International Film Festival, Locarno, Switzerland

2004 Canarias Media Festival, Las Palmas de Gran Canarias, Canary Islands, Spain

2003 New York Video Festival, Walter Reade Theater, Lincoln Center, New York, NY
Nueva Film Festival, Laforet Museum Harajuku, Tokyo, Japan
Tribeca Film Festival, New York, NY

2002 Impakt Film Festival, Utrecht, the Netherlands
ResFest, on tour in New York, NY, Los Angeles, CA, and San Francisco, CA
Telluride Film Festival, Telluride, CO

2001 BFI London Film Festival, London, UK
International Short Film Festival Oberhausen, Oberhausen, Germany

2000 Crossing Boundaries, Danish Film Institute, Copenhagen, Denmark
International Short Film Festival Oberhausen, Oberhausen, Germany
Regarding Beauty in Performance and Media Arts, Haus der Kunst, Munich, Germany

1998 Geneva International Film Festival, Geneva, Switzerland
International Film Festival Rotterdam, the Netherlands
RET.INEVITABLE, Brooklyn Bridge Anchorage, New York, NY

1997 Film + Arc—Graz 3, International Biennale, Graz, Austria
Montreal International Festival of New Cinema and New Media, Montreal, Canada
Video Divertimento, San Casciano dei Bagni, Italy

1996 Boston Film Festival, Boston, MA
Champ Libre, Sous la Passerelle, Montreal, Canada
International Festival of New Film and Video, Split, Croatia
New York Film Festival, Alice Tully Hall, Lincoln Center, New York, NY
New York Video Festival, Walter Reade Theater, Lincoln Center, New York, NY
Telluride Film Festival, Telluride, CO

Artist's Books

2015   *Station to Station*. New York, NY: DelMonico Books•Prestel.

2012   *SONG 1*. Washington, DC: Hirshhorn Museum and Sculpture Garden, Smithsonian Institution.

2011   *Black Mirror*. Athens, Greece: DESTE Foundation for Contemporary Art.
          The Sleepwalkers Box. New York, NY: Princeton Architectural Press/DFA Records.

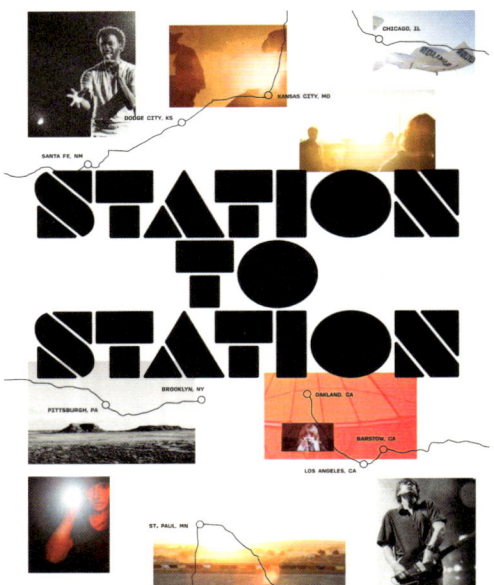

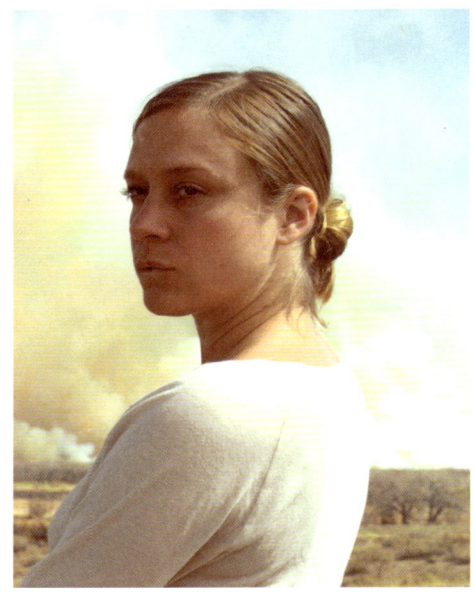

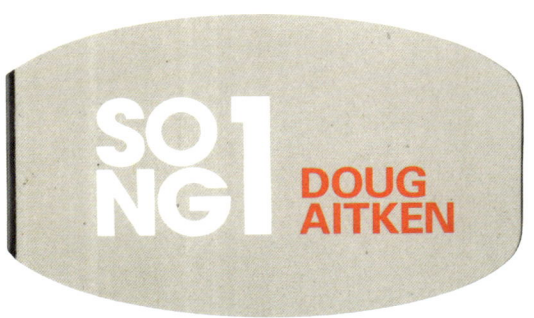

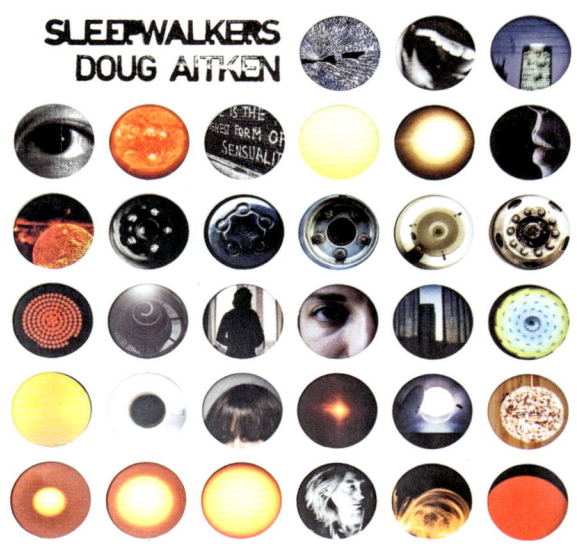

2010   *The Idea of the West*. New York, NY: D.A.P./
        Distributed Art Publishers; Los Angeles, CA:
        The Museum of Contemporary Art, Los Angeles;
        Zurich, Switzerland: JRP|Ringier.

2009   *Frontier*. Rome, Italy: Enel Contemporanea.

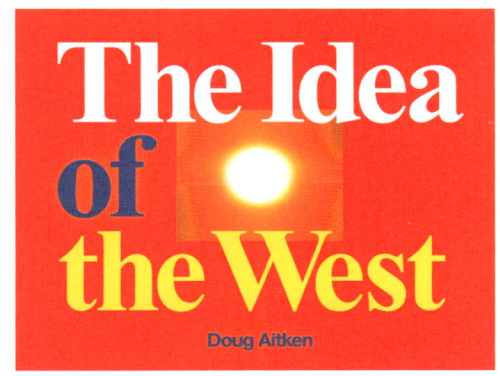

2005   *Broken Screen: Expanding the Image, Breaking
        the Narrative: 26 Conversations with Doug
        Aitken*. New York, NY: D.A.P./Distributed Art
        Publishers.
        ALPHA. Zurich, Switzerland: JRP|Ringier.

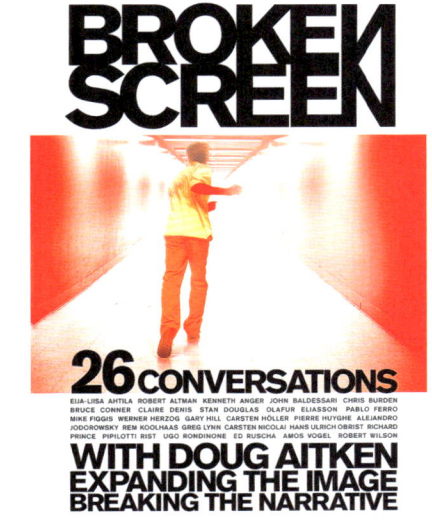

2008   *Write-In Jerry Brown President*. New York, NY:
        The Museum of Modern Art.

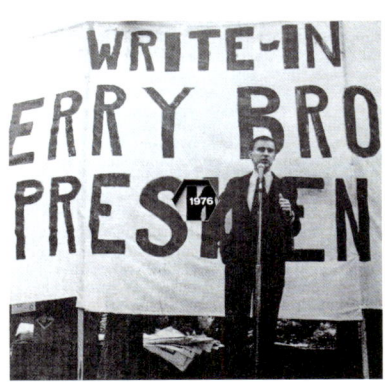

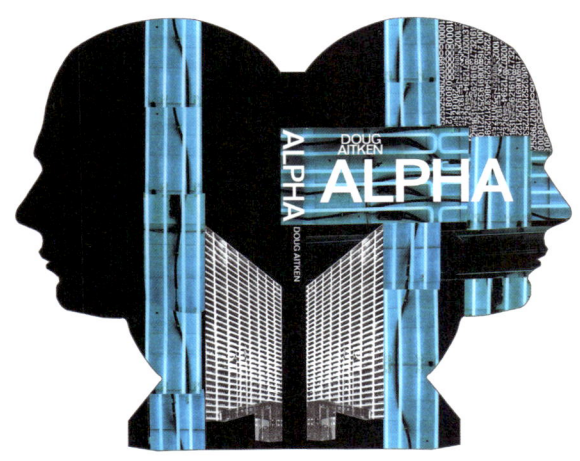

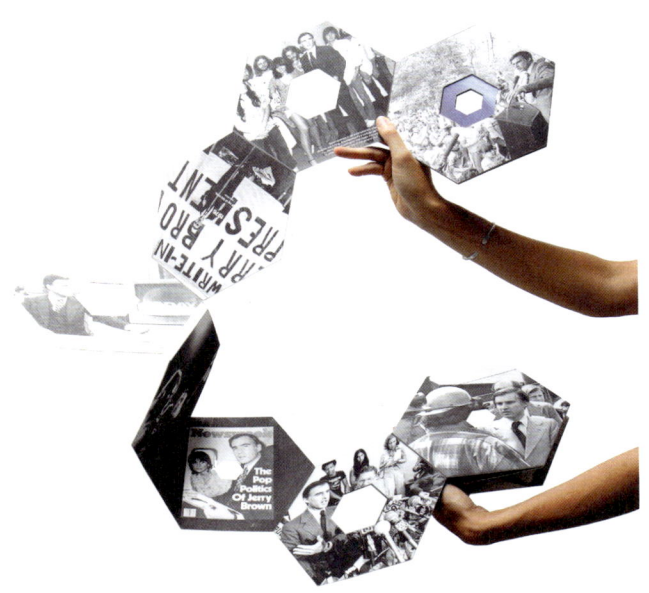

2003   *Doug Aitken: A-Z Book [Fractals]*. Philadelphia, PA: Fabric Workshop and Museum; Ostfildern, Germany: Hatje Cantz Publishers.

2002   *New Ocean*. Tokyo, Japan: Tokyo Opera City Art Gallery.

2001   *New Ocean*. London, UK: Serpentine Gallery.
        Notes for New Religions, Notes for No Religions. Ostfildern, Germany: Hatje Cantz Publishers.

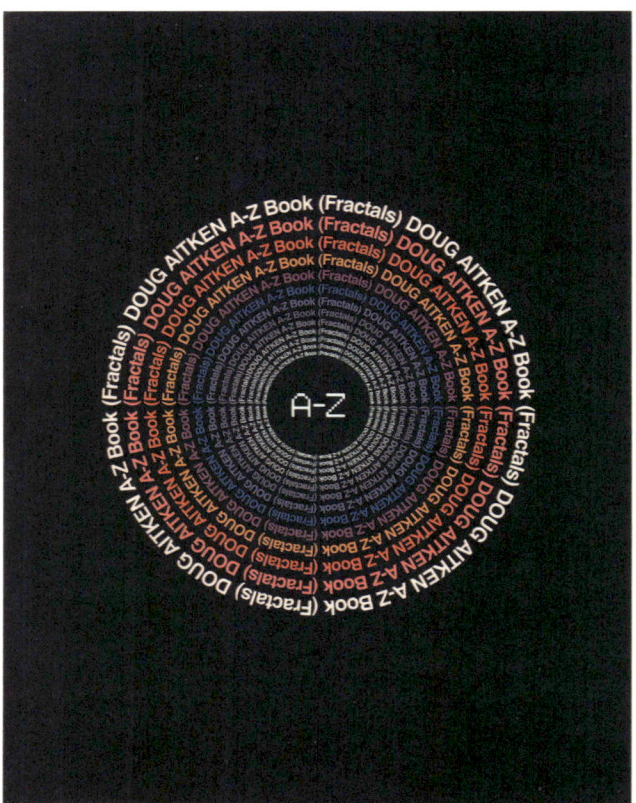

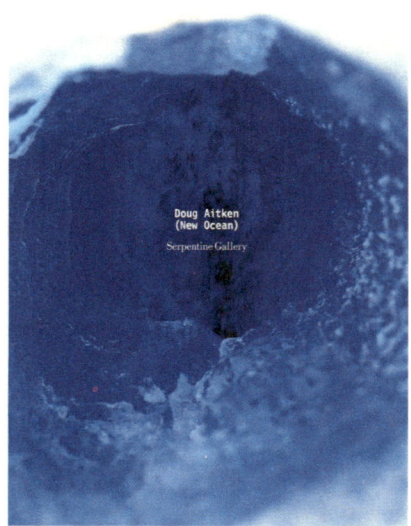

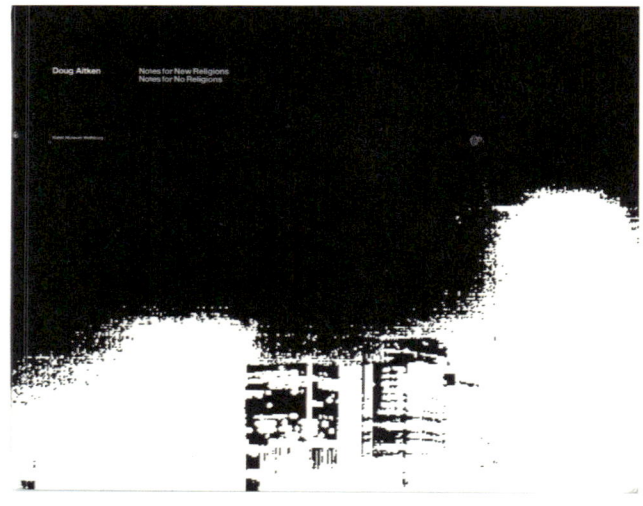

Selected Books and Catalogs

2000 *I AM A BULLET: Scenes from an Accelerating Culture*.
New York, NY: Crown Publishers.
Diamond Sea. London, UK: Book Works.

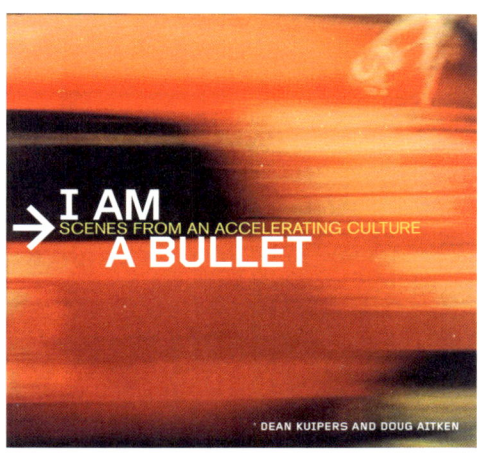

Diamond Sea

1998 *Metallic Sleep*. Tokyo, Japan: Taka Ishii Gallery.

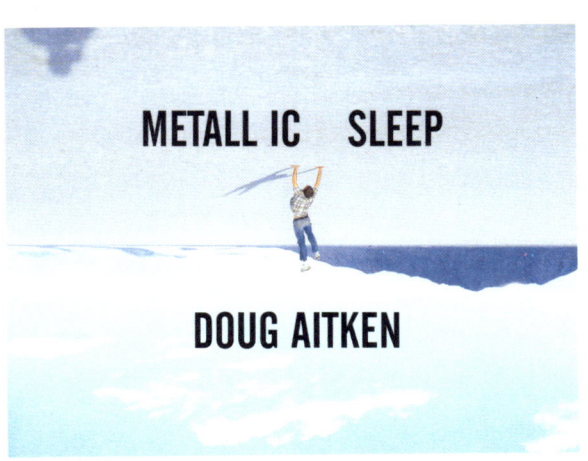

Doug Aitken

2015 Codognato, Mario. *HE: The Hergott Shepard Photography Collection*. Contributions by Richard Meyer and Ann Goldstein. Ann Arbor, MI: University of Michigan Museum of Art. Exh. cat.
Erickson, Steve. *Doug Aitken: Sculptures, 2001–2015*. Edited by Lionel Bovier. Zurich, Switzerland: JRP|Ringier.
Miller, Dana, ed. *Whitney Museum of American Art: Handbook of the Collection*. Introduction by Adam D. Weinberg. New York: The Whitney Museum of American Art.
Müller, Helmut, and Max Hollein, eds. *Doug Aitken*. Contributions by Mathias Ulrich, Jörg Heiser, Dominic Eichler, Martin Herbert, Joseph Akel, April Lamm, and Katya Tylevich. Frankfurt, Germany: Schirn Kunsthalle; Vienna: Verlag für moderne Kunst. Exh. cat.
Regen Projects 25. Contributions by George Baker, Ann Goldstein, Michael Maltzan, and Shaun Caley Regen. Los Angeles: Regen Projects/DelMonico Books • Prestel.
Rondeau, James, ed. *Society for Contemporary Art, 1940–2015*. Contributions by Barry Schwabsky, Carter Ratcliff, and Franz Schulze. Chicago: Art Institute of Chicago.

2014 *Doug Aitken: Electric Earth*. Yongin-si, Korea: Nam June Paik Center. Exh. cat.
Marta, Karen, ed. *Doug Aitken: 100 YRS*. Contributions by Francesco Bonami, Bice Curiger, Kerry Brougher, Aaron Betsky, Tim Griffin, and Hans Ulrich Obrist. New York: Rizzoli.
Obrist, Hans Ulrich, ed. *MAPPING IT OUT: An Alternative Atlas of Contemporary Cartographies*. Introduction by Tom McCarthy. London, UK: Thames & Hudson.

2013 Balsom, Erika. *Exhibiting Cinema in Contemporary Art*. Amsterdam: Amsterdam University Press.
Guiot, Nathalie. *Artists and Collectors*. Montreuil, France: BlackJack editions.
Holzwarth, Hans Werner, ed. *Art Now. Vol. 4*. Cologne, Germany: Taschen.
Little Water: Dojima River Biennale. Osaka, Japan: Dojima River Forum. Exh. cat.

2011 *Defining Contemporary Art—25 Years in 200 Pivotal Artworks*. Contributions by Daniel Birnbaum, Cornelia H. Butler, Suzanne Cotter, Bice Curiger, Okwui Enwezor, Massimiliano Gioni, Bob Nickas, and Hans Ulrich Obrist. New York: Phaidon.

2010 *Art Moves*. Toruń, Poland: Art Moves Festival. Exh. cat.

2009 Ebersberger, Eva, and Daniela Zyman, eds. *The Collection Book: Thyssen-Bornemisza Art Contemporary*. Cologne, Germany: Verlag der Buchhandlung Walther König.
Holzwarth, Hans Werner, ed. *100 Contemporary Artists*. Cologne, Germany: Taschen.

2008　*The Cinema Effect: Illusion, Reality, and the Moving Image.* Contributions by Kerry Brougher, Anne Ellegood, Kelly Gordon, Kristen Hileman, and Tony Oursler. Washington, DC: Hirshhorn Museum and Sculpture Garden/D Giles Limited. Exh. cat.

Doug Aitken: *99c Dreams.* Aspen, CO: Aspen Art Press. Exh. cat.

50 Years of Modern Art. Humlebæk, Denmark: Louisiana Museum of Modern Art. Stamp catalog.

Fogle, Douglas. *Life on Mars: 55th Carnegie International.* Pittsburgh, PA: Carnegie Museum of Art. Exh. cat.

Heiser, Jörg. *All of a Sudden: Things That Matter in Contemporary Art.* New York: Sternberg Press.

Holzwarth, Hans Werner, ed. *Art Now. Vol. 3.* Cologne, Germany: Taschen.

Lissoni, Andrea. "Video and Contemporary Art. History of a Not Too Invisible Ghost." In *Electronic Lounge: La Donazione Halevim al Museo del Novecento.* Poggibonsi [Siena], Italy: Carlo Cambi Editore. Exh. cat.

Red Eye: L.A. Artists from the Rubell Family Collection. Contributions by Mark Coetzee, Michael Darling, Michael Holte, and Jason Rubell. Miami, FL: RFC Miami. Exh. cat.

Ruf, Beatrix, ed. *Blasted Allegories: Works from the Ringier Collection.* Zurich, Switzerland: JRP|Ringier. Exh. cat.

2007　Birnbaum, Daniel. *Chronology.* 2nd ed. Berlin: Sternberg Press.

Fokidis, Marina, ed. *her[his]tory.* Athens: Museum of Cycladic Art. Exh. cat.

Hall, Emily, ed. *Doug Aitken: Sleepwalkers.* Contributions by Klaus Biesenbach, Peter Eleey, Glenn D. Lowry, and Anne Pasternak. New York: Museum of Modern Art. Exh. cat.

Peltason, Ruth A., ed. *Creative Time: The Book.* Contributions by Anne Pasternak, Lucy Lippard, Kriby Gookin, Linda Yablonsky, David Levi Strauss, Peter Eleey, Frances Richard, Michael Breson, and Lauren F. Friedman. New York: Princeton Architectural Press.

Roberts, Rebecca, ed. *MoMA, Highlights Since 1980: 250 Works from the Museum of Modern Art.* Introduction by Glenn D. Lowry. New York: Museum of Modern Art.

Silence. Listen to the Show. Turin, Italy: Fondazione Sandretto Re Rebaudengo/Electa. Exh. cat.

Sounding the Subject: Video Trajectories. Contributions by Daniel Birnbaum, Mechtild Widrich, and Caroline A. Jones. Introductions by Jane Farver and Pamela and C. Richard Kramlich. Cambridge, MA: MIT List Visual Art Center. Exh. cat.

Thomas, Rachel, ed. *All Hawaii Entrées: Lunar Reggae.* Dublin, Ireland: Irish Museum of Modern Art/Charta. Exh. cat.

Works in Progress: Herzog & de Meuron's Miami Art Museum. Miami: Miami Art Museum. Exh. cat.

2006　*Ecotopia: The Second ICP Triennial of Photography and Video.* New York: International Center for Photography/Steidl. Exh. cat.

Gan, Stephen, Ceclilia Dean, and James Kaliardos, eds. *Visionaire*, no. 48 *Magic.* New York: Visionaire/Van Cleef & Arpels.

2005　*Art Basel Conversations.* Basel, Switzerland: Art Basel/Hatje Cantz Publishers.

Bidibidobidiboo: Works from Collezione Sandretto Re Rebaudengo. Turin, Italy: Fondazione Sandretto Re Rebaudengo/Skira. Exh. cat.

Encounters in the Twenty-First Century: Polyphony: Emerging Resonances. Kanazawa, Japan: 21st Century Museum of Contemporary Art Kanazawa/Tankosha Publishing Company. Exh. cat.

Grosenick, Uta. *Art Now Vol. 2.* Cologne, Germany: Taschen.

Hüsch, Anette, Joachim Jäger, and Gabriele Knapstein, eds. *Beyond Cinema: The Art of Projection: Films, Videos and Installations from 1963 to 2005.* Berlin: Hamburger Bahnhof, Museum für Gegenwart/Hatje Cantz Publishers. Exh. cat.

Rothfuss, Joan, and Elizabeth Carpenter, eds. *Bits & Pieces Put Together to Present a Semblance of a Whole: Walker Art Center Collections.* Minneapolis, MN: Walker Art Center.

Sharp, Amanda. Interview with Doug Aitken. In *Press Play: Contemporary Artists in Conversation.* New York: Phaidon.

Universal Experience: Art, Life, and the Tourist's Eye. Chicago: Museum of Contemporary Art Chicago.

2004　Chillida, Alicia, ed. *Landscape and Memory.* Madrid, Spain: La Casa Encendida/El Centro Atlántico de Arte Moderno, Las Palmas. Exh. cat.

Couturier, Élisabeth. *L'art contemporain, mode d'emploi.* Paris: Éditions Filipacchi.

Gili, Marta, Jon Alain Guzik, and Chus Martínez. *Doug Aitken: We're Safe as Long As Everything is Moving.* Barcelona, Spain: CaixaForum. Exh. cat.

2003　*Defying Gravity: Contemporary Art and Flight.* Raleigh, NC: North Carolina Museum of Art. Exh. cat.

de Oliveira, Nicholas, Nicola Oxley, and Michael Petry. *Installations II: l'empire des sens.* London, UK: Thames & Hudson.

Imperfect Innocence: The Debra and Dennis Scholl Collection. Contributions by Nancy Spector, James Rondeau, and Michael Rush. Baltimore, MD: Contemporary Museum/D.A.P./Distributed Art Publishers. Exh. cat.

RISE: Doug Aitken. Humlebæk, Denmark: Louisiana Museum of Modern Art. Exh. cat.

Schwerfel, Heinze Peter. *Kino und Kunst: eine Liebesgeschicte.* Cologne, Germany: Dumont.

Spiritus. Stockholm, Sweden: Magasin 3 Stockholm Konsthall. Exh. cat.

2002　Grosenick, Uta, and Burkhard Riemschneider, eds. *Art Now: 137 Artists at the Rise of the New Millennium.* Cologne, Germany: Taschen.

Screen Memories. Mito-shi, Japan: Contemporary Art Gallery, Art Tower Mito. Exh. cat.

2001 *Doug Aitken*. Contributions by Daniel Birnbaum, Jörg Heiser, and Amanda Sharp. New York: Phaidon.
Hypermental: Rampant Reality 1950–2000 from Salvador Dali to Jeff Koons. Contributions by Sibylle Berg, Norman Bryson, Bice Curiger, Paul D. Miller, Griselda Pollock, Gero von Randow, and Peter Weibel. Zurich, Switzerland: Kunsthaus Zurich/Hatje Cantz Publishers. Exh. cat.

2000 Fischer, Tine, Arine Kirstein, and Synnøve Kjaerland. *Crossing Boundaries 2000*. Copenhagen, Denmark: Danish Film Institute.
Flight Patterns. Contributions by Cornelia H. Butler, Lee Weng Choy, and Francis Pound. Los Angeles: The Museum of Contemporary Art, Los Angeles. Exh. cat.
Form Follows Fiction. Contribution by Jeffrey Deitch. Turin, Italy: Castello di Rivoli, Museo d'Arte Contemporanea/Charta. Exh. cat.
Fresh Cream, Contemporary Art in Culture. New York: Phaidon.
McDonald, Ewen, ed. *Biennale of Sydney 2000*. Sydney, Australia: Biennale of Sydney Ltd. Exh. cat.
Speed of Vision: On the Construction and Perception of Time in Video Art. Ridgefield, CN: Aldrich Museum of Contemporary Art. Exh. cat.
Video Vibe: Arte, Musica e Video in Gran Bretagna. British School at Rome, Italy/Castelvecchi Editore. Exh. cat.
Vergne, Philippe, ed. *Let's Entertain: Life's Guilty Pleasures*. With contributions by Akiko Busch, Dike Blair, Susan Davis, Emma Duncan, and Joshua Gamson. Minneapolis, MN: Walker Art Center. Exh. cat.
Whitney Biennial: 2000 Biennial Exhibition. New York: Whitney Museum of American Art/Harry N. Abrams, Inc. Exh. cat.

1999 *Doug Aitken, Diamond Sea*. Dallas, TX: Dallas Museum of Art. Exh. cat.
EXTRAetORDINAIRE: Le Printemps de Cahors. Saint-Cloud, France: Le Printemps de Cahors/Actes Sud. Exh. cat.
Frohne, Ursula Anna, ed. *Video Cult/ures: Multimediale Installationen der 90er Jahre*. Karlsruhe, Germany: Zentrum für Neue Kunst/Dumont. Exh. cat.
Szeemann, Harald, and Cecilia Liveriero Lavelli, eds. *dAPERTutto: La Biennale di Venezia: 48a Esposizione internazionale d'arte*. Venice, Italy: La Biennale di Venezia/Marsilio Editori. Exh. cat.

1998 Bonami, Francsco, and Hans Ulrich Obrist, eds. *Dreams*. Turin, Italy: Fondazione Sandretto Re Rebaudengo/Castelvecchi Editore. Exh. cat.
I Love New York—Crossover of Contemporary Art. Cologne, Germany: Museum Ludwig Köln/Dumont. Exh. cat.
Unfinished History. Contributions by Douglas Fogle and Francesco Bonami. Minnesota, MN: Walker Art Center. Exh. cat.

1997 *film+arc.graz*. Graz, Austria: Third International Biennale. Exh. cat.
One Minute Scenario. Saint-Cloud, France: Le Printemps de Cahors/Actes Sud. Exh. cat.
22nd International Ljubljana Biennial of Graphic Art. Ljubljana, Slovenia: Cankarjev dom Cultural and Congress Centre, Modern Gallery and Tivoli Gallery. Exh. cat.
Whitney Biennial: 1997 Biennial Exhibition. New York: Whitney Museum of American Art/Harry N. Abrams. Exh. cat.

1996 *a/drift*. Annandale-on-Hudson, NY: Center for Curatorial Studies, Bard College. Exh. cat.
Campo 6: The Spiral Village. Turin, Italy: Galleria Civica d'Arte Moderna e Contemporanea/Skira. Exh. cat.

1995 *La Belle et la Bête: un choix de jeunes artistes américains*. Musée d'art moderne de la Ville de Paris. Exh. cat.

1994 *Audience 0.01: International Video*. Trevi, Italy: Trevi Flash Art Museum/Giancarlo Politi Editore. Exh. cat.

1993 *Okay Behavior*. New York: 303 Gallery.

Selected Articles and Reviews

2015 Aspden, Peter. "In Search of Perpetual Fluidity." *Financial Times*, June 27.
Barnes, Freire. "Art-Totally happening." *Time Out*, June 23, 86.
Bodin, Claudia. "Der Soundtrack des Lebens." *Art Das Kunstmagazin*, July, 64–73.
Callaghan, Jeremy. "Madre naturaleza." *Architectural Digest España*, no. 103 [June]: 100–109.
Carey-Kent, Paul. "Doug Aitken." *Border Crossings* 34, no. 4 [December–February]: 88–89.
Ellis-Petersen, Hannah. "Barbican Next Stop for Roaming Station to Station Art Project." Culture, TheGuardian.com, March 25.
Ellis-Petersen, Hannah. "Non-Stop Art: Why Doug Aitken Is a Man on a Mission." Culture, TheGuardian.com, June 24.
Ellis-Petersen, Hannah. "*Station to Station* Pulls Out All the Stops with Lineup as It Heads for Barbican." Culture, TheGuardian.com, May 26.
Gelt, Jessica. "Sundance Film Festival, New Frontier on Cutting Edge." *Los Angeles Times*, January 22.
Guttridge-Hewitt, Martin. "'It's Like a Cultural Particle Accelerator': Doug Aitken Explains the Ambitious Station to Station." FactMag.com, June 26.
Hubert, Craig. "The Diametric Extremes of Doug Aitken." *Modern Painters*, June, 31–33.
Jury, Louise. "Barbican Is Next Stop for the US Artist." *London Evening Standard*, June 29.
Law, Katie. "All change." *London Evening Standard*, June 25.
Merkel, Ronja. "Doug Aitken in der Schirn." *Journal Frankfurt*, July 3–16, 44–53.
Schneider, Iris. "Station to Station: Doug Aitken's Different Conversation." LAObserved.com, August 19.

Tehrani, Bijan. "Doug Aitken talks about Station to Station." CinemaWithoutBorders.com, August 19.
Thöne, Eva. "Multimedia-Star Aitken: Der Mann, der die Zeit einfängt." Spiegel.de, July 9.
Tylevich, Katya. "Doug Aitken: Nomad Art." Elephant, no. 21 [Winter]: 138–45.
Vankin, Deborah. "Art in Motion." Culture Monster, Los Angeles Times, August 19.

2014
Cooper, Ashton. "Art Reads: 'Doug Aitken 100 YRS.'" BlouinArtInfo.com, May 22.
Fitzpatrick, Kyle. "Doug Aitken Sign Spinning Performance." LAImYours.com, September 30.
Fitzpatrick, Kyle. "Doug Aitken at Regen Projects." LAImYours.com, August 1.
Oliver, Ellen. "Lots of Movement Around 'Still Life.'" Los Angeles Times, September 14.
Owens, Mitchell. "Social Studies." Architectural Digest, December, 92.
Stromberg, Matt. "Doug Aitken: Still Life at Regen Projects." DailyServing.com, September 24.
Symonds, Alexandria. "Exclusive Preview and Interview: 'The Source [Evolving],' Doug Aitken." Interview Magazine, January 17.
Vankin, Deborah. "Sign Spinners as Performance Art: Doug Aitken's 'Happening' Saturday." Culture Monster, LATimes.com, October 3.
Vartanian, Hrag. "ArtRx LA." Hyperallergic.com, September 2.
Zimskind, Lyle. "Framed: Doug Aitken's 'Native Land' Bombards Us with Electronic Messages." LAMag.com, September 19.

2013
Bell, Melissa. "Doug Aitken's Art Train Rolls out of Washington Saturday Afternoon." Going Out Guide, WashingtonPost.com, September 6.
Boucher, Brian. "Doug Aitken Demolishes 303 Gallery." ArtinAmerica.com, April 2.
Erickson, Steve. "Escape Artist." Smithsonian 44, no. 8 [December]: 72–77.
Griffin, Tim, and Doug Aitken. "Station to Station." Parkett, no. 93 [December]: 6–22.
Finkel, Jori. "Art Hits the Rails." Los Angeles Times, June 20.
Frere-Jones, Sasha. "Station to Station." NewYorker.com, October 2.
Kennedy, Randy. "A Public Art Project That Will Travel by Train." New York Times, June 21.
Mondloch, Kate. "Mirror Mirror." Millennium Film Journal 1, no. 58 [Fall]: 138–42.
Neilson, Laura. "A Mobile Platform for Art." Wall Street Journal, September 6.
Richard, Frances. Review of solo exhibition at 303 Gallery, New York. Artforum 51, no. 9 [May]: 325–26.
Roberts, Randall. "'Station' Rocks, Rolls into L.A." Los Angeles Times, September 28.
Sancken, Kristin. "Doug Aitken Tackles Time in '100 YRS.'" Whitewallmag.com, March 11.
Semuels, Alana. "They'll Be Working on the Railroad." Los Angeles Times, September 9.
Vankin, Deborah. "Inspiration at End of the Line." Los Angeles Times, October 6.
Vankin, Deborah. "This Train Is Bound to Inspire." Los Angeles Times, September 25.
Volk, Gregory. "Back on the Train: Doug Aitken's 'Station to Station.'" ArtinAmerica.com, September 20.

Watercutter, Angela. "Station to Station: Artist Transforms Train into Experimental Cross-Country Studio." Wired.com, June 20.
Wilkinson, Isabel. "Art's Big Road Trip." Newsweek, August 30.
Wilson, Michael. "Nomad's Land." Scene & Herd, Artforum.com, September 11.

2012
Barry, Robert. Review of solo exhibition at LUMA Foundation, Arles, France. Frieze, no. 144 [January/February]: 11.
Carter, Stinson. "Where I Work: Doug Aitken." Homes, Wall Street Journal, May 4.
Catlin, Roger. "Liquid Architecture." Washington Post, March 18.
Dayal, Geeta. "Doug Aitken's Song 1 Wraps Museum in 360-Degree Panoramic Video." Culture, Wired.com, April 18.
Gygax, Raphael. "Doug Aitken: Eva Presenhuber—Zurich." Flash Art, no. 286 [October]: 118.
Hanley, William. "First Look: Doug Aitken's Song 1 at the Hirshhorn." ArchitecturalRecord.com, April 18.
Hastings, Sophie. "Vibrations of Creativity." Financial Times, September 1.
Herbert, Martin. "Now See This." Art Review, no. 62 [October]: 24–29.
Kennicott, Philip. "Hirshhorn Piece Is All About Projection." Washington Post, March 23.
Rahma, Knazam. Review of solo exhibition at LUMA Foundation, Arles, France. Critics' Picks, Artforum.com, November 7.
Wildman, Sarah. "On the National Mall, Art in the Round." New York Times, March 18.
Yi, Esther. "When a Museum's Exterior Becomes a Canvas for Video Art." Culture, TheAtlantic.com, March 27.
"Mar. 19–24." Arts, The Week Ahead, New York Times, March 16.
"Thinking Outside the Circle: Exploring the Hirshhorn's 'SONG 1' Exhibit." Washington Post, March 23.

2011
Drohojowska-Philp, Hunter. "Doug Aitken: Museum of Contemporary Art and Regen Projects." ARTnews 110, no. 2 [February]: 114.
Rappolt, Mark. "Doug Aitken." Art Review, no. 53 [October]: 104.
Spears, Dorothy. "Can You Hear Me Now?" New York Times, July 24.
Yablonsky, Linda. "The Epic Performance." Art Newspaper, no. 225 [June]: 48–49.

2010
Boehm, Mike. "Video Artist Is on MOCA Party List." Los Angeles Times, June 19.
Finkel, Jori. "How 'West' Was Written." Los Angeles Times, November 10.
Gopnik, Blake. "For Hirshhorn's Exterior, Theater in the Round?" Washington Post, April 21.
Israel, Alex. "Myths of Decline." Artforum 48, no. 5 [January]: 67–68, 70.
Knight, Christopher. "An L.A. Assembly." Los Angeles Times, November 1.
Knight, Christopher. Review of solo exhibition at Regen Projects. Around the Galleries, Los Angeles Times, November 26.
Knight, Christopher. "Art World A-Twitter over Hirshhorn 'Purchase.'" Los Angeles Times, April 25.

Latimer, Quinn. "Video Stars at Art Basel." ArtinAmerica.com, June 17.
Moreno, Shonquis. "Listen to Doug Aitken." Mark, no. 25 (April–May): 47.
Yablonksy, Linda. "How the West Was Won." Scene & Herd, Artforum.com, November 19.

2009 Aitken, Doug. "Doug Aitken Workshop." Domus, no. 922 (February): 48–53.
Finkel, Jori. "Remastered." Modern Painters, October, 38–40.
Higgie, Jennifer. "Doug Aitken in Rome." Editor's Blog, Frieze.com, October 29.
Levin, Kim. Review of solo exhibition at 303 Gallery, New York. ARTnews 108, no. 1 (January): 110.
Lissoni, Andrea. "Tutti I sogni di Doug." Rolling Stone Italia, October, 46.
Pagel, David. Review of solo exhibitions at Regen Projects and Regen Projects II, Los Angeles. Around the Galleries, Los Angeles Times, September 25.
Pappalardo, Dario. "'Frontier' una luce in riva al Tevere." La Repubblica [Rome], October 19.
"Enel Contemporanea 2009? Per Roma Bonami sceglie Doug Aitken." Exibart.com, June 7.

2008 Ayerza, Josefina. "Doug Aitken." Lacanian Ink, no. 32 (Fall): 150–53.
Finkel, Jori. "At The Ready When Artists Think Big." New York Times, April 27.
Hirsch, Faye. Review of solo exhibition at 303 Gallery, New York. Art in America 96, no. 11 (December): 156.
Knight, Christopher. "Extraterrestrial Earthlings Find 'Life.'" Los Angeles Times, May 7.
Licht, Alan. "Reality Show." Art Review, no. 18 (January): 49–51.
McKenna, Kristine. "SoCal Color." New York Times Magazine, March 9, 150–51.
Nicolai, Carsten. "The Artists' Artists." Artforum 47, no. 4 (December): 98.
Smith, Roberta. "An Alien Sighting on Planet Pittsburgh." New York Times, May 9.
Review of solo exhibition at 303 Gallery. Goings on About Town, Art, New Yorker, October 13.

2007 Cash, Stephanie. "A Night in the Life." Art in America 95, no. 4 (April): 104–107.
Finkel, Jori. "MoMA's Off-the-Wall Cinema." New York Times, January 7.
Henry, Clare. "An Urban Drive-In Movie on Manhattan's Sidewalks." Financial Times [London], January 19.
Martin, Courtney J. "Doug Aitken: Sleepwalkers." Flash Art, no. 40 (March/April): 121.
Myers, Terry R. "Doug Aitken, the Flaneur." ArtReview, no. 7 (January): 68–73.
Smith, Roberta. "The Museum as Outdoor Movie Screen, Featuring Five Lives Lived After Dark." New York Times, January 18.
Thompson, Adam. Review of sleepwalkers at The Museum of Modern Art, New York. Art Papers 31, no. 3 (May/June): 69.
Vanderbilt, Tom. "City of Glass." Artforum 45, no. 5 (January): 45–46.
Vogel, Carol. "'Sleepwalkers' Video Is Tailored for Miami." New York Times, October 26.

2006 Bollen, Christopher. "Artists in Residence." New York Times Magazine, April 16, 52–56.
Eichler, Dominic. "Universal Experience." Frieze, no. 96 (January/February): 146–47.
Faucon, Teresa, and Damien Sausset. "Doug Aitken: l'évidence du temps/Doug Aitken: Signs of Time." Art Press, no. 319 (January): 20–27.
Hart, Hugh. "Art as a Prism for Ideas." Los Angeles Times, March 25.
Homes, A. M. "Doug Aitken." Vanity Fair, December, 374.
"Portfolio/Doug Aitken: What I Think About, When I Think About You, 2005." Mouvement, no. 38 (January–March): 108–15.
Teeman, Tim. "Around the World in Eighty Ways." The Knowledge, Times [London], September 24.

2005 Aitken, Doug. Interview with Andre Wiesmayr. Tokion, September/October, 78–81.
Aitken, Doug. Interview with Art Center College of Design. Boundless, no. 1, 8–13.
Demir, Anaid. "Ultraworld, une histoire sans début et sans fin." Le Journal des Arts, no. 226 (December): 2–15, 14.
Knight, Christopher. Review of solo exhibition at Regen Projects, Los Angeles. Around the Galleries, Los Angeles Times, September 30.
Miles, Christopher. Review of solo exhibition at Regen Projects, Los Angeles. Artforum 44, no. 4 (December): 285.
Moisdon, Stephanie. "Doug Aitken: à la recherche de mondes perdus." Beaux Arts Magazine, no. 257 (November): 52–57.
Schönwald, Cédric. "Ultraworld: Doug Aitken." Art 21, no. 5 (December/January): 52–54.
Schwerfel, Heinz Peter. "Ein Surfer durch Licht und Zeit." Art Das Kunstmagazin, no. 11 (November): 60–72.
Willis, Holly. "Time Machines." LA Weekly, September 16–25.

2004 Griffin, Tim. "Broken Screen: A Project by Doug Aitken." Artforum 43, no. 3 (November): 194–201.
Merino, José Luis. "Armonizar los contrarios." El País [Bilbao], November 8.
Rebollar, Mónica. "Fragmentary Beauty." Lápiz [Madrid], no. 208 (December): 50–65.
Ruscha, Ed. "Earth Is the Alien Planet: Doug Aitken Talks to Ed Ruscha." Frieze, no. 84 (June–August): 100–105.
Smith, Roberta. "Summertime at P.S. 1: Where Opposites Like Hands On/Hands Off Attract." New York Times, July 16.

2003 Bonacossa, Ilaria. "A Shifting Breakfast." Label [Warsaw], no. 9 (Spring): 92–97.
Eleey, Peter. Review of solo exhibition at The Fabric Workshop and Museum, Philadelphia, and 303 Gallery, New York. Frieze, no. 72 (January/February): 93.
Menin, Samuele, and Valentina Sansone. "Focus Video and Film: Contemporary Video Art Today (Part I)." Flash Art, no. 228 (January/February): 88–93.
Newhall, Edith. Review of solo exhibition at The Fabric Workshop and Museum. ARTnews 102, no. 5 (May): 159.
Smee, Sebastian. "Mesmerising Visions." Daily Telegraph [London], October 29.
Tegeder, Danielle. "Doug Aitken." Bomb, no. 83 (Spring): 44–46.

2002   Aitken, Doug. Interview with Tim Griffin. *Index Magazine,* September/October, 40–47.

Firstenberg, Lauri. "Urban Pornographic." *MAKE Magazine* [London], no. 92: 8–9

Griffin, Tim. Review of solo exhibition at 303 Gallery, New York. *Artforum* 41, no. 4 [December]: 137.

Heartney, Eleanor. Review of solo exhibition at 303 Gallery. *Art in America* 90, no. 11 [November]: 155–56.

Honigman, Ana Finel. Review of solo exhibition at 303 Gallery. *contemporary,* no. 45 [November]: 85.

Kastner, Jeffrey. "No Labels, No Boundaries: An Artist of the Moment." *New York Times,* October 6.

Morton, Tom. Review of solo exhibition at the Serpentine Gallery, London. *Modern Painters,* Winter, 102–103.

Newhall, Edith. "Too Much Information." *New York Magazine,* September 9, 70.

Smith, Roberta. Review of solo exhibition at 303 Gallery. *New York Times,* October 18.

2001   "Berlin." *Frankfurter Allgemeine Zeitung,* February 28.

Bishop, Claire. Review of solo exhibition at the Serpentine Gallery. *Evening Standard* [London], October 11.

Chapman, Peter. Review of solo exhibition at the Serpentine Gallery. Going Out, *Independent* [London], October 6.

Cork, Richard. "Flood Warnings." Review of solo exhibition at the Serpentine Gallery. *Times* [London], October 17.

Ebeling, Knut. "Parabeln der Unbehaustheit." *Berliner Zeitung,* March 6.

Firstenberg, Lauri. "Visualizing the Contemporary Vernacular: The Photography of Doug Aitken." *Camera Austria International,* no. 74 [May]: 6–17.

Franke, Anselm. "Doug Aitken. Variiert in seinen Installationen. Ensembles von Film, Video, Foto, Architektur, und Sound." *KW Magazine* [Berlin], February, 78, 86–87.

Franke, Anselm. "Doug Aitken: Videos als raumfullendes Gebilde." *Wolfsburger Allgemeine Zeitung,* February 16.

Fricke, Harald. "Leben unter dem Stroboskop." *Die Tageszeitung,* February 20.

Guzik, Jon Alain. "Calm, Cool, and Collected: The Art of Doug Aitken and Sharon Lockhart." *SOMA: Left Coast Culture,* no. 4 [May]: 42–45.

Januszczak, Waldemar. "Going Underground." *Sunday Times* [London], October 21.

Jothady, Manisha. "Reisen in den Inner Space." *FRAME Magazine,* January/February, 67–73.

Nehring, Lydia. Review of solo exhibition at The KW Institute for Contemporary Art, Berlin. *Berliner Morgenpost,* February 15.

Pardo, Patrick. "The Politics of Landscape." *NYArts* 6, no. 2 [February]: 75.

Reust, Hans Rudolf. Review of group exhibition "Hypermental" at Kunsthaus Zürich. *Artforum* 34, no. 10 [Summer]: 193–94.

Romano, Gianni. Review of solo exhibition at Secession, Vienna. *Flash Art,* no. 216 [January/February]: 121–22.

Spiegl, Andreas. Review of solo exhibition at Secession, Vienna. *Camera Austria International,* no. 73 [February]: 78–79.

Spinelli, Claudia. "Mediale Entgrenzung: Der Videokünstler Doug Aitken in Wolfsburg." *Neue Zürcher Zeitung,* April 26.

Vogel, Sabine V. "Die Welt im Zwichenraum, Zu Doug Aitkens Videoinstallationen." *Kunst-Bulletin,* no. 4 [April]: 12–17.

Walder, Gabriela. "Der Großstadtnomade von Los Angeles." *Die Welt* [Hamburg], March 8.

Wulffen, Thomas. "Amor vacui." *Frankfurter Allgemeine Zeitung,* February 26.

2000   Adams, Mark. "Accelerating Art: Aitken, 'I Am a Bullet.'" *Rolling Stone,* September 14, 105.

Aitken, Doug. "A Thousand Words: Doug Aitken Talks About Electric Earth." *Artforum* 38, no. 9 [May]: 160–61.

Baker, Kenneth. "The Fantasy World of Bollywood: Video Artist Explores Mystique of Movies." *San Francisco Chronicle,* July 12.

Birnbaum, Daniel. "Best of 2000." *Artforum* 39, no. 4 [December]: 126–27.

Bonami, Francesco. "Liquid Time." *Parkett,* no. 57, 29–32.

Bronson, A. A. "Doug Aitken, Glass Horizon, These Restless Minds, Wiener Secession." *Association of Visual Artists,* January 3.

Gerstler, Amy. "Man in Motion: The Video Nomad Goes Home." *Los Angeles Magazine,* November, 122–26.

Glueck, Grace. Review of group exhibition "Speed of Vision" at The Aldrich Contemporary Art Museum, Ridgefield, CT. *New York Times,* July 21

Grabner, Michelle. Review of group exhibition "Let's Entertain" at The Walker Art Center, Minneapolis. *Frieze,* no. 54 [September/October]: 125–26.

Green, Charles. Review of The Sydney Biennale. *Artforum* 39, no. 1 [September]: 186–87.

Guthmann, Edward. "India's 'Bollywood' Inspires Video Artist." *San Francisco Chronicle,* July 18.

Halle, Howard. "2000 and None: The Whitney Blows the Franchise." *Time Out New York,* April 6–13, 72.

Helfand, Glen. "Access Bollywood." *San Francisco Bay Guardian,* July 26–August 1.

McKenna, Kristine. "Biennial Man." *LA Weekly,* March 17–23.

Roberts, James. "Omega Man." *Parkett,* no. 57, 22–23.

van Assche, Christine. "Doug Aitken, the 'Stalker' of this Fin de Siècle." *Parkett,* no. 57, 54–58.

Willis, Holly. "Signal to Noise, Doug Aitken's Blow Debris." *LA Weekly,* December 8–14.

1999 Anton, Saul. "Doug Aitken's Moment." *Tate: The Art Magazine,* no. 19 [Winter]: 54-58.
Anton, Saul. Review of solo exhibition at 303 Gallery, New York." *Artbyte,* no. 2 [June-August]: 108.
Aspesi, Natalia. "Festa grande per artisti casalinghi." *La Repubblica* [Rome], June 10.
Cincinelli, Saretto. "Pitti Immagine Discovery." *Flash Art Italia,* no. 216 [June/July]: 118.
Guerrin, Michel. "Video et photographie scellent leurs noces au Printemps de Cahors." *Le Monde,* June 23.
Heiser, Jörg, and Andrew Gellatly. "Just Add Water." *Frieze,* no. 48 [September/October]: 66-71.
Krauss, Nicole. Review. *Art in America* 87, no. 3 [March]: 112.
Madoff, Steven Henry. "All's Fair." *Artforum* 38, no. 1 [September]: 145-54, 184, 190.
Robinson, Walter. "Hi Mom, I'm in Venice." Artnet.com, June 10.
Ryan, Orla. "Venice: Meaningful Instances and Laguna Lacunae." *Circa,* no. 89 [Autumn]: 14-18.
Saltz, Jerry. "New Channels." *Village Voice,* January 12.
Vetrocq, Marcia. "The Venice Biennale: Reformed, Renewed, Redeemed." *Art in America* 87, no. 9 [September]: 82-93.
Vogel, Carol. "At Venice Biennale, Art Is Turning into an Interactive Sport." *New York Times,* June 14.

1998 Akasaka, Hideto. "Mindscape." *Asahi Camera* [Tokyo], August.
Arning, Bill. Review. *Time Out New York,* January 7, 54.
Bonami, Francesco. "Doug Aitken: Making Work Without Boundaries." *Flash Art,* no. 200 [May/June]: 80-83.
Fogle, Douglas. "No Man's Land." *Frieze,* no. 39 [March/April]: 56-61.
Kimmelman, Michael. "The Art of the Moment [And Only For the Moment]." *New York Times,* August 1.
Pastami, Shumchi. "Doug." *Esquire* [Tokyo], September.
Woznicki, Krystian. "California on the Mind's Road Map." *Japan Times,* July 19, 13.

1997 Leggat, Graham. "All of These and None of These: The 1996 New York Video Festival." *Parkett,* no. 48, 162-65.
McKenna, Kristine. "It Happens Every Two Years." *Los Angeles Times,* March 9.
Newhall, Edith. "Glimmer Fields." *New York Magazine,* April 14, 148.
Pokorny, Sydney. Review of solo exhibition at 303 Gallery, New York. *Artforum* 35, no. 10 [Summer]: 137-38.
Searle, Adrian. "Nowhere to Run." *Frieze,* no. 34 [May]: 42-47.
Talkington, Amy. "Diamonds in the Desert." *Ray Gun,* no. 48 [August].

1996 Arning, Bill. "Down for the Kunst." *Time Out New York.*
Schmerler, Sarah. "Art in the Anchorage '96." *Time Out New York.*

1995 Di Genova, Arianna. "Una collezione d'arte." *Il Manifesto* [Rome], February 23.
Schwartz, Henry. Review of solo exhibition at 303 Gallery, New York. *Flash Art,* no. 181 [March/April]: 104-105.

1994 Colman, David. "Jump cuts." Short Takes, *Vogue,* December 1, 204.
Cork, Richard. "All Human Life Is Missing." *Times* [London], April 26.
Decter, Joshua. Review of solo exhibition at 303 Gallery, New York. *Artforum* 33, no. 4 [December]: 84.
Kastner, Jeffrey. "Beyond Belief." *Flash Art,* no. 177 [Summer]: 61.
Lillington, David. "Monkey Business—Beyond Belief." *Time Out London,* April 20-27, 41.
Muir, Gregor. "Beyond Belief." *World Art,* no. 2 [June]: 109.
Pokorny, Sydney. Review of solo exhibition at 303 Gallery. *Frieze,* no. 19 [November/December]: 61.
Saltz, Jerry. "Doug Aitken at AC Project Room." *Art in America* 82, no. 4 [April]: 128.
Weil, Benjamin. "Ouverture: Doug Aitken." *Flash Art,* no. 176 [May/June]: 104.

1993 Saltz, Jerry. "Mayday, Mayday, Mayday." *Art in America* 81, no. 9 [September]: 41-45.
Saltz, Jerry. "10 Artists for the '90s." *Art & Auction,* May, 122-25, 155.

1992 Bogan, Neill. *Art Papers,* [October/November]: 54.

Awards

2013 Smithsonian Magazine American Ingenuity Award: Visual Arts
2012 Nam June Paik Art Center Prize
2009 Aurora Award, Aurora Picture Show, Houston, TX
2007 German Film Critics Association Award, KunstFilmBiennale, Cologne, Germany
2000 Aldrich Award, Aldrich Museum of Contemporary Art, Ridgefield, CT
1999 International Prize—Golden Lion, Venice Biennale, Venice, Italy

Contributors

Joseph Grima

Joseph Grima is an architect, writer, and editor based in Genoa, Italy. Previously he was the editor of *Domus* magazine and directed Storefront for Art and Architecture, an independent gallery in New York. In 2012 he was co-curator of the first edition of the Istanbul Design Biennial. He has curated exhibitions and presented work in numerous international exhibitions including the Venice Architecture Biennale, New Museum of Contemporary Art, New York, and the Triennale di Milano.

Anna Katz

Anna Katz is the Wendy Stark Curatorial Fellow at The Museum of Contemporary Art, Los Angeles [MOCA], where she is the curatorial assistant for *Doug Aitken: Electric Earth*. Previously a Joan Tisch Teaching Fellow at the Whitney Museum of American Art from 2008 to 2013, she holds a Ph.D. from the Department of Art and Archaeology at Princeton University. Her doctoral dissertation is the first book-length study of sculptor Lee Bontecou's oeuvre during the most active period of her production, 1958 to 1971. Katz has recently contributed to the catalogues *Whitney Museum of American Art: Handbook of the Collection* [2015] and *Kerry James Marshall: Mastry* [2016].

Norman M. Klein

Norman M. Klein is a critic, urban and media historian, and novelist. His books include *The History of Forgetting: Los Angeles and the Erasure of Memory*; *Seven Minutes: The Life and Death of the American Animated Cartoon*; *The Vatican to Vegas: The History of Special Effects*; *Freud in Coney Island and Other Tales*; and the database novel *Bleeding Through: Layers of Los Angeles, 1920-86*. His essays, on subjects ranging from European cultural history to animation and architectural studies, from special effects to cinema and digital theory, from LA studies to fiction, media design, and documentary film, have appeared in anthologies, museum catalogues, newspapers, and scholarly journals.

Glenn D. Lowry

Glenn D. Lowry became director of The Museum of Modern Art in 1995; he was previously director of the Art Gallery of Ontario and curator of Near Eastern Art at the Smithsonian Institution's Sackler and Freer Galleries [he is a scholar of Islamic art]. Lowry lectures and writes in support of contemporary art, on the role of museums in society, and on other topics related to his research interests. Lowry's recent publications include *Design for the New Museum of Modern Art* [2004], *Oil and Sugar: Contemporary Art and Islamic Culture* [2009], and *The Museum of Modern Art in This Century* [2009].

Philippe Vergne

Philippe Vergne was appointed director of The Museum of Contemporary Art, Los Angeles [MOCA], in March 2014. Prior to his appointment at MOCA, Vergne served for five years as director of Dia Art Foundation, New York. Prior to leading Dia, Vergne held leadership roles as deputy director and chief curator at the Walker Art Center in Minneapolis, and as director of the Musée d'art Contemporain [MAC] in Marseille, France. Among his curatorial projects, Vergne has organized monographic exhibitions of the work of Carl Andre, Huang Yong Ping, and Kara Walker and thematic group exhibitions, including *Let's Entertain: Life's Guilty Pleasures* and *How Latitudes Become Forms: Art in a Global Age*; in 2006, Vergne co-curated the Whitney Biennial with Chrissie Iles.

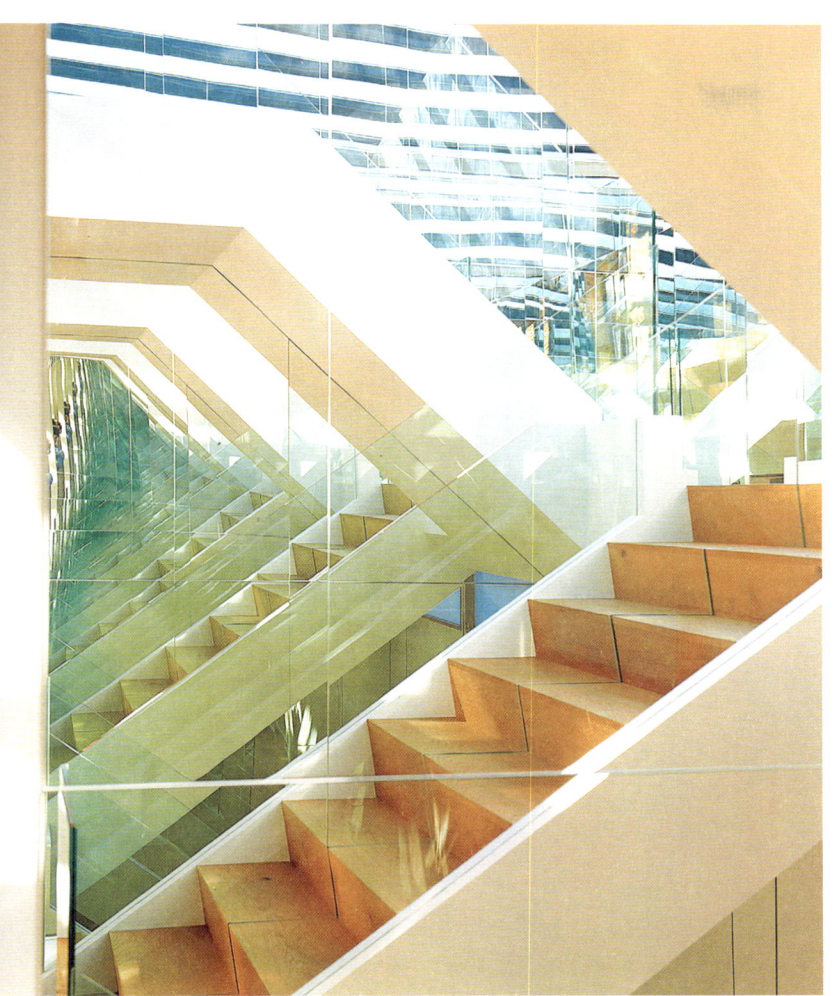
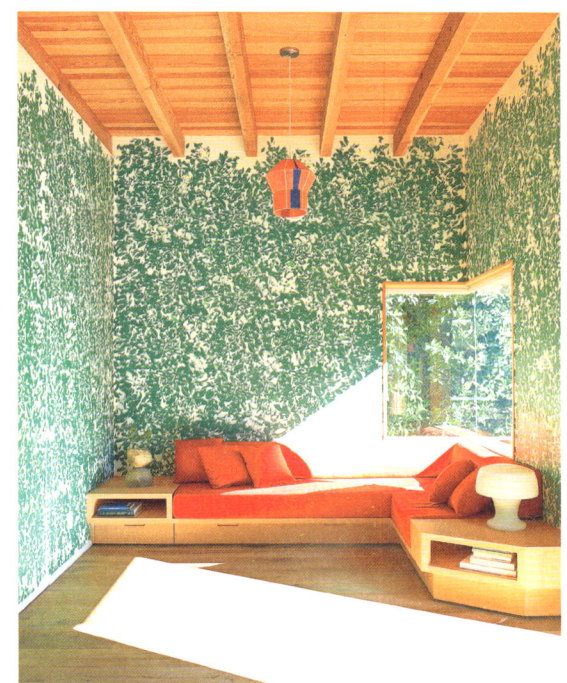
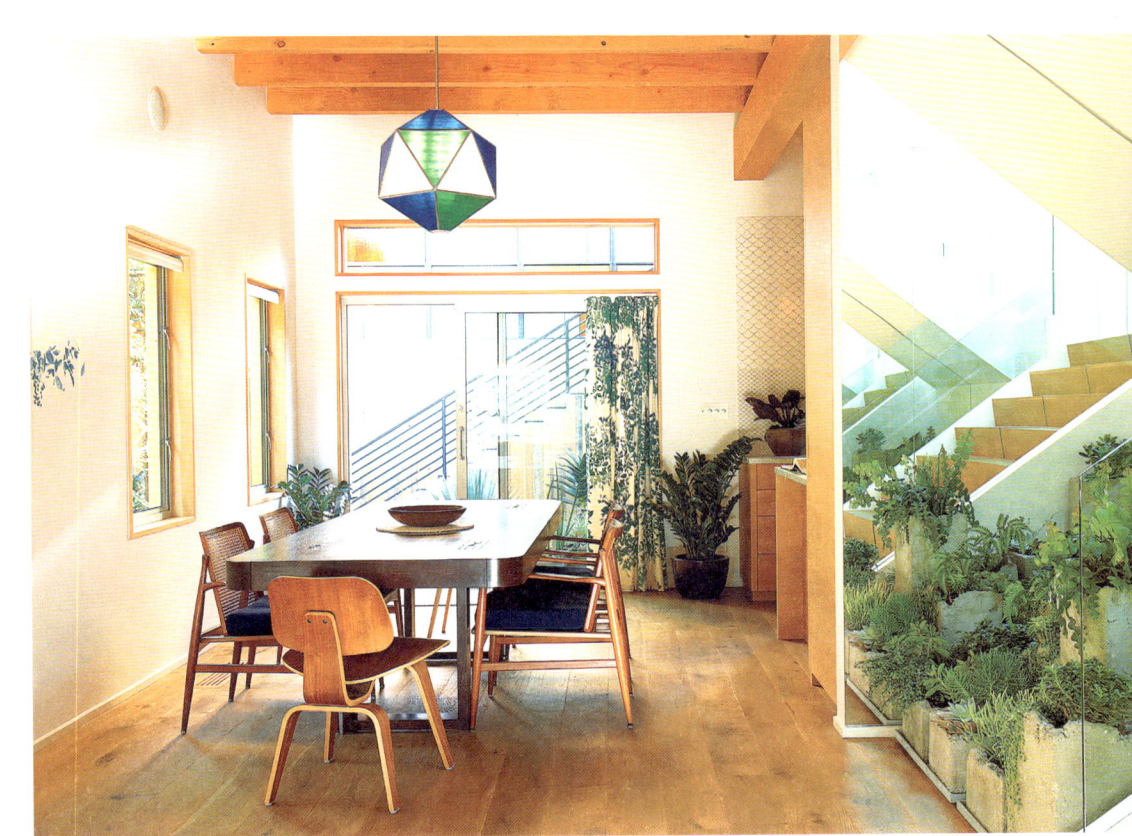

Acid Modernism, 2012

Photography Credits

Unless otherwise noted,
images © Doug Aitken Workshop

Stefan Altenburger
pp. 6, 106-107, 190

Hisham Bharoocha
p. 244 [bottom]

John Berens
pp. 4, 17-18, 20, 24 [top], 26, 34,
58-59, 102-103, 117, 119, 184, 189

© Frederick Charles
pp. 166-167, 198, 232

Charles Coleman
pp. 56-57

Brian Doyle
pp. 31 [bottom], 32 [top], 46 [left],
50-51, 200-201, 222, 244 [top]

Brian Forrest
pp. 24 [bottom], 66-67,
68-69 [left and center], 72-73, 116,
118, 131, 165

Reto Guntli
pp. 60-61

Aaron Koblin and Ben Tricklebank
p. 47 [left]

Mara Mckevitt
p. 46 [right]

Norbert Miguletz
pp. 84-85, 142-143, 168-171,
176-177

Ye Rin Mok
p. 44 [right]

Matthew Nauser
p. 221

Jason Schmidt
p. 259

Max Schwartz
pp. 48-49, 62-63, 69 [right], 70-71

Alayna Van Dervort
pp. 42-43, 47 [right]

Courtesy of 303 Gallery
pp. 101, 154-155

Courtesy of Victoria Miro Gallery
pp. 88-89, 230-231

Lenders to the Exhibition

Doug Aitken
Art Institute of Chicago
Cristina and Thomas Bechtler
Broad Art Foundation
Dallas Museum of Art
Jenny Emerson
Janet Friesen
Sammlung Goetz, München
Hirshhorn Museum and Sculpture
    Garden, Smithsonian
    Institution
Maja Hoffmann
Tracey Jacobs
La Colección Jumex, México
Kadist Art Foundation
Allison and Warren B. Kanders
Kramlich Collection
Kravis Collection
Gustavo Mana
Marciano Art Collection
Victoria Miro Gallery, London
The Museum of Modern Art, New York
New Art Trust
Ellen Pompeo
Galerie Eva Presenhuber, Zurich
Anthony and Jeanne Pritzker
Private collection
Gelila and Wolfgang Puck
Regen Projects, Los Angeles
The David Teiger Trust
303 Gallery, New York
Ruth and William True
Tom and Mila Tuttle

Board of Trustees 2015–16

Maurice Marciano, Co-Chair
Lilly Tartikoff Karatz, Co-Chair
Eugenio Lopez, Vice Chair
Lillian P. Lovelace, Vice Chair
Maria Seferian, Vice Chair
Clifford J. Einstein,
    Chair Emeritus
David G. Johnson, Chair Emeritus
Dallas Price-Van Breda,
    President Emeritus
Jeffrey Soros, President Emeritus

Wallis Annenberg
John Baldessari
Mark Bradford
Gabriel Brener
Steven A. Cohen
Charles L. Conlan II
Kathi B. Cypres
Laurent Degryse
Ariel Emanuel
The Honorable Eric Garcetti*
Susan Gersh
Aileen Getty
NancyJane Goldston
Laurence Graff
Mark Grotjahn
Michael Harrison*
Bruce Karatz
Barbara Kruger
Wonmi Kwon
Daniel S. Loeb
Mary Klaus Martin
Jamie McCourt
Edward J. Minskoff
Steven T. Mnuchin
Catherine Opie
Victor Pinchuk
Lari Pittman
Heather Podesta
Carolyn Powers
Steven F. Roth
Carla Sands
Chara Schreyer
Adam Sender
Darren Star
Sutton Stracke
Cathy Vedovi
Philippe Vergne*
Christopher Walker
Council President
    Herb J. Wesson Jr.*
Orna Amir Wolens

*Ex-Officio

Life Trustees

Eli Broad, Founding Chairman
Betye Monell Burton
Blake Byrne
Lenore S. Greenberg
Audrey Irmas
Frederick M. Nicholas
Thomas E. Unterman

MOCA Staff

Catherine Arias
Kate Baratta
Bryan Barcena
Patricia Bell
Beth Bernstein
David Bradshaw
Marco Braunschweiler
Tim Butler
Alyssa Cohen
Sarah Cohen
Hana Cohn
Colleen Russell Criste
Jill Davis
Sandy Davis
Aria Dean
Karen Dunbar
Aldo Espina
Priyanka Fernando
Kaileena Flores-Emnace
Christy Francois
Frieda Gossett-Clayton
Andrew Gould
Michael Harrison
Alanna Herrera
Jeanne Hoel
Anna Katz
Andy Kolar
Jean Lee
Walter Lopez
Rebecca Matalon
Caitlin Mitchell
Helen Molesworth
Rosenda Moore
Jay Myres
Kim O'Grady
Valerie Partridge
Niyah Rahmaan
Sergio Ramirez
Jessie Weinstein Rich
Sarika Sanyal
Woodburn Schofield Jr.
Eva Seta
Jodi Shapiro
Laura Sils
Bennett Simpson
Shannon Slater
Jin Son
Sarah Lloyd Stifler
Lanka Tattersall
Ace Ubas
Philippe Vergne
Santi Vernetti
Kim Vollstedt
Patrick Weber
Emily Willmann

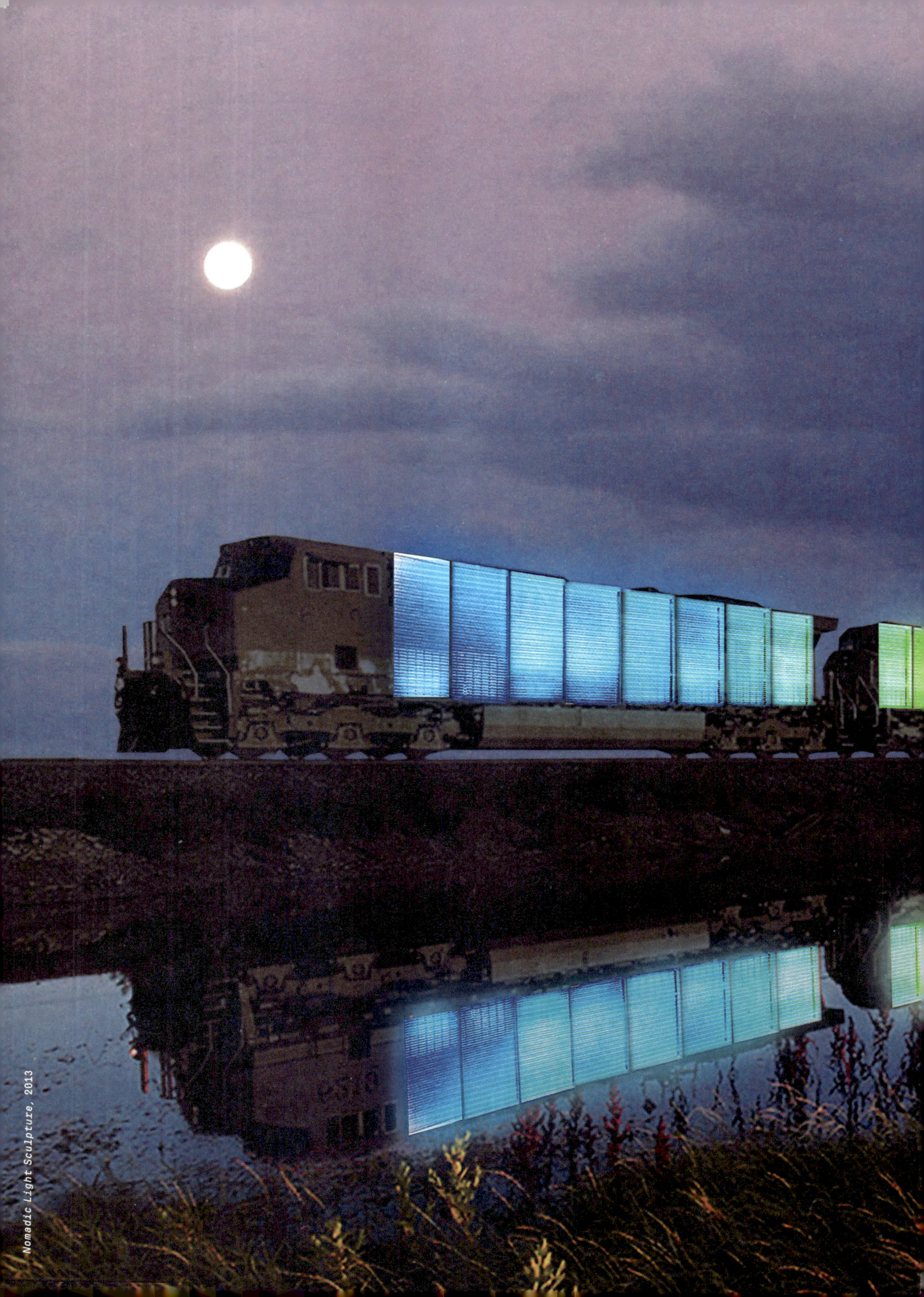

Nomadic Light Sculpture, 2013

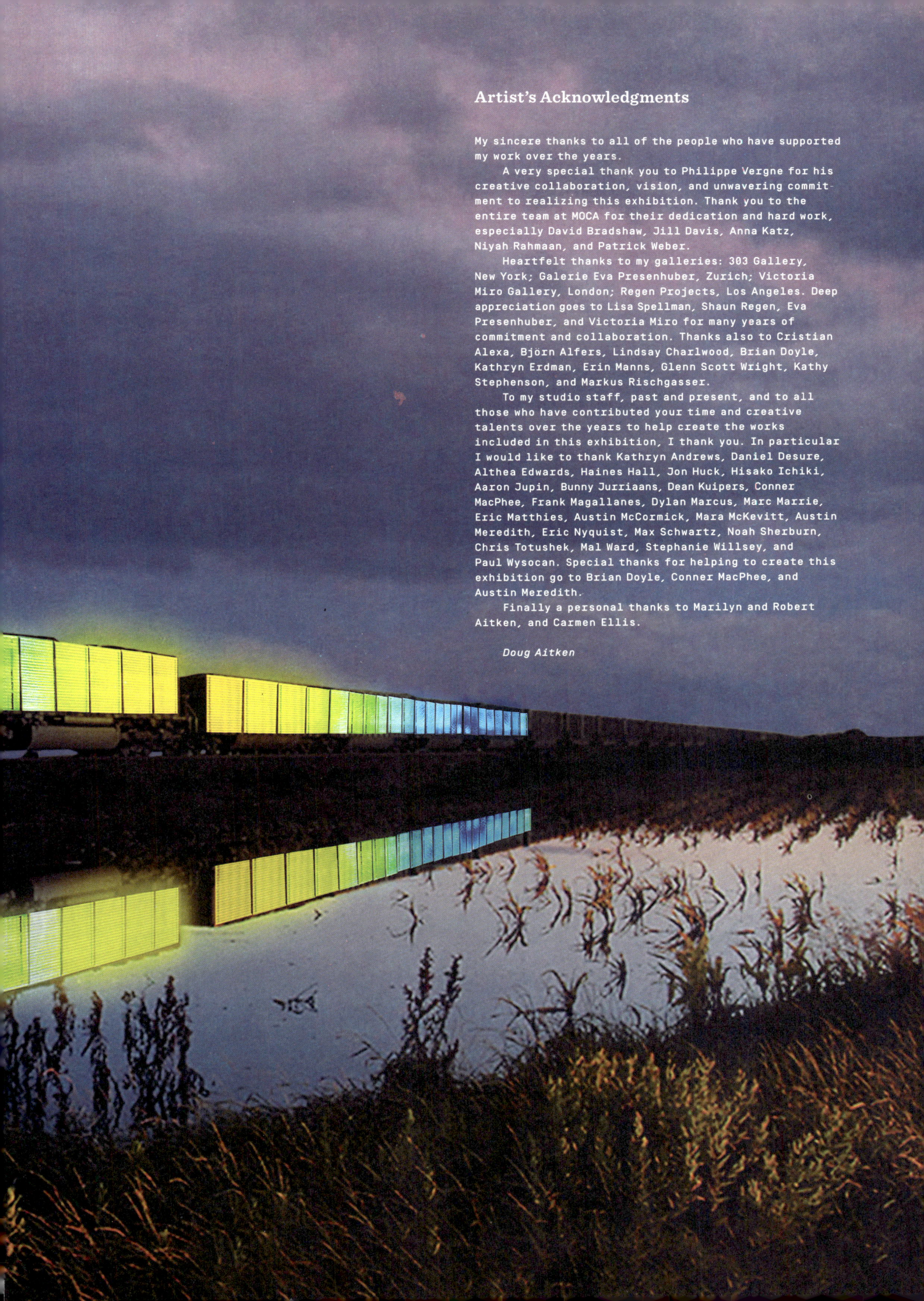

Artist's Acknowledgments

My sincere thanks to all of the people who have supported my work over the years.

A very special thank you to Philippe Vergne for his creative collaboration, vision, and unwavering commitment to realizing this exhibition. Thank you to the entire team at MOCA for their dedication and hard work, especially David Bradshaw, Jill Davis, Anna Katz, Niyah Rahmaan, and Patrick Weber.

Heartfelt thanks to my galleries: 303 Gallery, New York; Galerie Eva Presenhuber, Zurich; Victoria Miro Gallery, London; Regen Projects, Los Angeles. Deep appreciation goes to Lisa Spellman, Shaun Regen, Eva Presenhuber, and Victoria Miro for many years of commitment and collaboration. Thanks also to Cristian Alexa, Björn Alfers, Lindsay Charlwood, Brian Doyle, Kathryn Erdman, Erin Manns, Glenn Scott Wright, Kathy Stephenson, and Markus Rischgasser.

To my studio staff, past and present, and to all those who have contributed your time and creative talents over the years to help create the works included in this exhibition, I thank you. In particular I would like to thank Kathryn Andrews, Daniel Desure, Althea Edwards, Haines Hall, Jon Huck, Hisako Ichiki, Aaron Jupin, Bunny Jurriaans, Dean Kuipers, Conner MacPhee, Frank Magallanes, Dylan Marcus, Marc Marrie, Eric Matthies, Austin McCormick, Mara McKevitt, Austin Meredith, Eric Nyquist, Max Schwartz, Noah Sherburn, Chris Totushek, Mal Ward, Stephanie Willsey, and Paul Wysocan. Special thanks for helping to create this exhibition go to Brian Doyle, Conner MacPhee, and Austin Meredith.

Finally a personal thanks to Marilyn and Robert Aitken, and Carmen Ellis.

Doug Aitken

This book was published on the occasion of the exhibition

Doug Aitken
Electric Earth

The Museum of Contemporary Art, Los Angeles

Lead support is provided by the Annenberg Foundation, The Eli and Edythe Broad Foundation, Aileen Getty Foundation, Eugenio Lopez, LUMA Foundation, Maurice Marciano, Carolyn Powers, and Fondazione Sandretto Re Rebaudengo. Major support is provided by Mandy and Cliff Einstein, Mimi and Peter Haas Fund, and Panasonic. Generous support is provided by Jill and Peter Kraus, the National Endowment for the Arts, Maria Seferian, and Julia Stoschek Foundation e. V., Düsseldorf. Additional support is provided by Juliet McIver, Eileen and Peter Michael, and David and Angella Nazarian. Supporters of the exhibition catalogue include 303 Gallery, Galerie Eva Presenhuber, Regen Projects, Los Angeles, and Victoria Miro Gallery. Exhibitions at MOCA are supported by the MOCA Fund for Exhibitions with lead annual support provided by Delta Air Lines, Shari Glazer, Hästens, and Sydney Holland, founder of the Sydney D. Holland Foundation. Generous funding is also provided by Jerri and Dr. Steven Nagelberg, and Thao Nguyen and Andreas Krainer.

Exhibition Itinerary

The Museum of Contemporary Art, Los Angeles
September 10, 2016–January 15, 2017

Modern Art Museum of Fort Worth
May 27–September 24, 2017

Design: Lorraine Wild and Marina Mills Kitchen, Green Dragon Office, Los Angeles
Editorial: Donna Wingate, Artist and Publisher Services, New York
Proofreader: Sam Frank
Photo editor: Max Schwartz
Production coordinator: Luke Chase, DelMonico Books • Prestel

Printed and bound in China

This book is typeset in Sentinel and Simplon Mono.

Cover and end papers: Doug Aitken

Unless otherwise mentioned, all works © Doug Aitken

Library of Congress Cataloging-in-Publication Data

Aitken, Doug, 1968- artist.
  Doug Aitken: Electric Earth/ organized by Philippe Vergne; essays
    by Joseph Grima, Anna Katz, Norman M. Klein, Glenn D. Lowry, Philippe Vergne.
  Los Angeles: The Museum of Contemporary Art; New York:
    DelMonico Books-Prestel, 2016.
  | Includes bibliographical references.
LCCN 2016015170 | ISBN 9783791355696 [hardcover: alk. paper]

LCC N6537.A4 A4 2016 | DDC 700.92--dc23
LC record available at https://lccn.loc.gov/2016015170

A CIP catalogue record for this book is available from the British Library.

ISBN: 978-3-7913-5569-6

Published in 2016 by The Museum of Contemporary Art, Los Angeles, and DelMonico Books • Prestel

The Museum of Contemporary Art, Los Angeles
250 South Grand Avenue
Los Angeles, CA 90012
213-626-6222
www.moca.org

DelMonico Books, an imprint of Prestel, a member of Verlagsgruppe Random House GmbH

Prestel Verlag
Neumarkter Strasse 28
81673 Munich

Prestel Publishing Ltd.
14-17 Wells Street
London W1T 3PD

Prestel Publishing
900 Broadway, Suite 603
New York, NY 10003

www.prestel.com

All rights reserved. No part of this book may be reproduced or transmitted in any form or by any means, electronic or mechanical, including photocopy, recording, or any other information storage and retrieval system, or otherwise, without written permission from the publisher.

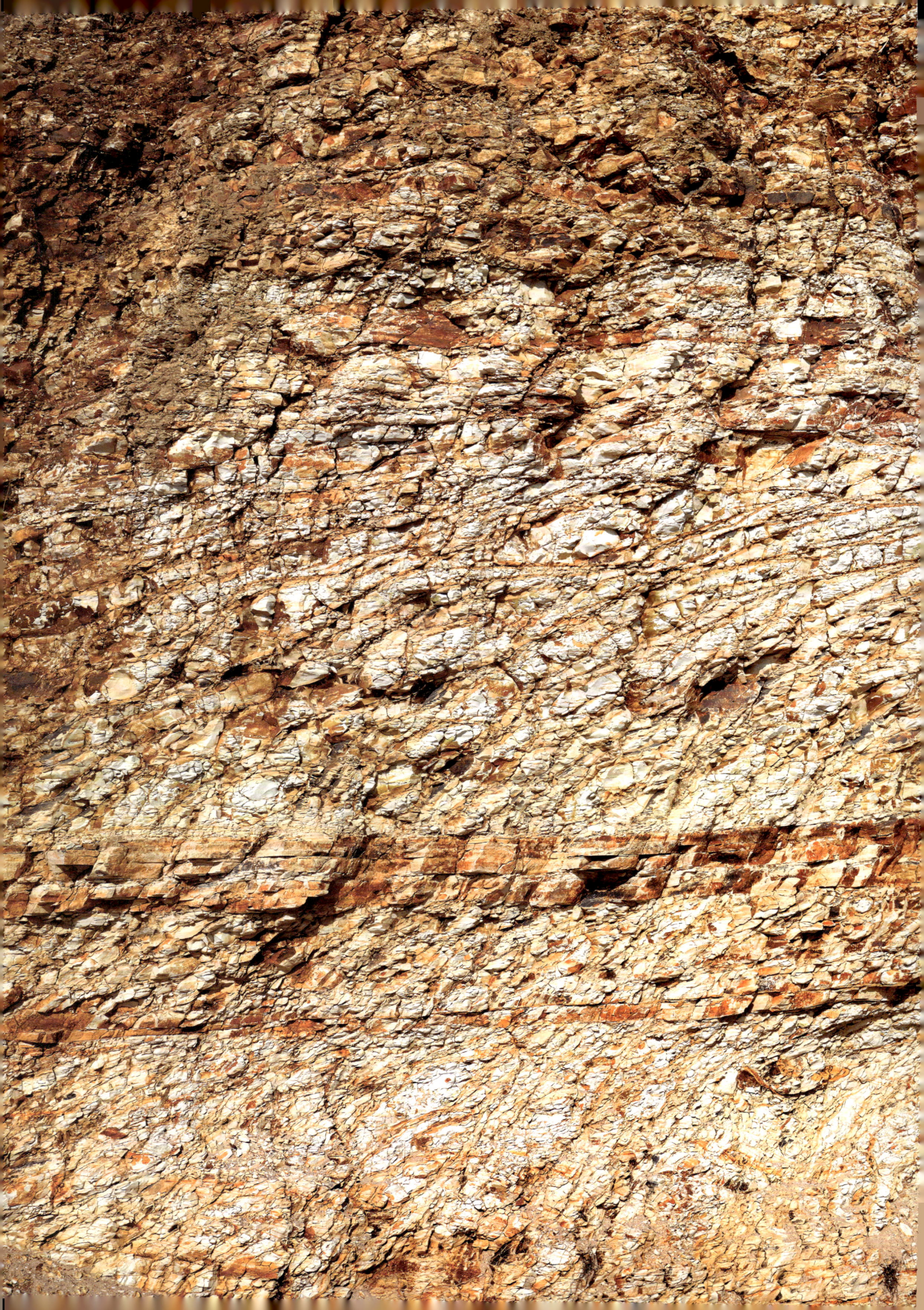